GO MATH

Grade 8

Assessment Resources

Cover Image Credits: ©Tom Grubbe/Flickr/Getty Images

Printed in the U.S.A.

ISBN 978-0-544-06671-7

6 7 8 9 10 0982 20 19 18 17 16 15 14

4500486618 B C D E F G

Contents

Introduction

Individual Student Profiles

Performance Tasks

Answer Sheets

Quizzes

Unit Tests and Performance Tasks

Benchmark Tests

Assessment Options

	Assessment Resources	Student Edition and Teacher's Edition	Online Personal Math Trainer Online Assessment and Intervention Online homework assignment available my.hrw.com
Diagnostic/ Entry Level	• Placement Test • Beginning-of-Year Diagnostic Test	• *Are You Ready?*	• Diagnostic Test • *Are You Ready?* Intervention and Enrichment
Formative/ Progress Monitoring	• Module Quizzes (Levels B, D)	• Your Turn • Math Talk • Reflect • Questioning Strategies • Essential Questions • Lesson Quizzes • *Ready to Go On?* Quizzes • Module Assessment Readiness	• *Ready to Go On?* Intervention and Enrichment • Online Homework • Module Assessment Readiness • Online Quizzes and Tests
Summative	• Unit Tests (Levels A, B, C, D) • Unit Performance Tasks • Quarterly Benchmark Tests • Mid-Year Test • End-of-Year Test	• Unit Assessment Readiness • Unit Performance Tasks	• Unit Assessment Readiness • Online Quizzes and Tests

Using the Assessment Resources

The *Assessment Resources* provides the following tests to assess mastery.

<table>
<tr>
<td>Diagnostic/ Entry Level</td>
<td>Placement Test
• Use to assess prerequisite skills mastery before beginning the school year.
• For students who require intervention, use the online Are You Ready? Intervention.</td>
<td>Beginning-of-Year Diagnostic Test
• Use to assess knowledge of the key objectives that will be taught in the current school year.
• Use as a baseline for a student's mastery of math concepts and skills, and to evaluate growth during the school year.</td>
</tr>
<tr>
<td>Formative/ Progress Monitoring</td>
<td colspan="2">Module Quizzes
• Use to assess mastery of the concepts and skills taught in the Modules.
• Use Level D for students who are considerably below level and require modified materials. For all other students use Level B.</td>
</tr>
<tr>
<td rowspan="2">Summative</td>
<td>Unit Tests
• Use to assess mastery of the concepts and skills taught in the Units.
• Level A: for students who are slightly below level
• Level B: for students who are on level
• Level C: for advanced students
• Level D: for students who are considerably below level and require modified materials</td>
<td>Benchmark Tests
• Use for test prep.
• There are four Benchmark Tests: two quarterly tests, the Mid-Year Test, and the End-of-Year Test.</td>
</tr>
<tr>
<td colspan="2">Performance Tasks
• Use to provide alternate assessment at the end of each Unit.
• These tasks are accessible to all students and suitable to be completed in a classroom.
• Before starting the Performance Task, provide students with the Scoring Rubric for Students to establish the expectations and scoring rubrics for the task. Use the Teacher's Guide Scoring Rubric to assess students' work and their competency with applying the Mathematical Practices.</td>
</tr>
</table>

Placement Test

Individual Student Profile

The Proficient? column provides a snapshot of a student's mastery of previous grade-level standards.

Each Student Edition Module begins with *Are You Ready?*, a tool to assess whether students have the prerequisite skills needed to be successful. *Are You Ready?* Intervention is also available online.

Name ______________________ **Date** ______________ **Class** ______________

COMMON CORE	Placement Test Items	Proficient? Yes/No	COMMON CORE	Placement Test Items	Proficient? Yes/No
7.EE.1	17		**7.RP.1**	34	
7.EE.2	25		**7.RP.2**	28, 33	
7.EE.3	31		**7.RP.3**	2, 8, 9	
7.EE.4	30		**7.SP.1**	10	
7.G.1	3, 29, 32		**7.SP.2**	1	
7.G.3	14		**7.SP.3**	6	
7.G.4	11, 19, 22, 24, 26		**7.SP.4**	6	
7.G.5	13		**7.SP.5**	12	
7.G.6	4, 5, 18		**7.SP.6**	15	
7.NS.1	30		**7.SP.7**	21, 27	
7.NS.2	16, 20		**7.SP.8**	7, 35	
7.NS.3	23				

Beginning-of-Year Diagnostic Test

Individual Student Profile

The Proficient? column provides a snapshot of a student's knowledge of key objectives that will be taught in this grade. The Diagnostic Test can be used as a baseline for a student's mastery of objectives and to evaluate growth.

Name ______________________ Date ______________ Class ______________

COMMON CORE	Student Edition Modules	Diagnostic Test Items	Proficient? Yes/No
8.EE.1	2	35	
8.EE.2	1	2, 75	
8.EE.3	2	3, 57, 63	
8.EE.4	2	49	
8.EE.5	3, 6	12, 15, 27	
8.EE.6	3, 4, 11	14, 27, 29, 65, 71, 72	
8.EE.7	7	13, 70	
8.EE.7a	7	34	
8.EE.7b	7	13, 51, 56, 70, 77	
8.EE.8a	8	31	
8.EE.8b	8	19, 20, 34, 56, 62	
8.EE.8c	8	19, 20, 31, 52, 56, 62	
8.F.1	6	12, 15, 55	
8.F.2	3, 4, 6	11, 27, 28	
8.F.3	4, 6	12, 17, 28, 29	
8.F.4	3, 4, 5, 6	7, 8, 9, 10, 11, 12, 14, 15, 27, 28, 29, 53, 64, 65, 68, 72, 80	
8.F.5	6	10, 12, 29	
8.G.1	9	32, 33, 36, 50, 59, 65	
8.G.2	9	59	
8.G.3	9	58	
8.G.4	10	4, 6, 16, 37, 61	
8.G.5	11	24, 30, 71	
8.G.6	12	22, 25	
8.G.7	12	22, 25	

Beginning-of-Year Diagnostic Test

Individual Student Profile (continued)

Name ______________________ **Date** ____________ **Class** ____________

COMMON CORE	Student Edition Modules	Diagnostic Test Items	Proficient? Yes/No
8.G.8	12	26, 69	
8.G.9	13	21, 23, 48, 67	
8.NS.1	1	1, 2, 75	
8.NS.2	1	5	
8.SP.1	5, 14	27, 38, 60	
8.SP.2	5	27	
8.SP.3	5, 14	27, 38, 54	
8.SP.4	15	39, 40, 41, 42, 43, 44, 45, 46, 47, 48	

Mathematical Practices

Performance Tasks

Teacher's Guide

Performance Tasks provide an alternate way for teachers to assess students' mastery of concepts. This method of assessment requires the student to create answers by using critical thinking skills.

Through observation or analysis of students' responses, teachers can determine what the students know, do not know, and whether the students have any misconceptions.

Assigning Performance Tasks

Discuss with students what is expected before they start the Performance Task. Provide the *Scoring Rubric for Students* to help them understand the scoring criteria.

- Encourage discussion of new ideas and viability of other students' reasoning and work.
- Encourage multiple approaches, and emphasize that not just one answer is correct.
- Encourage students to initiate a plan.
- Encourage students to manage, analyze, and synthesize information.
- Encourage students to use appropriate tools and math models to solve the problems, and remind students to attend to precision.

Use the *Teacher's Guide Scoring Rubric* to help assess the complex learning outcomes.

Performance Tasks

Scoring Rubric for Students

What you are expected to do:

- ☐ Make a plan. If the plan does not work, change it until it does work.
- ☐ Use accurate reasoning to represent the problem.
- ☐ Fully explain the steps that you used to find the solution.
- ☐ Use different methods and models to help you find the solution.
- ☐ Use appropriate tools such as rulers, geometry tools, and calculators.
- ☐ Use clear language to explain your answers. Check that your answers are accurate.
- ☐ Look for patterns and explain your reasoning using different representations such as symbols, words, or graphs.
- ☐ Find efficient ways to solve the problems, and explain general rules clearly.

Your teacher will need to see all your work. Be sure to include the following:

- ☐ Drawings, tables, and graphs to support your answers.
- ☐ Clearly written sentences to explain your reasoning.
- ☐ All the steps in your solution.
- ☐ The answer; check that it is reasonable and answers the question.

Performance Tasks

Teacher's Guide Scoring Rubric

Mathematical Practices	Level 4	Level 3	Level 2	Level 1
Make sense of problems and persevere in solving them.	Student makes a plan and follows it, or adjusts it to obtain a solution.	Student makes a viable plan but implementation has minor flaws.	Student makes a plan, but it has major flaws that the student is unable to address.	Student shows no evidence of making a plan.
Reason abstractly and quantitatively.	Student uses accurate reasoning to represent the problem.	Student reasoning shows a minor flaw.	Student reasoning is missing a critical step.	Student shows little evidence of mathematical reasoning.
Construct viable arguments and critique the reasoning of others.	Student fully explains the steps that lead to the conclusion.	Student skips a step in the explanation.	Student has missing or out-of-sequence steps in the explanation.	Student makes no attempt to explain the steps used.
Model mathematics [using graphs, diagrams, tables, formulas].	Student uses appropriate models and implements them correctly.	Student chooses an appropriate model, but makes minor error(s) in implementation.	Student chooses a model but is unable to relate it effectively to the problem.	Student is unable to model the relationship.
Use appropriate tools [e.g., ruler, paper/pencil, technology] strategically.	Student chooses appropriate tools and uses them effectively.	Student chooses an appropriate tool, but makes minor error(s) in its use.	Student chooses an appropriate tool, but cannot apply it properly to the problem.	Student chooses an inappropriate tool or none at all.
Attend to precision.	Student uses clear language and accurate calculations.	Student uses some vocabulary incorrectly and/or makes minor error(s) in calculations.	Student use of language is confusing and/or makes errors in calculations.	Student does not provide an explanation; calculations are inaccurate.
Look for and make use of structure.	Student finds and uses patterns and processes, and expresses them accurately.	Student finds and uses patterns and processes, but makes minor error(s) in expressing them.	Student finds patterns and processes, but cannot apply them successfully.	Student is unable to find patterns and processes that are appropriate.
Look for and express regularity in repeated reasoning.	Student finds shortcuts and/or generalizations and expresses them clearly.	Student finds shortcuts and/or generalizations, but makes minor errors.	Student finds a shortcut or generalization, but does not represent it effectively.	Student is unable to find shortcuts and/or generalizations.

Multiple-Choice Answer Sheet

Test Title ______________________________

1. Ⓐ Ⓑ Ⓒ Ⓓ
2. Ⓐ Ⓑ Ⓒ Ⓓ
3. Ⓐ Ⓑ Ⓒ Ⓓ
4. Ⓐ Ⓑ Ⓒ Ⓓ
5. Ⓐ Ⓑ Ⓒ Ⓓ
6. Ⓐ Ⓑ Ⓒ Ⓓ
7. Ⓐ Ⓑ Ⓒ Ⓓ
8. Ⓐ Ⓑ Ⓒ Ⓓ
9. Ⓐ Ⓑ Ⓒ Ⓓ
10. Ⓐ Ⓑ Ⓒ Ⓓ
11. Ⓐ Ⓑ Ⓒ Ⓓ
12. Ⓐ Ⓑ Ⓒ Ⓓ
13. Ⓐ Ⓑ Ⓒ Ⓓ
14. Ⓐ Ⓑ Ⓒ Ⓓ
15. Ⓐ Ⓑ Ⓒ Ⓓ
16. Ⓐ Ⓑ Ⓒ Ⓓ
17. Ⓐ Ⓑ Ⓒ Ⓓ
18. Ⓐ Ⓑ Ⓒ Ⓓ
19. Ⓐ Ⓑ Ⓒ Ⓓ
20. Ⓐ Ⓑ Ⓒ Ⓓ
21. Ⓐ Ⓑ Ⓒ Ⓓ
22. Ⓐ Ⓑ Ⓒ Ⓓ
23. Ⓐ Ⓑ Ⓒ Ⓓ
24. Ⓐ Ⓑ Ⓒ Ⓓ
25. Ⓐ Ⓑ Ⓒ Ⓓ
26. Ⓐ Ⓑ Ⓒ Ⓓ
27. Ⓐ Ⓑ Ⓒ Ⓓ
28. Ⓐ Ⓑ Ⓒ Ⓓ
29. Ⓐ Ⓑ Ⓒ Ⓓ
30. Ⓐ Ⓑ Ⓒ Ⓓ
31. Ⓐ Ⓑ Ⓒ Ⓓ
32. Ⓐ Ⓑ Ⓒ Ⓓ
33. Ⓐ Ⓑ Ⓒ Ⓓ
34. Ⓐ Ⓑ Ⓒ Ⓓ
35. Ⓐ Ⓑ Ⓒ Ⓓ
36. Ⓐ Ⓑ Ⓒ Ⓓ
37. Ⓐ Ⓑ Ⓒ Ⓓ
38. Ⓐ Ⓑ Ⓒ Ⓓ
39. Ⓐ Ⓑ Ⓒ Ⓓ
40. Ⓐ Ⓑ Ⓒ Ⓓ
41. Ⓐ Ⓑ Ⓒ Ⓓ
42. Ⓐ Ⓑ Ⓒ Ⓓ
43. Ⓐ Ⓑ Ⓒ Ⓓ
44. Ⓐ Ⓑ Ⓒ Ⓓ
45. Ⓐ Ⓑ Ⓒ Ⓓ
46. Ⓐ Ⓑ Ⓒ Ⓓ
47. Ⓐ Ⓑ Ⓒ Ⓓ
48. Ⓐ Ⓑ Ⓒ Ⓓ
49. Ⓐ Ⓑ Ⓒ Ⓓ
50. Ⓐ Ⓑ Ⓒ Ⓓ

Multiple-Choice Answer Sheet

Test Title ______________________

51. Ⓐ Ⓑ Ⓒ Ⓓ
52. Ⓐ Ⓑ Ⓒ Ⓓ
53. Ⓐ Ⓑ Ⓒ Ⓓ
54. Ⓐ Ⓑ Ⓒ Ⓓ
55. Ⓐ Ⓑ Ⓒ Ⓓ
56. Ⓐ Ⓑ Ⓒ Ⓓ
57. Ⓐ Ⓑ Ⓒ Ⓓ
58. Ⓐ Ⓑ Ⓒ Ⓓ
59. Ⓐ Ⓑ Ⓒ Ⓓ
60. Ⓐ Ⓑ Ⓒ Ⓓ
61. Ⓐ Ⓑ Ⓒ Ⓓ
62. Ⓐ Ⓑ Ⓒ Ⓓ
63. Ⓐ Ⓑ Ⓒ Ⓓ
64. Ⓐ Ⓑ Ⓒ Ⓓ
65. Ⓐ Ⓑ Ⓒ Ⓓ
66. Ⓐ Ⓑ Ⓒ Ⓓ
67. Ⓐ Ⓑ Ⓒ Ⓓ
68. Ⓐ Ⓑ Ⓒ Ⓓ
69. Ⓐ Ⓑ Ⓒ Ⓓ
70. Ⓐ Ⓑ Ⓒ Ⓓ
71. Ⓐ Ⓑ Ⓒ Ⓓ
72. Ⓐ Ⓑ Ⓒ Ⓓ
73. Ⓐ Ⓑ Ⓒ Ⓓ
74. Ⓐ Ⓑ Ⓒ Ⓓ
75. Ⓐ Ⓑ Ⓒ Ⓓ
76. Ⓐ Ⓑ Ⓒ Ⓓ
77. Ⓐ Ⓑ Ⓒ Ⓓ
78. Ⓐ Ⓑ Ⓒ Ⓓ
79. Ⓐ Ⓑ Ⓒ Ⓓ
80. Ⓐ Ⓑ Ⓒ Ⓓ
81. Ⓐ Ⓑ Ⓒ Ⓓ
82. Ⓐ Ⓑ Ⓒ Ⓓ
83. Ⓐ Ⓑ Ⓒ Ⓓ
84. Ⓐ Ⓑ Ⓒ Ⓓ
85. Ⓐ Ⓑ Ⓒ Ⓓ
86. Ⓐ Ⓑ Ⓒ Ⓓ
87. Ⓐ Ⓑ Ⓒ Ⓓ
88. Ⓐ Ⓑ Ⓒ Ⓓ
89. Ⓐ Ⓑ Ⓒ Ⓓ
90. Ⓐ Ⓑ Ⓒ Ⓓ
91. Ⓐ Ⓑ Ⓒ Ⓓ
92. Ⓐ Ⓑ Ⓒ Ⓓ
93. Ⓐ Ⓑ Ⓒ Ⓓ
94. Ⓐ Ⓑ Ⓒ Ⓓ
95. Ⓐ Ⓑ Ⓒ Ⓓ
96. Ⓐ Ⓑ Ⓒ Ⓓ
97. Ⓐ Ⓑ Ⓒ Ⓓ
98. Ⓐ Ⓑ Ⓒ Ⓓ
99. Ⓐ Ⓑ Ⓒ Ⓓ
100. Ⓐ Ⓑ Ⓒ Ⓓ

Name ______________________ Date ______________ Class ______________

Placement Test

1. What is the mean for the set of data shown below?

   27, 32, 14, 19, 24, 26, 22, 32, 29

   A 18   C 26

   B 25   D 32

2. Max drove 460 miles in 8 hours at a constant speed. How long would it take him to drive 661.25 miles at that speed?

   A 10.5 hours   C 11.5 hours

   B 11 hours   D 12 hours

3. A mural inspired by a photograph measures 108 inches by 180 inches. The scale factor is 12. What are the dimensions of the photograph?

   A 8 in. × 14 in.

   B 7.5 in. × 10.5 in.

   C 9 in. × 10.5 in.

   D 9 in. × 15 in.

4. The net of a square pyramid is shown below. What is the surface area of the pyramid?

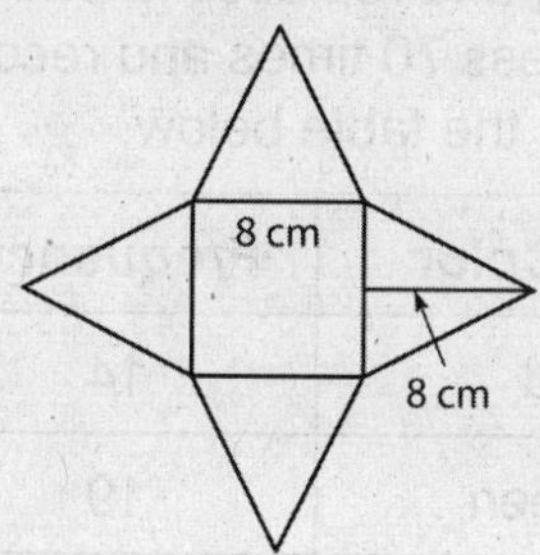

   A 100 cm^2 C 172 cm^2

   B 136 cm^2 D 192 cm^2

5. A gallon of paint covers 400 square feet. How many square feet will $2\frac{3}{8}$ gallons of paint cover?

   A 950 ft^2

   B 986 ft^2

   C 1,040 ft^2

   D 1,068 ft^2

6. Based on the dot plots below, which of the following is a true statement?

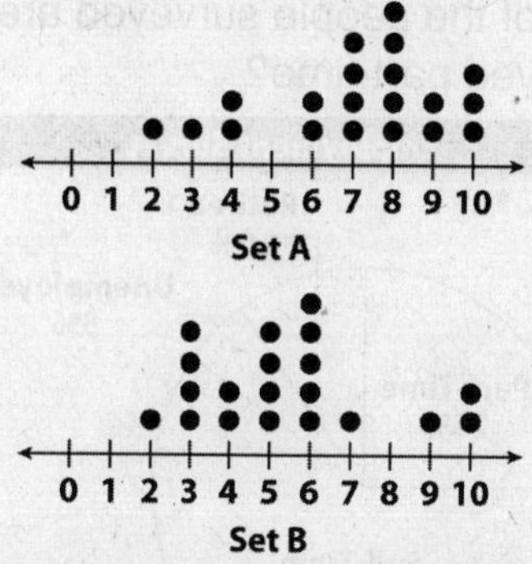

   A Set B is less symmetrical than Set A.

   B Set B has the lesser mean.

   C Set A has the greater range.

   D Set A has the lesser mode.

7. A deli makes sandwiches to order. A customer can choose ham, turkey, or roast beef, and have it served on white, wheat, or rye bread. They can also choose mustard, mayonnaise, ketchup, or hot sauce. How many different sandwiches of one meat, one bread, and one condiment can a customer order?

   A 28   C 36

   B 32   D 45

8. The Jenkins family's monthly budget is shown in the circle graph. The family has a monthly income of $4800. How much money do they spend on transportation each month?

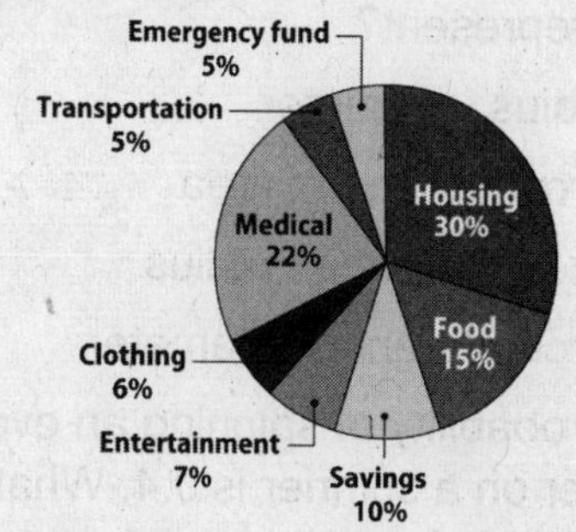

   A $200   C $240

   B $220   D $288

Name ______________________ Date ______________ Class ______________

Placement Test

9. The circle graph shows the results of an employment survey of 900 people. How many of the people surveyed are employed part-time?

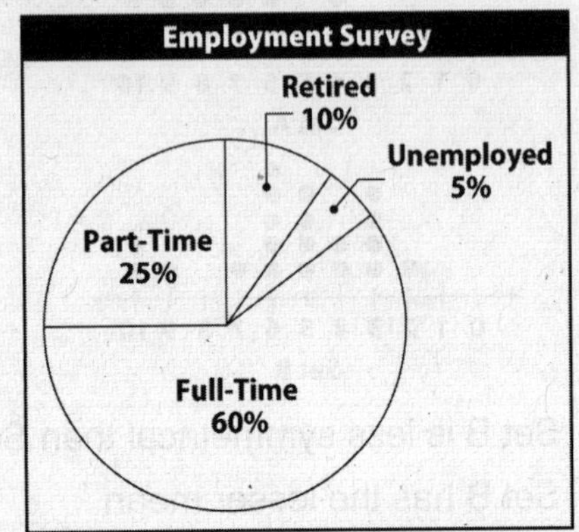

A 225 C 450

B 320 D 810

10. Which of the following is a random sample?

A A survey company asks radio station listeners to call in and tell their favorite radio station.

B 150 customers at an Italian restaurants are asked about their favorite food.

C A professional polling company surveys voters about who they would like to be elected as senator.

D Cameron emails students to find out how many have a computer at home.

11. In a circle of any size, what ratio does pi (π) represent?

A radius : diameter

B circumference : area

C circumference : radius

D circumference : diameter

12. The probability of spinning an even number on a spinner is 0.4. What is the probability of **not** spinning an even number, expressed as a percent?

A 90% C 40%

B 60% D 6%

13. What is the measure of $\angle RST$ in the diagram below?

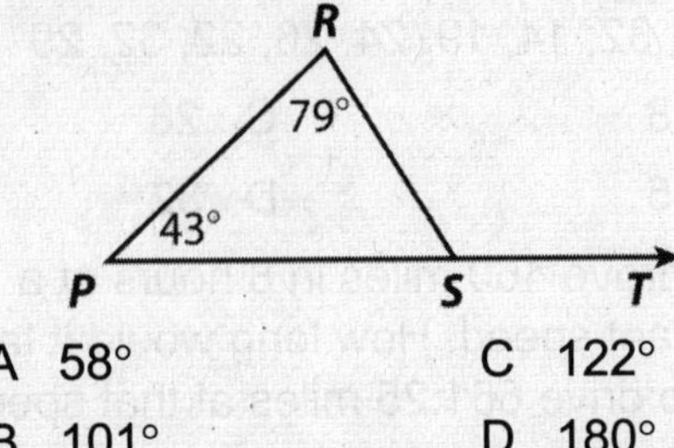

A 58° C 122°

B 101° D 180°

14. A horizontal plane intersects a triangular pyramid as shown below. What is the shape of the cross-section?

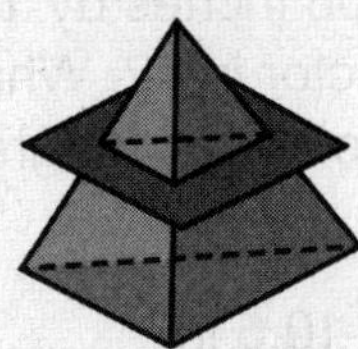

A triangle C pyramid

B parallelogram D rectangle

15. Juanita has a bag of marbles. Without looking, she removes one marble, notes the color, and replaces it. She repeats this process 70 times and records the results in the table below.

Color	Frequency
Red	14
Green	19
Blue	21
Yellow	16

What is the probability that she will pick a blue marble on her seventy-first try?

A $\frac{1}{5}$ C $\frac{19}{70}$

B $\frac{8}{35}$ D $\frac{3}{10}$

16. What is 64% of 40?

A 104 C 26

B 28.3 D 25.6

Name ______________________ Date ____________ Class ____________

Placement Test

17. Simplify $\frac{1}{3}(9a+b)-\frac{1}{2}(4a+2b)$.

A $a-\frac{2}{3}b$ C $2a+\frac{1}{2}b$

B $a+\frac{1}{3}b$ D $2a-b$

18. The volume of a rectangular prism is 240 cubic centimeters. A rectangular pyramid has the same length, width, and height as the prism. What is the volume of the pyramid?

A 720 cm^3 C 80 cm^3

B 360 cm^3 D 40 cm^3

19. Tim took a random survey of 20 sixth graders and 20 eighth graders. He asked how many hours a week each played sports. His data is shown in the two dot plots below.

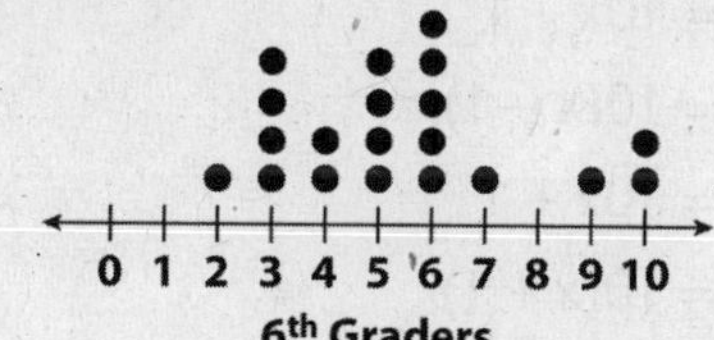

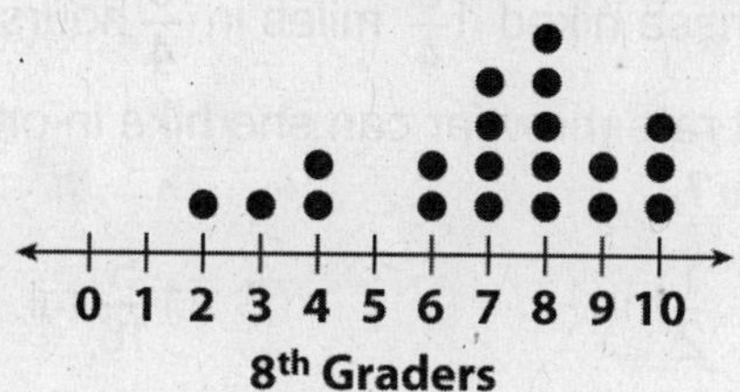

What is the difference between the median number of hours that 6th graders play sports and the median number of hours that 8th graders play sports?

A 4 h C 2 h

B 2.5 h D 1.65 h

20. What is the value of the expression below?

$$(-64) \div (-16)$$

A 4 C –4

B –1 D –8

21. A quarterback completes 65% of his passes. Out of his next 40 passes, how many can you expect to be completed?

A 22 passes C 26 passes

B 24 passes D 28 passes

22. The Canadian $1 coin has a diameter of 26.5 mm. What is the circumference of the coin? Use 3.14 for π.

A 83.21 mm C 158.64 mm

B 108.64 mm D 166.42 mm

23. Melissa bought a new dishwasher for $1,200. The manufacturer is offering a 15% rebate. How much will the dishwasher cost after the rebate?

A $180 C $1,020

B $1,000 D $1,380

24. What is the area of the figure below?

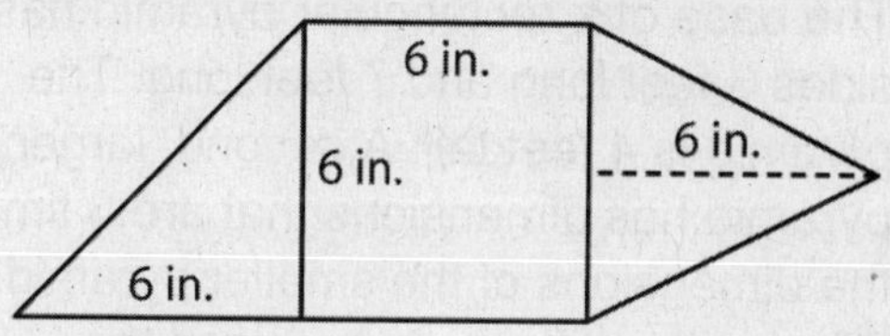

A 40 in^2 C 64 in^2

B 54 in^2 D 72 in^2

25. Evan wants to leave an 18% tip for the server at a restaurant. Which expression does **not** show how to calculate the tip if b is the total bill?

A $0.18b$ C $0.1b+0.08b$

B $b+0.18b$ D $b-0.82b$

26. What is the greatest integer that satisfies the inequality $3x-4 \leq 8$?

A 4 C 6

B 5 D 7

Name ______________________ Date ______________ Class ______________

Placement Test

27. Harry rolls a number cube. What is the probability that he will roll an even number **or** a number greater than 4?

A $\frac{1}{6}$
B $\frac{1}{3}$
C $\frac{1}{2}$
D $\frac{2}{3}$

28. Which of the following equations represents the linear relationship shown in the table below?

x	2	3	4	5
y	7	9	11	13

A $y = 2x - 3$
B $y = 2x + 3$
C $y = 3x - 2$
D $y = 3x + 2$

29. The base of a rectangular pyramid has sides 3 feet long and 7 feet long. The pyramid is 4 feet tall. A second, larger pyramid has dimensions that are 3 times the dimensions of the smaller pyramid. What is the difference between the volumes of the two pyramids?

A 28 ft^3
B 56 ft^3
C 728 ft^3
D 756 ft^3

30. The solution to which inequality is shown in the number line below?

A $3x + 2 < 4$
B $3x - 2 > 4$
C $3x + 2 \geq 4$
D $3x - 2 \leq 4$

31. Sal bought 3 CDs for $15.98 each, a computer cable for $39.95, and a case for his MP3 player for $24.99. Sales tax is 7%. To the nearest cent, what is the total cost of his purchases?

A $120.78
B $121.78
C $121.79
D $130.79

32. The triangles below are similar. What is the length of $\overline{ED}$?

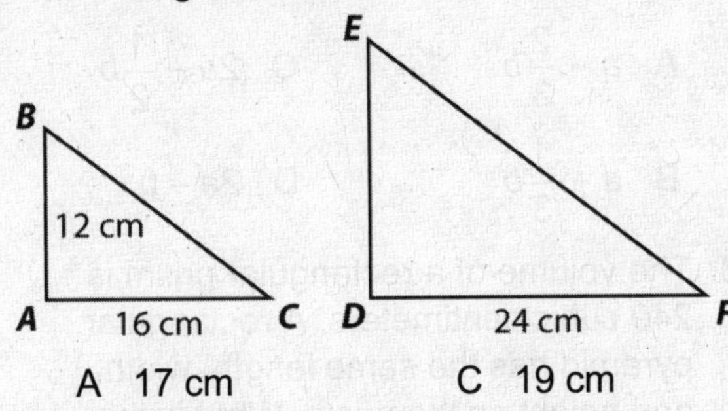

A 17 cm
B 18 cm
C 19 cm
D 20 cm

33. Which equation represents the data shown in the table below?

Fence Length (*y*)	100	150	180	240
Number of Posts (*x*)	11	16	19	25

A $y = 10x - 1$
B $y = 10(x - 1)$
C $y = 10x + 1$
D $y = 10(x + 1)$

34. Marissa hiked $1\frac{3}{4}$ miles in $\frac{3}{4}$ hours. At that rate, how far can she hike in one hour?

A $\frac{1}{2}$ mi
B $\frac{2}{3}$ mi
C $1\frac{5}{16}$ mi
D $2\frac{1}{3}$ mi

35. Nick tosses a standard number cube and spins a spinner. The spinner is divided into four equal sections colored red, blue, green, and yellow. What is the probability that Nick rolls an odd number and spins green?

A $\frac{1}{8}$
B $\frac{1}{6}$
C $\frac{1}{5}$
D $\frac{1}{4}$

Name ______________________ Date ______________ Class ______________

Beginning-of-Year Diagnostic Test

1. Which label could replace "A" in the diagram below?

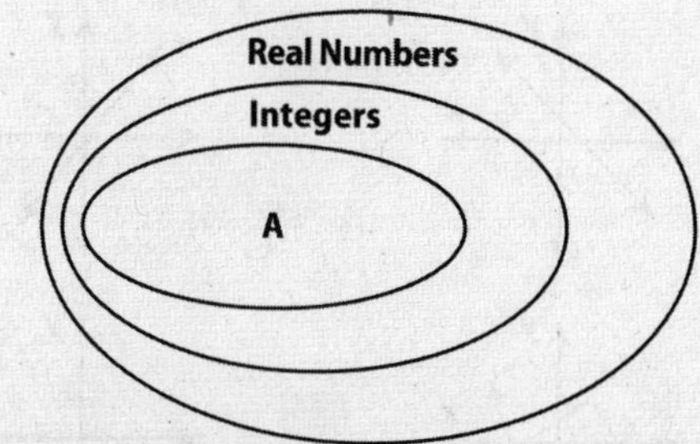

A Rational Numbers

B Whole Numbers

C Negative Numbers

D Irrational Numbers

2. Between which two integers does the value of $\sqrt{50}$ lie?

A 4 and 5

B 7 and 8

C 8 and 9

D 49 and 51

3. Alejandro wrote the number 6,240,000 in scientific notation. Which number did he write?

A 62.4×10^{-6}

B 6.24×10^{-5}

C 62.4×10^{5}

D 6.24×10^{6}

4. The gray figure is the image of the black figure after a dilation.

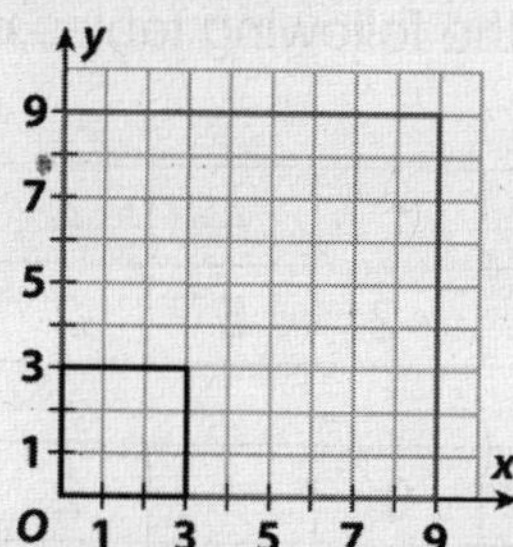

Which represents the dilation?

A $(x, y) \rightarrow \left(\frac{1}{2}x, \frac{1}{2}y\right)$

B $(x, y) \rightarrow (2x, 2y)$

C $(x, y) \rightarrow (3x, 3y)$

D $(x, y) \rightarrow (6x, 6y)$

5. The lengths in centimeters of four line segments are shown below.

$$3.1, 3.5, 3\frac{1}{5}, 4.2$$

Which list shows the lengths in order from **least** to **greatest**?

A $3.1, 3\frac{1}{5}, 3.5, 4.2$

B $3.1, 3.5, 3\frac{1}{5}, 4.2$

C $3\frac{1}{5}, 3.1, 3.5, 4.2$

D $4.2, 3.5, 3\frac{1}{5}, 3.1$

6. A figure is dilated by a factor of 3. Which statement about the measurements of the image is true?

A The perimeter of the original figure is multiplied by 3, and the area is multiplied by 9.

B The perimeter and area of the original figure are tripled.

C The perimeter of the original figure is multiplied by 9, and the area is multiplied by 27.

D The perimeter of the original figure is multiplied by 9, and the area is multiplied by 3.

7. The points $A(0, 0)$, $B(1, 1)$, $C(2, 2)$ and $D(3, 3)$ all lie on the line $y = x$. Ben calculated the slopes of $\overline{AB}$ and $\overline{CD}$. What can he conclude?

A The slopes are the same.

B The slope of $\overline{AB}$ is greater than the slope of $\overline{CD}$.

C The slope of $\overline{CD}$ is greater than the slope of $\overline{AB}$.

D The slopes of $\overline{AB}$ and $\overline{CD}$ are negative.

Name ________________________ Date ______________ Class ______________

Beginning-of-Year Diagnostic Test

8. What is the slope of the line described by the data in the table below?

x	0	1	2	3
y	2	4	6	8

A -2 C $-\frac{1}{2}$

B $\frac{1}{2}$ D 2

9. Which equation shows the relationship in the table below?

x	3	4	5	6
y	9	12	15	18

A $y = x$ C $y = 3x$

B $y = 2x$ D $y = 4x$

10. Which of the following is the equation of the line graphed below?

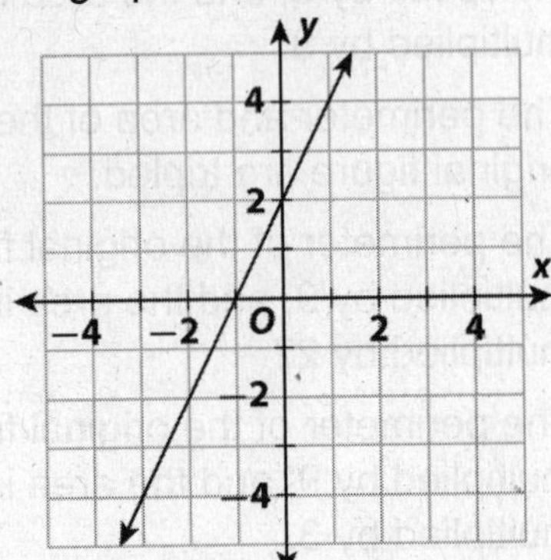

A $y = -2x + 2$ C $y = -2x - 2$

B $y = 2x - 2$ D $y = 2x + 2$

11. Carmella sells homemade pies for \$10 a pie. It costs \$2 for the ingredients to bake each pie. Carmella bought a new oven for \$600. How many pies must Carmella bake and sell before she recovers the cost of the oven?

A 50 C 75

B 60 D 95

12. Which of the following graphs does **not** show a linear relationship?

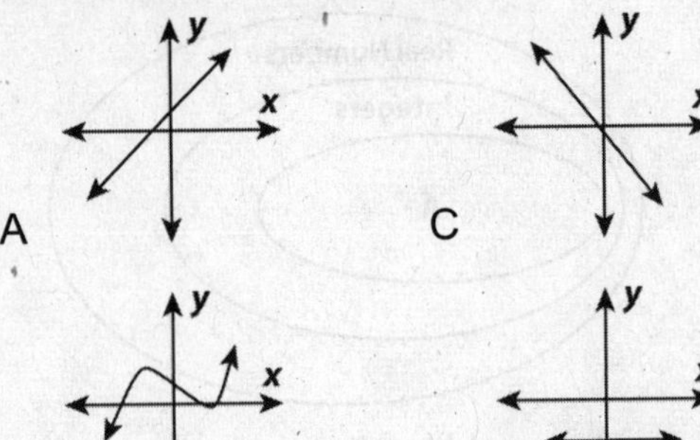

13. What is the value of n in the equation: $8n + 9 = -n$?

A -1

B $-\frac{7}{9}$

C 1

D 17

14. Which of the following equations represents a proportional relationship?

A $y = 5x$ C $y = \frac{5}{x}$

B $y = \frac{1}{2}x + 5$ D $y = x + \frac{1}{2}$

15. Which of the following tables represents a function?

A

x	1	4	4	5
y	−2	5	2	6

B

x	0	1	2	3
y	2	3	4	−3

C

x	0	1	2	2
y	1	5	5	8

D

x	0	1	2	1
y	8	9	8	−4

Name ______________________ Date ____________ Class ____________

Beginning-of-Year Diagnostic Test

16. Andrew graphed the triangle $X'Y'Z'$ by dilating triangle XYZ. Which of the following **must** be true?

   A The ratios of corresponding sides of triangles XYZ and $X'Y'Z'$ are equal.

   B The area of triangle $X'Y'Z'$ is greater than the area of triangle XYZ.

   C Triangle XYZ is congruent to triangle $X'Y'Z'$.

   D Triangle XYZ is an isosceles triangle.

17. A cell phone company charges $50 for the phone plus a monthly service charge of $30. The equation below describes the total cost y after x months.

$$y = 30x + 50$$

   Which is true of the relationship between x and y?

   A It is linear and proportional.

   B It is linear and non-proportional.

   C It is not linear and proportional.

   D It is not linear and non-proportional.

18. A leopard's speed was timed over a 50-yard distance. The leopard was running 50 miles per hour. Which equation shows the relationship between the distance in miles, y, and time, x, the leopard runs?

   A $y = 50x$ B $y = 60x + 50$

   C $y = 50x + 60$ D $y = 60x$

19. Which expression can you substitute in the indicated equation to solve the system of equations shown below?

$$\begin{cases} 4x + 3y = 4 \\ y = -3x - 2 \end{cases}$$

   A $-3x - 2$ for x in $4x + 3y = 4$

   B $-3x - 2$ for y in $4x + 3y = 4$

   C $4x + 3y$ for x in $y = -3x - 2$

   D $4x + 3y$ for y in $y = -3x - 2$

20. What is the solution to the system of equations shown below?

$$\begin{cases} -4x + y = -1 \\ 2x + 2y = -2 \end{cases}$$

   A (−5, 1) C (0, −1)

   B (−1, 2) D (−1, 0)

21. Ananya drew a cylinder with a radius of 3 inches and a height of 5 inches. She also drew a cone with the same radius and height. Which of the following is true?

   A The volumes are the same.

   B The volume of the cylinder is three times the volume of the cone.

   C The volume of the cone is three times the volume of the cylinder.

   D The volume of the cylinder is four-thirds the volume of the cone.

22. Martin used the diagram below to explain the Pythagorean theorem to a classmate. Which statement did Martin use in his explanation?

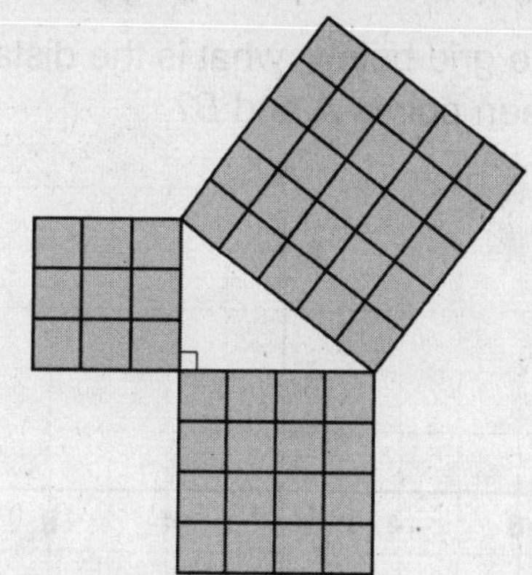

   A $3^2 + 4^2 < 5^2$

   B $5^2 + 4^2 = 3^2$

   C $3^2 + 5^2 = 4^2$

   D $3^2 + 4^2 = 5^2$

Name ______________________ Date ______________ Class ______________

Beginning-of-Year Diagnostic Test

23. A sphere has a radius of 3 centimeters. What is the volume of the sphere?

A 36π cm^3 C 144π cm^3

B 72π cm^3 D 288π cm^3

24. The figure shows two parallel lines intersected by a transversal. Which pair of angles is congruent?

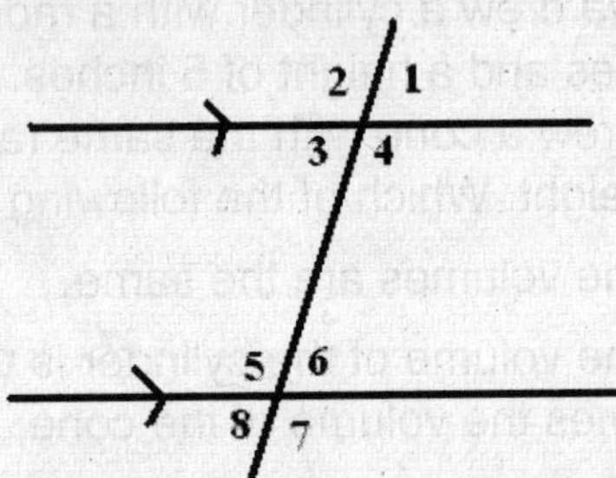

A ∠1 and ∠2 C ∠3 and ∠7

B ∠2 and ∠5 D ∠5 and ∠6

25. A diagonal shortcut across a rectangular lot is 100 feet long. The lot is 60 feet wide. What is the length of the lot?

A 40 ft C 80 ft

B 60 ft D 90 ft

26. On the grid below, what is the distance between points *A* and *B*?

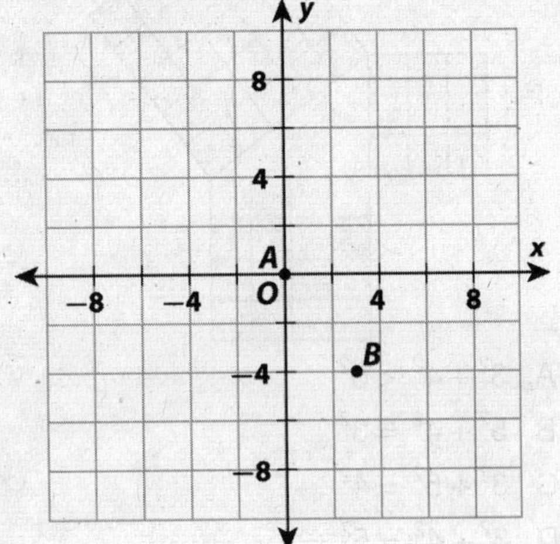

A 3 units C 5 units

B 4 units D 25 units

27. The table shows the amount of gas used by a household over time. What is the slope of the data in the table?

Number of Weeks	2	3	4	5	6
Gas Used (ft^3)	80	120	160	200	240

A −160

B −40

C 40

D 80

28. The equation below can be used to solve which of the following word problems?

$$2x + 15 = 4x$$

A The price of four books is $15 more than the price of two books. What is the price per book?

B The price of two books is $15 more than the price of four books. What is the price per book?

C The price of four books equals $15. What is the price per book?

D John bought a certain number of $2 books and $4 books for a total of $15. How many of each book did he buy?

29. Mariana rides her bicycle 5 miles per hour. Which graph represents this relationship?

A 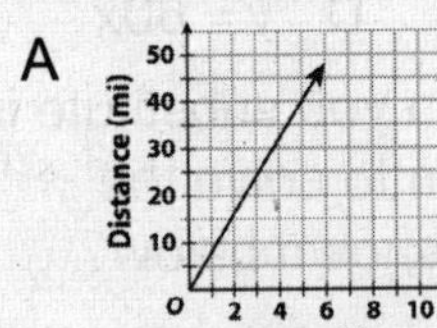

C 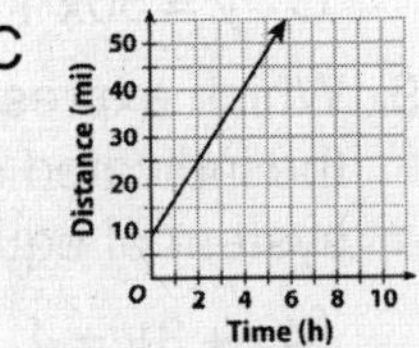

B 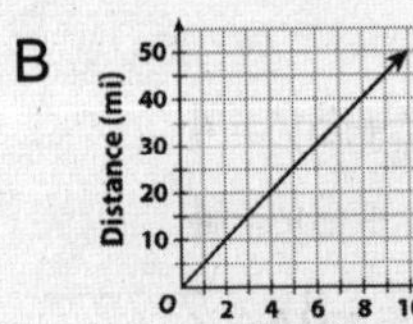

D 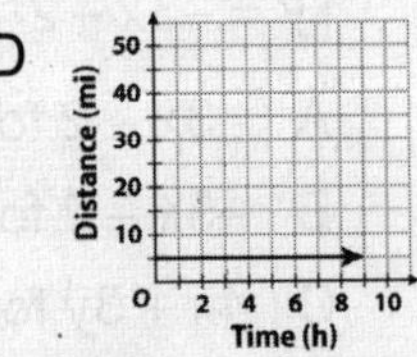

Name ______________________ Date ______________ Class ______________

Beginning-of-Year Diagnostic Test

30. The measures of the three angles of a triangle are $(x)°$, $(2x)°$ and $(3x)°$. What is the value of x?

    A 20   C 40

    B 30   D 50

31. What is the solution of the system of equations graphed below?

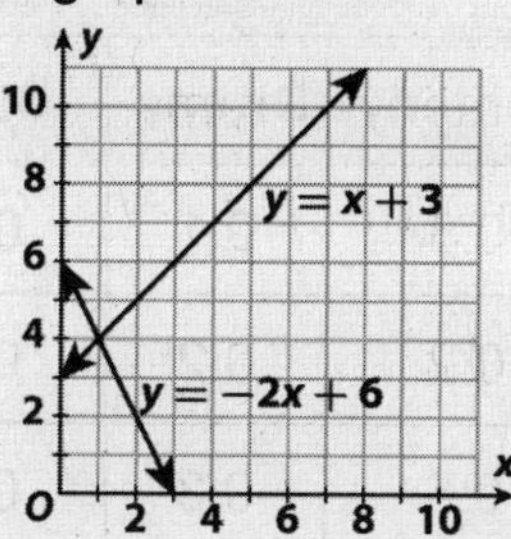

    A (0, 3)   C (1, 4)

    B (0, 6)   D (3, 0)

32. Under which transformation is orientation **not** preserved?

    A translation   C reflection

    B dilation   D rotation

33. Michael applied a transformation to triangle *ABC* to obtain triangle *A'B'C'*. The two triangles are **not** congruent. Which of the following could be the transformation Michael applied?

    A translation   C reflection

    B dilation   D rotation

34. Which of the following best describes the number of solutions to the system of equations shown below?

$$\begin{cases} 2x + y = 3 \\ -4x - 2y = -6 \end{cases}$$

    A no solutions

    B one solution

    C two solutions

    D infinitely many solutions

35. Which expression represents 64?

    A 2^3 C 2^5

    B 2^4 D 2^6

36. The vertices of a triangle are located at the points $A(0, 1)$, $B(2, 4)$ and $C(3, 0)$. The triangle is translated 5 units down to obtain triangle *A'B'C'*. What are the coordinates of the vertices of triangle *A'B'C'*?

    A $A'(0, -4)$, $B'(2, -1)$, $C'(3, -5)$

    B $A'(0, 6)$, $B'(2, 9)$, $C'(3, 5)$

    C $A'(-5, 1)$, $B'(-3, 4)$, $C'(-2, 0)$

    D $A'(5, 1)$, $B'(7, 4)$, $C'(8, 0)$

37. Jenya obtained the image of triangle *ABC* after a dilation with a scale factor of 3. The area of triangle *ABC* is 15 square centimeters, and its perimeter is 20 centimeters. Which of the following describes the area and perimeter of the new figure?

    A The area is 45 cm^2 and the perimeter is 60 cm.

    B The area is 135 cm^2 and the perimeter is 60 cm.

    C The area is 45 cm^2 and the perimeter is 180 cm.

    D The area is 135 cm^2 and the perimeter is 180 cm.

38. Which of the following best describes the relationship between the two variables in the scatter plot and trend line below?

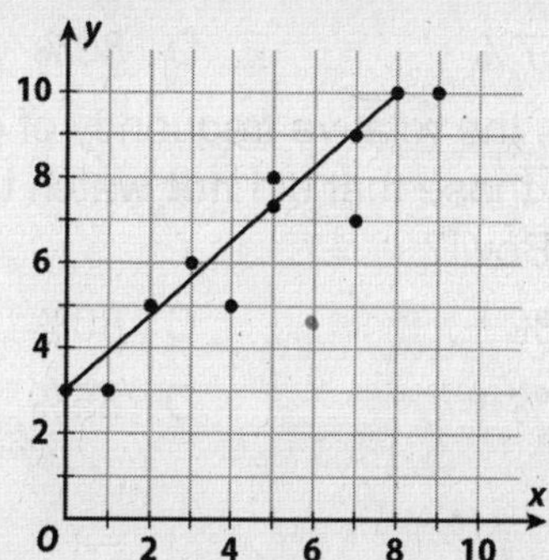

    A positive linear association

    B negative linear association

    C no association

    D quadratic association

Name ____________________ Date ____________ Class ____________

Beginning-of-Year Diagnostic Test

Use the table to answer questions 39–43.

Marlo collected data from students about whether they watched the latest Super Bowl game. The table below shows the results of Marlo's survey.

	Watched	Did Not Watch	TOTAL
Boys	80	20	100
Girls	40	60	100
Total	120	80	200

39. Of the students surveyed, how many watched the Super Bowl?

A 40 C 120
B 80 D 200

40. Of the students surveyed, how many girls did **not** watch the Super Bowl?

A 20 C 60
B 40 D 80

41. What is the relative frequency of students that watched the Super Bowl?

A 20% C 40%
B 30% D 60%

42. What is the relative frequency of boys among those that watched the Super Bowl?

A 33.3% C 75%
B 66.7% D 80%

43. What is the relative frequency of girls among those that did **not** watch the Super Bowl?

A 65% C 80%
B 75% D 85%

Use the table to answer questions 44–47.

Tina collected data from students about the type of movie they preferred: comedy, drama, or other. The two-way relative frequency table below shows the results of Tina's survey.

	Preferred Type of Movie			
Gender	**Comedy**	**Drama**	**Other**	**Total**
Boys	0.3	0.1	0.1	0.5
Girls	0.2	0.2	0.1	0.5
Total	0.5	0.3	0.2	1

44. What is the joint relative frequency of students surveyed who are boys and prefer comedy movies?

A 10% C 30%
B 20% D 40%

45. What is the joint relative frequency of students surveyed who prefer movies other than comedies or dramas?

A 10% C 30%
B 20% D 40%

46. What is the marginal relative frequency of students surveyed who prefer dramas?

A 10% C 30%
B 20% D 50%

47. What is the conditional relative frequency that a student prefers dramas, given that the student is a girl?

A 10% C 40%
B 20% D 50%

Name ______________________ Date ______________ Class ______________

Beginning-of-Year Diagnostic Test

48. A sphere has a radius of 1 inch. Which expression represents the volume of the sphere?

A π C $\frac{4}{3}\pi$

B $\frac{\pi}{2}$ D 2π

49. The mass of Earth in kilograms is about 6×10^{24}, and the mass of the Moon is about 7×10^{22}. What is the sum of the masses of Earth and its Moon?

A 1×10^2 C 6.07×10^{24}

B 7.06×10^{23} D 13×10^{46}

50. In what quadrant would the triangle be if it is rotated 90° clockwise about the origin?

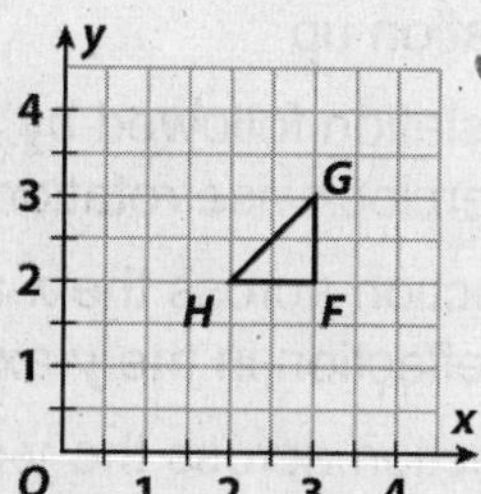

A Quadrant I C Quadrant III

B Quadrant II D Quadrant IV

51. What value of x is the solution to the equation?

$$4(x - 1) = 2(x + 1)$$

A –2 C 1

B 0 D 3

52. What is the value of x in the solution to the system of equations shown below?

$$\begin{cases} 7x + y = 14 \\ -2x - y = 6 \end{cases}$$

A –7 C 2.4

B 1.6 D 4

53. Which graph below shows a linear equation with a positive slope and a negative y-intercept?

A

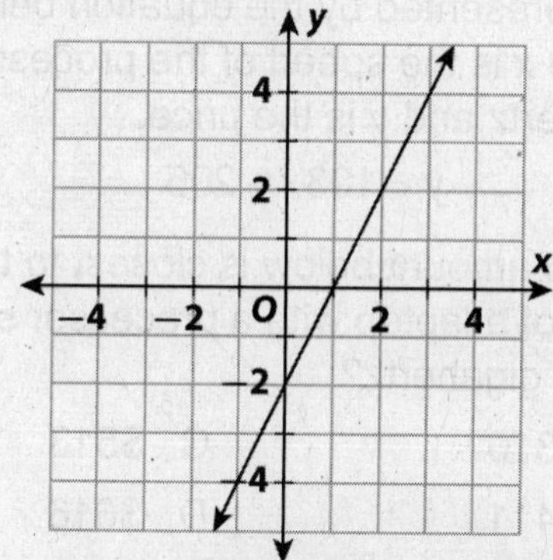

B

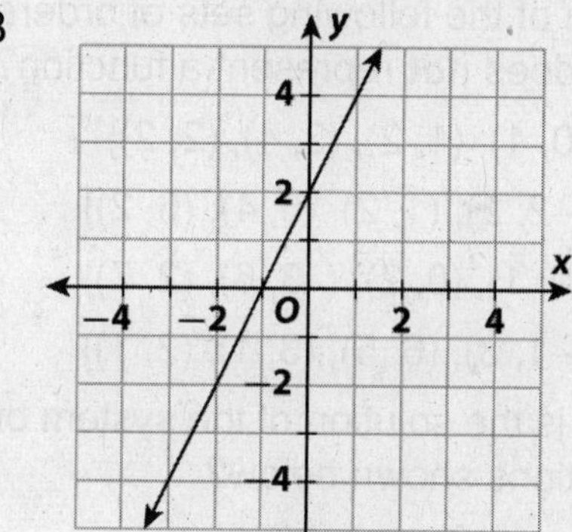

C

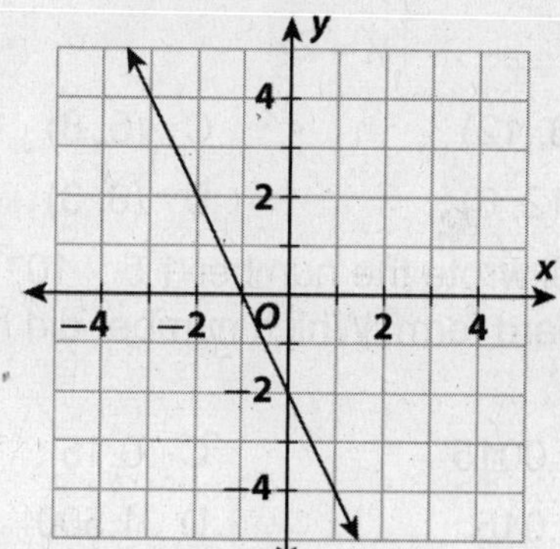

D

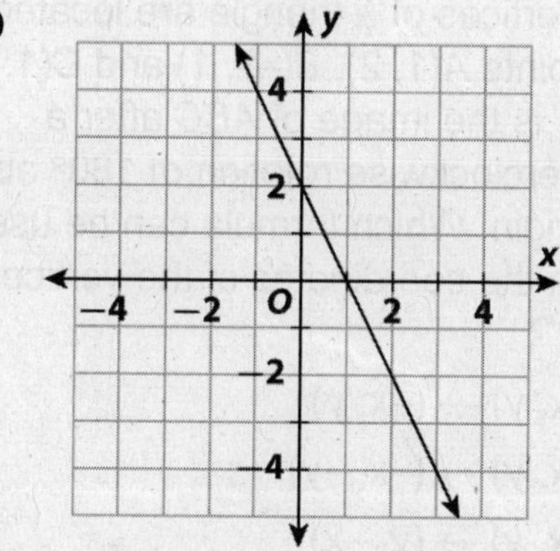

Name ______________________ Date ______________ Class ______________

Beginning-of-Year Diagnostic Test

54. Melvin analyzed prices of laptop computers based on the speed of the processor. He calculated the trend line to be represented by the equation below, where x is the speed of the processor in gigahertz and y is the price.

$$y = 103x + 205$$

Which amount below is closest to the price of a laptop with a processor speed of 2.0 gigahertz?

A \$310 C \$513
B \$411 D \$616

55. Which of the following sets of ordered pairs does **not** represent a function?

A {(0, 1), (1, 2), (3, 4), (2, 2)}
B {(–2, 2), (1, 2), (5, 4), (6, 2)}
C {(0, 1), (0, 2), (–3, 6), (2, 7)}
D {(–1, 3), (6, 5), (3, 1), (2, 1)}

56. What is the solution of the system of equations shown below?

$$\begin{cases} y = 3x - 6 \\ y = 2x \end{cases}$$

A (6, 12) C (6, 8)
B (12, 6) D (6, 3)

57. Reniel wrote the number 1.5×10^{-3} in standard form. Which number did he write?

A 0.0015 C 0.15
B 0.015 D 1,500

58. The vertices of a triangle are located at the points $A(1, 2)$, $B(-2, 1)$ and $C(1, 5)$. $A'B'C'$ is the image of ABC after a counterclockwise rotation of 180° about the origin. Which formula can be used to obtain the coordinates of the vertices of $A'B'C'$?

A $(x, y) \to (-x, y)$
B $(x, y) \to (-x, -y)$
C $(x, y) \to (y, -x)$
D $(x, y) \to (-y, x)$

59. Ashton applied a sequence of transformations to obtain triangle B from triangle A as shown below.

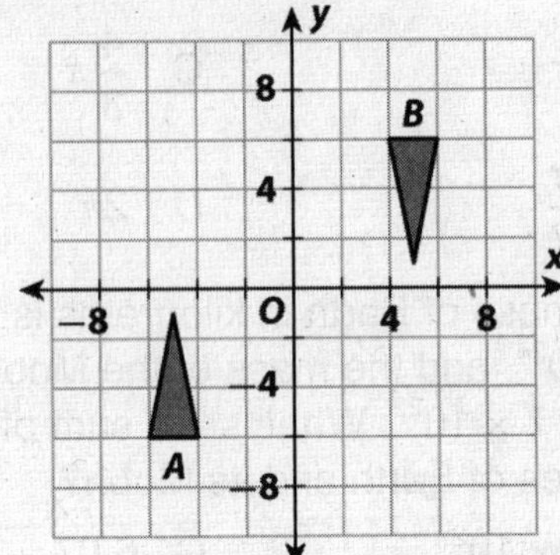

Which of the following describes a sequence of transformations that could have been used?

A a translation right followed by a translation up
B a translation followed by a 90° counterclockwise rotation
C a reflection across the x-axis followed by a reflection in the y-axis
D a reflection across the y-axis followed by a dilation

60. Lisa analyzed the scatter plot below.

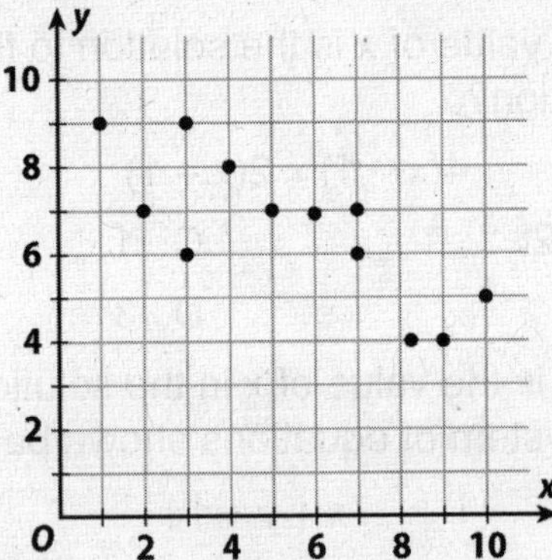

Which of the following best describes the relationship between the two variables?

A positive linear association
B negative linear association
C nonlinear association
D no association

Name ______________________ Date ____________ Class ____________

Beginning-of-Year Diagnostic Test

61. Juan drew a rectangle with a perimeter of 22 units. He then performed a dilation with scale factor of 2 on the rectangle. What is the perimeter of the resulting image?

 A 11 units C 24 units

 B 20 units D 44 units

62. What is the solution to the system of equations shown below?

$$\begin{cases} y = 3x + 20 \\ y = 5x + 2 \end{cases}$$

 A (9, 47) C (9, 27)

 B (9, 45) D (–11, –53)

63. Mary wrote the number 2.3×10^3 in standard form. Which number did she write?

 A 0.0023 C 23

 B 0.023 D 2,300

64. At the café, Padma can choose to earn $12 per hour plus a $100 starting bonus, or to earn $16 per hour with no starting bonus. After how many hours of work will she earn the same amount under both payment options?

 A 4 h C 50 h

 B 25 h D 84 h

65. The point (–2, –3) is rotated 180° about the origin. What are the coordinates of the resulting image?

 A (–2, 3) C (2, –3)

 B (2, 3) D (3, 2)

66. Which is the equation of the line that represents the data shown in the table below?

x	–1	0	1	2	3
y	5	8	11	14	17

 A $y = -3x + 8$ C $y = -3x - 8$

 B $y = 3x + 8$ D $y = 3x - 8$

67. The volume of a cone is 300 cubic centimeters. A cylinder has the same radius and height as the cone. What is the volume of the cylinder?

 A 200 cm^3 C 900 cm^3

 B 400 cm^3 D 2,700 cm^3

68. At a farmer's market, Paul can purchase 6 pears and one apple for the same price as 8 pears. The price of the apple is $0.80. What is the price of each pear?

 A $0.40 C $0.80

 B $0.60 D $1.60

69. To the nearest tenth, what is the distance between the points (–3, 3) and (1, 2)?

 A 2.2 units C 5.4 units

 B 4.1 units D 6.4 units

70. At a bookstore, the price of two notebooks plus a $40 backpack is the same as the price of 10 notebooks. Which equation could be used to find the price of each notebook?

 A $2x = 10x + 40$ C $40 = 2x + 10x$

 B $2x + 40 = 10x$ D $2x - 40 = 10x$

71. Triangles *ABC* and *XYZ* below are similar. What is the length of $\overline{XZ}$?

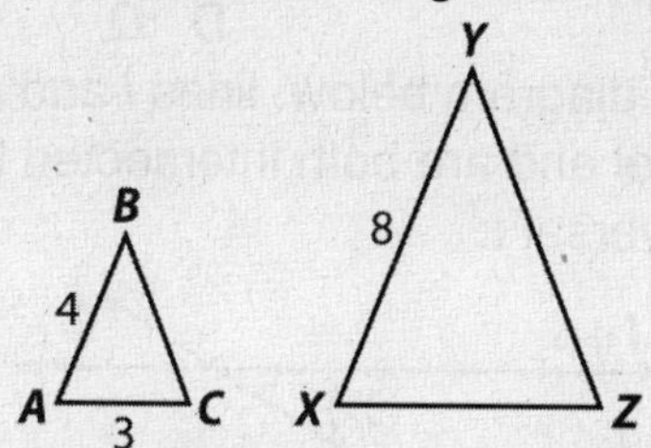

 A 1.5 units C 6 units

 B 3 units D 7 units

72. A produce stand sells a basket of 12 apples for $6. If the unit price of an apple is the same, what is the price for a basket of 18 apples?

 A $2 C $18

 B $9 D $36

Name ________________________ Date ______________ Class ______________

Beginning-of-Year Diagnostic Test

73. What is the y-intercept of the line graphed below?

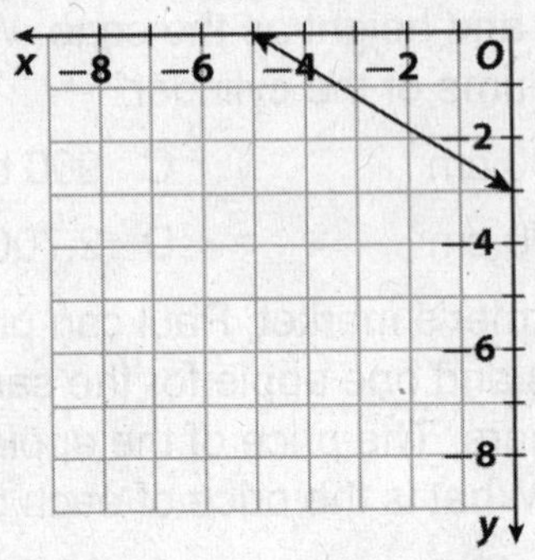

A -5 C $-\frac{3}{5}$

B -3 D 3

74. Janna has a rectangular yard that measures 20 feet by 48 feet. She wants to install a fence along the diagonal of the yard. How long will the fence be?

A 28 ft C 52 ft

B 34 ft D 136 ft

75. Which lettered point shows the position of $\sqrt{20}$ on the number line below?

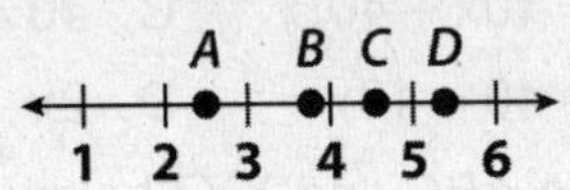

A *A* C *C*

B *B* D *D*

76. In the diagram below, lines *l* and *m* are parallel and are both intersected by transversal *t*.

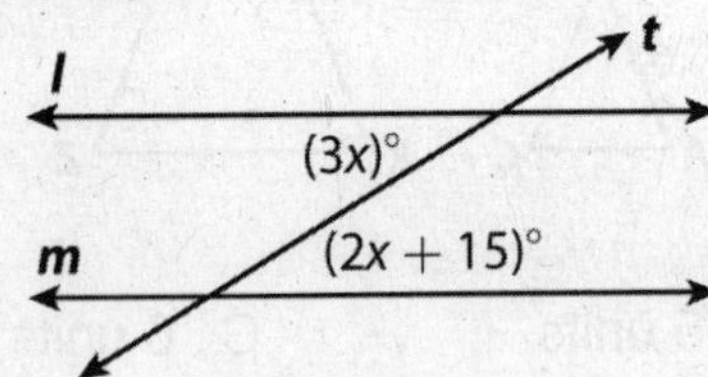

What is the value of x?

A 15 C 45

B 30 D 135

77. What is the solution to the equation below?

$$0.5x + 20 = 0.6x$$

A $x = -200$ C $x = 20$

B $x = 2$ D $x = 200$

78. What is the solution to the system of equations graphed below?

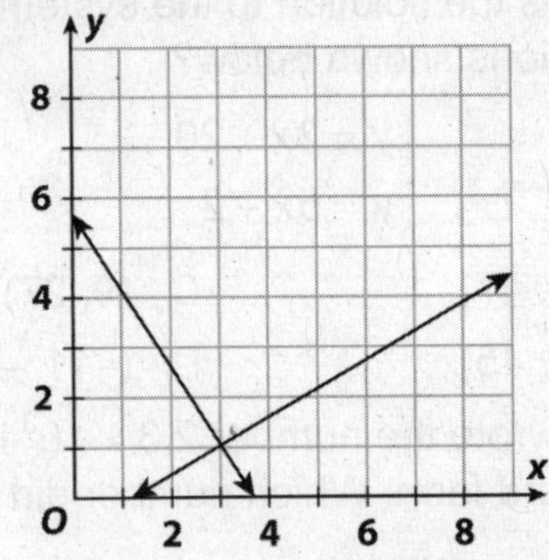

A (1, 3) C (0, –1)

B (3, 1) D (0, 5.5)

79. What is the value of x in the diagram below?

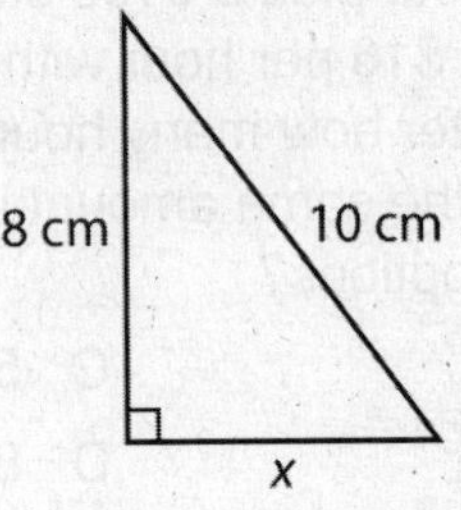

A 6 cm C 24 cm

B 9 cm D 34 cm

80. Which equation represents the data shown in the table below?

x	–1	0	1	2	3
y	3	1	–1	–3	–5

A $y = -2x - 1$ C $y = -2x + 1$

B $y = x + 1$ D $y = 2x + 1$

Name ______________________ Date __________ Class __________

MODULE 1

Real Numbers

Module Quiz: B

1. Which expression shows a decimal equivalent to the fraction $\frac{13}{32}$?

A 0.41 C 0.40625
B 0.406 D 0.4625

2. Which fraction equals a repeating decimal?

A $\frac{5}{80}$ C $\frac{17}{85}$
B $\frac{11}{88}$ D $\frac{18}{81}$

3. Which number is a perfect square?

A 249 C 265
B 256 D 281

4. If $\sqrt{n} = \frac{3}{2}$, what is $-\sqrt{n}$?

A $-\frac{3}{2}$ C $\frac{1}{2}$
B $-\frac{2}{3}$ D $\frac{2}{3}$

5. A square playing field has an area of 1,255 square yards. About how long is each side of the field?

A 12.55 yards C 35 yards
B 2.55 yards D 55 yards

6. Which is an estimate of $\sqrt{35}$ to the nearest hundredth?

A 3.5 C 5.91
B 5.29 D 5.92

7. Which value of *n* will make the rational number $-\frac{17}{n}$ an integer?

A 18 C 170
B 102 D none of these

8. Which of these is **most** likely to describe the change received from a cash purchase?

A whole number
B negative integer
C rational number
D irrational number

9. Which term for set A makes this diagram true?

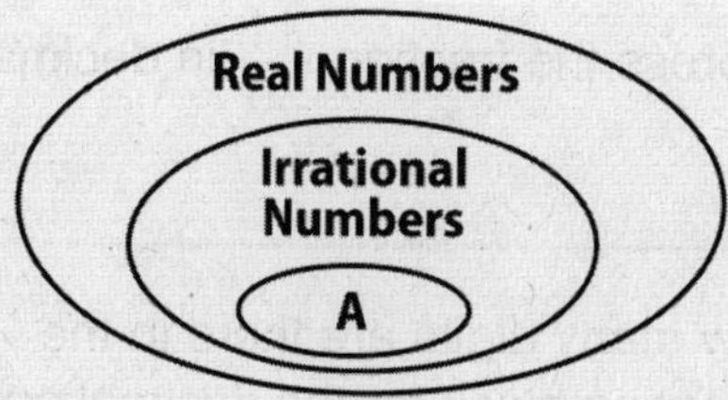

A Whole Numbers
B Rational Numbers
C Integers
D none of these

10. Which statement is false?

A Some integers are irrational.
B Some integers are whole numbers.
C Some rational numbers are integers.
D Some real numbers are irrational.

11. Which number is between $\frac{17}{4}$ and $\sqrt{20}$?

A $\sqrt{28} - 1.5$ C $2 + \sqrt{8}$
B $\pi + 1.2$ D $\frac{5\pi}{3}$

12. Which is the greatest number?

A $50 - 16\pi$ C $-\sqrt{20} + \frac{1}{2}$
B $16 - \sqrt{410}$ D $\frac{7}{3} - \frac{7\pi}{3}$

Name ____________________ Date ____________ Class ____________

MODULE 1 Real Numbers

13. Is $\frac{11}{128}$ equal to a terminating decimal or a repeating decimal? Explain how you know.

____

14. Write $2\frac{1}{16}$ as a decimal.

____

15. Express the fraction $\frac{11}{30}$ in decimal form.

____

16. How many digits are there in the repeating block for the decimal equivalent of $\frac{3}{7}$?

____

17. Find the two square roots of $\frac{9}{4}$.

____

18. A number line is numbered in tenths. Describe where you would plot $\sqrt{87.35}$.

____

19. Estimate $\sqrt{250}$ to two decimal places.

____

20. Classify $\frac{\sqrt{64}}{5}$ as a whole number, integer, rational number, irrational number, or real number. Write all the names that apply.

____

21. Write the principal square root of the integers between 320 and 325. Which of these is a rational number?

____

For 22–24, use the table.

Geometric Formulas	
area of a circle	$A = \pi r^2$
area of a triangle	$A = \frac{1}{2}bh$
perimeter of a square	$P = 4s$
volume of a sphere	$V = \frac{4}{3}\pi r^3$
surface area of a sphere	$SA = 4\pi r^2$

22. Which formulas contain a rational number that is not an integer?

____

23. Which formulas contain both a rational number and an irrational number?

____

24. What kinds of numbers would not be sensible for the values of the variables?

____

25. Find an integer between $\sqrt{30}$ and $\frac{4\pi}{3}$.

____

26. Arrange the numbers in order from greatest to least.

$\sqrt{150}$, $11\frac{4}{9}$, 4π

____

Name ____________________ Date ____________ Class ____________

MODULE 1

Real Numbers

Module Quiz: D

1. Which decimal equals the fraction $\frac{3}{8}$?

A 0.4
B 0.375
C 0.38

2. Which of these shows a repeating decimal?

A 5.66
B $5.\overline{6}$
C $5\frac{2}{3}$

3. Which number is **not** the square of a whole number?

A 100
B 400
C 800

4. How many square roots does the number 20 have?

A 0
B 1
C 2

5. A garden has an area of 9 square meters. Each square is 1 square meter.

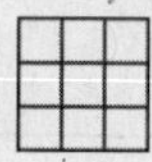

What is the length of one side of this garden?

A 1 meter
B 3 meters
C 16 meters

6. Between which two whole numbers is the square root of 18?

A 4 and 5
B 5 and 6
C 17 and 18

7. Which of these integers is **not** a whole number?

A –6
B 6
C 66

8. A teacher divided a class of students into 3 groups of the same size. Which term describes the number of students in each group?

A whole number
B not an integer
C irrational number

9. The diagram shows sets of numbers. Which set equals set A?

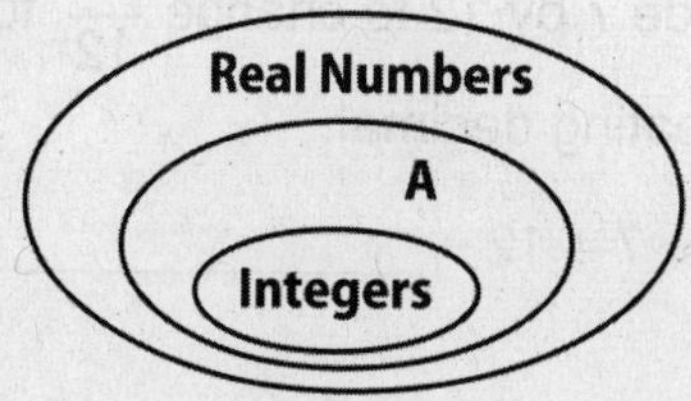

A Whole Numbers
B Rational Numbers
C Integers

10. Which of these **cannot** be a whole number?

A a positive integer
B a negative integer
C a rational number

11. Which number is between $6\frac{1}{8}$ and $\sqrt{64}$?

A $7\frac{1}{2}$
B $8.\overline{16}$
C $\sqrt{68}$

12. Which list is in order from least to greatest?

A $\pi + 10,\ \sqrt{20} + \frac{1}{2},\ \sqrt{100}$
B $\sqrt{100},\ \pi + 10,\ \sqrt{20} + \frac{1}{2}$
C $\sqrt{20} + \frac{1}{2},\ \sqrt{100},\ \pi + 10$

Name ____________________ Date ____________ Class ____________

MODULE 1

Real Numbers

13. Does $\frac{1}{15}$ equal a terminating decimal or a repeating decimal?

____

14. Write $12\frac{31}{100}$ as a decimal.

____

15. Divide 7 by 12 to change $\frac{7}{12}$ to a repeating decimal.

$\frac{7}{12} = 7 \div 12 =$ ____________

16. Write the next 4 digits in the repeating decimal $4.7\overline{15}$.

____

17. Use these facts.

$12 \times 12 = 144$

$-12 \times -12 = 144$

What are the two square roots of 144?

____

18. Between which two whole numbers would you place $\sqrt{40}$ on a number line?

____

19. Estimate the square root of 83 to the nearest whole number.

____

20. Is the square root of 13 a rational number or an irrational number?

____

21. Write the square roots of the even numbers from 10 to 20. Which of these is **not** an irrational number?

____

For 22–24, use the table.

Geometric Formulas	
area of a circle	$A = \pi r^2$
area of a triangle	$A = \frac{1}{2}bh$
perimeter of a square	$P = 4s$
volume of a sphere	$V = \frac{4}{3}\pi r^3$
surface area of a sphere	$SA = 4\pi r^2$

22. Which formulas contain an irrational number?

____

23. Which formulas contain a rational number?

____

24. Why would negative numbers not make sense for the values of the variables?

____

25. Find a whole number between $9\frac{4}{9}$ and $\sqrt{144}$.

____

26. Which number in this list is the greatest?

$8.\overline{33}, 3\pi, \frac{17}{2}, \sqrt{64}$

____

Name ______________________________ Date ________________ Class ______________

MODULE 2

Exponents and Scientific Notation

Module Quiz: B

1. Which shows 2.6×10^4 in standard notation?

   A 264 C 26,000

   B 2,600 D 26,104

2. The population of a large U.S. city is 1,703,210. Which of the following best expresses this population?

   A 1.7×10^6 C 1.703×10^6

   B 1.7×10^7 D 17.03×10^6

3. Find the value of 6^{-3}.

   A –36 C 216

   B –63 D –216

4. When changing 67,430,000 to scientific notation, how many places is the decimal point moved?

   A 4 C 7

   B 6 D 8

5. Let x be the first factor in an expression in scientific notation. Which describes this factor?

   A $0 \le x \le 1$ C $1 \le x \le 10$

   B $0 \le x < 1$ D $1 \le x < 10$

6. What is the standard notation for a distance of 9.302×10^{10} miles?

   A 9,302,000,000 miles

   B 9,302,107,000 miles

   C 93,020,000,000 miles

   D 93,200,000,000 miles

7. A number between 0 and 1 is written in scientific notation. Which of these describes the exponent?

   A fraction

   B whole number

   C positive integer

   D negative integer

8. What is the scientific notation for a length of 0.0000923 centimeter?

   A 9.23×10^{-6} cm C 92.3×10^{-5} cm

   B 9.23×10^{-5} cm D 923×10^{-5} cm

9. Simplify the expression $(7 - 2)^2 + (6 - 2)^3$.

   A 25 C 41

   B 64 D 89

10. A dollar bill is about 0.00011 meter thick. What is this thickness in scientific notation?

    A 11×10^{-6} meter

    B 1.1×10^{-4} meter

    C 1.1×10^{-3} meter

    D 11×10^{-3} meter

11. A distance of 6.5×10^{-8} is multiplied by 10. The result is written in scientific notation. What is the new exponent?

    A –80 C –7

    B –8 D –6

12. A square garden has an area of 1,600 square feet. How long is each side of the garden?

    A 16 feet C 80 feet

    B 40 feet D 160 feet

13. Which of these is most likely to describe the number of yards lost in a football game?

    A rational number

    B whole number

    C real number

    D integer

Name ____________________ Date ____________ Class ____________

MODULE 2

Exponents and Scientific Notation

14. Why is this number not in scientific notation?

    36.5×10^6

    ____

15. Write 3.65×10^5 in standard notation.

    ____

16. What power of ten makes this statement true?

    $78{,}000{,}000{,}000 = 7.8 \times$ ____

17. Write your answer in scientific notation.

    $(6.4 \times 10^3) + (5.2 \times 10^4)$

    ____

18. Round this population figure to two nonzero digits. Then write it in scientific notation.

    186,453,000 people

    ____

19. Change a length of 0.00000843 meter to scientific notation.

    ____

20. Write a diameter of 7.024×10^{-5} centimeter in standard notation.

    ____

21. Write a decimal between 0.0006 and 0.0007. Then write the number in scientific notation.

    ____

22. A small organism with a length of 7.5×10^{-6} meter tripled in size. Write the new length in standard notation.

    ____

For 23–26, use the table.

	Size (meters)
water molecule	3.2×10^{-10}
typical virus	7.5×10^{-8}
small transistor	1.6×10^{-5}
grain of salt	1.6×10^{-4}
large ant	2.5×10^{-2}
height of Mount Everest	8.9×10^{3}
diameter of the moon	3.5×10^{6}
diameter of the sun	1.4×10^{9}

23. How many zeros are needed to write the diameter of the sun in standard notation?

    ____

24. Write the diameter of the transistor in standard notation.

    ____

25. How many digits are there in the standard notation for the height of Mount Everest?

    ____

26. An object is 100 times greater than the grain of salt. Describe the size of this object in scientific notation.

    ____

27. Arrange the numbers in order from greatest to least.

    $4.\overline{3}, \frac{\pi}{4}, \sqrt{75}, \frac{20}{13}$

    ____

28. Write your answer in scientific notation.

    $(5.1 \times 10^7) + (1.3 \times 10^6)$

    ____

Name ______________________ Date ______________ Class ______________

MODULE 2

Exponents and Scientific Notation

Module Quiz: D

1. Which number is equal to the following?

   9×10^3

   A 90
   B 93
   C 9,000

2. Which factor in 5.32×10^9 shows a power of 10?

   A 5.32
   B 9
   C 10^9

3. Which is the correct power to change 810,000 into scientific notation?

   $810{,}000 = 8.1 \times$ ____

   A 10^5
   B 10^6
   C 10^7

4. Which describes the first factor of a number written in scientific notation?

   A less than 0
   B greater than 10
   C greater than or equal to 1 and less than 10

5. Find the value of 2^3.

   A 6
   B 8
   C 23

6. What is a population of 930,000 people written in scientific notation?

   A 9.3×10^5
   B 9.3×10^6
   C 93×10^6

7. In 9.3×10^{-8} the exponent is a negative number. Which of these describes the value of a number in scientific notation that includes a negative exponent?

   A negative
   B very small
   C very large

8. What is this length in standard notation?

   0.7×10^{-4} inch

   A 0.000007 inch
   B 0.00007 inch
   C 0.0007 inch

9. What is this distance in scientific notation?

   0.0065 meter

   A 6.5×10^{-4} meter
   B 6.5×10^{-3} meter
   C 65×10^{-3} meter

10. Simplify the expression $(5 - 1)^2 - (6 - 5)^3$.

    A 15
    B 16
    C 17

11. Which number is the greatest?

    A 2.3×10^{-3}
    B 1.5×10^{-4}
    C 8.6×10^{-2}

12. A square floor has 100 tiles. Each tile is 1 square foot. What is the length of one side of this square floor?

    A 10 feet
    B 20 feet
    C 25 feet

13. A student divided 10 meters of wire into 6 equal parts. Which type of number describes the length of each part?

    A whole number
    B integer
    C rational number

Name ______________________ Date ______________ Class ______________

MODULE 2

Exponents and Scientific Notation

14. This number is written in scientific notation. What is the exponent?

    3.5×10^6

    ____

15. The value of 10^4 is 10,000. Use this fact to change 5.2×10^4 to standard notation.

    $5.2 \times 10^4 = 5.2 \times$ ______ $=$

    ____

16. Complete the steps to change 4,700 to scientific notation.

    $4,700 = 4.7 \times 1,000 =$

    ____________ $\times$ ____________

17. Write your answer in scientific notation.

    $(3 \times 10^3) - (1.4 \times 10^2)$

    ____

18. Write 8.5×10^6 in standard notation.

    ____

19. Use a negative exponent to complete this equation.

    $0.005 = 5 \times 10^?$

    ____

20. $0.00087 = 8.7 \times 10^{-4}$

    How many places does the decimal point move to change 0.00087 into scientific notation?

    ____

21. Write 0.0007 in scientific notation.

    ____

22. Write 1.4×10^{-2} in standard notation.

    ____

For 23–26, use the table.

	Size (meters)
water molecule	3.2×10^{-10}
small transistor	1.6×10^{-5}
grain of salt	1.6×10^{-4}
large ant	2.5×10^{-2}
height of Mount Everest	8.9×10^3
diameter of the sun	1.4×10^9

23. Write the height of Mount Everest in standard notation.

    ____

24. Write the size of the ant in standard notation.

    ____

25. Write the largest number in standard notation.

    ____

26. Which is larger, the transistor or the grain of salt?

    ____

27. Which number in this list is the greatest?

    $\pi,\ 4.\overline{666},\ \sqrt{30},\ \frac{18}{5}$

    ____

28. Write your answer in scientific notation.

    $(5.3 \times 10^7) - (1.1 \times 10^4)$

    ____

Name _______________ Date _______________ Class _______________

MODULE 3

Proportional Relationships

Module Quiz: B

Use the table for 1–3.

Dan's Dog-Walking Business

Time (h)	2	5	9	11
Charge ($)	30		135	165

1. Dan charges $15 per hour for walking dogs. What is the missing number in the table?

   A 50   C 75

   B 60   D 82.5

2. What is the constant of proportionality for the data in the table?

   A $k = 2$ C $k = 15$

   B $k = 11$ D $k = 30$

3. Which equation shows the relationship in the table?

   A $y = 15x$ C $y = x + 15$

   B $y = 30x$ D $y = \frac{15}{x}$

4. Which table shows a constant rate of change?

A

Time (h)	6	12	18
Distance (mi)	225	450	750

B

Time (h)	6	12	18
Distance (mi)	225	500	750

C

Time (h)	6	12	20
Distance (mi)	225	450	675

D

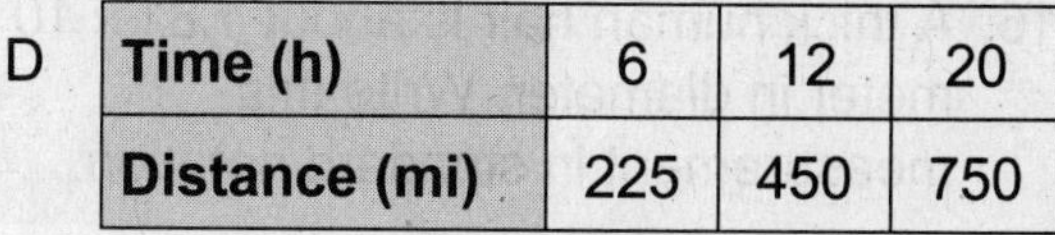

Time (h)	6	12	20
Distance (mi)	225	450	750

Use the graph for 5–6.

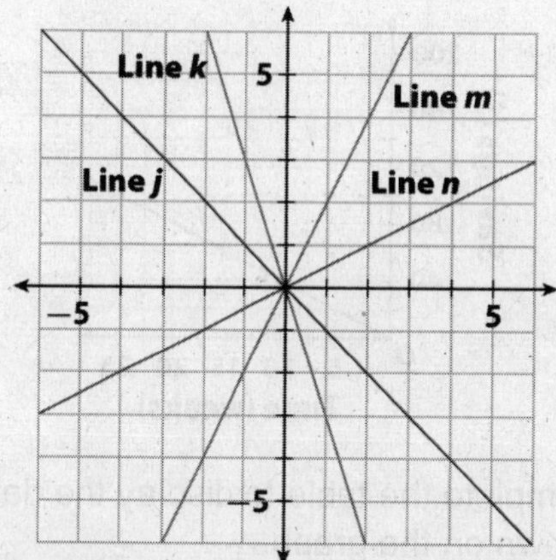

5. Which line has a slope of –3?

   A line *j*   C line *m*

   B line *k*   D line *n*

6. What is the slope of line *n*?

   A –2   C $\frac{1}{2}$

   B $-\frac{1}{2}$ D $\frac{2}{3}$

7. Every 2.5 hours, a machine produces 150 baskets. What is the unit rate of this proportional relationship?

   A 2.5/h   C 25/h

   B 16.6/h   D 60/h

8. Which of the following is a negative rational number that is **not** an integer?

   A $-\pi$ C –2

   B –4.5   D $\sqrt{5}$

Name ______________________ Date ______________ Class ______________

MODULE 3

Proportional Relationships

Use the graph for 9–10.

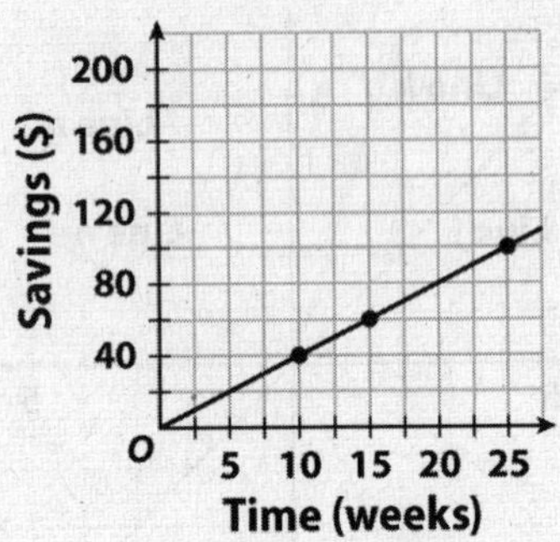

9. Complete the table to display the data shown on the graph.

Time (weeks)			
Savings ($)			

10. Find the constant of proportionality and write an equation for the relationship.

____

11. Carla is renting a canoe. It costs \$80 for 2 hours and \$110 for 4 hours. What is the rate of change for this situation?

____

12. Draw a line through the origin that has a slope of $-\frac{4}{3}$.

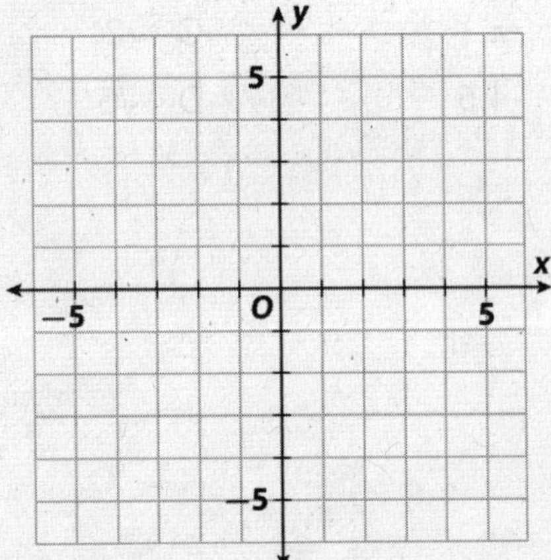

Use the graph for 13–14.

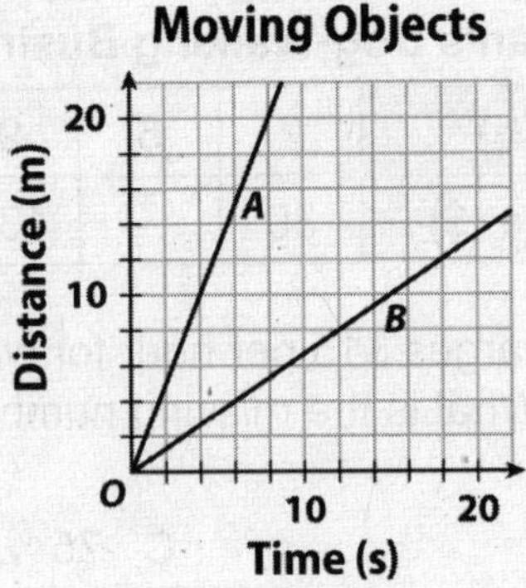

13. The graph shows two objects moving at a constant speed. Use the graph to compare the unit rates.

____

____

14. The data in this table represents another moving object, Object C. Explain how this unit rate compares to those shown on the graph.

Time (s)	5	10	20
Distance (m)	7.5	15	30

____

____

____

15. Hiking at a constant rate, Fred covers 20 miles in 4 hours. Predict how far he can hike in 10 hours.

____

16. A thick human hair is about 1.81×10^{-4} meter in diameter. Write this measurement in standard notation.

____

Name ______________________________ Date ______________ Class______________

MODULE 3

Proportional Relationships

Module Quiz: D

Use the table for 1–3.

Dan's Dog-Walking Business

Time (h)	1	2	3	4
Charge ($)	5	10	15	

1. How much does Dan charge per hour for walking dogs?

   A $1

   B $5

   C $20

2. What is the missing number in the table?

   A 16

   B 20

   C 40

3. Which equation shows the relationship in the table?

   A hours = 5 × dollars

   B dollars = 5 + hours

   C dollars = 5 × hours

4. Which table shows a car moving at a constant speed?

   A

Time (h)	1	2	3
Distance (mi)	50	150	250

   B

Time (h)	1	2	3
Distance (mi)	50	100	150

   C

Time (h)	1	2	3
Distance (mi)	50	500	5,000

Use the graph for 5–6.

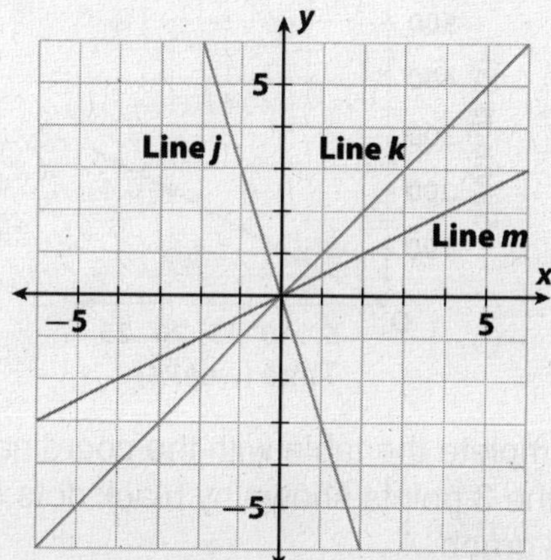

5. Which line has a negative slope?

   A line *j*

   B line *k*

   C line *m*

6. What is the slope of line *m*?

   A −2

   B $\frac{1}{2}$

   C $\frac{2}{3}$

7. Every 3 hours, a machine produces 60 baskets. What is the unit rate?

   A 3 per hour

   B 20 per hour

   C 57 per hour

8. Which of the following is a negative rational number?

   A −4.5

   B $-\pi$

   C $-\sqrt{5}$

Name ______________________ Date ____________ Class ____________

MODULE 3

Proportional Relationships

Use the graph for 9–10.

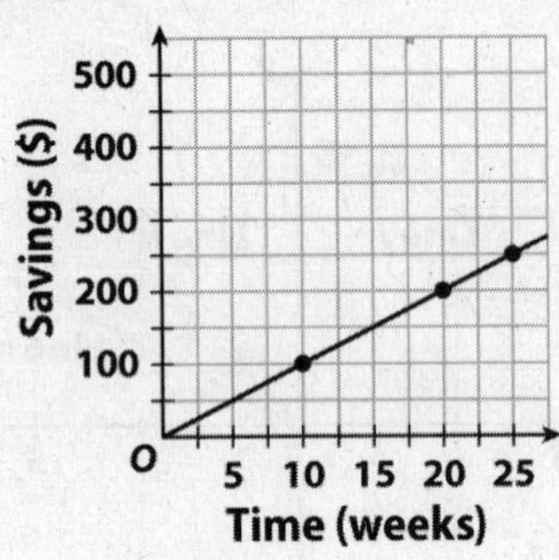

9. Complete the table with the coordinates of the 3 points shown by black dots on the graph.

Time (weeks)			
Savings ($)			

10. Write an equation in the form $y = kx$ for the line on the graph.

____

11. Carla is renting a canoe. It costs $80 for 2 hours and $160 for 4 hours. What is the rate per hour?

____

12. Plot points at (0, 0) and (3, 4). Draw a line through the points. What is the slope of your line?

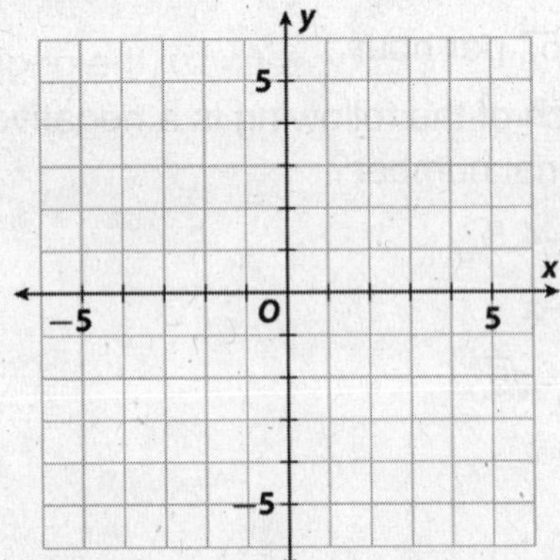

Use the graph for 13–14.

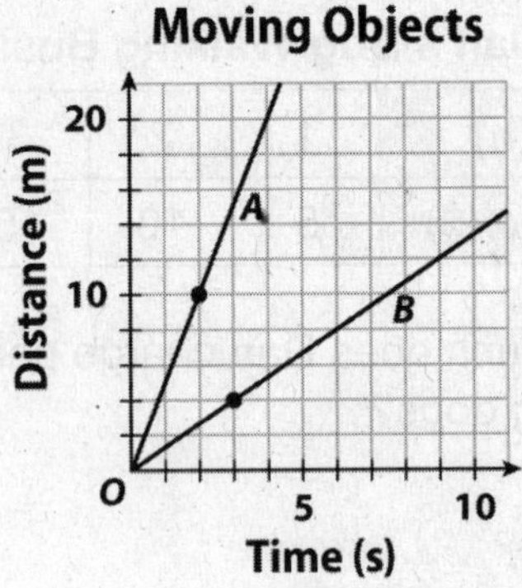

13. The graph shows 2 objects moving at a constant speed. Find the speed of Object *A* in meters per second.

____

14. Which moving object has a greater unit rate? Explain how you know.

____

____

____

15. Hiking at a constant rate, Fred covers 5 miles in 1 hour. Predict how far Fred can hike in 10 hours.

____

16. A thin human hair is about 1.7×10^{-5} meter in diameter. Write this measurement in standard notation.

____

Name ______________________ Date ______________ Class ______________

MODULE 4

Nonproportional Relationships

Module Quiz: B

1. This table shows a proportional relationship.

x	–4	–2	0	2	4
y	–14	–7	0	7	14

Which ordered pair could also belong to this relationship?

A (–6, 21) C (1, 3)

B (–1, –3) D (6, 21)

2. Which line has a slope of $\frac{1}{2}$ and a negative y-intercept?

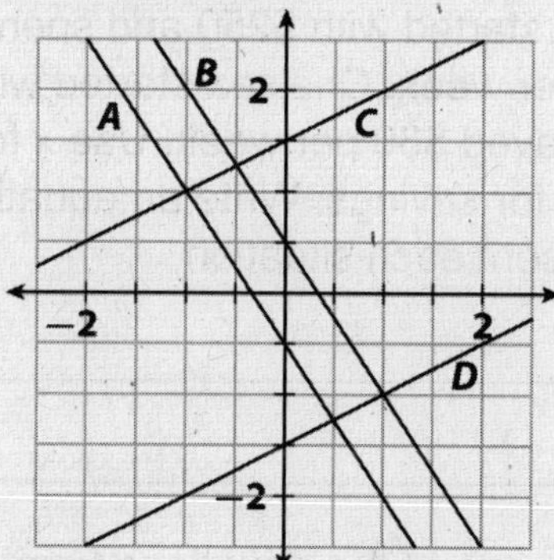

A line A C line C

B line B D line D

Use this situation for 3–4.

On a two-week job, a repairman works a total of 70 hours. He charges $75 plus $40 per hour. An equation shows this relationship, where x is the number of hours and y is the total fee.

3. Which number is the slope of the line shown by the equation?

A 14 C 70

B 40 D 75

4. Which number is the y-intercept?

A 14 C 70

B 40 D 75

5. Which statement **cannot** be true of the graph of a proportional relationship?

A It is not linear.

B It is a straight line.

C It includes the origin.

D It shows a constant ratio.

6. Which equation shows a proportional relationship?

A $y = \frac{1}{2}x - \frac{1}{2}$ C $y = \frac{1}{2}x$

B $y = 2x - 2$ D $y = \frac{2}{x}$

7. These two lines are graphs of nonproportional relationships. What makes them nonproportional?

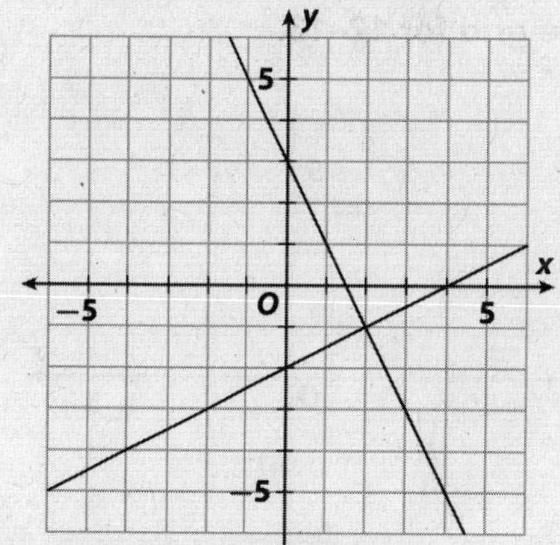

A They are not straight.

B They are not linear

C They do not go through the origin.

D They do not show a constant ratio.

8. What is 3.4 million in scientific notation?

A 3.4×10^6 C 34×10^{-1}

B 3.4×10^7 D 34×10^2

Name ______________________ Date ______________ Class ____________

MODULE 4

Nonproportional Relationships

9. A company prints designs on T-shirts. They charge $40 for set-up costs plus $12 per shirt. Complete the table of values for this situation.

Shirts	1	5	10	50
Cost ($)				

10. Find the slope and y-intercept of the line with equation $2y + x = -6$.

slope = ______ y-intercept: ______

11. Find the slope and y-intercept of the line through the points $(-3, -4)$ and $(0, -1)$.

slope = ______ y-intercept: ______

Use the grid for 12–13.

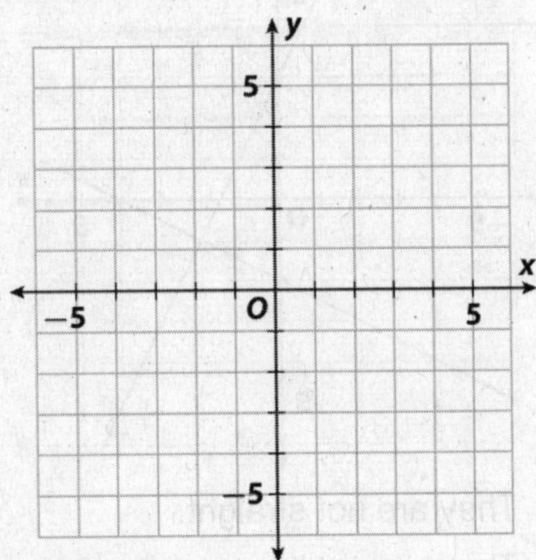

12. Graph $y = -\frac{4}{3}x + 2$ using the slope and y-intercept.

slope = ______ y-intercept: ______

13. Graph $2x - 5y = 10$ by making a table of ordered pairs.

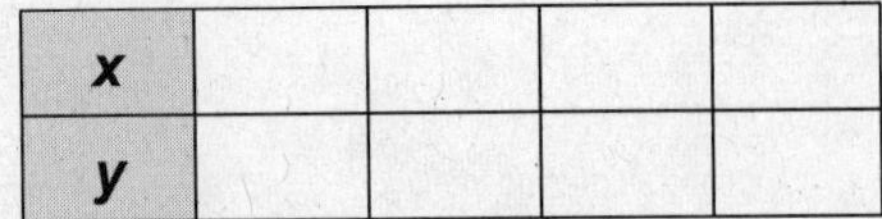

x				
y				

14. Which lines show linear relationships? Which show proportional relationships?

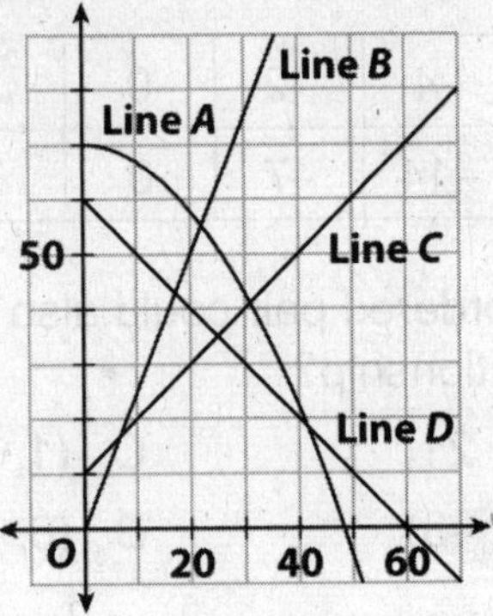

____

15. Steve started with $250 and spent $25 per week. Chelsea started with $30 and saved $30 per week. Use x for time and y for savings. Write an equation to represent each situation.

____

____

16. Graph one of the equations from Exercise 15.

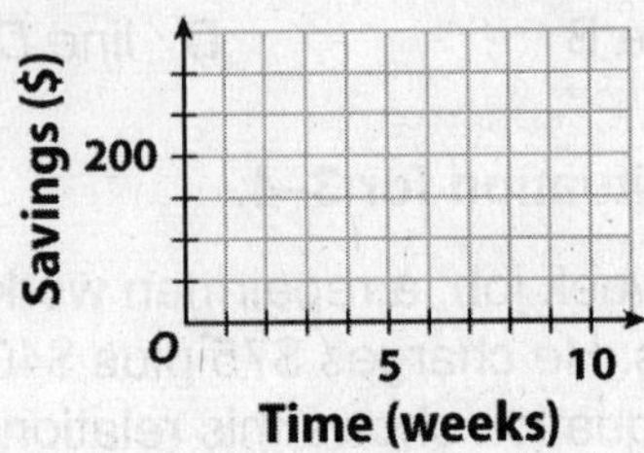

17. Compare. Write >, <, or =.

$\sqrt{5} + \pi \bigcirc \frac{19}{3}$

Name ______________________ Date ______________ Class ______________

MODULE 4

Nonproportional Relationships

Module Quiz: D

1. This table shows a proportional relationship.

x	–4	–2	0	2	4
y	–14	–7	0	7	14

What is the constant ratio, $\frac{y}{x}$?

A –4

B –7

C 3.5

2. Which line has a positive slope and a positive y-intercept?

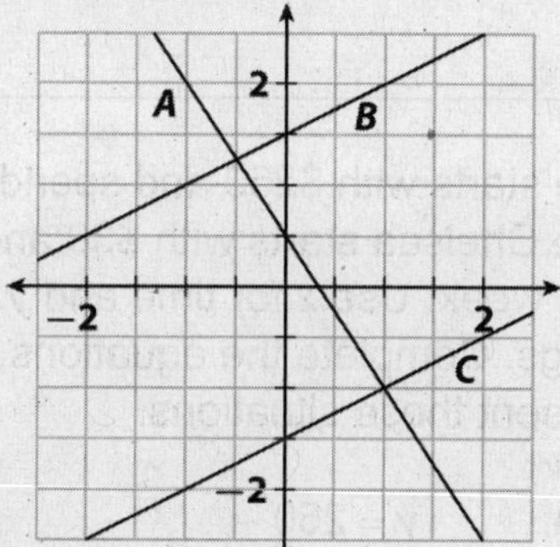

A line A

B line B

C line C

Use this situation for 3–4.

A repairman works 70 hours. He charges $75 plus $40 per hour.

3. Which equation shows this situation?

A $y = 40x + 75$

B $y = 75x + 40$

C $y = 70x + 75$

4. What is the initial value, the cost when the time is 0 hours?

A 0

B 40

C 75

5. What does the graph of a proportional relationship look like?

A a straight line through (0, 0)

B a vertical line through (10, 0)

C a horizontal line through (0, 10)

6. Which is **not** a proportional relationship?

A $y = x$

B $y = x + 2$

C $y = 2x$

7. These two lines are graphs of nonproportional relationships. What makes them nonproportional?

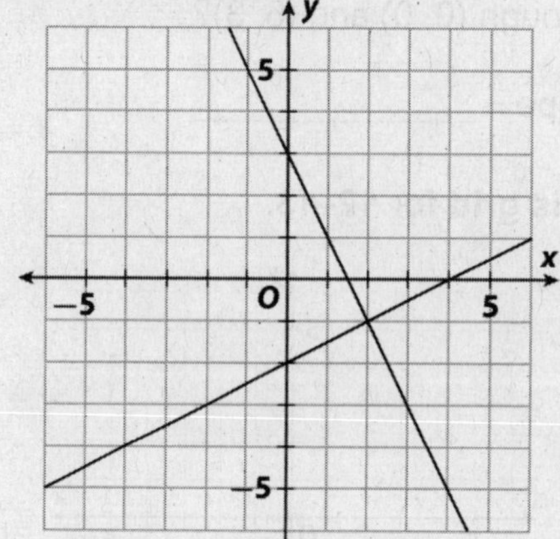

A They are not straight.

B They do not go through the origin.

C They do not show a constant ratio.

8. What is thirty-four thousand in scientific notation?

A 3.4×10^4

B 3.4×10^5

C 34×10^5

Name ________________________ Date ______________ Class ______________

MODULE 4

Nonproportional Relationships

9. A company prints T-shirts. They charge \$40 plus \$12 per shirt. So, the cost for n shirts is $40 + (12 \times n)$. Complete the table that shows this situation.

Shirts	1	2	3	4
Cost (\$)				

10. The y-intercept is the value of y when x equals 0. What is the y-intercept of the line with the equation $y = 2x + 8$?

y-intercept: ____________

11. What is the slope of the line that goes through (0, 0) and (6, 3)?

slope = ____________

Use this grid for 12–13.

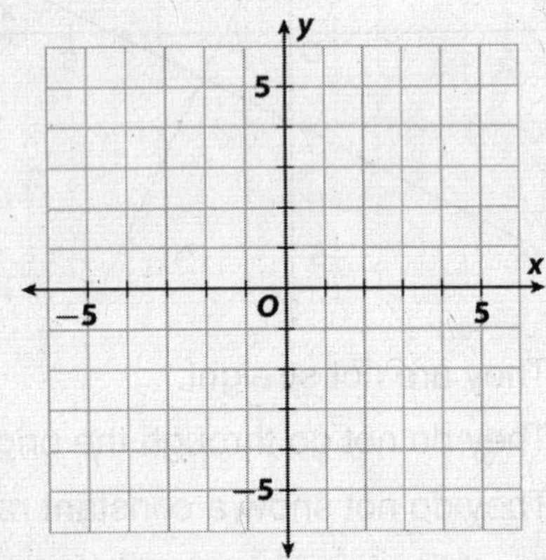

12. Graph $y = 2x - 3$ using the slope and y-intercept.

slope = ________ y-intercept: ________

13. Graph $x - y = 3$ by making a table of ordered pairs.

x				
y				

14. Which line shows a proportional relationship? Explain why.

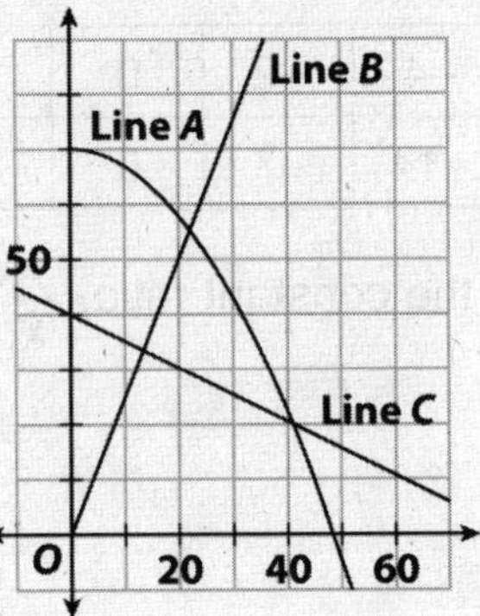

____

____

15. Steve starts with \$250 and spends \$25 a week. Chelsea starts with \$30 and saves \$30 a week. Use x for time and y for savings. Complete the equations that represent these situations.

Steve: $y = 250 -$ ________

Chelsea: $y =$ ________ $+ 30x$

16. The graphs show the equations from Exercise 15.

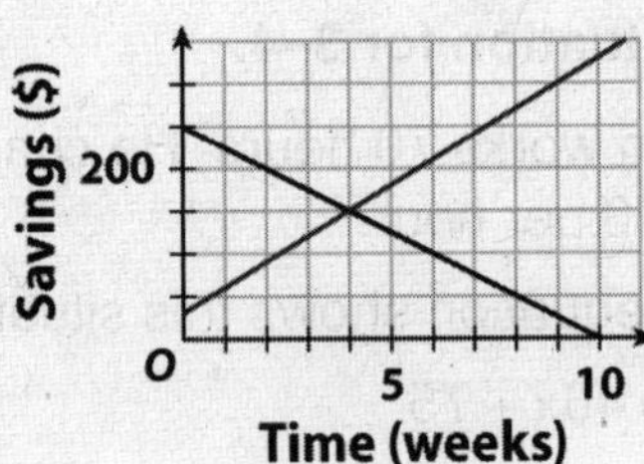

Is either of the relationships proportional? Explain.

____

17. Compare. Write >, <, or = .

$\sqrt{15}$ ◯ π

Name ______________________ Date ______________ Class ______________

MODULE 5

Writing Linear Equations

Module Quiz: B

1. Which graph shows a linear relationship?

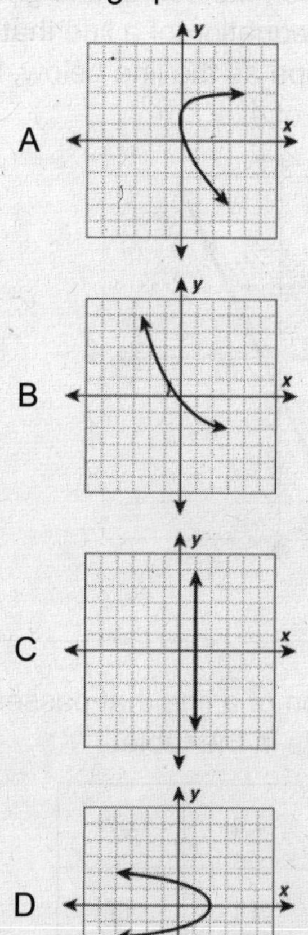

2. A furnace operates at 2,300°F. Before it can be used to extract metal from an ore, the temperature must be raised to 3,600°F. This takes place at a rate of 250°F per quarter hour. Which equation gives the furnace temperature *T* after *q* quarter hours?

   A $T = 250q + 2300$

   B $T = 250q + 3600$

   C $T = 2300q + 250$

   D $T = 3600q + 250$

3. Give the slope and *y*-intercept of the relationship shown in the table.

x	–100	0	100
y	75	50	25

   A slope: $-\frac{1}{4}$; *y*-intercept: –50

   B slope: $-\frac{1}{4}$; *y*-intercept: 50

   C slope: $\frac{1}{4}$; *y*-intercept: –50

   D slope: $\frac{1}{4}$; *y*-intercept: 50

4. An electronics company refurbishes ink-jet printers. The table shows the revenue produced for the number of units sold.

***u* (units)**	30	32	34	36
***R* ($000)**	8	9	10	11

   How much revenue will be produced for 45 units?

   A $1,550

   B $2,000

   C $15,500

   D $20,000

5. Biking at a constant rate, Elise travels 35 miles in 7 hours. If she travels at the same speed, how far will Elise bike in 9 hours?

   A 5 mi

   B 44 mi

   C 45 mi

   D 63 mi

Name ________________________ Date ______________ Class ______________

MODULE 5

Writing Linear Equations

6. A line with a slope of 4 passes through the point (2, 1). What is the equation of this line?

____

7. Find the equation of a line that fits the data shown in the graph below.

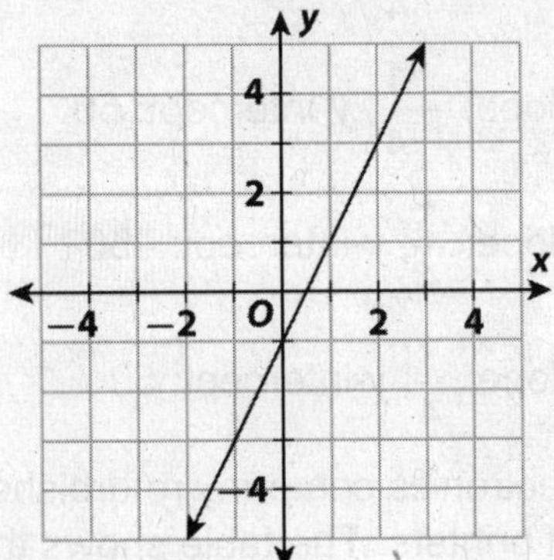

____

8. A line passes through the points (−1, 4) and (2, −2). What is the equation of this line?

____

9. A line with a slope of $\frac{1}{2}$ passes through the point (2, −1). What is the equation of this line?

____

10. A line passes through the points (−3, −1) and (−5, 4). What is the slope of this line?

____

11. A line is graphed on the coordinate grid below. Write the equation of a line that has the same slope as the line below, but has a *y*-intercept of 4.

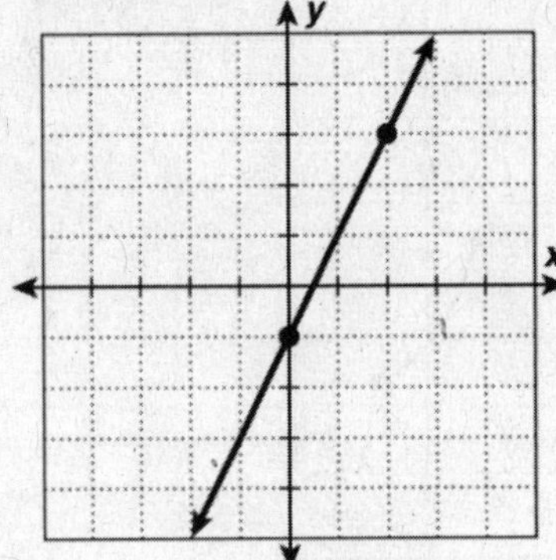

____

12. Write the equation of a line that passes through the points in the table.

x	−1	−4	−7
y	5	11	17

____

13. For every 5 hours that he works, Andrew is paid $60.20. How much is Andrew paid in dollars per hour?

____

Name ______________________ Date ______________ Class ______________

MODULE 5

Writing Linear Equations

Module Quiz: D

1. Find the slope and y-intercept of the line that is graphed on the coordinate grid below.

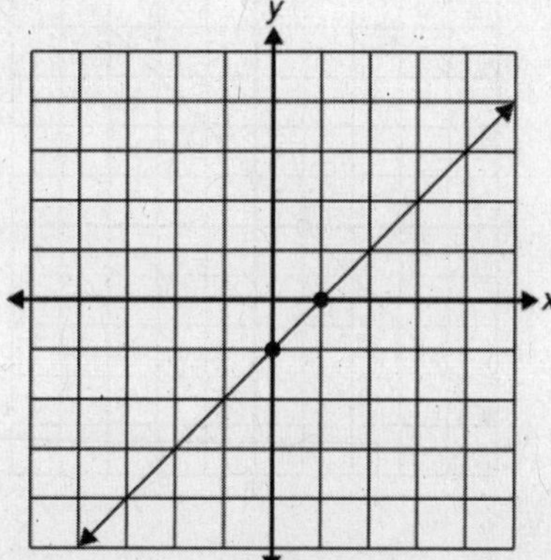

A slope: –1; y-intercept: –1

B slope: –1; y-intercept: 1

C slope: 1; y-intercept: –1

2. Which of the following equations has a slope of –3 and a y-intercept of 8?

A $y = -3x - 8$

B $y = -3x + 8$

C $y = 8x - 3$

3. The rain gauge shows 3 centimeters of rainwater. Which of the equations below gives the height, h, if it rains at a rate of 0.25 centimeters per hour after t hours?

A $h = 0.25t + 3$

B $h = 3t + 0.25$

C $t = 0.25h + 3$

4. Which of the following equations fits the data shown in the table?

x	0	1	2
y	3	5	7

A $y = -2x$

B $y = 2x$

C $y = 2x + 3$

5. Which of the following equations has a slope of zero?

A $x = 0$

B $y = -4$

C $y = x$

6. Which of the following equations represents the line that is graphed on the coordinate grid below?

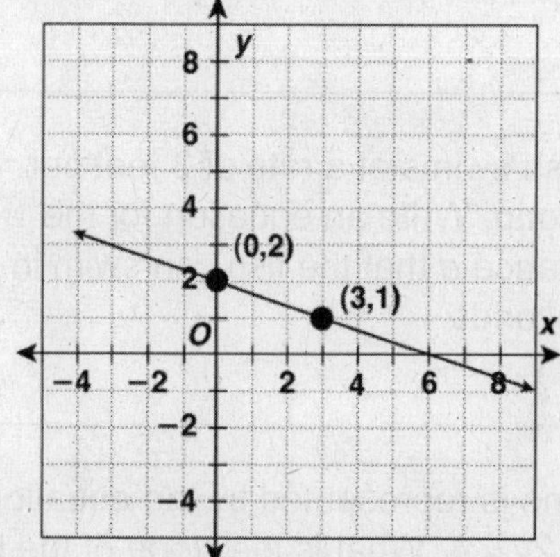

A $y = -3x + 2$

B $y = -\frac{1}{3}x - 6$

C $y = -\frac{1}{3}x + 2$

7. Which of the following equations has a positive slope?

A $x + y = 0$

B $y = -4$

C $y = x$

8. Which of the following equations shows direct variation?

A $y = \frac{x}{3} + 1$

B $y = 3x$

C $y = \frac{3}{x}$

Name ______________________ Date ______________ Class ______________

MODULE 5

Writing Linear Equations

9. A line has a slope of 1 and a y-intercept of -2. What is an equation that could represent this line?

____

10. A line is represented by the equation $y = \frac{2}{3}x + 1$. What is the slope of the line with that equation?

____

11. A fish swims at a rate of 3 feet per second. Write an equation for the distance d that the fish can swim in t seconds.

____

12. A line is represented by the equation $x + 2y = 4$. What is the slope of the line with that equation?

____

13. The data shown in the table below can be graphed as a straight line. What are the three missing y-values?

x	5	6	7	8	9
y	10				18

____

14. A line is graphed on the coordinate grid below. What is the equation of this line?

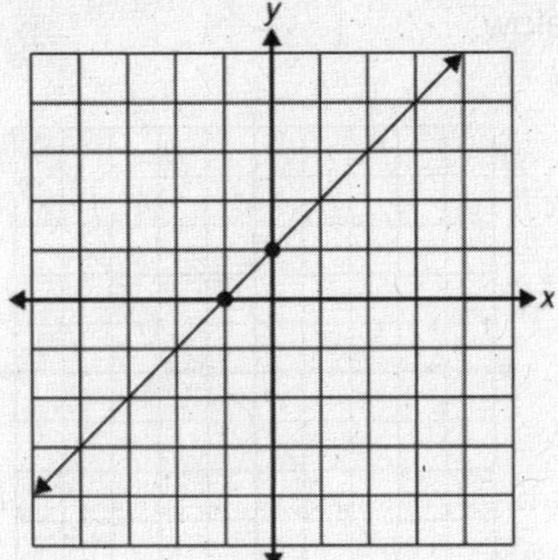

____

15. A line is represented by the equation $y + 1 = x$. What is the y-intercept of the line represented by the equation?

____

16. At a tennis club, the cost, c, of renting a tennis court is \$6 per hour. Write an equation that relates the cost, c, to the time t that a player rents the tennis court.

____

17. A straight line has a slope of 0. Write one possible equation that might represent this line.

____

18. A straight line is represented by the equation $y = \frac{1}{5}x$. What is the constant of variation in this equation?

____

Name ______________________ Date ______________ Class ______________

MODULE 6

Functions

Module Quiz: B

Choose the best answer.

1. A cheetah's speed was timed over a 100-yard distance. The cheetah was clocked running 70 miles per hour. Which equation shows the relationship between the distance, y, and time, x, the cheetah runs?

   A $y = 100x$ C $y = 100x + 70$

   B $y = 70x + 100$ D $y = 70x$

2. The graph of a linear relationship passes through (0, 2), (1, 5), and (3, 11) but not through (2, 7). Which of the following is the equation for this linear relationship?

   A $y = 2x + 3$ C $y = 5x$

   B $y = 3x + 2$ D $y = 4x - 1$

3. Norma made the graph below to show the relationship between the age and value of 12 cars. Which value, when removed from the graph, would result in the relationship being a function?

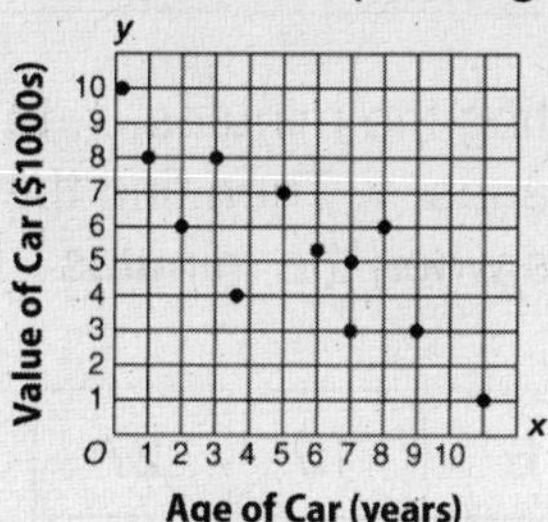

   A (3.5, 4) C (6, 5.25)

   B (9, 3) D (7, 5)

4. Which of the graphs shows a bike rider riding at an increasing speed and then stopping off to visit a friend?

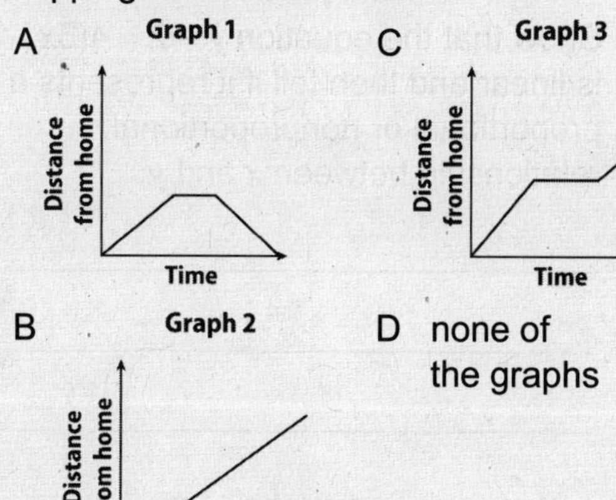

   D none of the graphs

Use the information, graph, and table below for 5–6.

Ben and Sally eat at the same restaurant. Then they each drive from the restaurant, which is a different distance from their homes, to the same park.

Ben

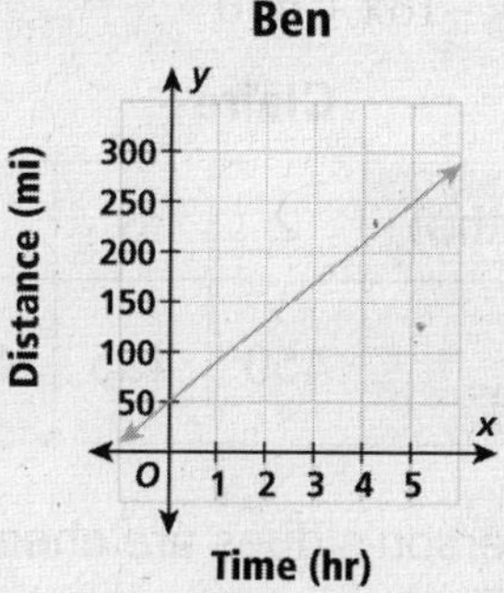

Sally

Time (h)	2	3	4	5
Distance (mi)	55	70	85	100

5. How much farther is Ben's home from the restaurant than Sally's home?

   A 25 mi C 75 mi

   B 50 mi D 150 mi

6. How fast is Sally driving?

   A 5 mi/h C 25 mi/h

   B 15 mi/h D 40 mi/h

Name ______________________ Date ______________ Class ______________

MODULE 6

Functions

Use the information and the table below for 7–8.

Marshall and Claire pay their monthly adventure club dues from their checking accounts according to the equation and table shown, where x is months and y is the amount left in each checking account.

Marshall: $y = -18x + 550$

Claire

Time (months)	2	3	4	5
Account Balance ($)	450	435	420	405

7. Which person's dues are cheaper per month? Explain.

8. Which person will be able to pay their dues for more months, assuming neither person deposits more money into their account? Explain.

9. Draw a graph in the space below that shows walking to the library at a constant speed, stopping at the library for an hour, then walking home at a constant speed.

10. What is the slope of this line? Explain how you found the slope.

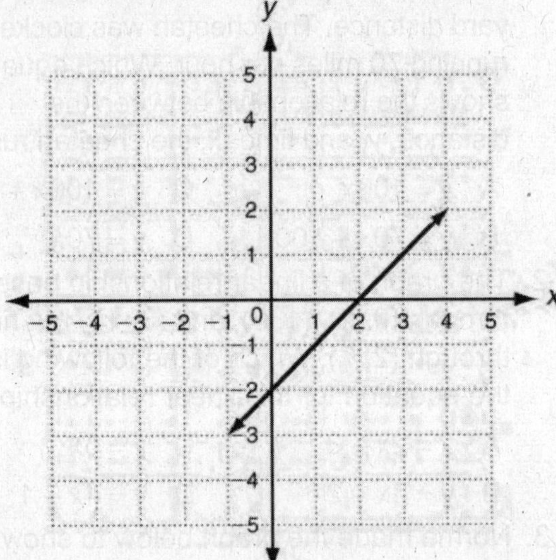

11. Write a rule relating the minutes, x, to the number of pages, y. Then find the number of pages when the minutes equal 72.

Minutes	6	15	27
Pages	20	50	90

12. Show that the equation $y - 2 = 4(3x + 5)$ is linear and then tell if it represents a proportional or nonproportional relationship between x and y.

Name ______________________ Date ______________ Class ______________

MODULE 6

Functions

Module Quiz: D

1. An elk was clocked running 45 miles per hour. Which equation shows the relationship between the distance, *y*, and time, *x*, that the elk ran?

   A $y = 45x$
   C $y = 5x + 40$
   B $y = x + 45$

2. The graph of a linear relationship passes through (0, 3), and (3, 9). Which is an equation for this linear relationship?

   A $y = 3x$
   C $y = 2x + 3$
   B $y = x + 6$

Use the diagrams below for 3.

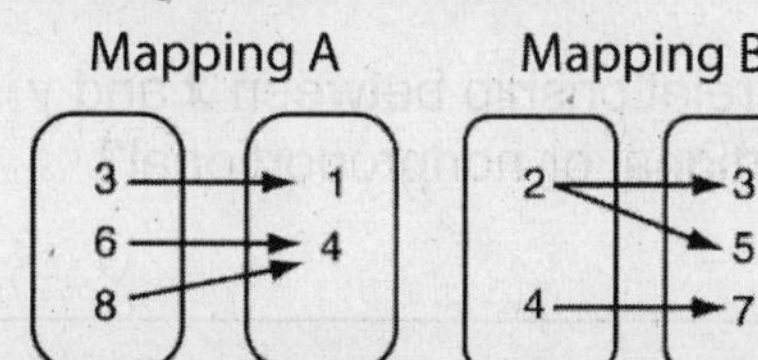

3. Which mapping diagram represents a relationship that is a function?

   A Mapping A
   B Mapping B
   C both Mapping A and Mapping B

4. Which graph shows a person walking, stopping for a while, then continuing at a slower speed?

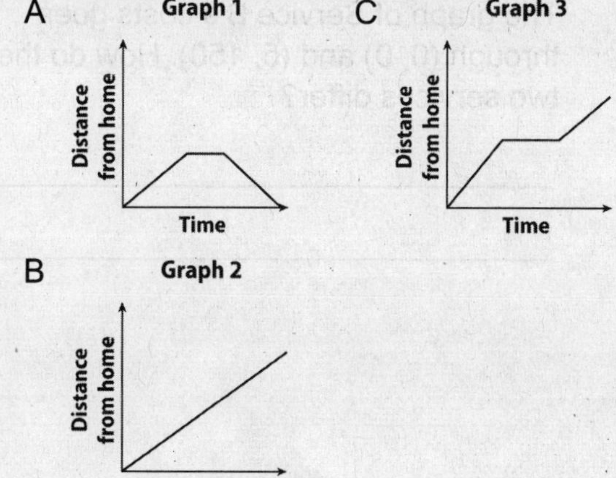

5. Which of the following is **not** a function?

   A {(2, 1), (4, 3), (6, 5), (8, 7)}
   B {(2, 1), (4, 1), (6, 5), (5, 4)}
   C {(2, 1), (4, 3), (6, 5), (2, 7)}

6. A cell phone company charges $50 for the phone plus a monthly service charge of $30. The equation $y = 30x + 50$ gives the cost *y* after *x* months. Which is true of the relationship between *x* and *y*?

   A It is linear and proportional.
   B It is linear and nonproportional.
   C It is not linear.

7. Which input/output table shows solutions to the equation $y = x^2 + 2$?

A

Input, *x*	−2	−1	0	1	2
Output, *y*	6	3	2	3	6

B

Input, *x*	−2	−1	0	1	2
Output, *y*	−2	−1	2	4	6

C

Input, *x*	−2	−1	0	1	2
Output, *y*	−2	0	2	3	6

8. The cost in dollars, *y*, to participate *x* days in a bike tour is a linear function. Lin's bike tour is described by the equation $y = 5x + 50$. The cost of Max's bike tour is $120 for a 14-day bike tour.

   If both Lin and Max take 14-day tours, whose bike tour costs less?

   A Lin's
   B Max's
   C The cost is the same for both.

Name ______________________ Date ______________ Class ______________

MODULE 6

Functions

9. Sketch a graph that shows Maria walking for a while at an increasing speed, stopping to talk to a friend, then continuing to walk at that speed.

10. Determine whether the relationship shown in the table below is a function. Write *function* or *not a function*.

Input	9	8	9	10
Output	27	32	36	40

____

11. The graph shows the total cost if a customer buys 1, 2, 3, 4, 5, or 6 gizmos. Determine whether the relationship is a function. Write *function* or *not a function*.

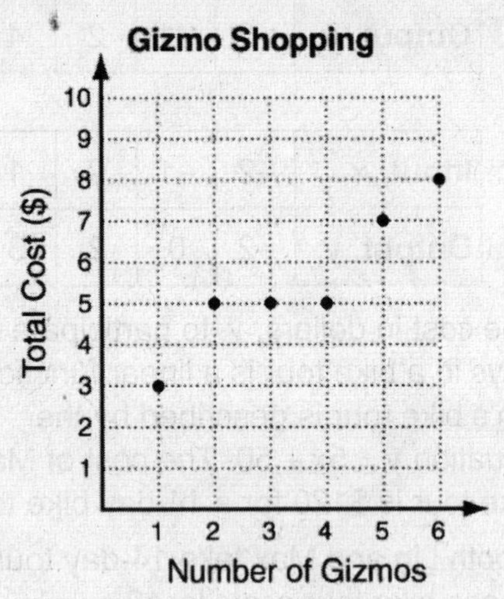

____

Use the graph for 12–13.

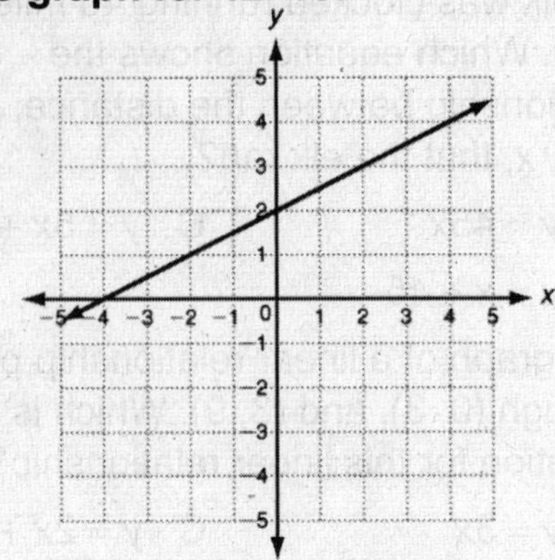

12. What is the slope of this line?

____

13. Is the relationship between *x* and *y* proportional or nonproportional?

____

14. Write the equation $y - 2 = 6x + 3$ in $y = mx + b$ form.

____

15. Two lawn-mowing services are compared. The monthly cost, *y* dollars, is compared to the number of times the yard is mowed, *x*. The monthly cost of Service A is represented by $y = 30x + 20$. The graph of Service B's costs goes through (0, 0) and (5, 150). How do these two services differ?

____

____

Name ______________________ Date ______________ Class ______________

MODULE 7

Solving Linear Equations

Module Quiz: B

Use the table for 1–2.

Computer Repair Service	Cost
ABC Tech	\$75 service charge plus \$50 an hour
Tech Squad	\$25 service charge plus \$70 an hour

1. At how many hours of service do the repair services cost the same? Choose the equation you could solve to find out.

   A $75x + 50 = 25x + 70$

   B $75x - 50 = 25x - 70$

   C $75 + 50x = 25 + 70x$

   D $(75 + 50)x = (25 + 70)x$

2. Steven estimates how long his computer repairs will take. He discovers that ABC Tech and Tech Squad will charge the same amount. What is Steven's estimate of the repair time?

   A 0.4 h C 2.5 h

   B 0.42 h D 5 h

3. Which of the following is an irrational number?

   A $\frac{4}{7}$ C -45

   B 61.2 D $\sqrt{17}$

4. What is the solution to the equation below?

   $$3 + 2.7x = 9.6 + 3.2x$$

   A $x = -25.2$ C $x = 13.2$

   B $x = -13.2$ D $x = 25.2$

5. Mike weighs 200 pounds and plans to lose 1.5 pounds a week. Jeff weighs 180 pounds and plans to lose 0.5 pounds a week. When will Mike and Jeff weigh the same?

   A in 2 weeks C in 20 weeks

   B in 10 weeks D never

6. Carla and Rob left a 20% tip after having lunch at a restaurant. The amount of the tip was \$6. Carla's lunch cost \$15. Which equation can you use to find x, the cost of Rob's lunch?

   A $0.2x + 15 = 6$ C $2(x + 15) = 6$

   B $0.2(x + 15) = 6$ D $0.2x = 15 + 6$

7. Larry saves 15% of his annual salary for retirement. This year his salary was \$2,000 more than last year, and he saved \$3,300. What was his salary last year?

   A \$15,000 C \$20,000

   B \$18,000 D \$22,000

8. For the equation $2(4x + 10) = 8x + k$, which value of k will create an equation with infinitely many solutions?

   A 4 C 20

   B 8 D 24

9. Which of the following equations has no solution?

   A $2(6 + x) = 14 + 2x$

   B $5x - 10 = x + 20$

   C $2(4 + x) = 8 + 2x$

   D $10x + 5 = 3(5x + 7)$

10. Which of the following is equivalent to 235,000,000,000?

    A 2.35×10^{-9} C 2.35×10^{11}

    B 2.35×10^{-10} D 2.35×10^{12}

Name ______________________ Date ______________ Class ______________

MODULE 7

Solving Linear Equations

11. Write and solve an equation for the relationship described below.

Four times a number plus three is the same as five plus the number.

equation: ______________________

solution: ______________________

12. A chess club has 500 members but is losing 30 members each year. A computer club has 150 members and is gaining 20 members per year. Write and solve an equation to find the number of years it will take for the two clubs to have the same number of members.

equation: ______________________

solution: ______________________

13. Is $0.\overline{33}$ a rational or irrational number? Explain.

____

____

____

____

14. Solve the equation below.

$$5 - \frac{1}{2}x = \frac{5}{8}x + 2$$

____

15. Two groups of hikers start at the same time and hike at the same average speed. Mark's group hikes for 2.5 hours. Sally's group hikes for 4.7 hours and covers another 7.7 miles. Write and solve an equation to find how fast the hikers are going.

equation: ______________________

solution: ______________________

16. Janice earns a 10% bonus based on her annual salary plus the number of sales she makes.She made 250 sales and earned a $5,000 bonus last year. Write and solve an equation to find her salary last year.

equation: ______________________

solution: ______________________

17. Solve the equation below.

$$\frac{1}{3}(12 + x) = -8(6 - x)$$

____

18. Tell whether the equation has one, zero, or infinitely many solutions.

$$2\left(x - \frac{1}{2}\right) = 8 + 2x$$

____

19. Complete the equation so it has one solution of $x = 2$.

$4(5x - 4) = 4x +$ ______________________

20. Write 15,000,000 in scientific notation.

____

Name ______________________ Date ______________ Class ______________

MODULE 7

Solving Linear Equations

Module Quiz: D

Use the table for 1 and 2.

Computer Repair Service	Cost
Tech Rite	\$75 service charge plus \$50 an hour
Best Byte	\$25 service charge plus \$70 an hour

1. Use x for the number of hours. Which expression shows the total charges for Tech Rite?

   A $75 + 50x$

   B $(75 + 50)x$

   C $75x + 50x$

2. For how many hours of service will the costs charged by the two companies be equal? Solve the equation below to find out.

   $$75 + 50x = 25 + 70x$$

   A 0.4 h

   B 2.5 h

   C 5 h

3. Which of the following is an irrational number?

   A $\frac{1}{4}$

   B 60

   C $\sqrt{3}$

4. What is the solution to the equation below?

   $$3 + 5.2x = 1 - 2.8x$$

   Start by adding $2.8x$ to both sides.

   A $x = -0.25$

   B $x = -1.2$

   C $x = -4$

5. Roy weighs 150 pounds and plans to lose 1.5 pounds a week. Luis weighs 200 pounds and plans to lose 2.5 pounds a week. Which equation shows when Roy and Luis will weigh the same? Use x for the number of weeks.

   A $150 + 1.5x = 200 + 2.5x$

   B $150 - 1.5x = 200 - 2.5x$

   C $150 + 1.5x = 200 - 2.5x$

6. Chad and Eric left a 20% tip after having lunch at a restaurant. The amount of the tip was \$5. Chad's lunch cost \$10. Which equation can you use to find x, the cost of Eric's lunch?

   A $0.2x + 10 = 5$

   B $0.2(x + 10) = 5$

   C $0.2x = 10 + 5$

7. Anita saves 15% of her annual salary for retirement. This year her salary was \$2,000 more than last year, and she saved \$3,300. What was her salary last year? Solve the equation below to find out.

   $$0.15(x + 2,000) = 3,300$$

   A \$15,000

   B \$18,000

   C \$20,000

8. How many solutions does the equation below have?

   $$2(4x + 10) = 8x + 20$$

   A 0

   B 1

   C infinitely many

9. Which of the following is equivalent to 435,000,000?

   A 4.35×10^8

   B 4.35×10^9

   C 4.35×10^{10}

Name ______________________ Date ______________ Class ______________

MODULE 7

Solving Linear Equations

10. Complete and solve an equation for the relationship described below.

    Three times a number minus five equals two times the number.

    equation: ______________________

    solution: ______________________

11. A games club has 50 members but is losing 3 members each year. A sports club has 15 members and is gaining 2 members per year.

    Use x for the number of years. Complete the equation to show when the two clubs will have the same number of members.

    $50 - 3x =$ ______________________

    Solve the equation to find the number of years.

    ____

12. Tell whether $\frac{4}{5}$ is a rational or irrational number.

    ____

13. Solve the equation below.

    $$5 - \frac{1}{2}x = 12$$

    ____

14. Two groups are hiking at about the same speed. Mario's group hikes for 2.5 hours. Seema's group hikes for 4.7 hours and covers 8.8 more miles. How fast are the hikers going? Solve the equation below to find out.

    $$4.7x = 2.5x + 8.8$$

    solution: ______________________

15. Ayesha earns a 10% bonus based on her annual salary plus the number of sales she makes. She made 250 sales and earned a $5,000 bonus last year. Solve the equation below to find her salary last year.

    $$0.1(x + 250) = 5{,}000$$

    solution: ______________________

16. Solve the equation below.

    $$12 + x = -3(4 - x)$$

    ____

17. Complete the equation so it has one solution of $x = 2$.

    $20x - 16 = 4x +$ ______________

18. Write 1,000,000 in scientific notation.

    ____

Name ______________________ Date ______________ Class ______________

MODULE 8

Solving Systems of Linear Equations

Module Quiz: B

1. Solve this system by graphing. Use the grid below.

$$\begin{cases} 2x + y = 3 \\ y = x - 3 \end{cases}$$

Which point is the solution?

A (–2, –1) C (–1, 2)

B (–1, –2) D (2, –1)

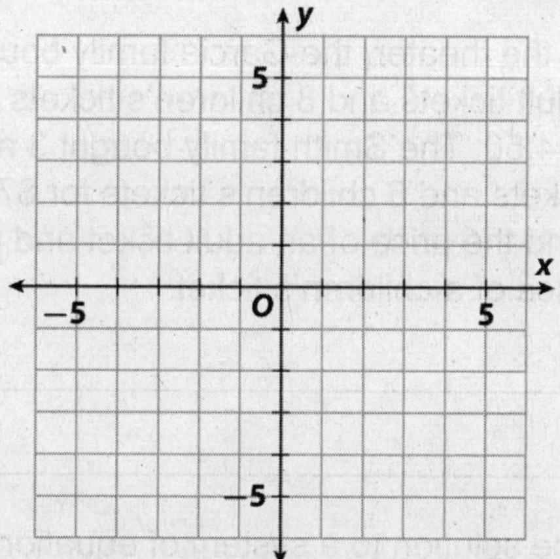

2. Which expression can you substitute in the indicated equation to solve the system below?

$$\begin{cases} 5x + y = 8 \\ x + 4y = 2 \end{cases}$$

A $2 - 4y$ for x in $5x + y = 8$

B $8 + 5x$ for y in $5x + y = 8$

C $2 + 4y$ for x in $x + 4y = 2$

D $5 + 8x$ for y in $x + 4y = 2$

3. Which is the solution to $\begin{cases} 4x - y = 8 \\ 6x + y = 2 \end{cases}$?

A (–4, 1) C (–2, 4)

B (1, –4) D (2, –4)

4. Which set of numbers is ordered from least to greatest?

A $2\pi, \sqrt{7}, 2.\overline{66}$ C $2\pi, \sqrt{7}, 2.\overline{66}$

B $\sqrt{7}, 2.\overline{66}, 2\pi$ D $2.\overline{66}, 2\pi, \sqrt{7}$

5. At the shopping mall, Joaquin bought 4 pretzels and a bottle of water for \$11.50. Kelly bought 3 pretzels and a bottle of water for \$9.00. What is the price of a bottle of water?

A \$0.50 C \$2.50

B \$1.50 D \$4.00

6. Which step could you use to start solving the system of equations below?

$$\begin{cases} 3x + 3y = 9 \\ -6x - 4y = -14 \end{cases}$$

A Multiply $3x + 3y = 9$ by 2 and add it to $-6x - 4y = -14$.

B Multiply $-6x - 4y = -14$ by 2 and subtract it from $3x + 3y = 9$.

C Substitute $3y - 9$ for x in $-6x - 4y = -14$.

D Add $3x + 3y = 9$ to $6x + 4y = 14$.

7. What is the solution to the system of linear equations shown on the graph?

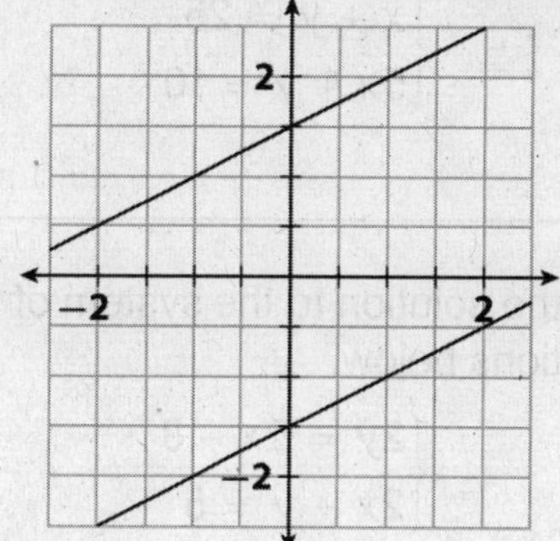

A 0

B (–2, 2)

C The system has no solution.

D The system has infinitely many solutions.

8. When $x = 3$, $y = 4$. What is y when $x = 12$?

A 3 C 12

B 4 D 16

Name ______________________ Date ____________ Class ____________

MODULE 8

Solving Systems of Linear Equations

9. Steve started with \$250 and spent \$25 per week. Chelsea started with \$30 and saved \$30 per week. Use x for time and y for savings. Write and graph equations to represent each situation. When did Steve and Chelsea have the same amount of money?

Steve: ______________________

Chelsea: ______________________

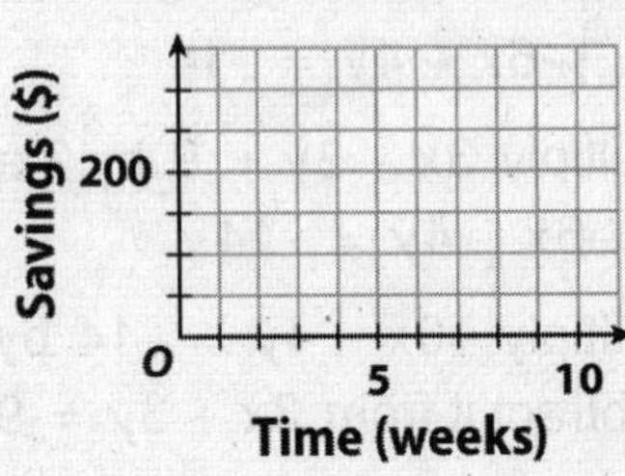

solution: ______________________

10. Determine the expression you can substitute for x in $5x + y = 10$ to solve the system below.

$$\begin{cases} x + y = 25 \\ 5x + y = 10 \end{cases}$$

____

11. Find the solution to the system of equations below.

$$\begin{cases} 2y = 2x - 8 \\ 2x + y = 5 \end{cases}$$

____

12. Order the numbers from least to greatest.

$$\frac{5}{4},\ 3\sqrt{3},\ \pi$$

____

13. At an office supply store, Samantha bought 5 notebooks and 2 pens for \$9. Jeffrey bought 3 notebooks and 2 pens for \$6. Find the price of a notebook and the price of a pen.

____

____

14. At the theater, the Garcia family bought 2 adult tickets and 3 children's tickets for \$44.50. The Smith family bought 3 adult tickets and 6 children's tickets for \$78. Find the price of an adult ticket and the price of a children's ticket.

____

____

15. The solution to a system of equations is graphed below. Does the system have a solution? Explain.

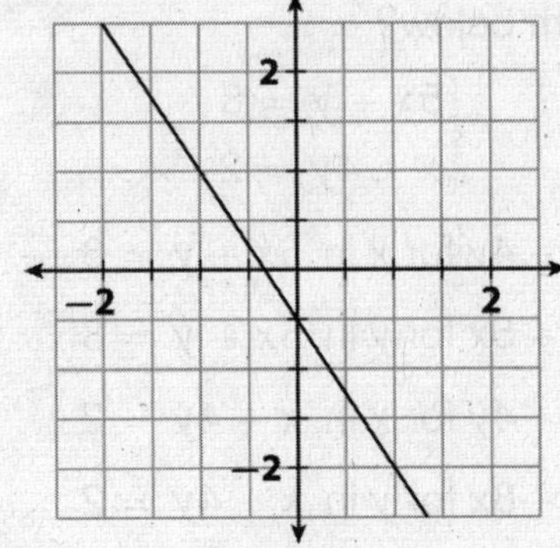

____

____

____

16. When $x = 8$, $y = 3$. What is y when $x = 24$?

____

Name ______________________ Date ______________ Class ______________

MODULE 8

Solving Systems of Linear Equations

Module Quiz: D

1. Solve this system by graphing. The first equation is graphed for you below.

$$\begin{cases} 2x + y = 3 \\ y = x - 3 \end{cases}$$

Which point is the solution?

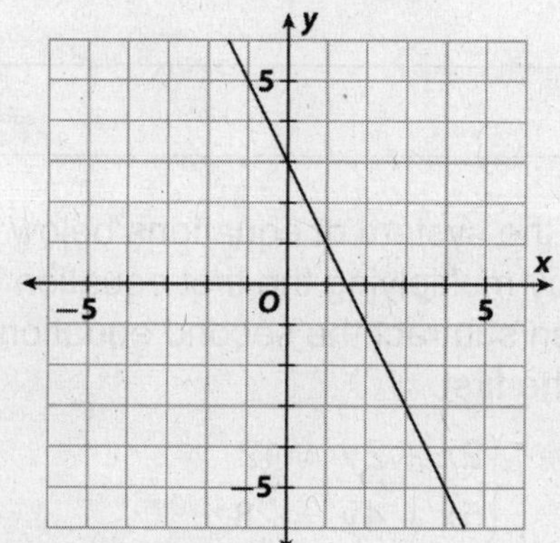

A (−2, −1)

B (−1, 2)

C (2, −1)

2. Which expression can you substitute for *x* in $5x + y = 8$ to solve the system below?

$$\begin{cases} 5x + y = 8 \\ x + 4y = 2 \end{cases}$$

A $2 - 4y$

B $-2 - 4y$

C $2 + 4y$

3. Add the equations to find the solution to the system $\begin{cases} 4x - y = 8 \\ 6x + y = 2 \end{cases}$.

A (−4, 1)

B (1, −4)

C (2, −4)

4. Which set of numbers is ordered from least to greatest?

A $2, \sqrt{7}, \frac{1}{3}$

B $\sqrt{7}, 2, \frac{1}{3}$

C $\frac{1}{3}, 2, \sqrt{7}$

5. Ricky bought an apple and a bottle of juice for $3. Noel bought 3 apples and a bottle of juice for $7. How much is a bottle of juice?

A $1

B $2

C $3

6. Which step could you use to start solving the system of equations below?

$$\begin{cases} x + y = 3 \\ -3x - 2y = -7 \end{cases}$$

A Multiply $x + y = 3$ by 3 and add it to $-3x - 2y = -7$.

B Multiply $-3x - 2y = -7$ by 2 and subtract it from $x + y = 3$.

C Add $x + y = 3$ to $-3x - 2y = -7$.

7. The graph of a system of linear equations results in the lines shown. They do not intersect at any points. What does this mean about the solution?

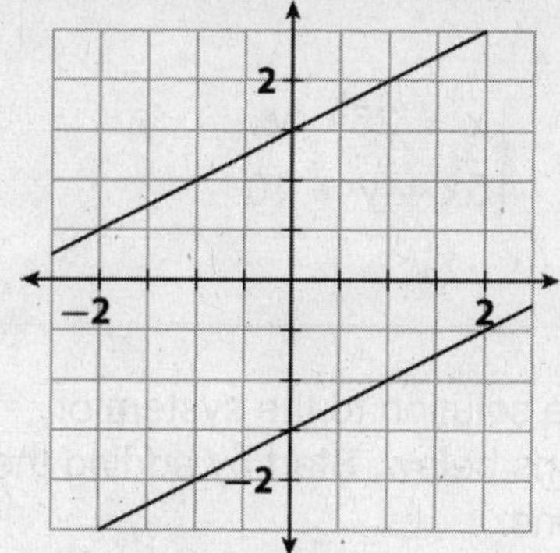

A The solution is 0.

B The system has no solution.

C The system has infinitely many solutions.

8. Solve for *y*.

$$\frac{3}{4} = \frac{6}{y}$$

A 3

B 8

C 12

Name ______________________ Date ______________ Class ______________

MODULE 8 Solving Systems of Linear Equations

9. Larissa starts with \$250 and spends \$25 a week. Chucho starts with \$30 and saves \$30 a week. Use x for time and y for savings. Complete the equations to represent each situation.

   Larissa: $y = 250 -$ ______

   Chucho: $y =$ ______ $+ 30x$

   The graph shows the equations.

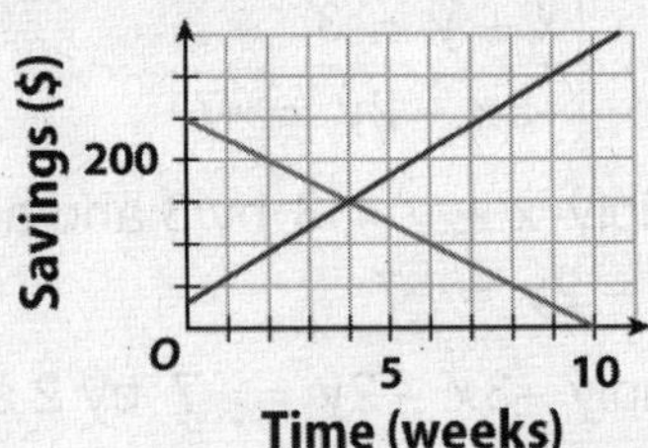

   When do Larissa and Chucho have the same amount of money?

   ____

10. Find the expression you can substitute for x in $5x + y = 10$ to solve the system below.

$$\begin{cases} x = 25 - y \\ 5x + y = 10 \end{cases}$$

   ____

11. Find the solution to the system of equations below. Start by adding the equations.

$$\begin{cases} -2x + 2y = -8 \\ 2x + y = 5 \end{cases}$$

   ____

12. Order the numbers from least to greatest.

$$\pi, \frac{1}{4}, \sqrt{3}$$

   ____

13. Solve the system of equations below. Start by subtracting the second equation from the first equation.

$$\begin{cases} 2x + 2y = 12 \\ 3x + 2y = 17 \end{cases}$$

   ____

   ____

14. Solve the system of equations below. Start by multiplying the first equation by 2. Then subtract the second equation from the first.

$$\begin{cases} 2x + 2y = 12 \\ 5x + 4y = 28 \end{cases}$$

   ____

   ____

15. The solution to a system of two linear equations is graphed below. The solution is a single line, which means the system has infinitely many solutions. Name one possible solution to the system.

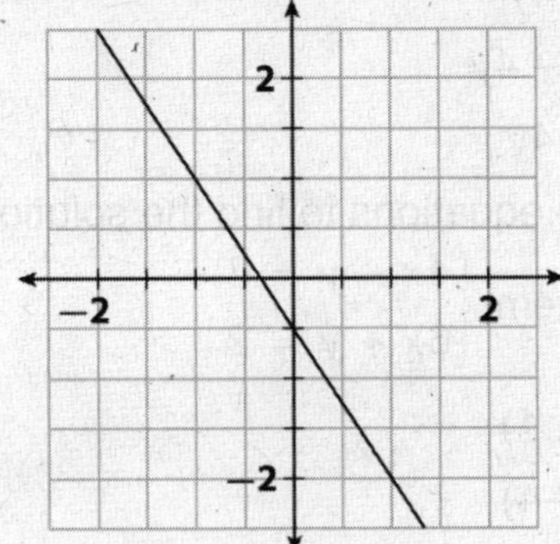

   ____

16. Solve for y.

$$\frac{8}{3} = \frac{16}{y}$$

   ____

Name ______________________ Date ______________ Class ______________

MODULE 9

Transformations and Congruence

Module Quiz: B

Use the diagram for 1–3.

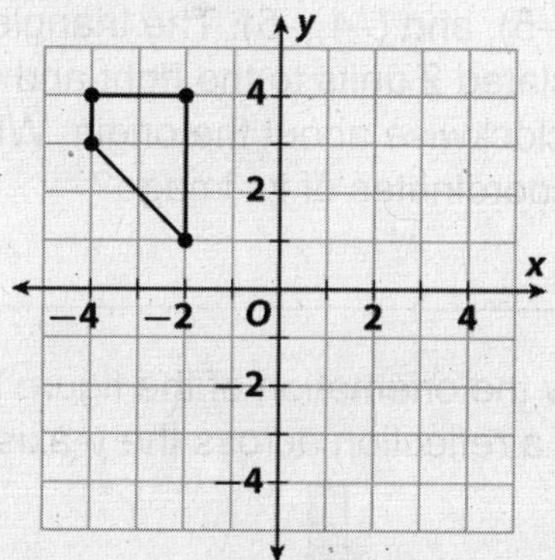

1. The quadrilateral shown is translated 7 units to the right and 5 units down. In which quadrant is the image of the quadrilateral located?

   A I   C III
   B II   D IV

2. The quadrilateral shown is reflected across the *y*-axis. In which quadrant is the image of the quadrilateral located?

   A I   C III
   B II   D IV

3. The quadrilateral shown is rotated 90° clockwise about the origin. In which quadrant is the image of the quadrilateral located?

   A I   C III
   B II   D IV

4. The vertices of a trapezoid are located at (1, –2), (3, –1), (3, –5), and (1, –4). The trapezoid is translated 3 units to the left and rotated 180° about the origin. What are the coordinates of its image?

   A (2, –2), (0, –1), (0, –5), (2, –4)
   B (–2, 2), (0, 1), (0, 5), (–2, 4)
   C (–1, –2), (–3, 1), (–3, 5), (–1, 4)
   D (–1, 0), (–3, 1), (0, 5), (–1, 4)

5. Which number is between $\frac{\sqrt{6}}{2}$ and $\sqrt{8}$?

   A 1   C 3
   B 2   D 4

6. What would be the orientation of the figure below after a reflection across the *x*-axis?

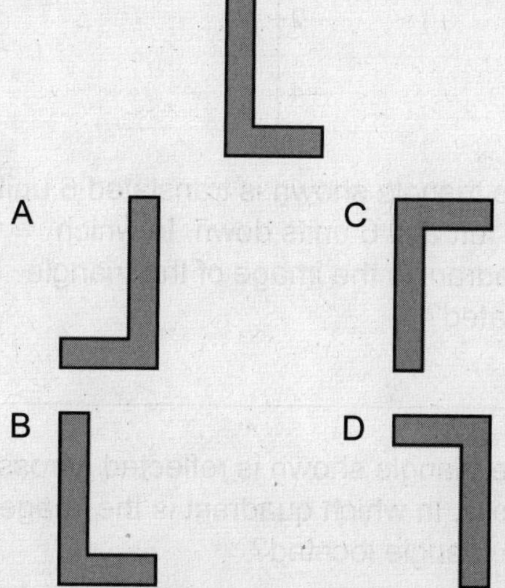

7. An irregular pentagon is rotated 180° about the origin. Which of the following statements is **not** true?

   A The new pentagon is the same size as the original pentagon.
   B The new pentagon is the same shape as the original pentagon.
   C The new pentagon is in the same orientation as the original pentagon.
   D The *x*-coordinates of the new pentagon are the same as the *x*-coordinates of the original pentagon.

8. Figure A is a parallelogram. It is translated 2 units to the right and 1 unit down and then rotated 90 degrees clockwise about origin. Which of the following is **not** true about its image A′?

   A A′ is the same shape as A.
   B A′ has the same orientation as A.
   C A′ is a parallelogram
   D A′ is the same size as A.

Name ______________________ Date ______________ Class ______________

MODULE 9

Transformations and Congruence

Use the diagram for 9–11.

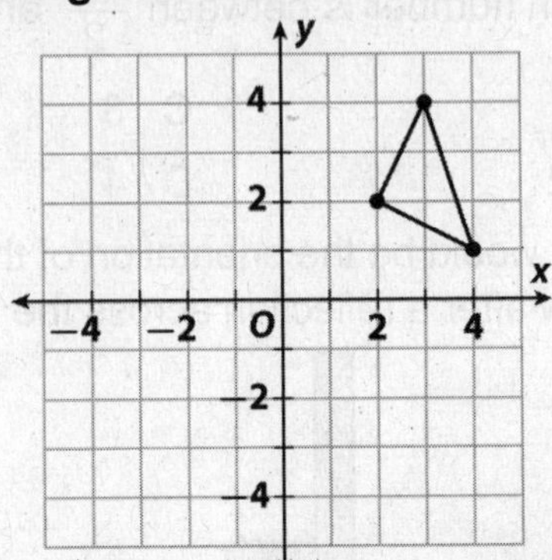

9. The triangle shown is translated 6 units to the left and 6 units down. In which quadrant is the image of the triangle located?

____

10. The triangle shown is reflected across the *x*-axis. In which quadrant is the image of the triangle located?

____

11. The triangle shown is rotated 90° counterclockwise about the origin. In which quadrant is the image of the triangle located?

____

12. How can you describe all the images of the triangle in Exercises 9–11?

____

13. Order the numbers below from least to greatest.

$$2.3, \frac{\sqrt{13}}{3}, \sqrt{11}$$

____

14. A triangle has vertices at (–2, –2), (–2, –5), and (–4, –5). The triangle is translated 2 units to the right and rotated 90° clockwise about the origin. What are the coordinates of its image?

____

15. Draw the orientation of the figure below after a reflection across the *y*-axis.

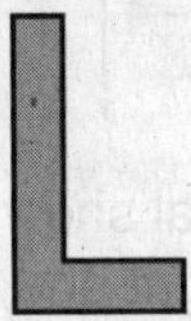

____

16. A trapezoid has been rotated 90° clockwise about the origin. Is it true that the *y*-coordinates of the new trapezoid are the same as the *y*-coordinates of the original trapezoid? Explain.

____

17. A parallelogram has vertices at (4, 4), (7, 4), (5, 2), and (2, 2). The parallelogram is translated 7 units down and reflected across the *y*-axis. What are the coordinates of its image?

____

18. The measures of the three angles of a triangle are given by $2x + 6$, x, and $3x$. What is the measure of the largest angle?

____

Name ________________________ Date ________________ Class ________________

MODULE 9

Transformations and Congruence

Module Quiz: D

Use the diagram for 1–3.

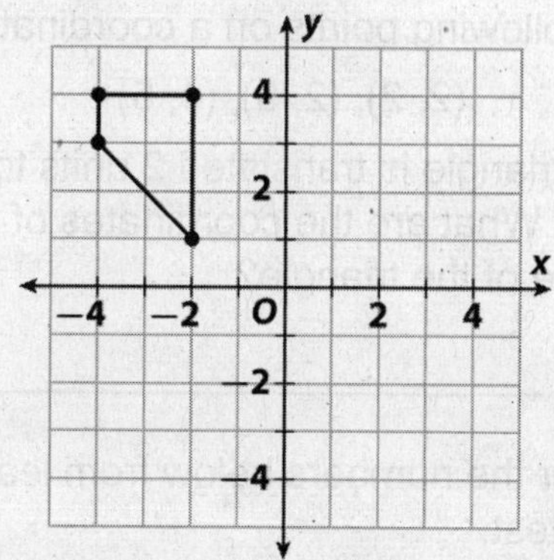

1. Where would the shape be located after a translation of 5 units to the right?

   A Quadrant I

   B Quadrant II

   C Quadrant III

2. Where would the shape be located after a reflection across the *x*-axis?

   A Quadrant I

   B Quadrant II

   C Quadrant III

3. Where would the shape be located after a rotation of 90° clockwise about the origin?

   A Quadrant I

   B Quadrant II

   C Quadrant III

4. Which number is between $\frac{5}{2}$ and $\sqrt{11}$?

   A 1

   B 2

   C 3

5. The vertices of a trapezoid are located at the following points on a coordinate grid.

   (1, 2), (3, 1), (3, 5), (1, 4)

   The trapezoid is translated 2 units to the right. What are the coordinates of the image of the trapezoid?

   A (3, 2), (5, 1), (5, 5), (3, 4)

   B (–3, 2), (–5, 1), (–5, 5), (–3, 4)

   C (1, 4), (3, 3), (3, 7), (1, 6)

6. What would the figure below look like after a reflection across the *x*-axis?

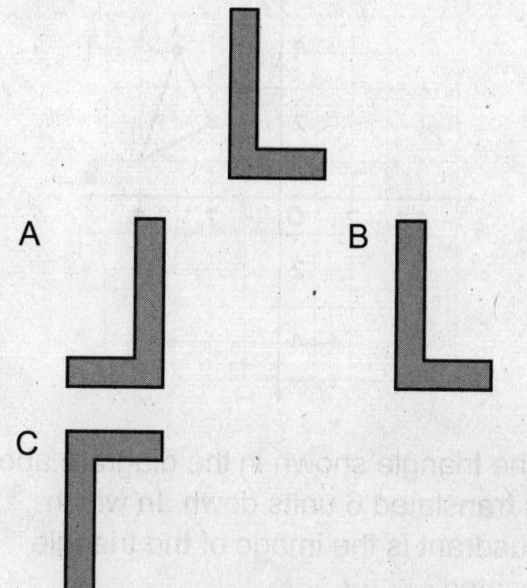

7. A scalene triangle is rotated 90° clockwise about the origin. Which of the following statements is **not** true?

   A The new triangle is the same size as the original triangle.

   B The new triangle is the same shape as the original triangle.

   C The *x*-coordinates of the new triangle are the same as the *x*-coordinates of the old triangle.

8. Describe the image when a scalene triangle is rotated 180 degrees counterclockwise about the origin.

   A It is a smaller scalene triangle than the original triangle.

   B It is a same size scalene triangle as the original triangle.

   C It is a larger scalene triangle than the original triangle.

9. The measures of the three angles of a triangle are given by *x*, 2*x*, and 2*x*. What is the value of *x*?

   A 5°

   B 36°

   C 70°

Name ______________________ Date ______________ Class ______________

MODULE 9

Transformations and Congruence

Use the diagram for Exercises 10–13.

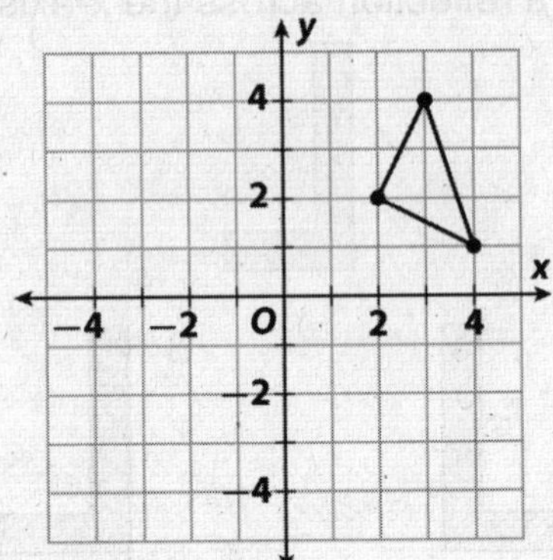

10. The triangle shown in the diagram above is translated 6 units down. In which quadrant is the image of the triangle located?

____

11. The original triangle shown in the diagram above is reflected across the *y*-axis. In which quadrant is the image of the triangle located?

____

12. The original triangle shown in the diagram above is rotated 90° clockwise about the origin. In which quadrant is the image of the triangle located?

____

13. When you translate, rotate, or reflect a figure, how does the image compare to the original figure?

____

14. The vertices of a triangle are located at the following points on a coordinate grid.

    (2, 2), (2, 5), (4, 5)

    The triangle is translated 2 units to the right. What are the coordinates of the image of the triangle?

____

15. Order the numbers below from least to greatest.

    $2.5, -\sqrt{2}, 7$

____

16. Draw the orientation of the figure below after it has been reflected across the *y*-axis.

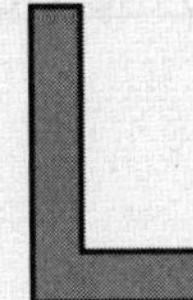

____

17. A trapezoid has been rotated 180°. Is it true that the new trapezoid is the same size as the original trapezoid?

____

18. The vertices of a triangle are located at the following points on a coordinate grid.

    (1, 1), (1, 5), (4, 1)

    The triangle is reflected across the *y*-axis. What are the coordinates of the image of the triangle?

____

19. The measures of the three angles of a triangle are given by $x + 4$, x, and $2x$. What is the value of x?

____

Name ______________________ Date ______________ Class______________

MODULE 10

Transformations and Similarity

Module Quiz: B

1. Which of the following describes a dilation?

   A a transformation that preserves size

   B a transformation that preserves shape

   C a translation that preserves size

   D a translation that preserves shape

2. How is the image of a figure that is dilated related to the original figure?

   A It is equivalent.

   B It is congruent.

   C It is similar.

   D It is rotated.

3. Which inequality represents the solution to the inequality below?

   $$\frac{2}{3}m + 3 < m - 4$$

   A $m < 21$ C $m > 21$

   B $m < 18$ D $m > 18$

4. The gray figure below is the image of the black figure after a dilation. Which represents the dilation?

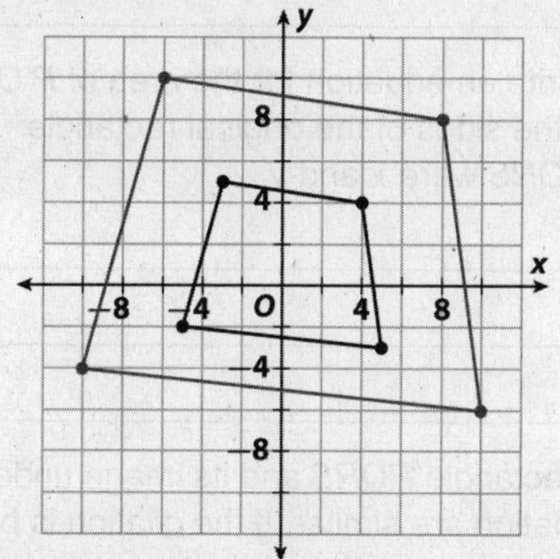

   A $(x, y) \rightarrow (2x, 2y)$

   B $(x, y) \rightarrow (1.5x, 2y)$

   C $(x, y) \rightarrow (2x, 1.5y)$

   D $(x, y) \rightarrow (1.5x, 1.5y)$

5. A quadrilateral has vertices at (1, 4), (7, 3), (3, –5), and (8, –4). The quadrilateral is dilated by a scale factor of 3.5 with the origin as its center. What are the coordinates of the vertices of the image of the quadrilateral?

   A (3, 12), (21, 9), (9, –15), (24, –12)

   B (3.5, 12), (24.5, 9), (10.5, –15), (28.5, –12)

   C (3.5, 14), (24.5, 10.5), (10.5, –17.5), (28, –14)

   D (3, 14), (21, 10.5), (9, –17.5), (24, –14)

6. A triangle has vertices at $A(-6, -3)$, $B(1, 5)$, and $C(4, -4)$. The triangle is dilated according to the transformation below. The center of dilation is the origin.

   $$(x, y) \rightarrow (2x, 2y)$$

   What are the vertices of the image of the triangle?

   A $A'(-12, -6)$, $B'(2, 10)$, $C'(8, -8)$

   B $A'(-3, -1.5)$, $B'(0.5, 5)$, $C'(2, -2)$

   C $A'(-12, 6)$, $B'(2, 10)$, $C'(8, 8)$

   D $A'(-12, -3)$, $B'(2, 5)$, $C'(8, -4)$

7. A figure is dilated by a factor of 3. Which of the following statements about the image of the figure is true?

   A The perimeter decreases.

   B The area decreases.

   C Both the area and the perimeter decrease.

   D Both the area and the perimeter increase.

Name ______________________ Date ______________ Class ______________

MODULE 10

Transformations and Similarity

8. Do the figures below show a dilation? If so, is it an enlargement or a reduction? What is the scale factor?

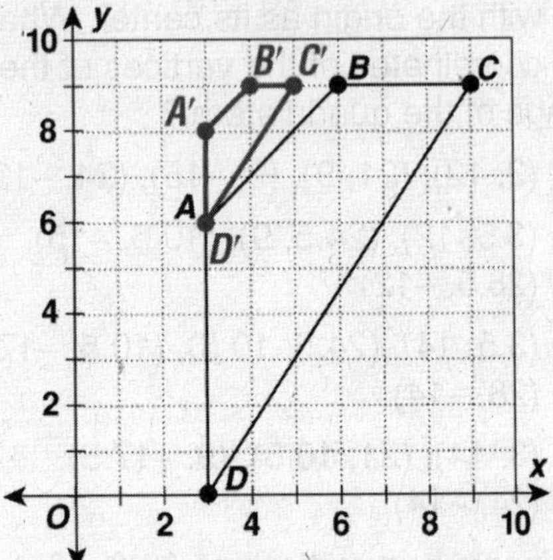

9. Graph the image of the figure after a dilation with the origin as its center and a scale factor of $\frac{1}{2}$. Draw your answer on the same grid. Then write an algebraic rule to describe the dilation.

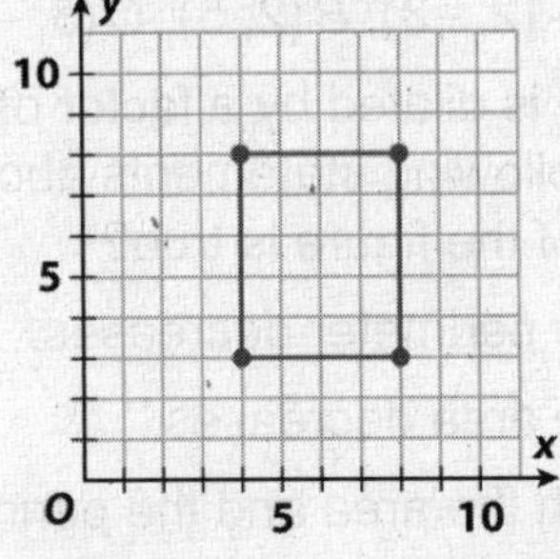

10. Write an inequality to represent the relationship described below.

Six more than three times a number is less than or equal to two times the number minus one.

Solve the inequality. Show your work.

Use this information for 11–13.

Rectangle $P'R'S'T'$ is a dilation of rectangle $PRST$, and the scale factor is 3.

11. Write an equation for the perimeter of $P'R'S'T'$ if the sides of the original rectangle $PRST$ were x and y.

12. Write an equation for the area of $P'Q'R'S'$ if the sides of the original rectangle $PQRS$ were x and y.

13. Rectangle $PQRS$ and its image under a dilation are similar. If the dilation is by a factor greater than 1, is the image larger or smaller?

If the dilation is by a factor less than 1, is the image larger or smaller?

Name ______________________ Date ______________ Class ______________

MODULE 10

Transformations and Similarity

Module Quiz: D

1. Which of the following describes a figure and its image under a dilation?

   A They are equivalent.

   B They are congruent.

   C They are similar.

2. Which inequality represents the solution to the inequality below?

   $$8p - 5 > 13 - p$$

   A $p < 2$

   B $p > 2$

   C $p > 9$

3. The only transformation that does not preserve size is a __________

   A translation

   B reflection

   C dilation

4. The black triangle was transformed to make the gray triangle. Which represents the transformation?

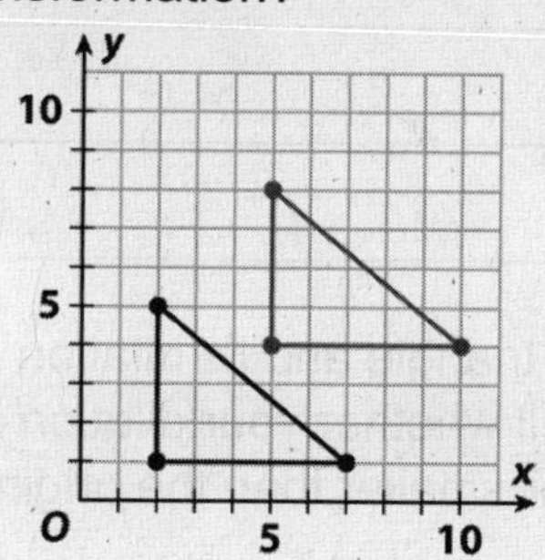

   A $(x, y) \to (x + 3, y + 3)$

   B $(x, y) \to (3x, 3y)$

   C $(x, y) \to (x - 2, y - 2)$

5. Which of the following is **not** a rational number?

   A $\sqrt{4}$

   B $\sqrt{9}$

   C $\sqrt{-1}$

6. The vertices of a square are located at (2, 2), (5, 2), (5, 5), and (2, 5). The square is dilated by a scale factor of 2. The center of dilation is the origin (0, 0). What are the coordinates of the vertices of the image of the square?

   A (4, 4), (10, 4), (10, 10), (4, 10)

   B (1, 1), (2.5, 1), (1, 2.5), (2.5, 2.5)

   C (4, 4), (7, 4), (4, 7), (7, 7)

7. *KLMN* is a rectangle. What is its image under a dilation with a scale factor of $\frac{1}{3}$?

   A a larger rectangle

   B a smaller rectangle

   C a smaller square

8. A triangle with angles of 30 degrees, 60 degrees and 90 degrees is dilated by a scale factor of 3. What happens to the angles?

   A They are tripled.

   B They are divided by 3.

   C They stay the same.

Name ________________________ Date ________________ Class ________________

MODULE 10

Transformations and Similarity

9. Draw the letter below to show its orientation after it is reflected across the y-axis.

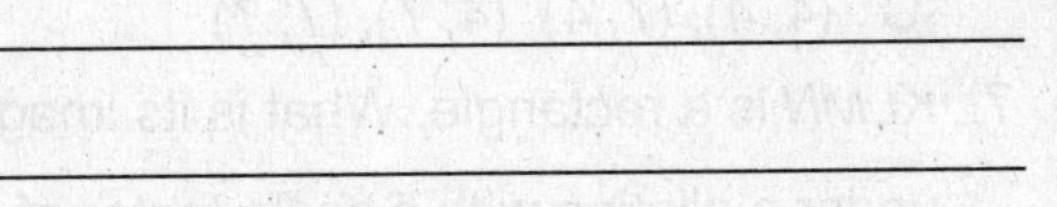

10. A dilation of a triangle is drawn using a scale factor less than 1. Will the image be larger than the original triangle or smaller than the original triangle? Explain how you know.

____

____

____

____

____

11. Identify the transformation shown on the grid below. Justify your choice.

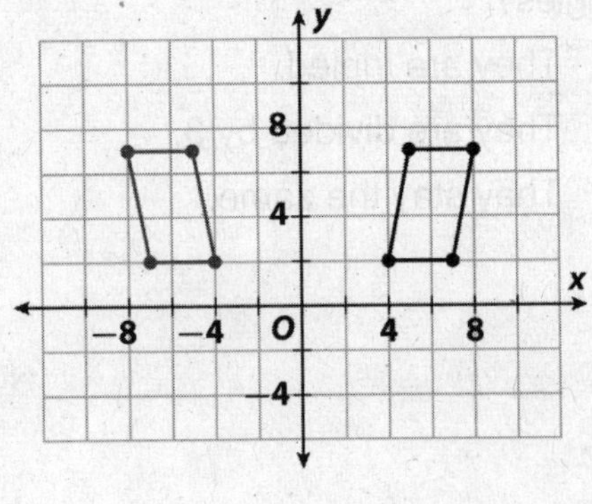

____

____

____

12. Square $ABCD$ has a side length of 4 inches. The square is dilated by a scale factor of 4 to form square $A'B'C'D'$. How can you transform square $A'B'C'D'$ back to square $ABCD$?

____

____

____

____

13. A figure is dilated by a scale factor of $\frac{1}{3}$. Explain whether the image is larger than, smaller than, or the same size as the original figure.

____

____

____

____

____

14. Draw a triangle and its dilation on the grid. Tell whether your dilation image is larger or smaller than the original image.

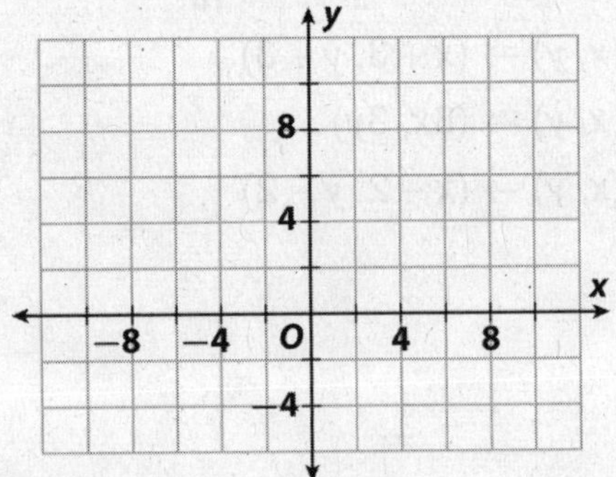

Name ______________________ Date ______________ Class ______________

MODULE 11

Angle Relationships in Parallel Lines and Triangles

Module Quiz: B

Use the figure for 1 and 2.

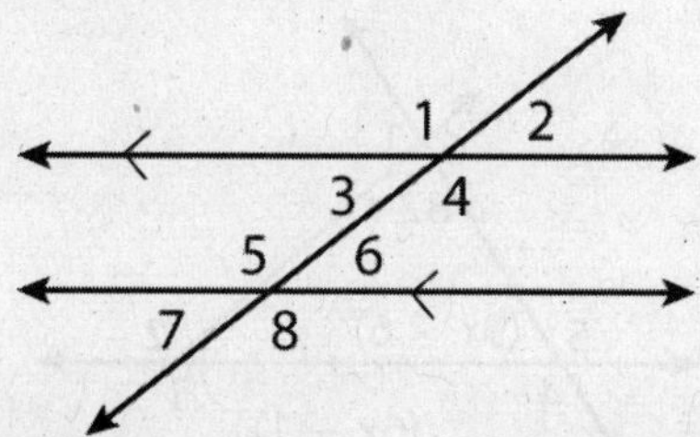

1. Which pair of angles are alternate exterior angles?

   A $\angle 7$ and $\angle 4$

   B $\angle 2$ and $\angle 6$

   C $\angle 8$ and $\angle 1$

   D $\angle 2$ and $\angle 8$

2. Which of these angles is **not** congruent to $\angle 5$?

   A $\angle 8$ C $\angle 1$

   B $\angle 6$ D $\angle 4$

3. The measures of three angles of a triangle are given by $(8x - 5)°$, $(2x)°$, and $(3x - 10)°$. What is the measure of the largest angle?

   A 15° C 35°

   B 115° D 95°

4. Which of the following linear equations is shown by the table below?

x	2	4	7	9	12
y	5	9	15	19	25

   A $y = 2x + 1$

   B $y = x + 2$

   C $y = 3x - 1$

   D $y = 2x - 1$

5. Which of the following equations shows a proportional function?

   A $y = x + 3$

   B $y = 2x - 1$

   C $y = x - 2$

   D $y = 4x$

6. What is the measure of $\angle A$ in the triangle below?

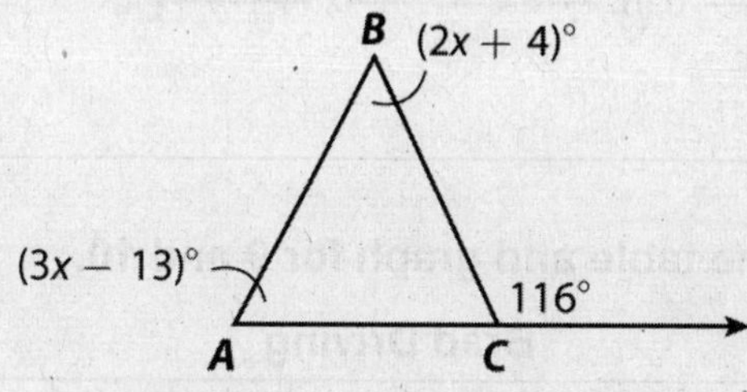

   A 116°

   B 25°

   C 62°

   D 54°

7. Which of the following is **not** an exterior angle of triangle *BHE*?

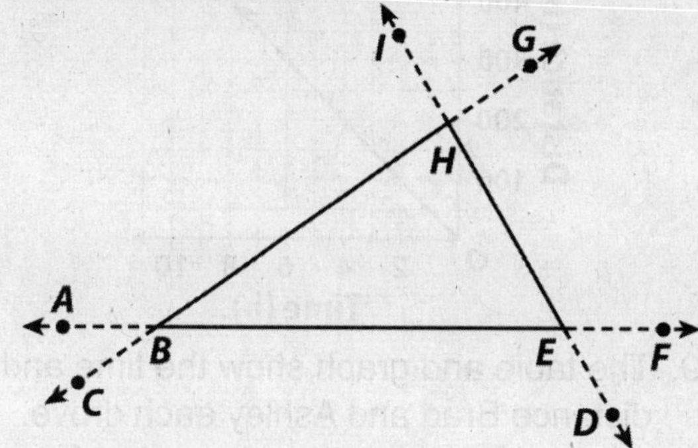

   A $\angle GHE$

   B $\angle ABH$

   C $\angle DEB$

   D $\angle FED$

Name ______________________ Date ______________ Class ______________

MODULE 11

Angle Relationships in Parallel Lines and Triangles

8. What is the measure of x?

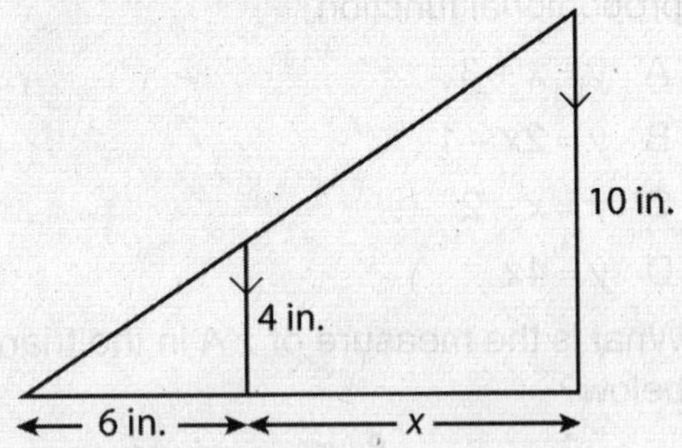

____

Use the table and graph for 9 and 10.

Brad Driving

Time (h)	3	4	6	7	9
Distance (mi)	144	192	288	336	432

Ashley Driving

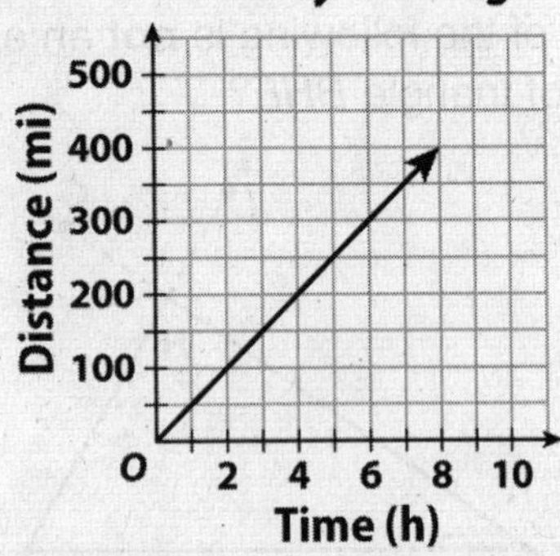

9. The table and graph show the time and distance Brad and Ashley each drove. Which driver drove at a faster rate?

____

10. How many miles per hour faster did the faster driver drive?

____

Use the diagram for 11–14.

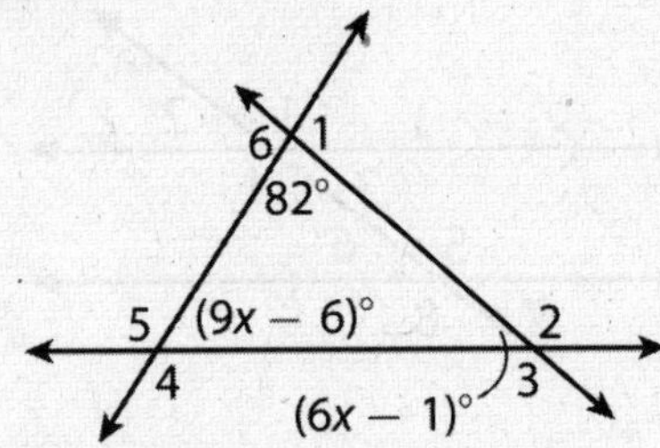

11. What is the measure of ∠1?

____

12. What is the measure of ∠2?

____

13. What is the measure of ∠4?

____

14. What is the measure of ∠5?

____

15. Are the triangles below similar? Explain your reasoning.

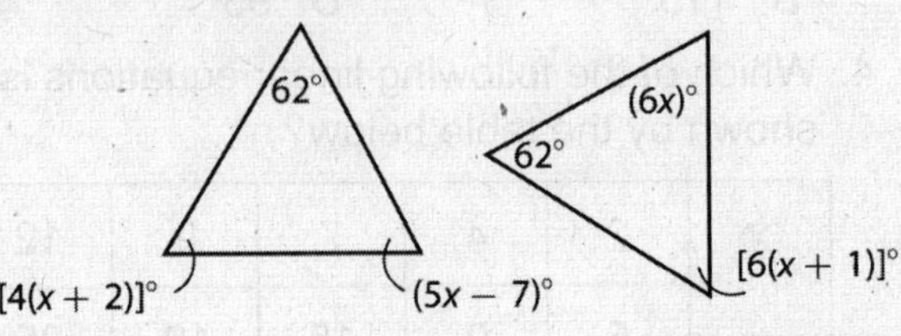

____

____

____

____

Name ______________________ Date ______________ Class ______________

MODULE 11

Angle Relationships in Parallel Lines and Triangles

Module Quiz: D

Use the figure for 1–3.

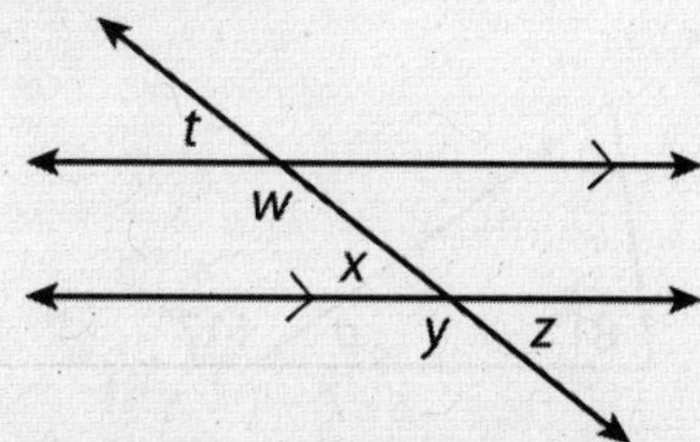

1. Which of the following terms best describes the relationship between $\angle w$ and $\angle x$?

   A corresponding angles

   B same-side interior angles

   C alternate interior angles

2. Which of the following pairs of angles are corresponding angles?

   A $\angle z$ and $\angle x$

   B $\angle t$ and $\angle x$

   C $\angle w$ and $\angle t$

3. Which of the following pairs of angles are congruent?

   A $\angle w$ and $\angle z$

   B $\angle y$ and $\angle x$

   C $\angle w$ and $\angle y$

4. Emma earns 120 frequent flyer miles for every $40 of merchandise she buys with her credit card.
   Which of the following equations could be used to graph this function?

   A $3y = 40x$

   B $y = 40x + 120$

   C $y = 3x$

5. What is the measure of the unlabeled angle of the triangle below?

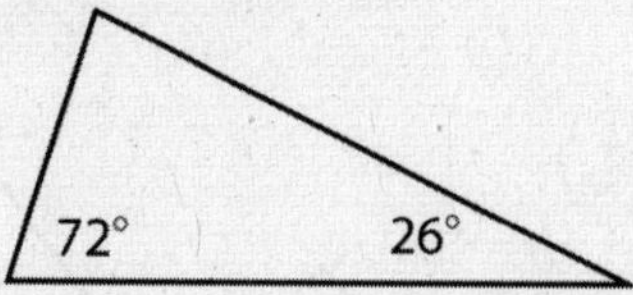

   A 90°

   B 82°

   C 98°

Use the figure for 6–8.

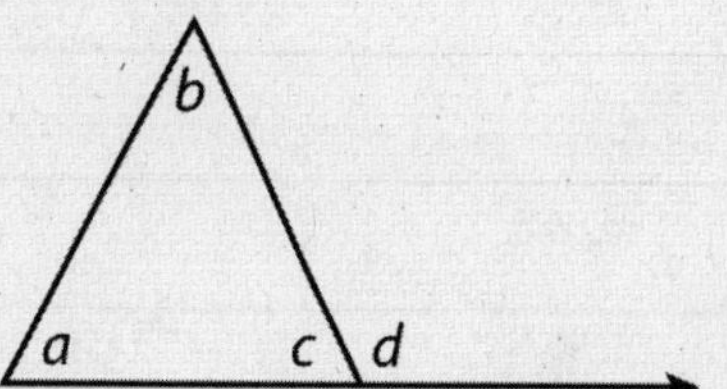

6. Which of the following angle or angles are remote interior angle(s) to $\angle d$?

   A $\angle a$

   B $\angle a$ and $\angle b$

   C $\angle c$

7. Which of the following expressions is equal to the measure of $\angle d$?

   A $m\angle a + m\angle b$

   B $m\angle c + m\angle b$

   C $m\angle a$

8. Which of the following terms best describes $\angle d$?

   A remote interior angle

   B corresponding angle

   C exterior angle

Name ______________________ Date ______________ Class ______________

MODULE 11 Angle Relationships in Parallel Lines and Triangles

9. Are the triangles below similar? Explain your answer.

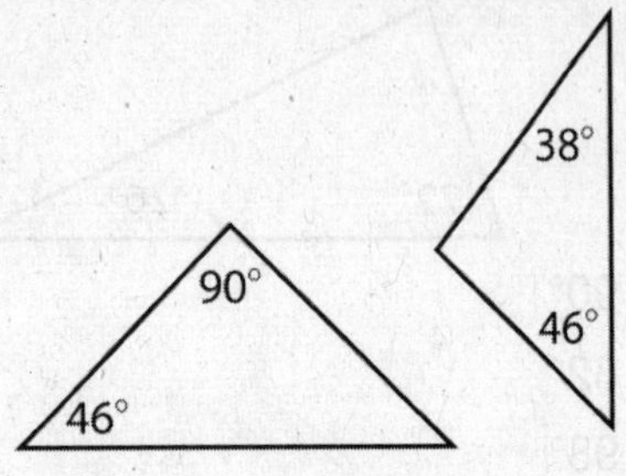

10. Is the relationship shown in the table a function? Explain your answer.

Input	19	12	15	14	12
Output	4	6	8	12	14

11. What is the measure of $\angle b$? Show your work.

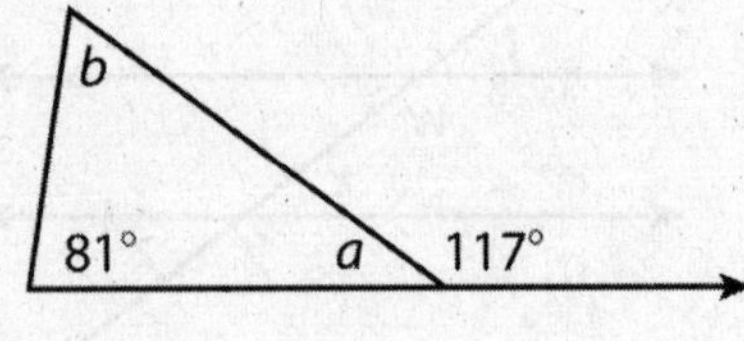

12. The table below shows the distance a car traveled over the times shown. At what rate did the car travel?

Car Driving on Highway

Distance (mi)	159	265	318	477
Time (h)	3	5	6	9

13. In the space below, draw a triangle and all of its exterior angles. Label each exterior angle with a letter, starting with *A*.

Name ______________________ Date ______________ Class ______________

MODULE 12

The Pythagorean Theorem

Module Quiz: B

1. What is the length of the hypotenuse of the triangle below?

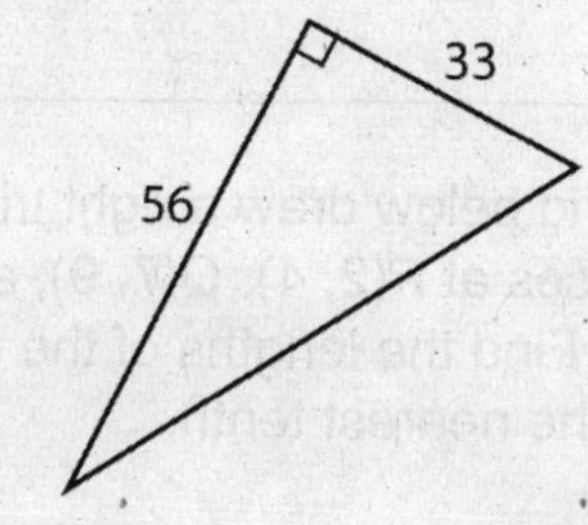

A 23
B 45.2
C 65
D 89

2. A diagonal shortcut across an empty rectangular lot is 97 feet. The lot is 72 feet long. What is the other dimension of the lot?

A 65 feet
B 84.5 feet
C 120.8 feet
D 169 feet

3. An isosceles right triangle has legs that are 10 inches long. How long is the hypotenuse?

A 10 in.
B 14.1 in.
C 20 in.
D 28.2 in.

Use this figure for 4 and 5.

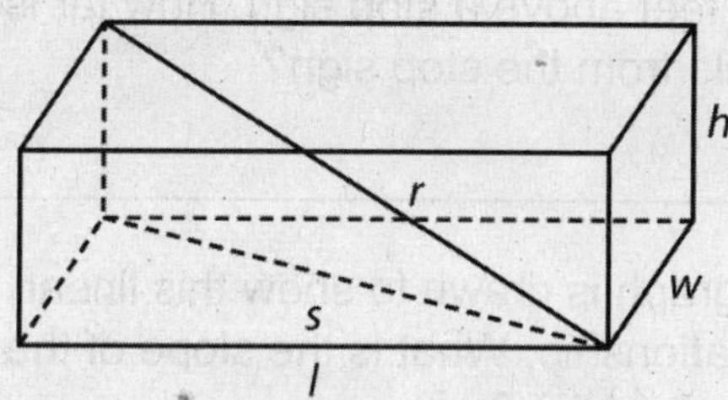

4. The box above is 15 centimeters long, 4 centimeters wide, and 3 centimeters tall. What is the length of the diagonal *s* of the bottom side?

A 4.4 cm
B 14.5 cm
C 15.5 cm
D 19 cm

5. What is the length of the diagonal *r* of the box?

A 4.7 cm
B 5 cm
C 15.8 cm
D 22 cm

6. Which set of three numbers can be used to make a right triangle?

A 39, 41, 45
B 39, 49, 59
C 39, 69, 99
D 39, 80, 89

7. Why is it **not** possible to make a right triangle using lengths of 10 feet, 60 feet, and 65 feet?

A $10 + 60$ is greater than 65.
B $65 - 60$ does not equal 10.
C $10^2 + 60^2$ does not equal 65^2.
D $(10 + 60)^2$ does not equal 65^2.

8. What is the distance between two points with coordinates at (8, 40) and (20, 5)?

A 35.3
B 37
C 47
D 54.1

9. What is the distance between points *W* and *X* to the nearest hundredth?

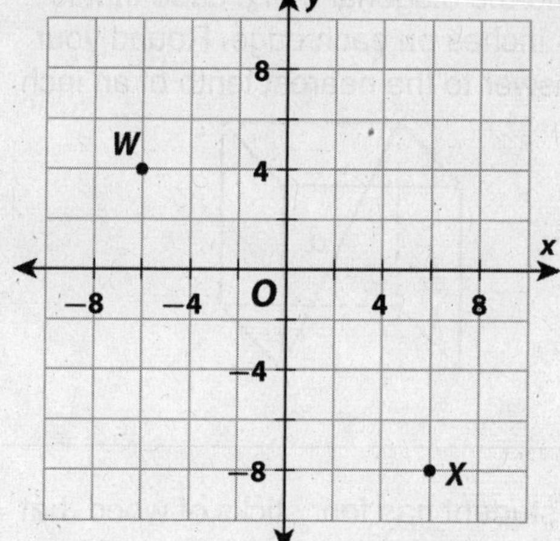

A 8.49
B 12
C 16.97
D 24

10. What is the scientific notation for 568 billion?

A 5.68×10^8
B 5.68×10^9
C 5.68×10^{11}
D 5.68×10^{12}

Name ______________________ Date ______________ Class ______________

MODULE 12

The Pythagorean Theorem

11. What is the missing side length in the triangle below?

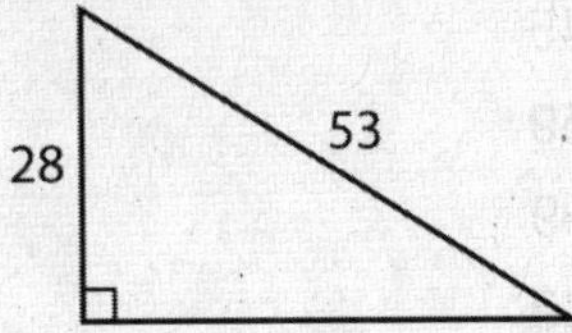

____

12. A right triangle has legs of 15 centimeters and 22 centimeters. What is the length of the hypotenuse to the nearest tenth of a centimeter?

____

13. A carpenter added a diagonal brace to a gate that measures 45 inches wide and 55 inches tall. How long is the brace to the nearest tenth of an inch?

____

14. Find the diagonal d of a cube that is 14 inches on each edge. Round your answer to the nearest tenth of an inch.

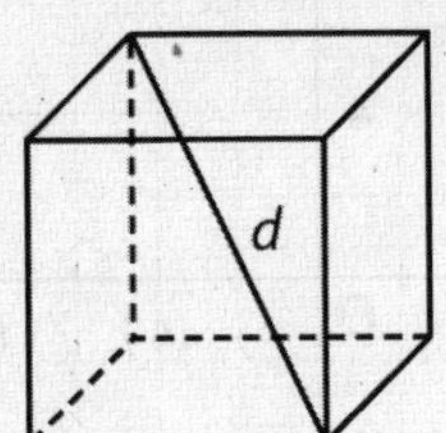

____

15. A student has four sticks of wood that measure 12 inches, 15 inches, 18 inches, and 30 inches. Can the student use three of these to make a right triangle with a hypotenuse of 30 inches? Explain your answer.

____

____

16. What is the distance between the origin and a point at (–15, 8)?

____

17. On the grid below draw a right triangle with vertices at $P(2, 4)$, $Q(7, 9)$, and $R(10, 6)$. Find the lengths of the three sides to the nearest tenth.

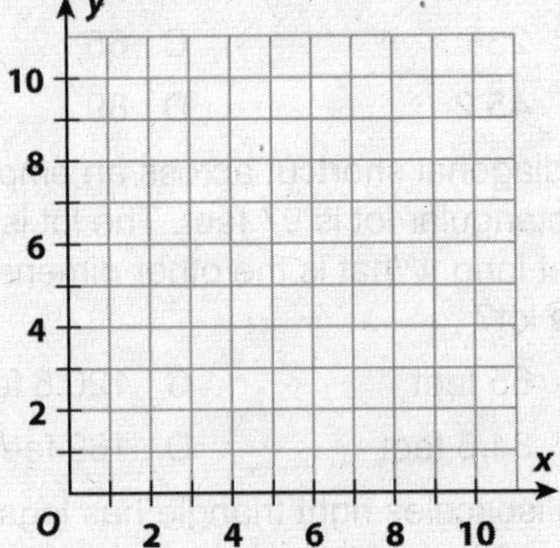

____

____

18. A child is flying a kite and has let out all 80 feet of the kite's string. The kite is 35 feet above a stop sign. How far is the child from the stop sign?

____

19. A graph is drawn to show this linear relationship. What is the slope of the graphed line?

Time (x)	3.5 h	5.5 h
Distance (y)	240 mi	320 mi

____

Name ______________________ Date ______________ Class ______________

MODULE 12

The Pythagorean Theorem

Module Quiz: D

1. What is the length of the hypotenuse of the triangle below?

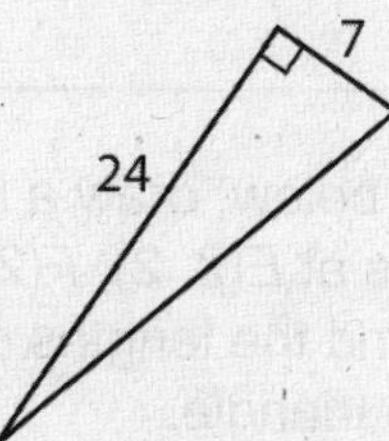

A 25 B 89
C 31

2. A rectangle is 80 inches long. The diagonal is 100 inches. How wide is the rectangle?

A 20 in.
B 60 in.
C 180 in.

3. Two legs of a right triangle each measure 10 inches. How long is the hypotenuse?

A 10 in.
B 14.1 in.
C 20 in.

Use the figure for 4 and 5.

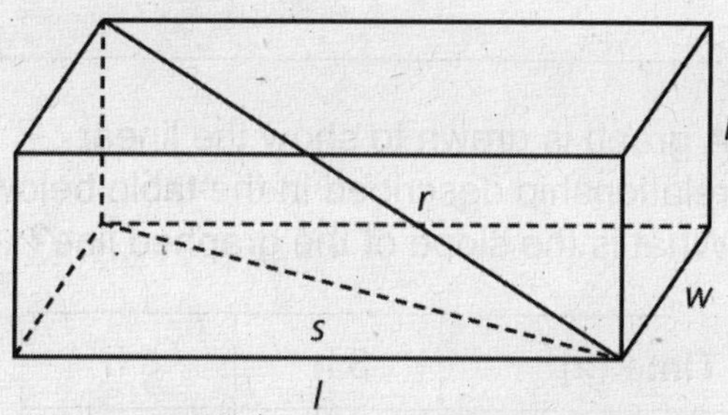

4. In the figure above, $l = 15$ cm, $w = 4$ cm, and $h = 3$ cm. What is the length of s?

A 4.4 cm
B 14.5 cm
C 15.5 cm

5. What is the length of diagonal r?

A 15.8 cm
B 22 cm
C 27.8 cm

6. Which set of three numbers can be used to make a right triangle?

A 3, 4, 5
B 4, 5, 6
C 5, 6, 7

7. Why is it **not** possible to make a right triangle using lengths of 4 feet, 8 feet, and 10 feet?

A $4 + 8$ is greater than 10.
B $10 - 8$ does not equal 4.
C $4^2 + 8^2$ does not equal 10^2.

8. What is the distance between two points with coordinates at (12, 0) and (0, 35)?

A 35.3
B 37
C 47

9. What is the distance between points P and Q on the grid below?

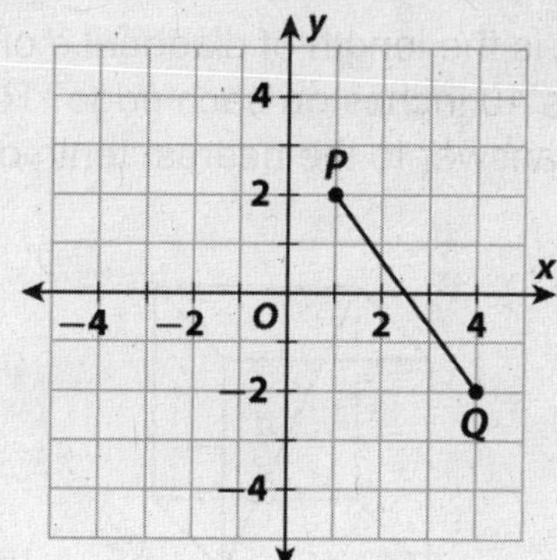

A 3
B 4
C 5

10. What is the scientific notation for 56 million?

A 5.6×10^6
B 5.6×10^7
C 5.6×10^8

Name ____________________ Date ______________ Class ______________

MODULE 12 The Pythagorean Theorem

11. What is the missing side length in the triangle below?

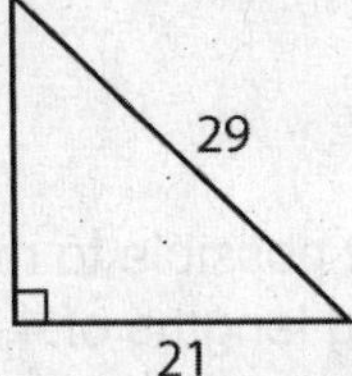

____

12. A right triangle has legs of 9 centimeters and 40 centimeters. What is the length of the hypotenuse?

____

13. A carpenter added a diagonal brace to a gate. The gate is 80 inches wide and 60 inches tall. How long is the brace?

____

14. What is the length of diagonal *d* of a cube that is 10 inches on each edge? Round your answer to the nearest tenth of an inch.

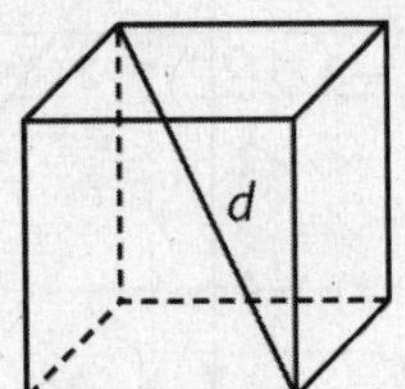

____

15. A student has four sticks of wood that measure 3 inches, 4 inches, 5 inches, and 6 inches. Can the student use any three of these sticks to make a right triangle? Explain why or why not.

____

____

____

16. What is the distance between (0, 0) and a point at (15, 8)?

____

17. On the grid below, draw a right triangle with vertices at *E*(2, 2), *F*(2, 8), and *G*(10, 8). Find the lengths of the three sides of the triangle.

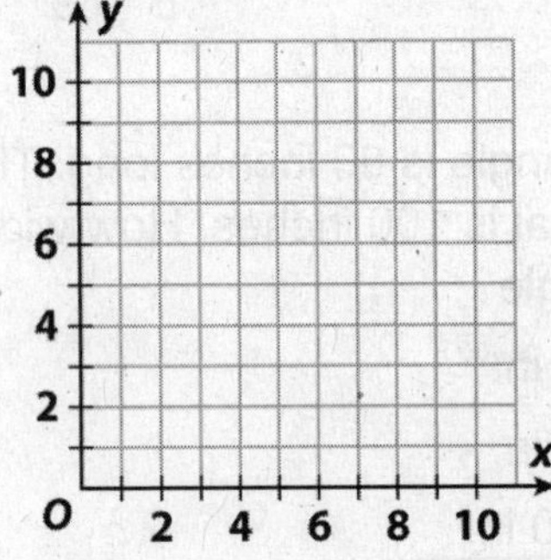

____

____

18. A kite is flying 40 feet above a stop sign. The child flying the kite is standing 30 feet away from the stop sign. How long is the string from the child to the kite?

____

19. A graph is drawn to show the linear relationship described in the table below. What is the slope of the graphed line?

Time (*x*)	3 h	5 h
Distance (*y*)	90 mi	150 mi

____

Name ________________________ Date ____________ Class ____________

MODULE 13

Volume

Module Quiz: B

Use 3.14 for π. Round answers to the nearest hundredth.

1. A can of soup has the shape of a cylinder. The diameter of the base is 3.4 inches, and the height of the can is 4.5 inches. What is the volume of the can?

   A 24.02 in^3

   B 40.84 in^3

   C 108.09 in^3

   D 163.34 in^3

2. A regulation bowling ball has a diameter of 8.5 inches. What is the volume of the bowling ball?

   A 302.49 in^3

   B 75.62 in^3

   C 2,571.14 in^3

   D 321.39 in^3

3. What is the measure of $\angle B$?

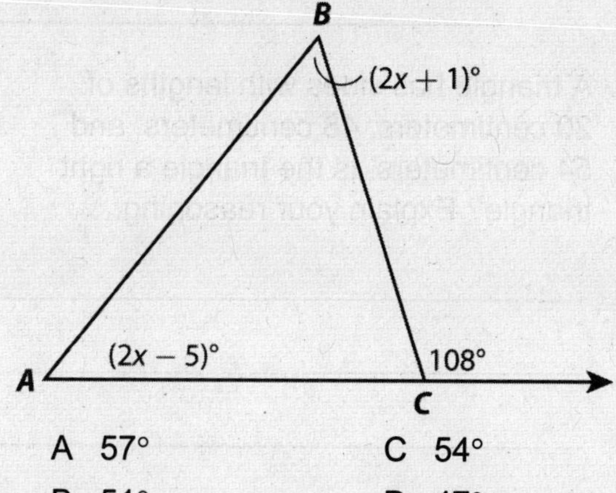

   A 57° C 54°

   B 51° D 47°

4. A cone has a height of 8.4 centimeters and a base with a radius of 5.2 centimeters. What is the volume of the cone?

   A 75.62 cm^3

   B 237.74 cm^3

   C 713.21 cm^3

   D 2,571.14 cm^3

5. Tomato paste is sold in a cylindrical can. The can has a radius of 1.5 inches and a height of 4.8 inches. What is the volume of the can?

   A 22.61 in^3

   B 108.52 in^3

   C 33.91 in^3

   D 13,565 in^3

6. A cylindrical stylus has a diameter of 0.1875 inch and is 6.2 inches long. What is the volume of the stylus?

   A 171.1 in^3

   B 17.11 in^3

   C 1.71 in^3

   D 0.17 in^3

7. What is the missing measure?

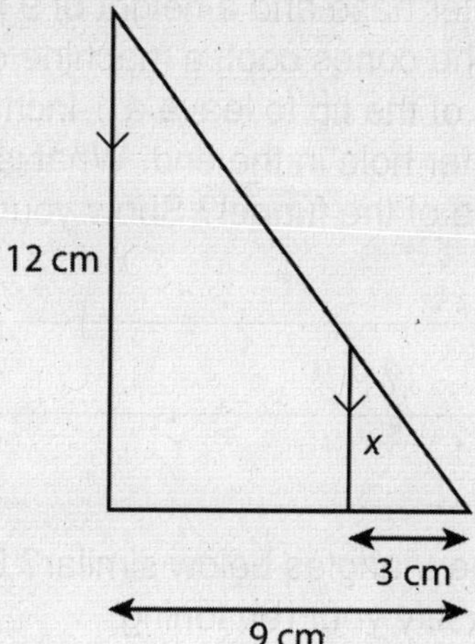

   A 8 cm C 6 cm

   B 4 cm D 3 cm

8. The volume of a cone is 294.38 cm^3. The radius of the base is 7.5 cm. Which of the following could be the height of the cone?

   A 4 cm C 6 cm

   B 5 cm D 7 cm

Name ______________________ Date ______________ Class ______________

MODULE 13 Volume

9. A cylindrical can of cat food has a diameter of 3.5 inches and a height of 1.25 inches. A second brand of cat food is packaged in a cylindrical can with a radius of 1.2 inches and a height of 1.25 inches. What is the difference between the volumes of the cans? Show your work.

____

____

____

____

10. A manufacturer makes conical funnels for professional painters. The funnels are formed from plastic with an 8-inch diameter base and a height of 9 inches. After the cones cool, a machine cuts off 1 inch of the tip to leave a 1-inch diameter hole in the end. What is the volume of the funnel? Show your work.

____

____

____

11. Are the triangles below similar? Explain and justify your reasoning.

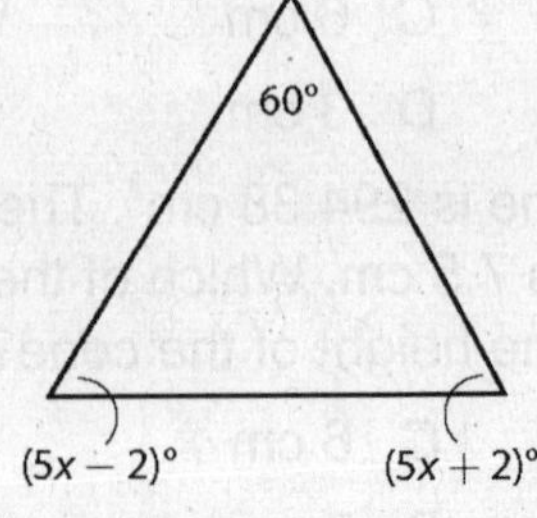

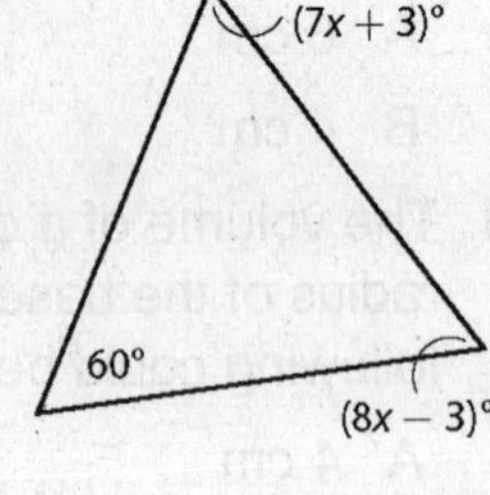

____

____

____

____

12. The volume of a cylinder is 713.21 in^3. The radius of the cylinder is 5.2 inches. What is the height of the cylinder? Show your work.

____

____

____

____

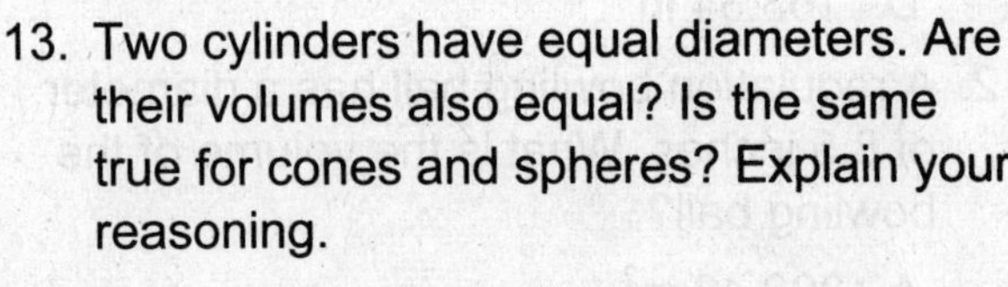

13. Two cylinders have equal diameters. Are their volumes also equal? Is the same true for cones and spheres? Explain your reasoning.

____

____

____

____

14. A triangle has sides with lengths of 20 centimeters, 48 centimeters, and 54 centimeters. Is the triangle a right triangle? Explain your reasoning.

____

____

____

____

____

Name ______________________ Date ______________ Class ______________

MODULE 13

Volume

Module Quiz: D

Use 3.14 for π. Round your answers to the nearest hundredth.

1. What is the volume of the cylinder below?
   Use the formula $V = \pi r^2 h$.

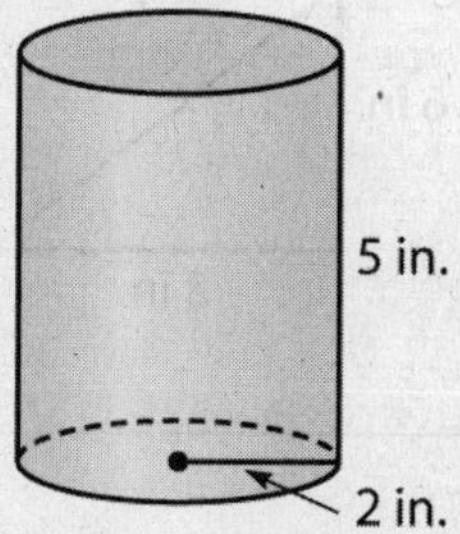

A $31.4\ \text{in}^3$

B $157\ \text{in}^3$

C $62.8\ \text{in}^3$

2. What is the volume of the cone below?
   Use the formula $V = \frac{1}{3}\pi r^2 h$.

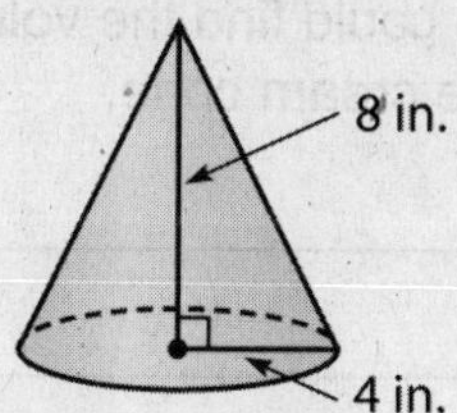

A $133.97\ \text{in}^3$

B $267.95\ \text{in}^3$

C $33.49\ \text{in}^3$

3. What is the measure of $\angle C$?

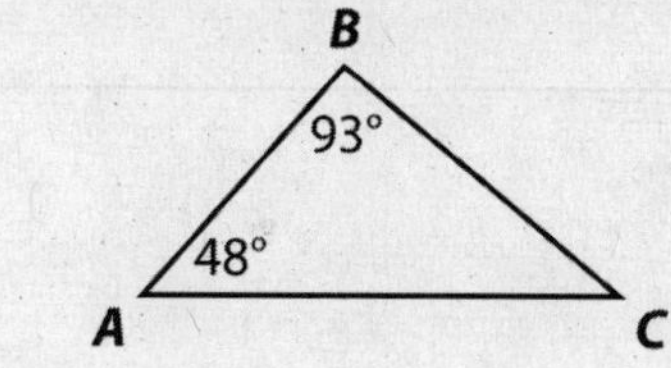

A 44°

B 39°

C 49°

4. What is the volume of the sphere below?
   Use the formula $V = \frac{4}{3}\pi r^3$.

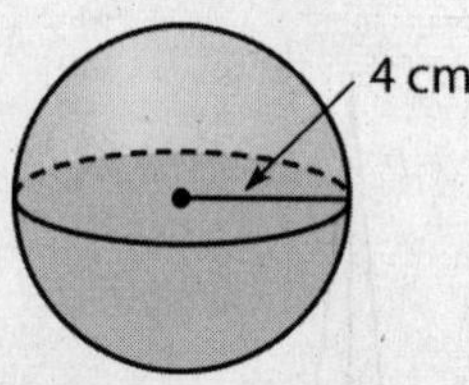

A $16.75\ \text{cm}^3$

B $66.99\ \text{cm}^3$

C $267.95\ \text{cm}^3$

5. What is the volume of the cylinder below?
   Use the formula $V = \pi r^2 h$.

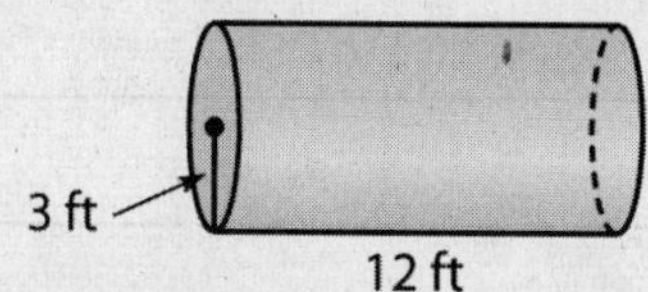

A $113.04\ \text{ft}^3$

B $1{,}356.48\ \text{ft}^3$

C $339.12\ \text{ft}^3$

6. What is the volume of the sphere below?
   Use the formula $V = \frac{4}{3}\pi r^3$.

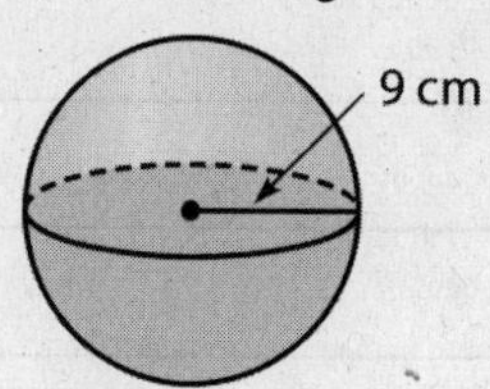

A $339.12\ \text{cm}^3$

B $3{,}052.08\ \text{cm}^3$

C $37.68\ \text{cm}^3$

Name ______________________ Date ______________ Class ______________

MODULE 13

Volume

7. What is the volume of this cone? Use the formula $V = \frac{1}{3}\pi r^2 h$. Show your work.

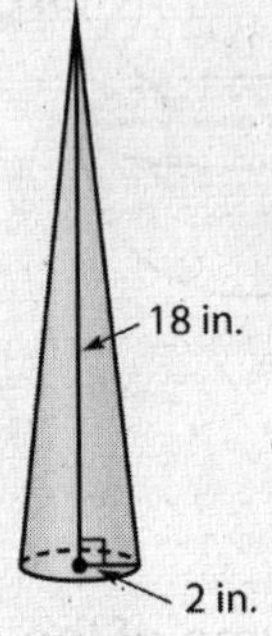

8. The formula for the volume of a cone is $V = \frac{1}{3}\pi r^2 h$. Which part of the formula represents the area of the base? How do you know?

9. A cone has the same radius as a cylinder, and exactly the same height. Which has a greater volume, the cone or the cylinder? Explain how you know.

10. Use the Pythagorean Theorem, $a^2 + b^2 = c^2$, to find the measure of the hypotenuse in this triangle. Show your work.

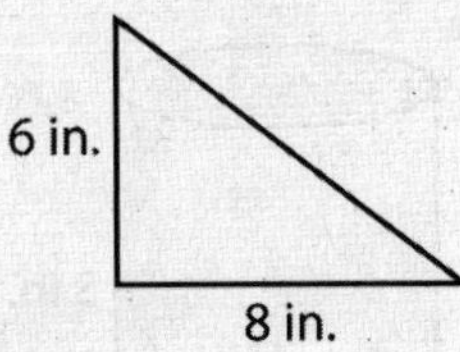

11. An ice cream cone is made of a cone shape and half a sphere shape. Explain how you could find the volume of the entire ice cream cone.

Name ________________________ Date ______________ Class ______________

MODULE 14

Scatter Plots

Module Quiz: B

1. Which scatter plot could have a trend line whose equation is $y = x + 15$?

A 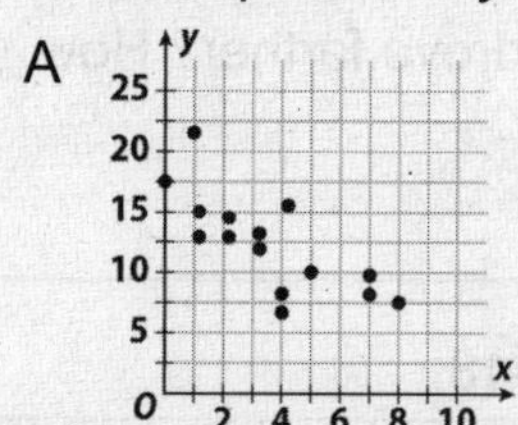

C 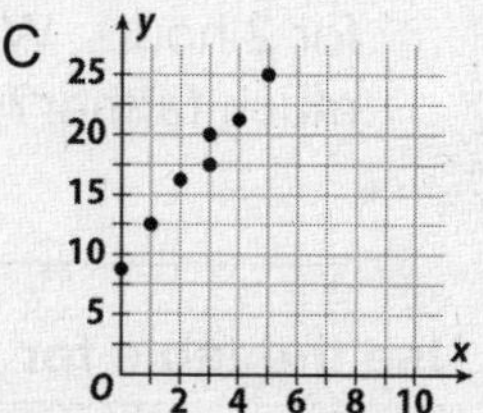

B 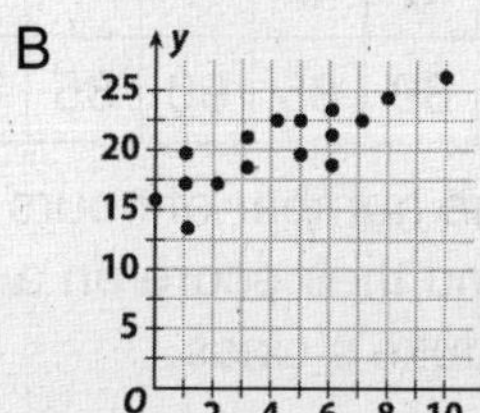

D 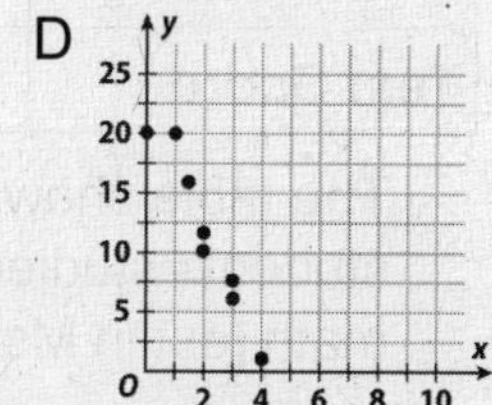

2. What type of association would you expect between a person's height and weight?

A positive C none

B negative D quadratic

3. Which of the following is **not** shown on the scatter plot below?

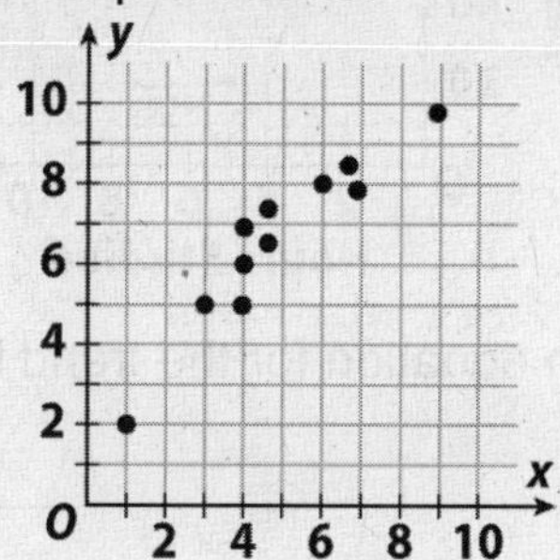

A a cluster

B negative association

C positive association

D an outlier

4. The distance between two stars in the solar system is 14,000,000,000,000 miles. What is this distance expressed in scientific notation?

A 1.4×10^{-13} C 1.4×10^{13}

B 14×10^{-12} D 14×10^{12}

5. The distance on a map between Lynwood and Forest Hill is 3.75 inches. According to the map key, 0.25 inch on the map is equivalent to 1 mile. What is the actual distance in miles between Lynwood and Forest Hill?

A 10 C 14

B 12 D 15

6. For the data shown in the scatter plot below, which point is an outlier?

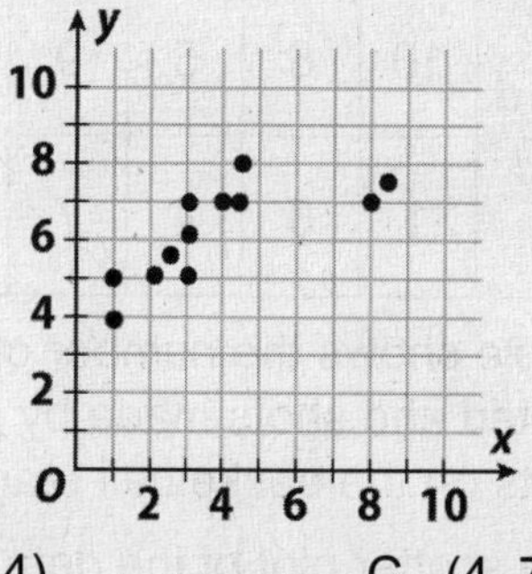

A (1, 4) C (4, 7)

B (3, 3) D (8, 7)

7. Colby graphed a scatter plot of student exam scores (y) and the number of hours each student had slept the night before the exam (x). She drew the trend line and calculated its equation to be $y = \frac{9}{2}x + 60$. What is the predicted score for a student who slept 6 hours the night before the exam?

A 82 C 93

B 87 D 95

8. Marissa says that the number y is equal to 8 more than 20 times x. Which of the following equations could be used to find the value of y?

A $y = 20x + 8$ C $y = 8x - 20$

B $y = 8x + 20$ D $y = -20x + 8$

Name ________________________ Date ______________ Class ______________

MODULE 14

Scatter Plots

9. Explain why a trend line is not a good model to use when explaining human growth in height from birth to age 50.

____

____

____

Use the table for 10–12.

Shots Attempted	10	8	5	9	4	7
Shots Made	1	6	4	7	3	5

The table shows the number of shots attempted and shots made by six students on the basketball team.

10. Make a scatter plot of the data.

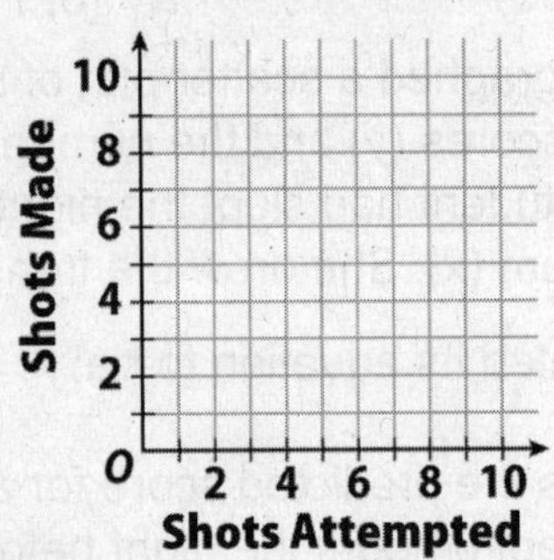

11. Are there are any clusters in the data? Explain.

____

____

____

12. Are there any outliers in the data? Explain.

____

____

____

13. Andrew drove 60 miles per hour for 1.5 hours. Devon drove 50 miles an hour for 2 hours. Who drove farther? How much farther?

____

Use the table for 14–18.

Hours Studied	1	3	3	4	4	2
Test Score	70	80	85	90	85	75

The table shows the number of hours students studied and their score on a math test in Ms. Aduke's class.

14. Make a scatter plot of the data and draw a trend line.

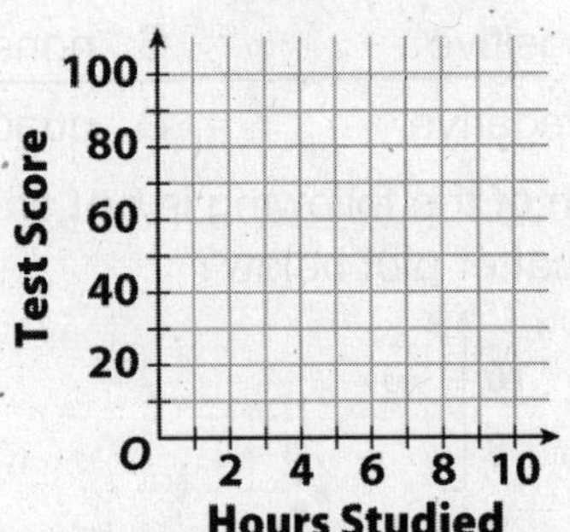

15. Write an equation for the trend line.

____

16. What type of association does the trend line show?

____

17. Predict the test score a student would get if he or she studied for 5 hours.

____

18. Are there any limitations to using the linear model to predict the test score? Explain.

____

____

Name ______________________ Date ______________ Class ______________

MODULE 14

Scatter Plots

Module Quiz: D

1. Which scatter plot could have a trend line whose equation is $y = x + 2$?

A

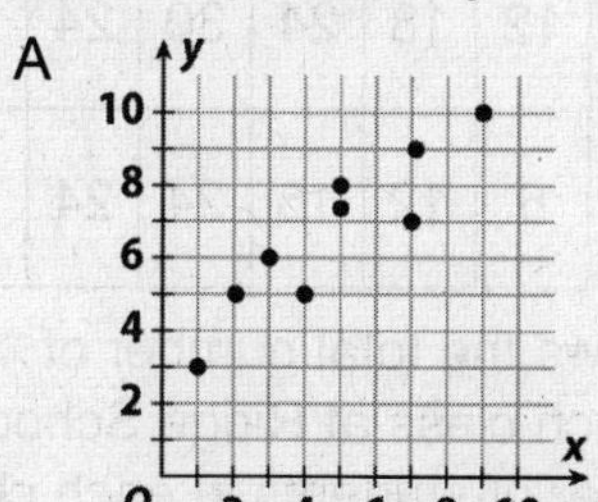

B

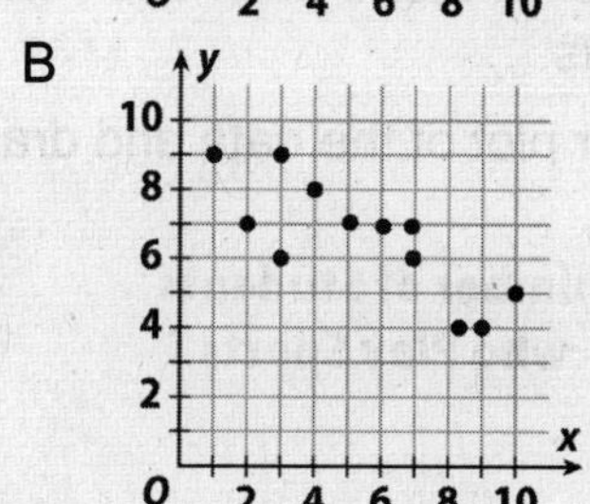

C

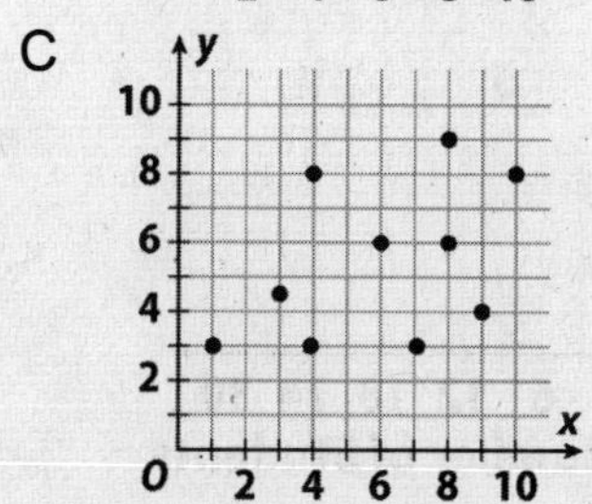

2. Which type of association would you expect between number of hours studied for a test and the score on the test?

A none

B positive

C negative

3. Which of the following is shown on the scatter plot below?

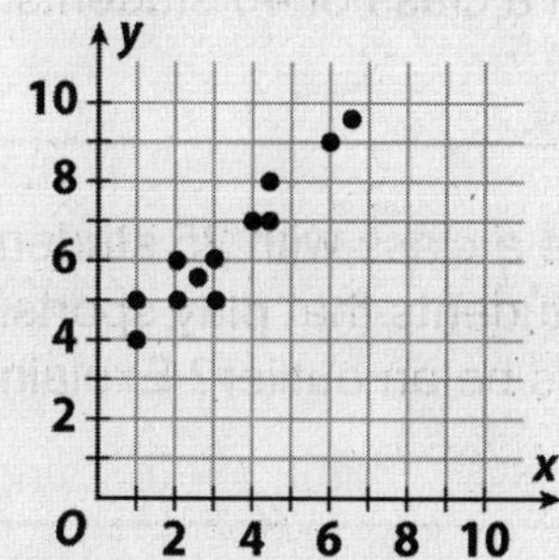

A cluster

B negative association

C outlier

4. The distance between two planets in the solar system is 560,000 miles. What is this distance expressed in scientific notation?

A 5.6×10^{-5}

B 5.6×10^{5}

C 56×10^{4}

5. For the data shown in the scatter plot below, which point is an outlier?

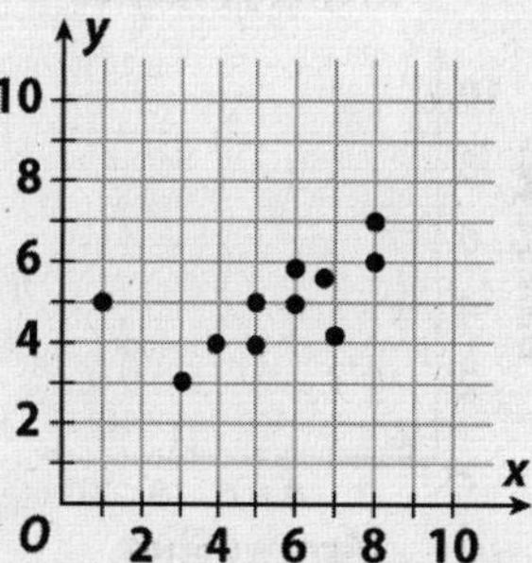

A (1, 5)

B (3, 3)

C (5, 4)

6. Jenya graphed a scatter plot of number of potholes (y) and length of a road in miles (x). She drew the trend line and calculated its equation to be $y = 3x + 5$. What is the predicted number of potholes for a road that is 10 miles long?

A 18

B 25

C 35

7. Cole says that the number y is equal to 50 times x. Which of the following equations could be used to find the value of y?

A $y = 50x$

B $y = x + 50$

C $y = \frac{x}{50}$

Name ______________________ Date ______________ Class ______________

MODULE 14

Scatter Plots

Use the table for 8–10.

Arrows Shot	9	7	8	6	5	6
Bull's Eyes	2	6	5	6	5	5

The table shows the number of arrows Johnny shot and the number of times he hit the bull's eye.

8. Make a scatter plot of the data.

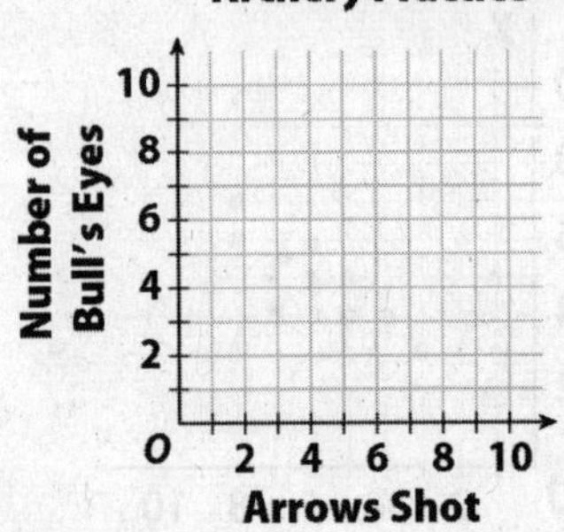

9. Are there are any clusters in the data? Explain.

____

____

____

10. Are there any outliers in the data? Explain.

____

____

____

11. Andrew drove 60 miles per hour for 2 hours. What is the total distance he traveled?

____

12. Sandra calculated the trend line for a scatter plot to be $y = 3x + 10$. What is the predicted value of y if $x = 40$?

____

Use the table for 13–17.

Number of Students	12	18	24	30	24	18
Students Who Play Sports	6	12	15	24	24	9

The table shows the total number of students in each class at Ridge School and the number of students in each class who play sports.

13. Make a scatter plot of the data and draw a trend line.

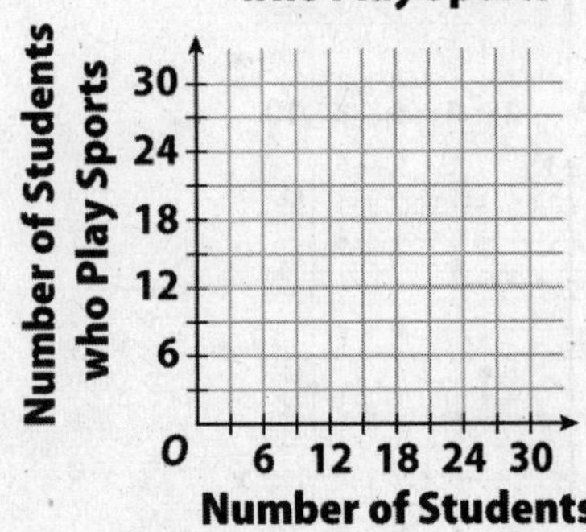

14. Write an equation for the trend line.

____

15. What type of association does the trend line show?

____

16. Predict the number of students who play sports in a class of 40 students.

____

17. Suppose a class with 25 students has only 3 students that play sports. Would this class be an outlier? Explain.

____

____

____

Name ______________________ Date ______________ Class ______________

MODULE 15

Two-Way Tables

Module Quiz: B

Use the situation and table below for 1–4.

A chef collected data on customers' ages and where they got information about the restaurant. The results are shown below.

	Under 40	40 and Older	Total
Internet	?	30	165
TV Newspaper	45	90	135
Total	180	120	300

1. How many customers under 40 years old, got their information on the Internet?

   A 45 C 165

   B 135 D 180

2. What is the relative frequency of a customer getting information from TV or newspaper?

   A 13.5% C 45%

   B 27% D 55%

3. What is the relative frequency of a customer 40 years or older getting information from the Internet?

   A 0.182 C 0.25

   B 0.222 D 0.4

4. Using the data in the table, which statement is true?

   A Most people under 40 use TV or newspaper as sources of information.

   B People who get information from the Internet are more likely to be 40 or over.

   C There is no association between a customer's age and the source they used for information.

   D There is an association between a customer's age and the source they used for information.

Use the situation and table below for 5–7

West Junior High rack club has members that run either the hurdles or in relay races. No student runs in both. The results are shown below.

	Hurdles	Relays	Total
Boys	8	12	20
Girls	15	15	?
Total	23	27	50

5. How many members of the track club are girls?

   A 15 C 30

   B 20 D 50

6. What is the joint relative frequency of track club members who are boys that prefer relays?

   A 0.16 C 0.3

   B 0.24 D 0.4

7. What is the marginal relative frequency of track club members who are girls?

   A 0.16 C 0.4

   B 0.3 D 0.6

8. Which action is shown by the graph?

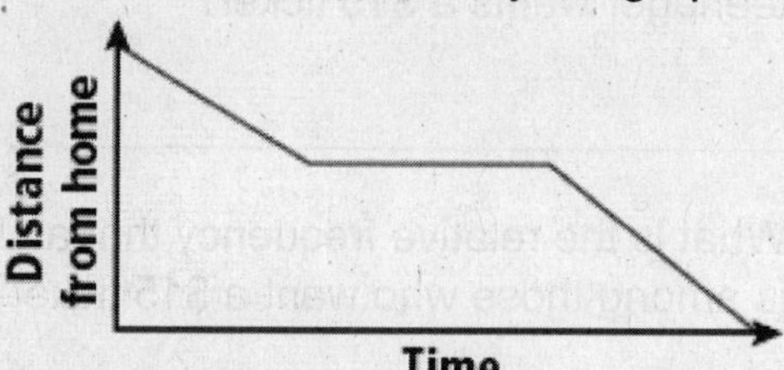

   A Ian starts at home and walks downhill. After he rests, he goes on walking downhill.

   B Ian leaves school and walks toward home. He stops at a store and then walks homes.

   C Ian leaves the library and runs all the way home.

   D Ian leaves the store and jogs to the library. Then he goes back to the store.

Name ________________ Date ____________ Class ____________

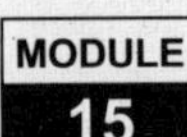

Two-Way Tables

Module Quiz: B

Use the table and situation for 9–14.

There were 80 teenagers in line for tickets to a concert. Forty percent were boys. Twenty-six girls wanted $10 tickets. The rest wanted $15 tickets. The results are shown below.

	$10	$15	Total
Boys	?	18	?
Girls	26	22	?
Total	40	40	80

9. How many of the teenagers in line are boys?

____

10. How many boys wanted tickets for $10?

____

11. How many of the teenagers in line are girls?

____

12. What is the relative frequency that a teenager wants a $15 ticket?

____

13. What is the relative frequency that a girl is among those who want a $15 ticket?

____

14. Is there an association between being a boy and wanting a $10 ticket? Explain.

____

____

____

____

Use the table and situation for 15–18.

A store tested customers by offering two items for sale for 2 months. Each item was marked 50% off one month and marked "Buy 1, Get 1 Free" the other month. The number of items sold each month is shown below.

	50% Off	Buy 1, Get 1 Free	Total
Item 1	12	8	20
Item 2	20	10	30
Total	32	18	?

15. What is the joint relative frequency for Item 1 when it was sold at 50% off?

____

16. What is the marginal relative frequency of selling items marked "Buy 1, Get 1 Free?"

____

17. What is the conditional relative frequency of selling Item 2 given that the price is 50% off?

____

18. What is the conditional relative frequency of selling an item marked 50% off, provided the item sold is Item 2?

____

19. Describe the action shown by the graph.

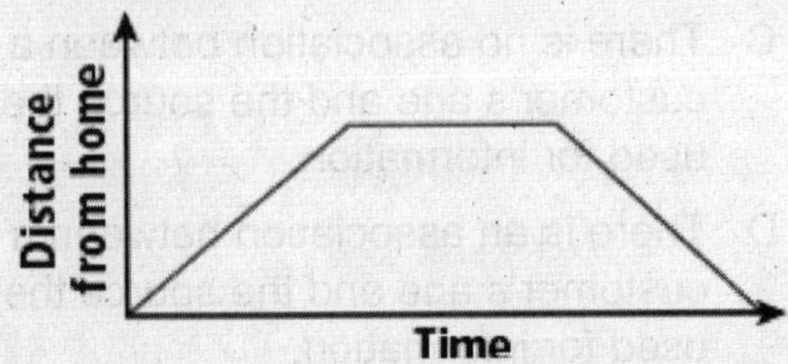

____

Name ______________________ Date ______________ Class ______________

MODULE 15

Two-Way Tables

Module Quiz: D

Use the situation and table for 1–4.

A car dealer collected data on customers' ages and where they got information about the cars they were interested in buying. The results are shown below.

	Under 40	40 and Older	Total
Internet	?	20	60
TV or Magazines	10	30	40
Total	50	50	100

1. How many customers under 40 years old, got their information on the Internet?

A 20 C 60

B 40

2. What is the relative frequency of a customer getting information from TV or magazines?

A 10% C 40%

B 30%

3. What is the relative frequency of a customer 40 years or older getting information from the Internet?

A 20% C 50%

B 40%

4. Using the data in the table, which statement is true?

A There is an association between the age of a customer and where that customer gets information about the cars they are interested in buying.

B There is no association between the age of a customer and where that customer gets information about the cars they are interested in buying.

C Most people 40 and over use the Internet to find information about the cars they are interested in buying.

Use the situation and table for 5–7.

In one track club some members call themselves the "Jumping Js." Each member of the Jumping Js competes in either the long jump or the triple jump. No student competes in both. The results are shown below.

	Long Jump	Triple Jump	Total
Boys	2	4	6
Girls	1	3	?
Total	3	7	10

5. How many members of the Jumping Js are girls?

A 3 C 6

B 4

6. What is the joint relative frequency of Jumping Js members who are girls that compete in the triple jump?

A 0.1 C 0.43

B 0.3

7. What is the marginal relative frequency of Jumping Js members who are girls?

A 0.4 C 0.6

B 0.5

8. Which action is shown by the graph?

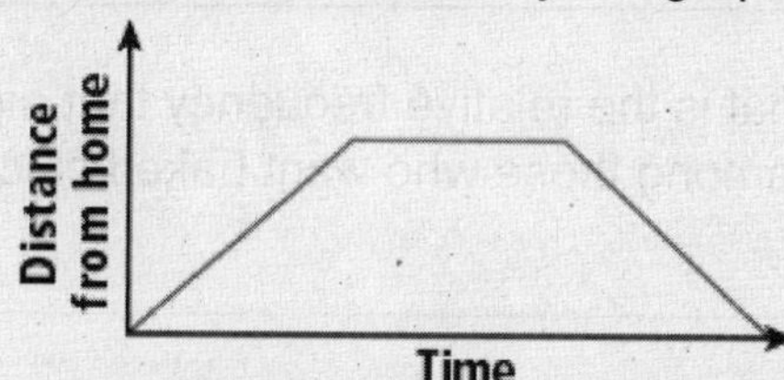

A Bill starts at home, walks to the store, then walks on to school.

B Bill starts at home, walks to the store and shops for a while, then walks back home.

C Bill walks around the block.

Name ______________________ Date ______________ Class ______________

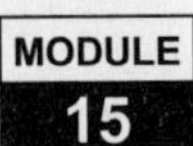

Two-Way Tables

Module Quiz: D

Use the situation and table for 9–14.

There were 20 teenagers at a restaurant. Forty percent were boys. Eight girls wanted salads. Five boys and four girls wanted baked chicken. The results are shown below.

	Salads	Baked Chicken	Total
Boys	?	5	?
Girls	8	4	12
Total	11	9	20

9. How many of the teenagers at the restaurant are boys?

____

10. How many boys wanted salads?

____

11. How many of the teenagers are girls who wanted baked chicken?

____

12. What is the relative frequency that a teenager wants a salad?

____

13. What is the relative frequency that a girl is among those who want baked chicken?

____

14. Is there an association between being a girl and wanting baked chicken? Explain.

____

____

____

____

Use the situation and table for 15–18.

East Junior High is deciding on a new school mascot. Below are the results of a survey.

	Tigers	Lions	Total
Girls	360	140	500
Boys	240	260	500
Total	600	400	?

15. How many students answered the survey at East Junior High?

____

16. What is the joint relative frequency for Lions as the mascot when voted for by boys?

____

17. What is the marginal relative frequency of Tigers being chosen as the mascot?

____

18. What is the conditional relative frequency of a student voting for Lions given that the student is a girl?

____

19. What action is shown by the graph?

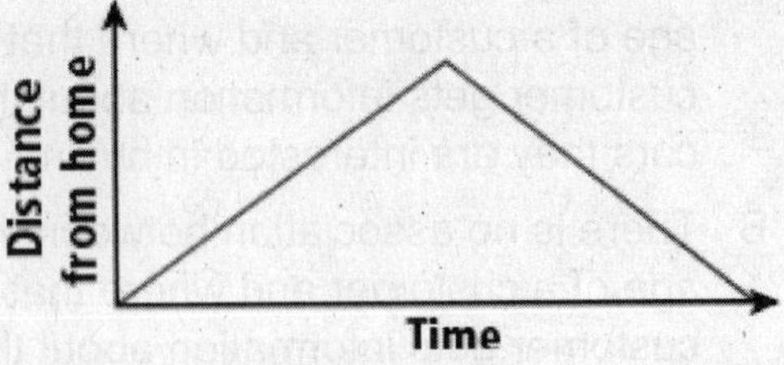

____

____

____

Name ______________________ Date ______________ Class ______________

UNIT 1

Real Numbers, Exponents, and Scientific Notation

Unit Test: A

1. Which fraction equals a repeating decimal?

   A $\frac{3}{10}$ C $\frac{6}{12}$

   B $\frac{1}{3}$ D $\frac{3}{4}$

2. A small square garden has an area of 25 square yards. How long is each side of the garden?

   A 2 yards

   B 2.5 yards

   C 5 yards

   D 5.2 yards

3. Which is an estimate of $\sqrt{15}$ to one decimal place?

   A 1.5 C 3.9

   B 3.8 D 4.1

4. What is the value of 3^{-5}?

   A 33333 C –243

   B –33333 D $\frac{1}{243}$

5. Which statement is true?

   A No whole numbers are integers.

   B No integers are whole numbers.

   C No rational numbers are real.

   D No integers are irrational.

6. Which is the best name for numbers that describe distances on a map?

   A whole numbers

   B positive integers

   C negative integers

   D rational numbers

7. Which of the following are true?

   I. $\sqrt{14} > \pi$

   II. $\frac{17}{5} < \sqrt{40}$

   III. $\sqrt{17 + 8} > 20$

   A only I and II

   B only II and III

   C none of them

   D all of them

8. Which number is between π and $\sqrt{14}$?

   A 1.5 C 3.5

   B 2.5 D 4.5

9. The population of a South American country is about 17,400,000. Which expression shows this number in scientific notation?

   A 1.7×10^7 C 1.8×10^7

   B 1.74×10^7 D 17.4×10^6

10. What is the answer in scientific notation?

    $(3.3 \times 10^7) + (7.7 \times 10^8)$

    A 8.03×10^9

    B 8.03×10^8

    C 11×10^8

    D 11×10^9

11. One type of insect is 0.0052 meter long. What is this length in scientific notation?

    A 5.2×10^{-3} meter

    B 5.2×10^{-2} meter

    C 52×10^3 meters

    D 52×10^4 meters

Name ____________________ Date ______________ Class ______________

UNIT 1

Real Numbers, Exponents, and Scientific Notation

12. Write $12\frac{1}{4}$ as a decimal.

____

13. Express the fraction $\frac{7}{9}$ in decimal form.

____

14. Compare the decimal forms of $\frac{2}{5}$ and $\frac{4}{9}$. How are they alike and how are they different?

____

____

15. Find the two square roots of 400.

____

16. Estimate $\sqrt{150}$ to the nearest tenth.

____

17. How are the values of -4^3 and 4^{-3} alike and how do they differ?

____

18. Choose two of the following terms for A and B to make this diagram true: whole numbers, integers, rational numbers, irrational numbers, real numbers.

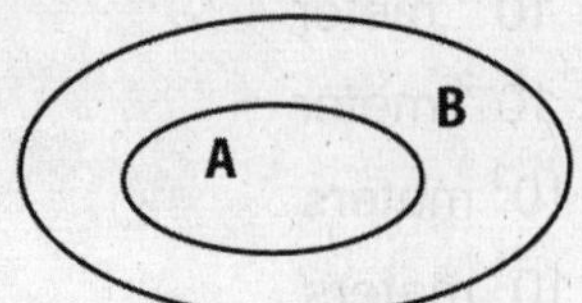

Set A: ________________

Set B: ________________

19. Find an integer between $-\sqrt{9}$ and $\frac{3}{2}$.

____

20. A number line shows the integers from −20 to 20. Describe where you would plot $\sqrt{30} + 6.2$.

____

21. Write the answer in scientific notation.
$(5.4 \times 10^8)(3.2 \times 10^6)$

____

For 22–24, use the table.

Diameter (meters)	
nucleus of an atom	7.2×10^{-15}
insulin molecule	5.3×10^{-9}
red blood cell	8.4×10^{-6}
grain of sand	2.4×10^{-3}
Moon	3.5×10^{6}
Sun	1.4×10^{9}
Milky Way galaxy	1.54×10^{21}

22. What is the standard notation for the diameter of the Sun?

____

23. Write the diameter of a red blood cell in standard notation.

____

24. About how many times larger than the diameter of the Moon is the diameter of the Sun? Write your answer in scientific notation.

____

Name ______________________ Date ______________ Class ______________

UNIT 1

Real Numbers, Exponents, and Scientific Notation

Unit Test: B

1. Which fraction equals a repeating decimal?

   A $\frac{5}{30}$ C $\frac{30}{50}$

   B $\frac{13}{25}$ D $\frac{13}{10}$

2. A square rug has an area of 225 square feet. How long is each side of the rug?

   A 15 feet

   B 22.5 feet

   C 23 feet

   D 25 feet

3. Which is an estimate of $\sqrt{14}$ to the nearest hundredth?

   A 1.4 C 3.47

   B 3.7 D 3.74

4. What is the value of 4^{-3}?

   A 444 C $\frac{1}{64}$

   B –444 D –64

5. Which statement is false?

   A All whole numbers are integers.

   B All irrational numbers are real.

   C Some integers are irrational.

   D Some integers are whole numbers.

6. Which of these is least likely to describe a distance below sea level?

   A whole number

   B integer

   C rational number

   D real number

7. Which of the following are true?

   I. $\sqrt{14} + 6.2 < 3\pi - 8.2$

   II. $\frac{17}{5} + \sqrt{64} > 8 + \pi$

   III. $35 - \sqrt{40} > 6\pi$

   A only I and II

   B only II and III

   C none of them

   D all of them

8. Which number is between $\frac{3}{25}$ and $\sqrt{14}$?

   A $\frac{1}{14}$ C $\sqrt{20}$

   B $\frac{13}{4}$ D $2 + \pi$

9. The population of a large U.S. city is 2,707,210. Which of the following best expresses this population?

   A 2.7×10^6 C 2.707×10^6

   B 2.7×10^7 D 27.07×10^6

10. What is the answer in scientific notation?

    $(5.1 \times 10^6) - (4.3 \times 10^5)$

    A 0.8×10^6

    B 0.8×10^5

    C 4.67×10^5

    D 4.67×10^6

11. One type of ant is 0.0035 meter long. What is this length in scientific notation?

    A 3.5×10^{-4} meter

    B 3.5×10^{-3} meter

    C 35×10^{-3} meter

    D 35×10^{-5} meter

Name ______________________ Date ______________ Class ______________

UNIT 1

Real Numbers, Exponents, and Scientific Notation

12. Write $4\frac{3}{8}$ as a decimal.

____

13. Express the fraction $\frac{5}{12}$ in decimal form.

____

14. Compare the decimal forms of $\frac{1}{4}$ and $\frac{25}{99}$. How are they alike and different?

____

15. Find the two square roots of $\frac{1}{16}$.

____

16. Estimate $\sqrt{40}$ to two decimal places.

____

17. How are $(-5)^5$ and 5^5 alike and how do they differ?

____

18. Choose three of the following terms for A, B, and C to make this diagram true: whole numbers, integers, rational numbers, irrational numbers, real numbers.

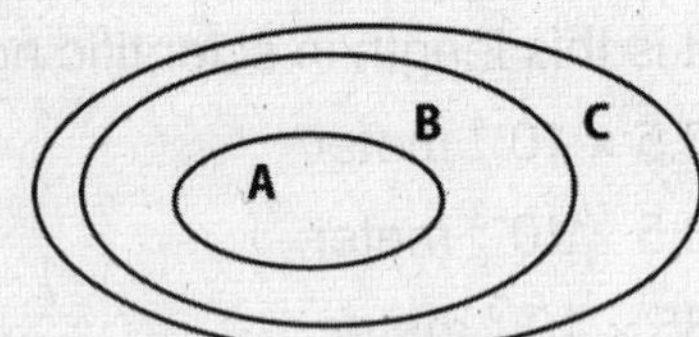

Diagram A: _______________

Diagram B: _______________

Diagram C: _______________

19. Find an integer between $\sqrt{40}$ and $\frac{7\pi}{2}$.

____

20. A number line is numbered in tenths. Describe where you would plot $\sqrt{43} - \pi$.

____

21. Write the answer in scientific notation.
$(7.3 \times 10^6) \div (3.2 \times 10^4)$

____

For 22–24, use the table.

22. How many zeros are needed to write the diameter of the Milky Way in standard notation?

Diameter (meters)	
nucleus of an atom	7.2×10^{-15}
insulin molecule	5.3×10^{-9}
red blood cell	8.4×10^{-6}
grain of sand	2.4×10^{-3}
Moon	3.5×10^{6}
Sun	1.4×10^{9}
Milky Way galaxy	1.54×10^{21}

____

23. Write the diameter of an insulin molecule in standard notation.

____

24. About how many times larger than the diameter of a red blood cell is the diameter of a grain of sand? Write your answer using a power of ten.

____

Name ______________________ Date ______________ Class ______________

UNIT 1

Real Numbers, Exponents, and Scientific Notation

Unit Test: C

1. Which fraction equals a repeating decimal with a 3-digit repeating block?

   A $\frac{5}{85}$ C $\frac{11}{155}$

   B $\frac{7}{111}$ D $\frac{5}{600}$

2. The area of the top of a small square table is 0.25 square meter. What are the dimensions of the table top?

   A 0.05 m × 0.05 m

   B 0.25 m × 0.25 m

   C 0.25 m × 1 m

   D 0.5 m × 0.5 m

3. Which is the best estimate of $\sqrt{0.65}$?

   A 0.065 C 0.81

   B 0.086 D 0.86

4. What is always true about a positive integer raised to a negative integer power?

   A It is positive

   B It is negative.

   C It is divisible by 3.

   D It is less than the integer.

5. What is **always** true when two whole numbers are subtracted?

   A The answer is irrational.

   B The answer is an integer.

   C The answer is a whole number.

   D The answer is not a real number.

6. A student used the area of a square to find its side length. Which probably describes the numerical result?

   A rational C negative

   B irrational D integer

7. Which of the following are false?

   I. $\sqrt{14} + 6.2 < 3\pi - 8.2$

   II. $\frac{17}{5} + \sqrt{64} > 8 + \pi$

   III. $35 - \sqrt{40} > 6\pi$

   A only I

   B only II

   C I and II

   D II and III

8. Which number is **not** between $\frac{-7\pi}{6}$ and $-\sqrt{30}$?

   A −5 C −4

   B −4.5 D −3.5

9. A website gives the population of a European country as 16,714,683. What is this population to three significant digits?

   A 1.67×10^7 C 16.7×10^7

   B 1.67×10^8 D 167×10^8

10. What is the answer in scientific notation? $(6.4 \times 10^9)\ (3.2 \times 10^3)$

    A 2.0×10^6

    B 2.048×10^{13}

    C 2.048×10^{12}

    D 2.048×10^{27}

11. The wingspan of one type of insect is 0.2 millimeter. Which expression shows the numerical value of the wingspan in meters?

    A 2.0×10^{-1} meter

    B 2.0×10^{-3} meter

    C 2.0×10^{-4} meter

    D 2.0×10^{-5} meter

Name ______________________ Date ______________ Class ______________

UNIT 1

Real Numbers, Exponents, and Scientific Notation

12. Write the decimal equivalent to the improper fraction $\frac{53}{16}$.

____

13. How many digits are there in the repeating block of the decimal equivalent to $8\frac{4}{7}$?

____

14. A fraction with a denominator of 7 equals a terminating decimal. What must be true of the numerator of this fraction?

____

15. Use a radical sign to indicate the negative square root of 34.68. Then evaluate the expression to two decimal places using a calculator.

____

16. The difference between the two square roots of a whole number is about 5.3. What is the number?

____

17. Is a positive integer raised to a negative power always positive? Explain with an example.

____

18. Explain why an integer cannot also be an irrational number.

____

____

19. Find an irrational number between $\sqrt{40}$ and $\frac{7\pi}{2}$.

____

20. Why is it not possible to plot the value of this expression on a number line?

$$\frac{(5\pi)^2}{\sqrt{25}-5}$$

____

21. Write the answer in scientific notation.
$(8.8 \times 10^5) \div (2.2 \times 10^3)$

____

For 22–24, use the table.

Diameter (meters)	
nucleus of an atom	7.2×10^{-15}
insulin molecule	5.3×10^{-9}
red blood cell	8.4×10^{-6}
grain of sand	2.4×10^{-3}
Moon	3.5×10^{6}
Sun	1.4×10^{9}
Milky Way galaxy	1.54×10^{21}

22. Write the second largest number in standard notation.

____

23. How many decimal places are there in the standard notation for the diameter of the red blood cell?

____

24. About how many times larger than the diameter of the nucleus of an atom is the diameter of the Milky Way?

____

Name ______________________ Date ______________ Class ______________

UNIT 1

Real Numbers, Exponents, and Scientific Notation

Unit Test: D

1. Which of these shows a repeating decimal?

   A 2.222

   B $4.0\overline{14}$

   C $6\frac{3}{10}$

2. A square floor has 16 tiles. Each tile is 1 square foot.

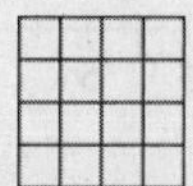

   What is the length of one side of this square floor?

   A 1 foot

   B 4 feet

   C 16 feet

3. Between which 2 whole numbers is the square root of 50?

   A 5 and 6

   B 6 and 7

   C 7 and 8

4. What is the value of 4^3?

   A 16

   B 43

   C 64

5. Which of these **cannot** be a rational number?

   A an integer

   B an irrational number

   C a real number

6. A student divided 5 feet of ribbon into 3 equal parts. Which type of number describes the length of each part?

   A whole number

   B integer

   C rational number

7. Which of the following are true?

   I. $\sqrt{36} > 5$

   II. $7 < \sqrt{10}$

   III. $\sqrt{17-8} > \sqrt{17+8}$

   A only I

   B only II

   C all of them

8. Which number is between $5\frac{3}{4}$ and $\sqrt{36}$?

   A $5\frac{1}{2}$

   B $\sqrt{25}$

   C 5.999

9. What is the correct power to change 760,000 into scientific notation?

   $760{,}000 = 7.6 \times$ ______

   A 10^5

   B 10^6

   C 10^7

10. What is the answer in scientific notation?

    $(1.2 \times 10^9) + (7.6 \times 10^8)$

    A 1.96×10^8

    B 1.96×10^9

    C 8.8×10^9

11. The width of a large butterfly is about 0.08 meter. What is the width when it is written in scientific notation?

    A 0.08×10^{-2} meter

    B 8.0×10^{-2} meter

    C 8.0×10^{-1} meter

Name ________________ Date ________ Class ________

UNIT 1

Real Numbers, Exponents, and Scientific Notation

12. Write $6\frac{27}{100}$ as a decimal.

____

13. Divide 5 by 6 to change $\frac{5}{6}$ to a repeating decimal.

____

14. Write the next 3 digits in the repeating decimal $0.27\overline{3}$.

____

15. Use these facts.

$6 \times 6 = 36 \quad -6 \times -6 = 36$

What are the two square roots of 36?

____

16. Estimate the square root of 60 to the nearest whole number.

____

17. A positive integer raised to the –3 power is always ____________.

18. Use this diagram to complete the statement below.

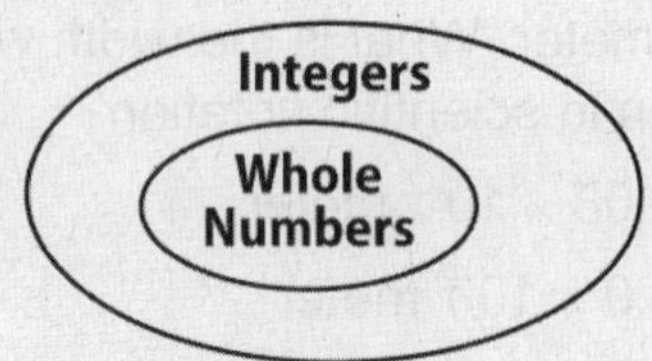

Every ________________ is also in the set of ____________.

19. Find a whole number between 3.75 and $\sqrt{36}$.

____

20. A number line shows the whole numbers from 0 to 10. Describe where you would plot $\sqrt{30}$.

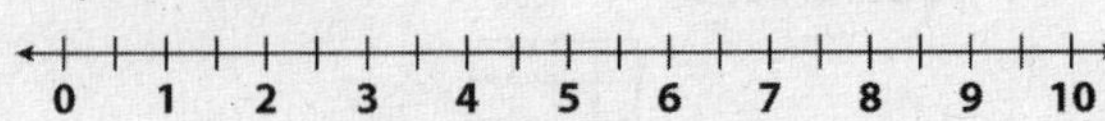

____

21. Write the answer in scientific notation.

$(1.3 \times 10^5)(2.2 \times 10^3)$

____

For 22–24, use the table.

Diameter (meters)	
red blood cell	8.4×10^{-6}
grain of sand	2.4×10^{-3}
Moon	3.5×10^{6}
Sun	1.4×10^{9}

22. Write the largest number in standard notation.

____

23. Write the diameter of a grain of sand in standard notation.

____

24. Which is larger, the red blood cell or the grain of sand?

____

Name ______________________ Date ______________ Class ______________

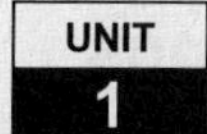

Expressions and the Number System

Performance Task

The Ants Go Marching

Ants are pretty small and the Earth is pretty large. Imagine a trail of ants marching around the Earth at the equator. How many ants would that be?

You Will Need

Tools	Calculator (graphing calculator is not needed)	
Data	Length of ant	3.4×10^{-3} meters
	Radius of Earth	6.378×10^{6} meters
Formulas	Circumference of circle	$C = 2\pi r$ *r* is the radius
	Distance formula	$D = rt$ *r* is the speed, *t* is the time

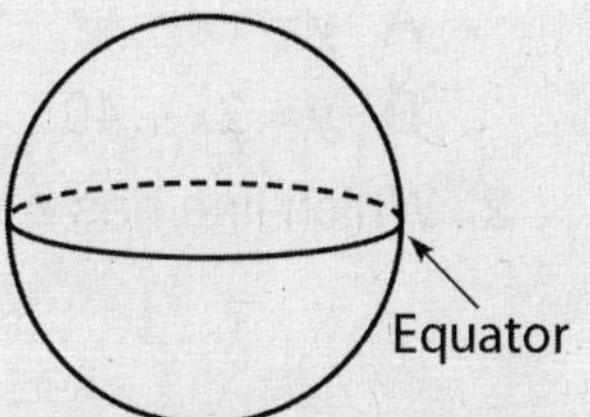

1. The length of the ant in inches is about $\frac{1}{8}$ inch. Write this as a decimal. Then write the ant's length in meters in standard form, in centimeters, and in one other form.

____

2. The circumference formula has both letter variables and numbers. Describe the numbers as rational or irrational. Which is greater?

____

3. Using the π (pi) key on your calculator, find the circumference of the Earth in meters. Round your answer to a reasonable degree of precision. Write both the standard form and scientific notation.

____

4. Divide the circumference by the ant length in meters. About how many ants would make a trail around the Earth? Write the standard form, the scientific notation, and one other form.

____

5. Decide on a reasonable speed for an ant in meters per hour. Use your speed to find how many days it would take an ant to go around the Earth.

____

6. Compare your solutions to problems 4–5 with those of another student. Be prepared to explain your steps.

____

Name ______________________________ Date ________________ Class ________________

UNIT 2

Proportional and Nonproportional Relationships and Functions

Unit Test: A

1. Which equation shows the relationship in the table?

Weeks (x)	2	5	10
Trees Planted (y)	40	100	200

A $y = 2x$ C $y = 20x$

B $y = 2x + 40$ D $y = 40x$

2. Which line has a slope of –2?

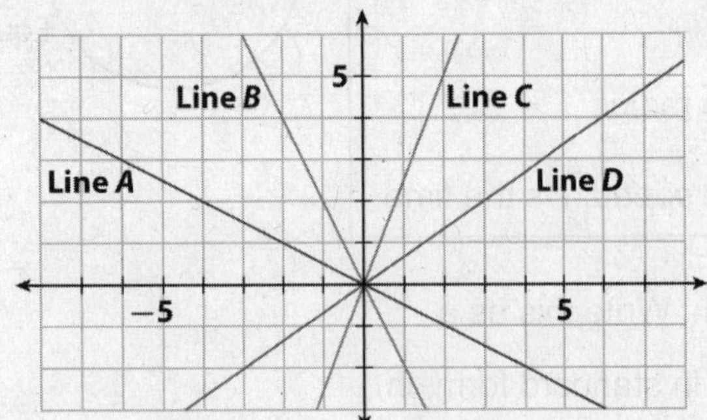

A line A C line C

B line B D line D

Use this graph for 3–4.

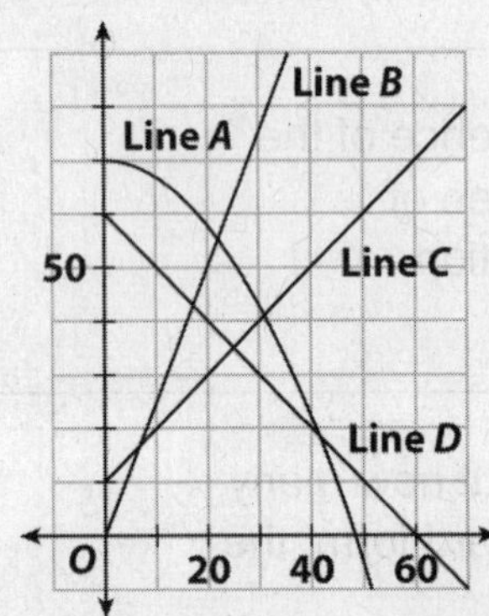

3. What is the equation for line C?

A $y = 2.5x$ C $y = 10 - x$

B $y = x + 10$ D $y = 10x + 10$

4. Which graph is **not** linear?

A line A C line C

B line B D line D

5. What ordered pair represents the y-intercept of the graph of $x + y = 9$?

A (0, 9) C (9, 0)

B (0, –9) D (–9, 0)

6. It costs $6 to take 1 dog to the dog beach. It costs $1 more for each additional dog. Which equation shows this situation, when $x \geq 1$?

A $y = x + 5$ C $y = 6x$

B $y = x + 6$ D $y = 6x + 2$

7. Which statement compares the data on these graphs?

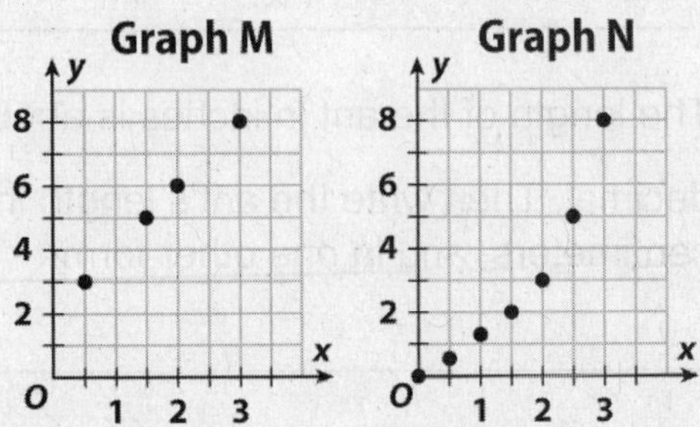

A Both graphs are linear.

B Neither graph is linear.

C M is linear. N is not linear.

D N is linear. M is not linear.

8. Which ordered pair belongs to the function shown by this mapping diagram?

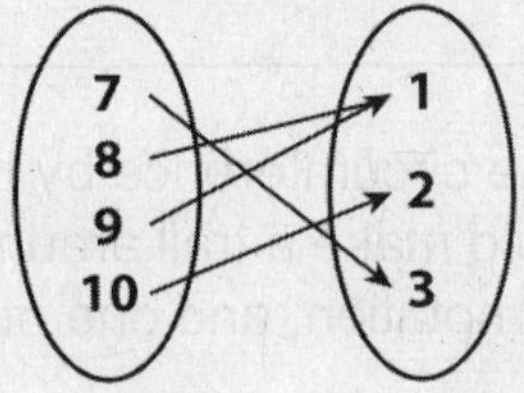

A (1, 7) C (7, 4)

B (2, 8) D (8, 1)

Name ____________ Date ____________ Class ____________

UNIT 2 Proportional and Nonproportional Relationships and Functions

9. The graph and the table show 2 different bicycle riders. Each rider travels at a constant speed.

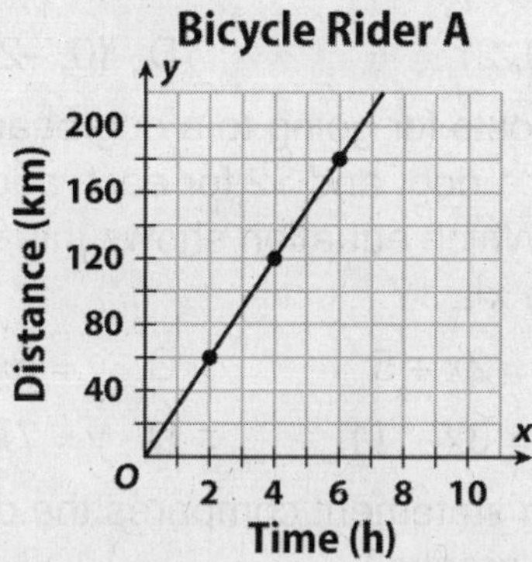

Bicycle Rider B

Time (h)	3	5	8
Distance (km)	72	120	192

Compare the speeds of the two riders.

____

10. Write equations for the two bicycle riders in problem 9.

Rider A: ____________

Rider B: ____________

11. Graph the equation $y = 2x - 3$.

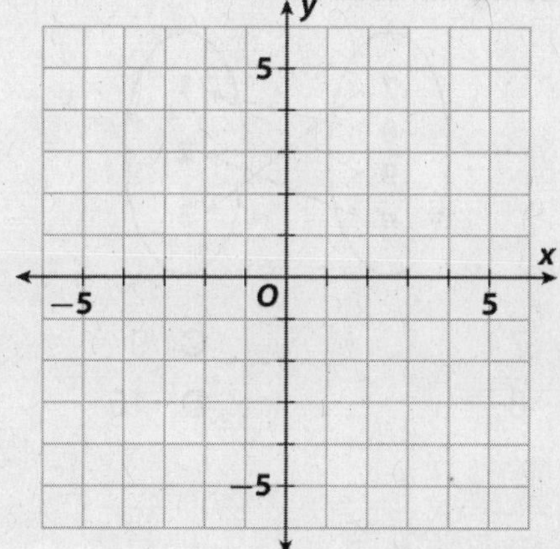

12. What is the slope and y-intercept of the graph of $y = 3x + 5$?

slope = ____________

y-intercept = ____________

13. Look at the graph. During what time(s) was Ziba increasing her distance from home?

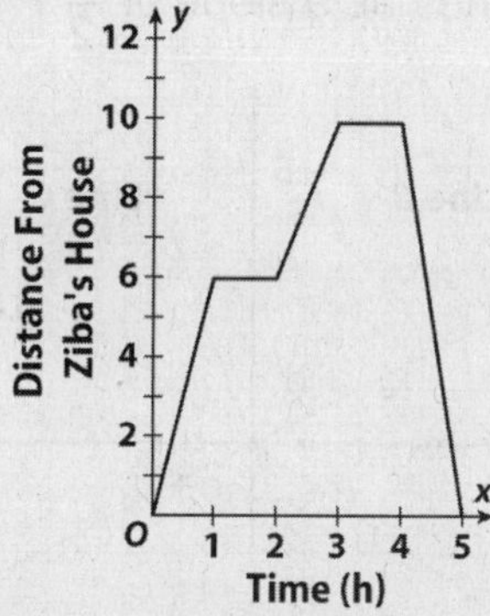

____

The functions on the graph and the table show two cars on a 500-mile trip.

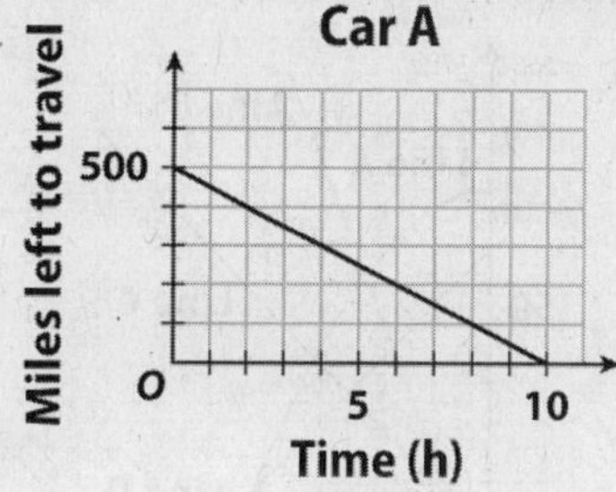

Car B

Time (h)	0	5	10	12
Miles Left	500	425	200	68

14. Which function is linear? Why?

____

15. Which car gets home first? Explain how you know.

____

Name ______________________ Date ______________ Class ______________

UNIT 2

Proportional and Nonproportional Relationships and Functions

Unit Test: B

1. Which equation shows the proportional relationship in the table?

Time (weeks)	2	5	10
Trees Planted	130	325	650

A $y = 2x$ C $y = 130x$

B $y = 65x$ D $y = 2x + 130$

2. Which line has a slope of $\frac{5}{2}$?

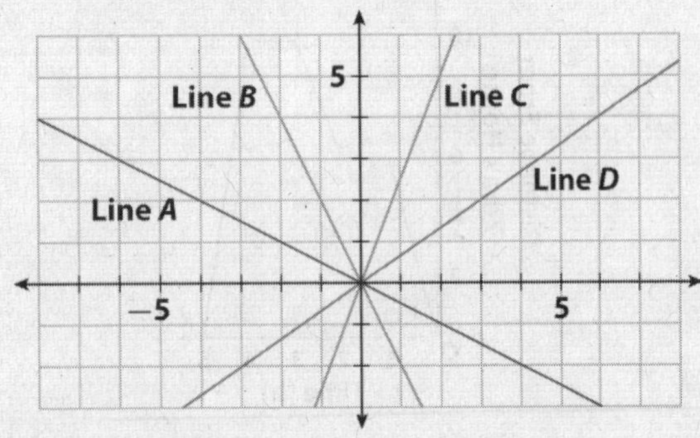

A line *A* C line *C*

B line *B* D line *D*

Use this graph for 3–4.

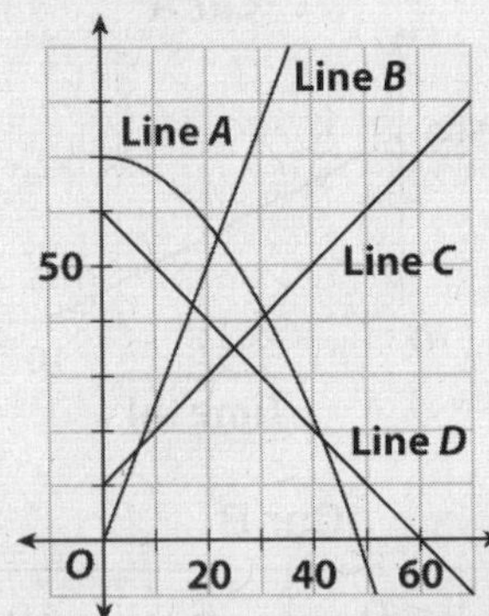

3. What is the equation for line *D*?

A $y = 2.5x$ C $y = 10 - x$

B $y = x + 10$ D $y = 60 - x$

4. Which graph shows a proportional relationship?

A line *A* C line *C*

B line *B* D line *D*

5. What ordered pair represents the *y*-intercept of the graph of $y = 2x - 3$?

A (0, 3) C (0, −3)

B (0, 2) D (0, −2)

6. The costs for going to a dog beach are \$7 for 1 dog, and \$2 for each additional dog. Which equation shows this situation, where $x \geq 1$?

A $y = 2x + 5$ C $y = 5x + 2$

B $y = 3x + 11$ D $y = 7x + 11$

7. Which statement compares the data on these graphs?

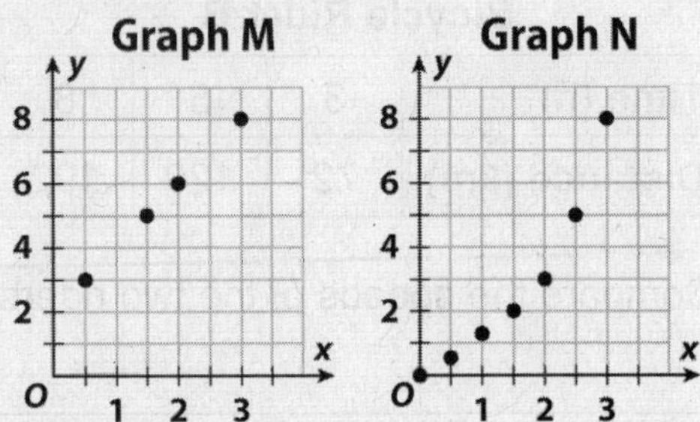

A M is linear. N is not linear.

B M is increasing. N is decreasing.

C Both have the same *y*-value for $x = 2$.

D Both show proportional relationships.

8. The mapping diagram shows a function. What could be a possible value for the missing number *n*?

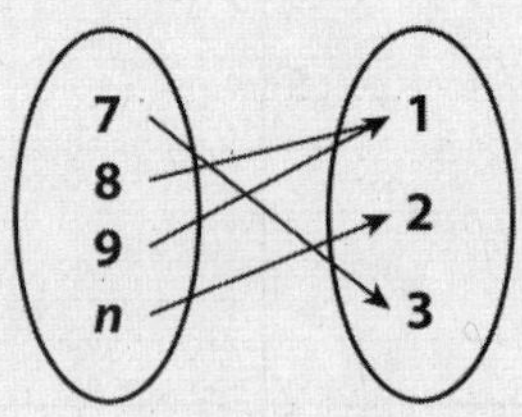

A 7 C 9

B 8 D 15

Name ______________________ Date ______________ Class ______________

UNIT 2

Proportional and Nonproportional Relationships and Functions

9. This graph shows a bicyclist moving at a constant rate.

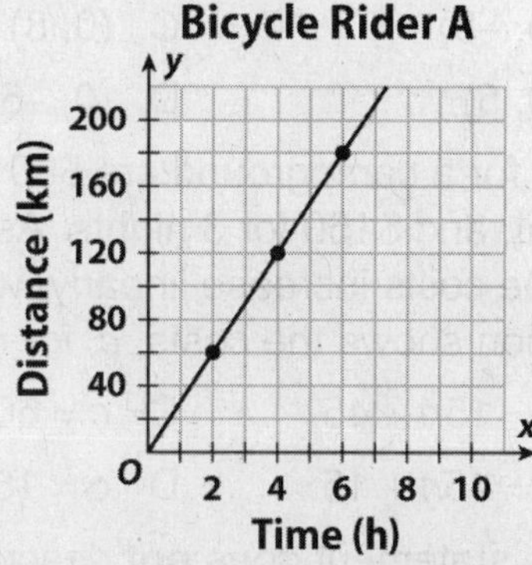

This table shows another bicyclist. How does the unit rate in the table compare with the unit rate on the graph?

Bicycle Rider B

Time (h)	3	5	8
Distance (km)	72	120	192

____

10. Write equations for the two bicycle riders in problem 9. How far will each go in 15 hours?

Rider A: ______________________

Rider B: ______________________

11. Graph the equation $y = \frac{1}{2}x - 2$.

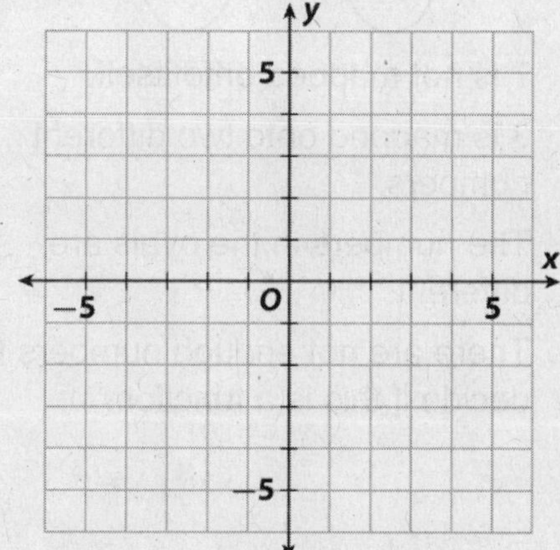

12. Find the slope and y-intercept of the graph in problem 11.

slope = ______________________

y-intercept = ______________________

13. Look at the graph. At what distances is it likely that Jackie stopped and visited with friends? Explain.

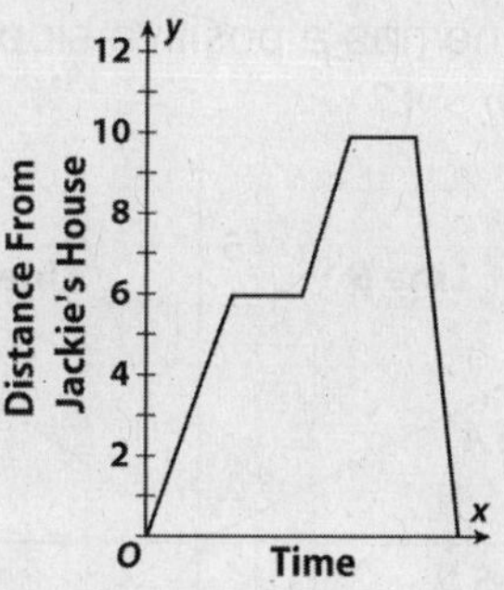

____

____

The functions on the graph and the table show two cars on a 650-mile trip.

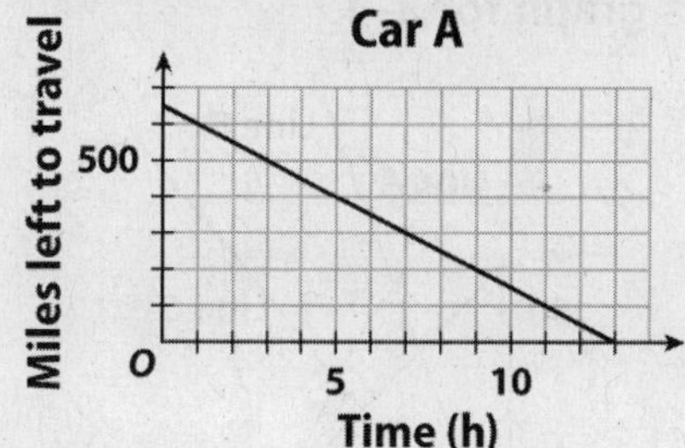

Car B

Time (h)	0	5	10	14
Miles Left	650	575	350	62

14. Which functions are linear? Which are proportional?

____

15. Which car gets home first? Explain how you know.

____

Name ________________________ Date ______________ Class______________

UNIT 2

Proportional and Nonproportional Relationships and Functions

Unit Test: C

1. Use the data in the table. Which equation shows the number of trees planted per day? Use a 5-day workweek.

Time (weeks)	2	5	10
Trees Planted	130	325	650

A $y = 13x$ C $y = 130x$

B $y = 65x$ D $y = 325x$

2. Which line has a positive slope m, where $m > 1$?

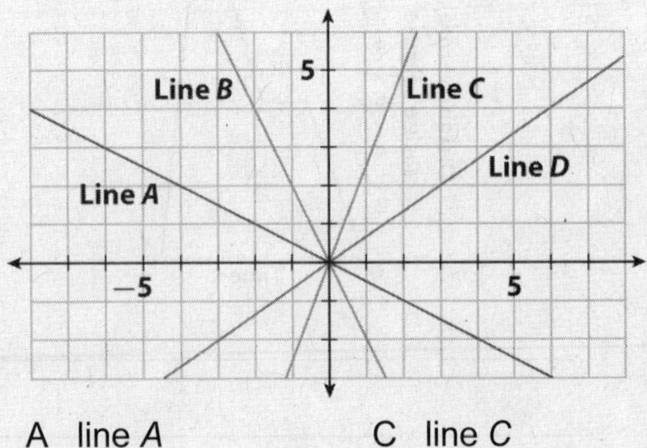

A line A C line C

B line B D line D

Use this graph for 3–4.

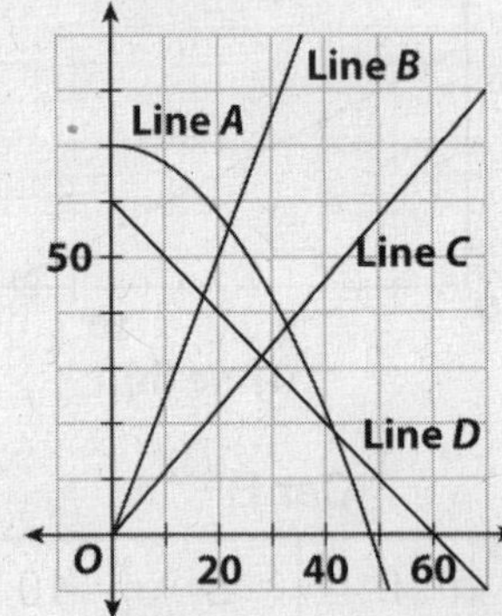

3. Which graph does **not** have an equation in the form $y = mx + b$?

A line A C line C

B line B D line D

4. Which graph shows a linear non-proportional relationship?

A line A C line C

B line B D line D

5. What ordered pair represents the y-intercept of the graph of $5x + y = 8$?

A (0, −8) C (0, 8)

B (0, 5) D (0, −5)

6. Costs for a campground are $60 for 1 night, and $150 for 3 nights. Assuming that the costs increase linearly, which equation shows the costs, c, for n nights?

A $c = 15n + 45$ C $c = 60n + 150$

B $c = 45n + 15$ D $c = 180n$

7. Which statement does **not** describe these graphs?

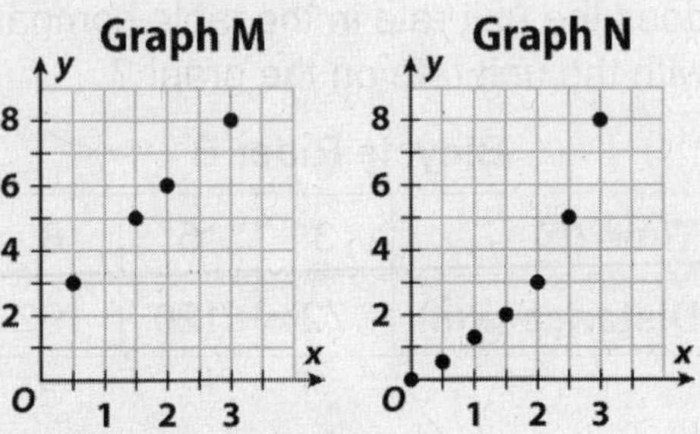

A Both show discrete data.

B Both show increasing values.

C Both are linear.

D Neither are proportional relationships.

8. Why is this **not** a function?

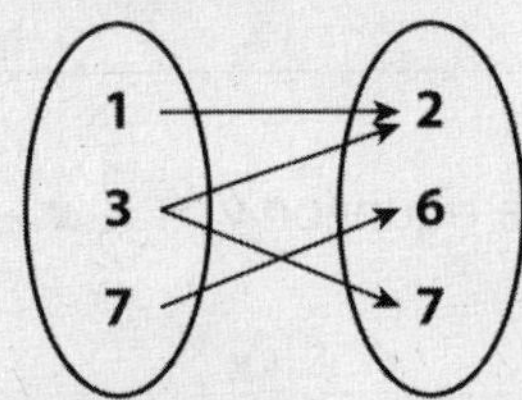

A 7 is not mapped onto itself.

B 3 is mapped onto two different numbers.

C The numbers in the ovals are different.

D There are not enough numbers to decide if this is a function.

Name ________________ Date ________________ Class ________________

Proportional and Nonproportional Relationships and Functions

Use the graph and table for 9–10.

Bicycle Rider A

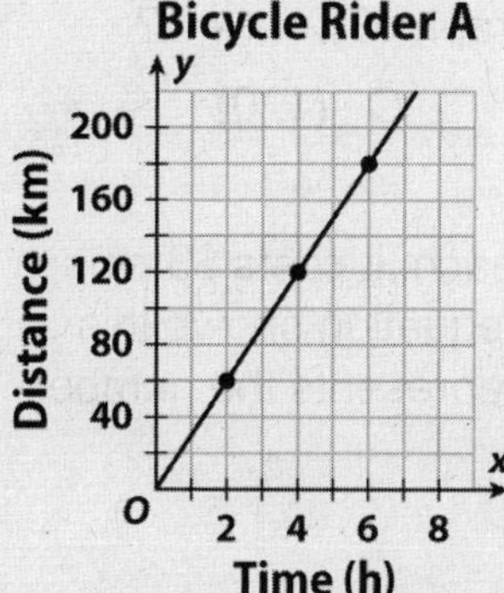

Bicycle Rider B

Time (hours)	Distance (km)
3	72
5	120
8	192

9. What conclusions can you reach using the data in the graph and table?

____

____

____

10. Write equations for the two riders. How long does it take each rider to go 150 km?

Rider A: ________________

Rider B: ________________

11. Graph the equation $3x - 2y = 8$.

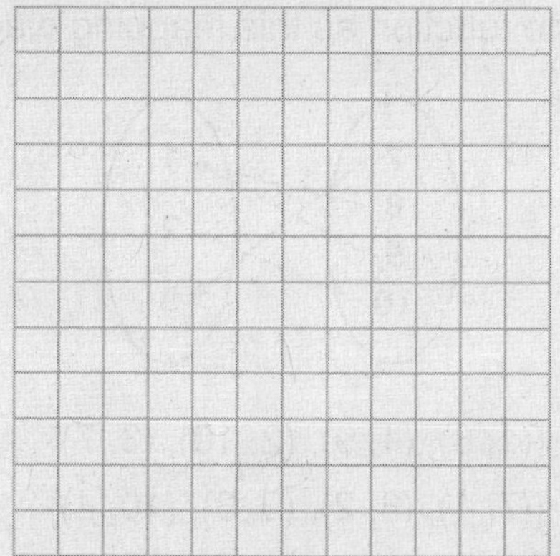

12. Find the slope and y-intercept of the graph in problem 11.

slope = ________________

y-intercept = ________________

13. Write a situation from this graph.

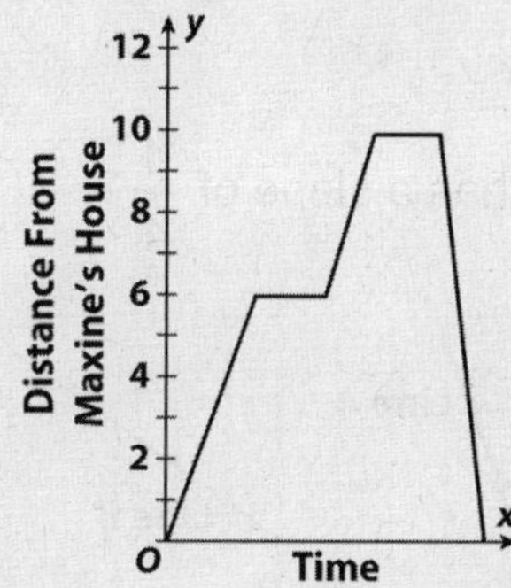

____

Use the graph and table for 14–15.

Car A

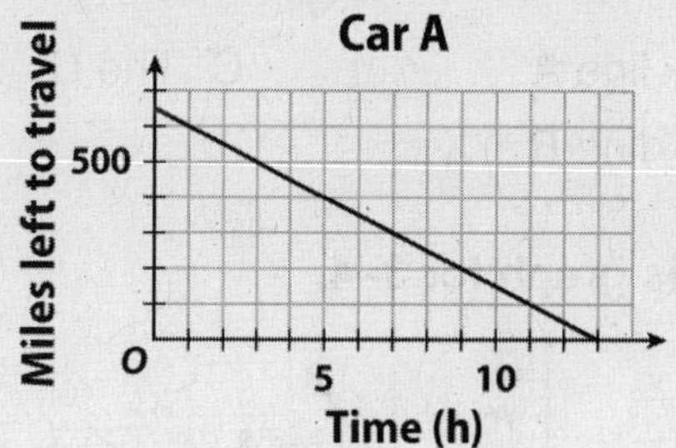

Car B

Time (h)	0	5	10	14
Miles Left	650	575	350	62

14. Describe the two functions.

____

____

15. Which car gets home first?

____

Name ________________________ Date ______________ Class ______________

UNIT 2

Proportional and Nonproportional Relationships and Functions

Unit Test: D

1. Which equation shows how the number of trees planted, y, is related to the number of weeks, x?

Weeks (x)	1	2	3
Trees Planted (y)	20	40	60

A $y = 2x$ C $y = x + 19$

B $y = 20x$

2. Which line has a slope of $\frac{1}{4}$?

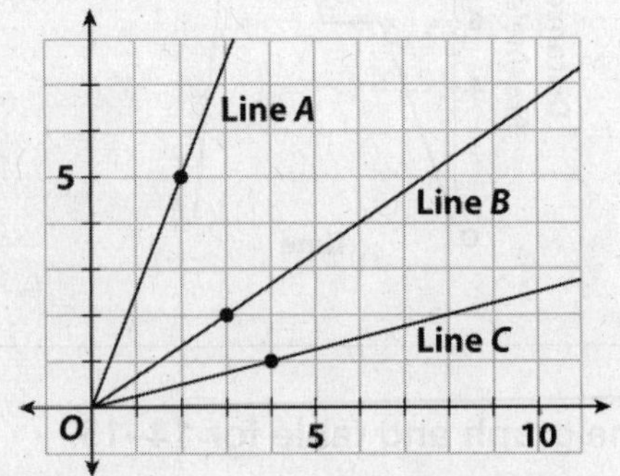

A line A C line C

B line B

Use this graph for 3–4.

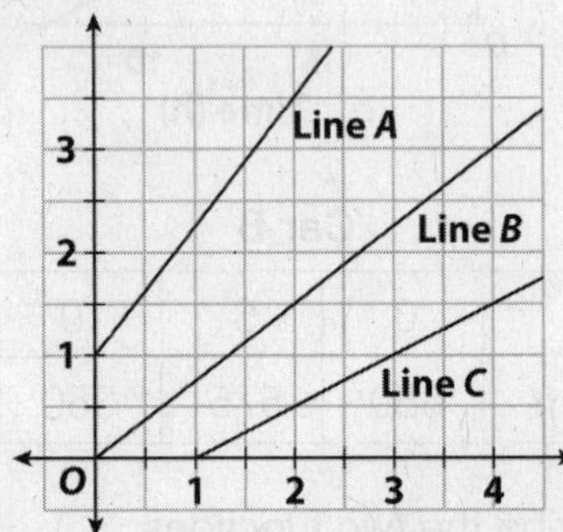

3. Which is the equation for line B?

A $y = \frac{3}{4}x$ C $y = \frac{3}{2}x$

B $y = \frac{4}{3}x$

4. Which graph shows a proportional relationship?

A line A C line C

B line B

5. What ordered pair represents the y-intercept of the graph of $y = x + 1$?

A (0, 0) C (1, 0)

B (0, 1)

6. To go to the dog beach, it costs \$3 plus \$2 per dog. Which equation shows this situation, where x represents the number of dogs?

A $y = 2x + 3$

B $y = 3x + 2$

C $y = 2x - 3$

7. Which graph shows a linear relationship?

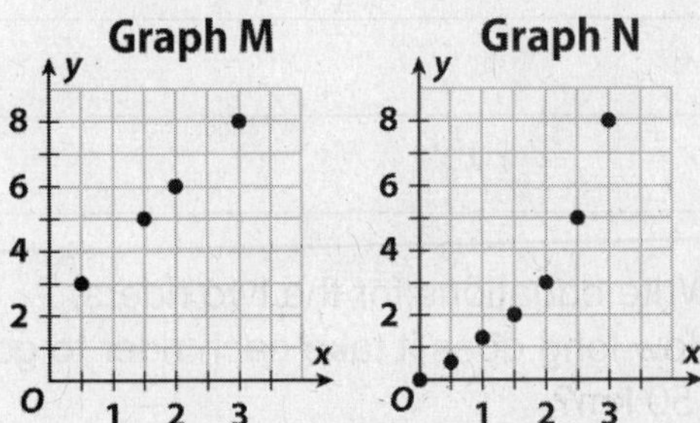

A Graph M

B Graph N

C Neither graph is linear.

8. Which set of ordered pairs shows the same function as this mapping diagram?

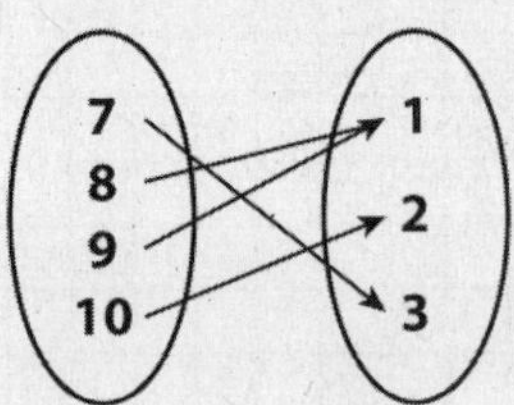

A {(1, 8), (1, 9), (2, 10), (3, 7)}

B {(7, 1), (8, 2), (9, 3), (10, 4)}

C {(7, 3), (8, 1), (9, 1), (10, 2)}

Name ______________________ Date ______________ Class ______________

UNIT 2

Proportional and Nonproportional Relationships and Functions

9. The graph shows the distance traveled by a bicycle rider. She moves at a constant speed. Find the slope of the line. What does this tell you about the speed?

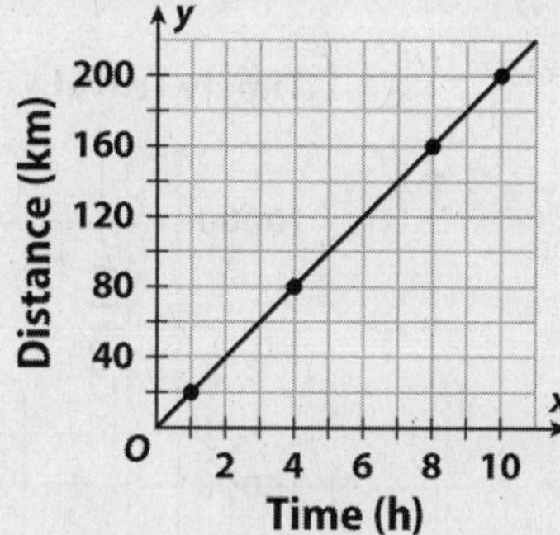

slope = ______________________

____

____

10. Write an equation for the bicycle rider in problem 9. Use y for the distance and x for the time.

$y =$ ______________________

11. Graph the equation $y = x + 2$.

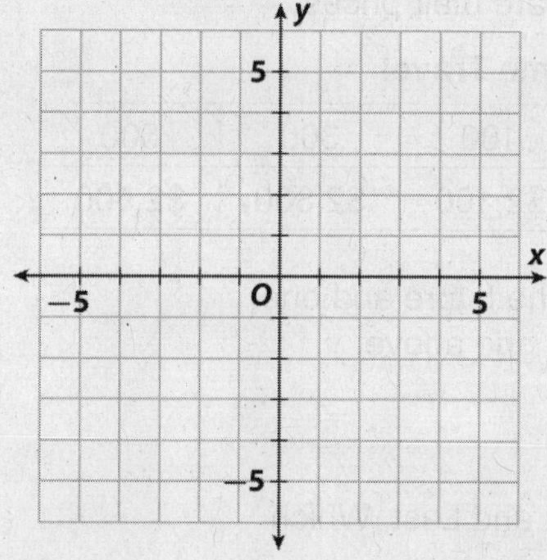

12. What is the y-intercept of the graph of $y = 3x + 5$? (Hint: Let x equal 0, and solve for y.)

y-intercept = ______________

13. What does line e on this graph indicate?

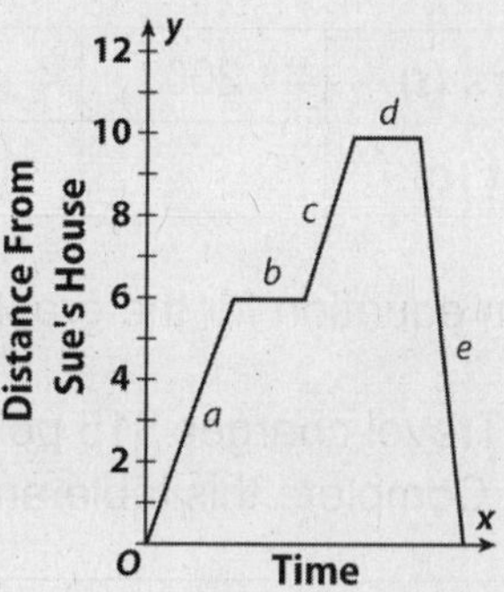

____

____

The functions on the graph and the table show two cars on a 500-mile trip.

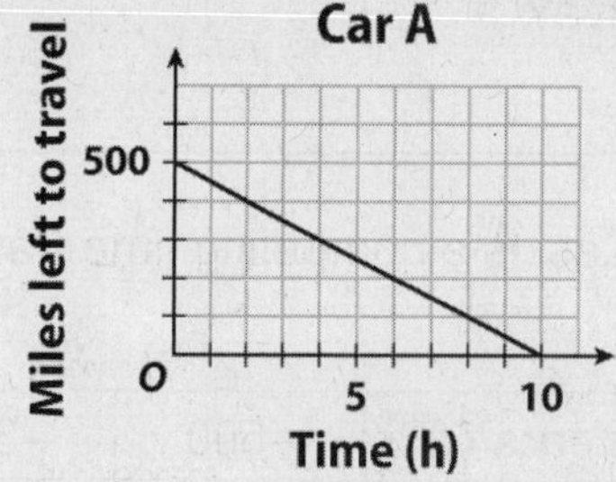

Car B

Time (h)	0	1	2	3
Miles Left	500	497	488	473

14. Why is the function in the table **not** linear?

____

15. It takes Car B almost 13 hours to get home. Which car gets home first? Explain how you know.

____

Name ______________________ Date ______________ Class ______________

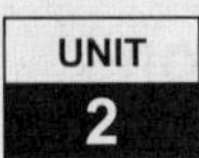

Proportional and Nonproportional Relationships and Functions

Performance Task

Back to the Future

Although time travel often occurs in movies and books, it isn't possible in real life. But if it were possible, companies would probably exist to sell trips!

1. Imagine that Timely Travel charges $5 per year to go forward in time. Complete the table for this relationship. Draw the graph on the grid at the right.

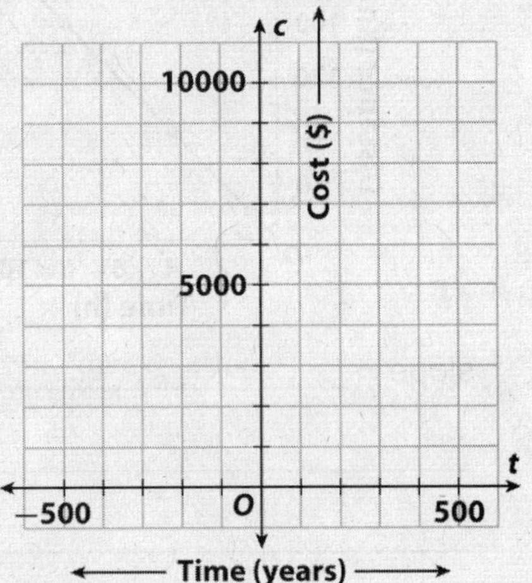

Years (*t*)	200	400	500
Cost (*c*)			

2. Write an equation for the graph. ______________

3. Timely Travel charges $15 per year to go backward in time. Complete this table and draw the graph.

Years (*t*)	–200	–400	–500
Cost (*c*)			

4. Write an equation for the graph.______________

5. Compare the constants of proportionality. Why is one positive and one negative?

____

First and Last is a competing time-travel company. Here are their prices.

First and Last Time Travel

Years (*t*)	–500	–300	–100	100	300	500
Cost (*c*)	$3,300	$3,100	$2,900	$2,100	$2,300	$2,500

6. Find the two equations, one for traveling forward to the future and one for traveling backward in time. Add the graphs to the grid above.

forward ($t > 0$) ______________ backward ($t < 0$) ______________

7. Compare the functions for Timely with those for First and Last. Which are linear? Which are proportional?

____

8. When does Timely cost more than First and Last?

____

Name ______________________ Date ______________ Class ______________

UNIT 3

Solving Equations and Systems of Equations

Unit Test: A

1. José and Nancy take care of animals when owners are away. José charges \$15 plus \$2 per animal. Nancy charges \$5 plus \$3 per animal. For how many animals do they charge the same amount? Solve the equation below to find out.

$$15 + 2x = 5 + 3x$$

A 3 animals C 10 animals

B 4 animals D 15 animals

2. A minivan and an SUV are traveling at the same speed. The minivan drives 4 hours. The SUV drives another half hour and goes 35 more miles. Let x be the speed of the cars. Which equation can be solved to find how fast the cars are going?

A $4x + 35 = 4.5x$ C $4x = 4.5x + 35$

B $4x + 35 = 3.5x$ D $4x = 3.5x + 35$

3. Ximena and Darius left a 20% tip after having dinner at a restaurant. The amount of the tip was \$5. Ximena's dinner cost \$15. Which equation can you use to find x, the cost of Darius's dinner?

A $0.2(x + 15) = 5$ C $20(x + 15) = 5$

B $0.2x + 15 = 5$ D $0.2x = 15 + 5$

4. For the equation $21 + 3x = 3x + k$, which value of k will create an equation with no solutions?

A x C 15

B $3x$ D 21

5. To start solving the system of equations below, which number would you multiply the equation $-2x - 5y = -1$ by?

$$\begin{cases} -2x - 5y = -1 \\ 8x + 4y = 16 \end{cases}$$

A 2 C 6

B 4 D 8

6. What ordered pair represents the y-intercept of the graph of $y = 4x$?

A (0, 4) C (4, 0)

B (0, –4) D (0, 0)

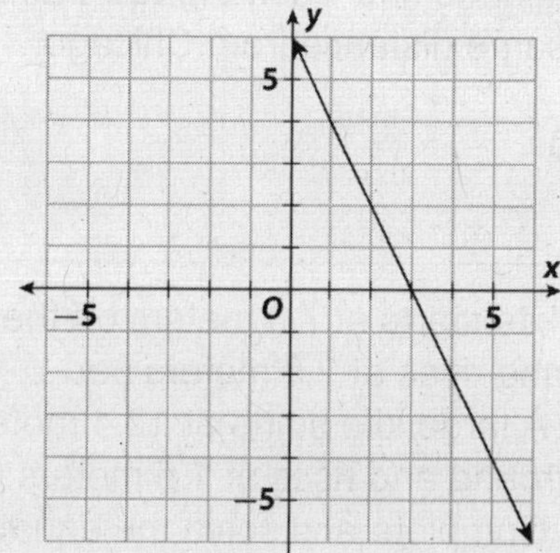

7. Which expression can you substitute in the indicated equation to solve the system below?

$$\begin{cases} x + y = 6 \\ 12x + y = 5 \end{cases}$$

A $5 + 12x$ for y in $x + y = 6$

B $5 - x$ for y in $x + y = 6$

C $6 - y$ for x in $12x + y = 5$

D $6 + y$ for x in $12x + y = 5$

8. Which is the solution to $\begin{cases} -x + 3y = 15 \\ x + 7y = 5 \end{cases}$?

Start by adding the equations.

A (–9, 2) C (–2, 9)

B (9, –2) D (2, –9)

9. The graph of a system of two linear equations is a pair of lines that intersect at a single point. How many solutions does the system have?

A 0 C 2

B 1 D infinitely many

Name ______________________ Date ______________ Class ______________

UNIT 3

Solving Equations and Systems of Equations

10. A train leaves Chicago traveling west at 60 miles per hour. An hour later, another train leaves Chicago traveling east at 80 miles per hour. Complete and solve the equation to find when the two trains are the same distance from Chicago.

    $60x + 60 =$ ______________________

    answer: ______________________

11. A small kite starts at 7.3 meters off the ground and rises at 2.5 meters per second. A large kite starts at 12.4 meters off the ground and rises at 1.5 meters per second. Complete and solve the equation to determine when the kites are at the same height.

    $7.3 + 2.5x =$ ______________________

    answer: ______________________

12. Mrs. Hernandez saves 4% of her earnings for retirement. This year, she earned \$200 more than last year, and she saved \$900. Complete and solve the equation to find her earnings last year.

    $0.04(x + 200) =$ ______________________

    solution: ______________________

13. Complete the equation so it results in a true statement and has infinitely many solutions.

    $3(2 + x) = 3x +$ ______________________

14. At the zoo, the Spencers bought 3 adult tickets and 2 children's tickets for \$23.50. The Yangs bought 2 adult tickets and 4 children's tickets for \$25. Solve the system of equations to find x, the price of an adult ticket and y, the price of a children's ticket.

$$\begin{cases} 3x + 2y = 23.5 \\ 2x + 4y = 25 \end{cases}$$

____

15. Anisa bought \$100 worth of stock and gained \$25 per year. Kevin bought \$400 worth of stock and lost \$35 per year. Use x for time and y for stock value. Graph the equations that represent each situation. When did Anisa and Keith have the same amount of stock value?

    Anisa: $y = 100 + 25x$
    Keith: $y = 400 - 35x$

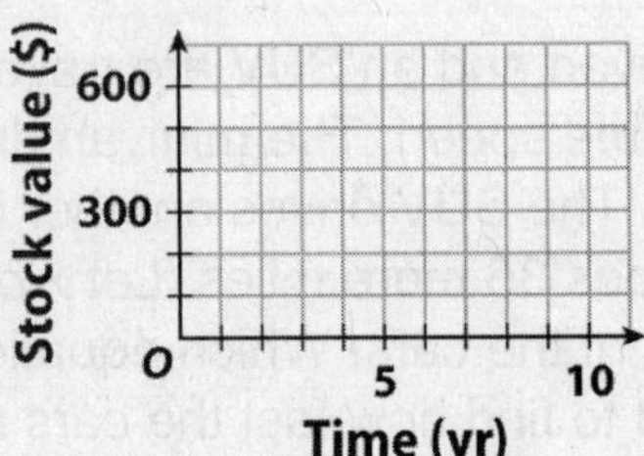

    answer: ______________________

16. Determine the expression you can substitute for x in $4x + 2y = 3$ to solve the system below.

$$\begin{cases} 4x + 2y = 3 \\ x + 6y = 4 \end{cases}$$

____

17. Find the solution to the system of equations below. Start by adding the equations.

$$\begin{cases} -5x + 2y = -7 \\ 5x + 3y = 2 \end{cases}$$

____

18. The graph of a system of two equations is a pair of parallel lines that do not have any points of intersection. Does the system have a solution?

____

Name ________________________ Date ______________ Class ______________

UNIT 3

Solving Equations and Systems of Equations

Unit Test: B

1. Jake and Hannah wash windows. Jake charges \$50 plus \$2 per window. Hannah charges \$20 plus \$5 per window. For how many windows washed do they charge the same amount?

   A 7 windows C 15 windows
   B 10 windows D 70 windows

2. A red car and a blue car are traveling at the same speed. The red car drives 3 hours. The blue car drives another half hour and goes 25 more miles. Which equation can be solved to find how fast the cars are going?

   A $3x + 25 = 3.5x$ C $2.5x + 25 = 3x$
   B $3x + 25 = 2.5x$ D $3.5x + 25 = 3x$

3. Anna and David left an 18% tip after having dinner at a restaurant. The amount of the tip was \$9. Anna's dinner cost \$28. Which equation can you use to find x, the cost of David's dinner?

   A $0.18(x + 28) = 9$ C $18(x + 28) = 9$
   B $0.18x + 28 = 9$ D $0.18x = 28 + 9$

4. For the equation $3(7 + x) = 3x + k$, which value of k will create an equation with no solutions?

   A x C 15
   B $3x$ D 21

5. Which step could you use to start solving the system of equations below?

$$\begin{cases} 2x + 5y = 1 \\ 8x + 4y = 16 \end{cases}$$

   A Substitute $5y - 1$ for x in $8x + 4y = 16$.
   B Multiply $2x + 5y = 1$ by 4 and subtract it from $8x + 4y = 16$.
   C Multiply $2x + 5y = 1$ by 4 and add it to $8x + 4y = 16$.
   D Add $2x + 5y = 1$ to $8x + 4y = 16$.

6. Solve this system by graphing both equations. Use the grid below.

$$\begin{cases} y = -2x + 6 \\ y = 4x \end{cases}$$

   Which point is the solution?

   A $(-1, -4)$ C $(1, -4)$
   B $(-1, 4)$ D $(1, 4)$

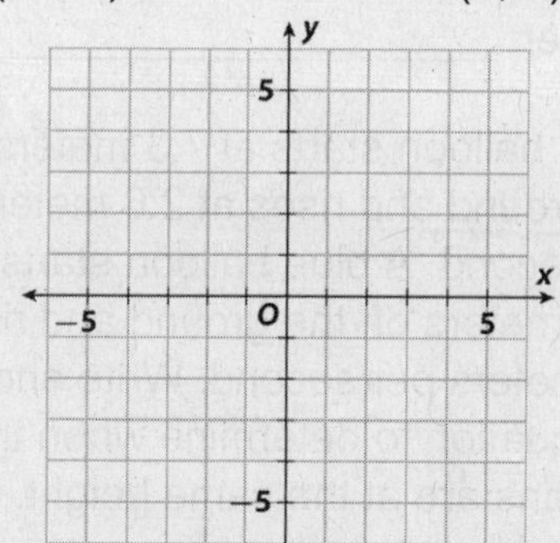

7. Which expression can you substitute in the indicated equation to solve the system below?

$$\begin{cases} x + 9y = 6 \\ 12x + y = 5 \end{cases}$$

   A $5 + 12x$ for y in $x + 9y = 6$
   B $5 - x$ for y in $x + 9y = 6$
   C $6 - 9y$ for x in $12x + y = 5$
   D $6 + 9y$ for x in $12x + y = 5$

8. Which is the solution to $\begin{cases} -x + 3y = 15 \\ x + 7y = 5 \end{cases}$?

   A $(-9, 2)$ C $(-2, 9)$
   B $(9, -2)$ D $(2, -9)$

9. The graph of a system of two linear equations is a pair of lines that intersect at the origin. Which statement is true of the system?

   A The solution is zero.
   B The solution is (0, 0).
   C The system has no solution.
   D The system has infinitely many solutions.

Name ______________________ Date ______________ Class ______________

UNIT 3

Solving Equations and Systems of Equations

10. A train leaves Buffalo traveling west at 60 miles per hour. An hour later, another train leaves Buffalo traveling east at 80 miles per hour. When are the two trains the same distance from Buffalo? Show the equation you use.

    equation: ______________________

    answer: ______________________

11. A red balloon starts at 7.3 meters off the ground and rises at 2.6 meters per second. A blue balloon starts at 12.4 meters off the ground and rises at 1.5 meters per second. Write and solve an equation to determine when the balloons are at the same height.

    equation: ______________________

    answer: ______________________

12. Nina saves 40% of her summer job earnings for college. This summer, she earned \$200 more than last summer, and she saved \$900. Write and solve an equation to find her earnings last summer.

    equation: ______________________

    solution: ______________________

13. Complete the equation so it has infinitely many solutions.

    $3(2 + x) = 3x +$

14. At the museum, the O'Rourke family bought 3 adult tickets and 2 children's tickets for \$23.50. The Patel family bought 2 adult tickets and 4 children's tickets for \$25. Find the cost of each type of ticket.

    ____

15. Art bought \$100 worth of stock and gained \$25 per year. Kiley bought \$400 worth of another stock and lost \$35 per year. Use x for time and y for stock value. Write and graph equations to represent each situation. When did Art and Kiley have the same amount of stock value?

    Art: ______________________

    Kiley: ______________________

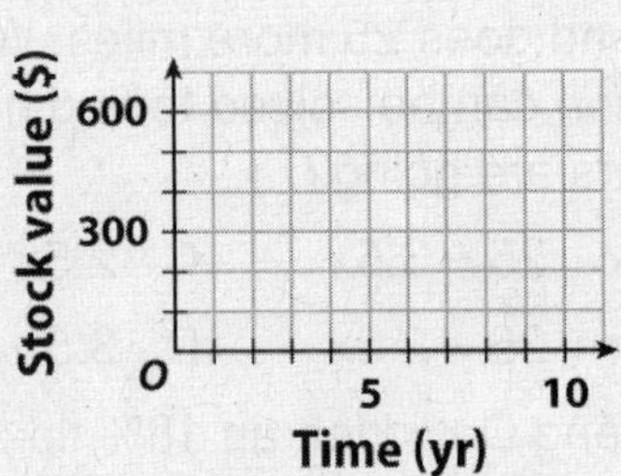

    answer: ______________________

16. Determine the expression you can substitute for x in $4x + 2y = 3$ to solve the system below.

    $$\begin{cases} 4x + 2y = 3 \\ 6y = 4 - x \end{cases}$$

    ____

17. Find the solution to the system of equations below.

    $$\begin{cases} 2y = 5x - 7 \\ 5x + 3y = 2 \end{cases}$$

    ____

18. The graph of a system of two equations is a pair of parallel lines. Does the system have a solution? Explain.

    ____

    ____

Name ______________________ Date ______________ Class______________

UNIT 3

Solving Equations and Systems of Equations

Unit Test C

1. Pedro and Paula clean boats. Pedro charges a fee of \$50 plus \$2 per square foot. Paula's fee is \$30 less than Pedro's, but she charges \$3 more per square foot. For how many square feet cleaned do they charge the same amount?

A 7 ft^2 C 15 ft^2

B 10 ft^2 D 70 ft^2

2. A red car and a blue car are traveling at the same speed. The red car drives 3 hours. The blue car drives another half hour and goes 25 more miles. A yellow car starts 12 minutes after the red car and travels 10 mi/h faster. How long does the yellow car drive before it catches up with the red car?

A 0.75 h C 1.25 h

B 1 h D 1.5 h

3. Rita and Eddie left an 18% tip after having dinner at a restaurant. The amount of the tip was \$9. Rita had an \$8 salad and a \$20 entrée. Eddie also ordered an \$8 salad and an entrée. What was the cost of Eddie's entrée?

A \$8 C \$14

B \$10 D \$22

4. For the equation below, which value of k will create an equation with no solutions?

$$2(4 + x) + (13 + x) = 3x + k$$

A x C 15

B $3x$ D 21

5. Solve the system of equations below.

$$\begin{cases} 2x + 5y = 1 \\ 8x + 4y = 16 \end{cases}$$

A $\left(-1\frac{3}{8}, -\frac{3}{4}\right)$ C $\left(2\frac{3}{8}, -\frac{3}{4}\right)$

B $\left(1\frac{3}{8}, \frac{3}{4}\right)$ D $\left(-2\frac{3}{8}, \frac{3}{4}\right)$

6. Bianca bought 2 apples and a pear and spent \$6. A pear costs four times as much as an apple. Graph a system of linear equations to represent the situation. Use the grid below.

What is the cost of a pear?

A \$1 C \$3

B \$2 D \$4

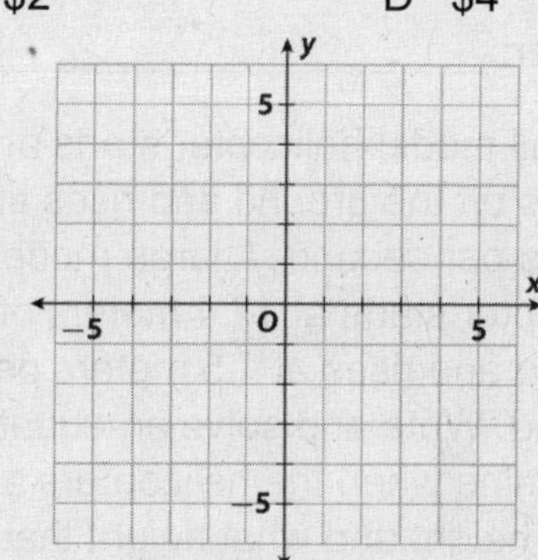

7. Which expression can you substitute in the indicated equation to solve the system below?

$$\begin{cases} 9y = 6 - x \\ 12x = 5 - y \end{cases}$$

A $5 + 12x$ for y in $9y = 6 - x$

B $5 - x$ for y in $9y = 6 - x$

C $6 - 9y$ for x in $12x = 5 - y$

D $6 + 9y$ for x in $12x = 5 - y$

8. Which is the solution to $\begin{cases} 3y = 15 + x \\ x + 7y = 5 \end{cases}$?

A (–9, 2) C (–2, 9)

B (9, –2) D (2, –9)

9. Two linear equations have the same slope and y-intercept. How many solutions does a system of these same linear equations have?

A 0 C 2

B 1 D infinitely many

Name ________________ Date ____________ Class ____________

UNIT 3

Solving Equations and Systems of Equations

10. At 11:45 a.m., a train leaves Denver traveling west at 60 miles per hour. At 12:45 p.m., another train leaves Denver traveling east at 80 miles per hour. When are the two trains the same distance from Denver?

    equation: ________________

    answer: ________________

11. A small model helicopter starts at 7.3 meters off the ground and rises at 2.6 meters per second. A large model helicopter starts at 12.4 meters off the ground and rises at 1.5 meters per second. Write and solve an equation to determine when the helicopters are at the same height and what height that is.

    equation: ________________

    answer: ________________

12. Evelyn saves 40% of her summer job earnings for college. This summer, she earned $200 more than last summer, and she saved $900. Write and solve an equation to find her earnings last summer and this summer.

    equation: ________________

    answer: ________________

13. Complete the equation so it has infinitely many solutions.

    $18 + 3(3 + 5x) = 15x +$ ________

14. At the zoo, the Spencer family bought 3 adult tickets and 2 children's tickets for $23.50. The Yang family bought 2 adult tickets and 4 children's tickets for $25. How much would the Diaz family spend if they bought 3 adults tickets and 1 children's ticket?

    ____

15. Babette bought $100 worth of stock and gained $25 per year. Han bought $400 worth of another stock and lost $35 per year. Use x for time and y for stock value. Write and graph equations to represent each situation. When did Babette and Han have the same amount of stock value? What was the value of their stock?

    Babette: ________________

    Han: ________________

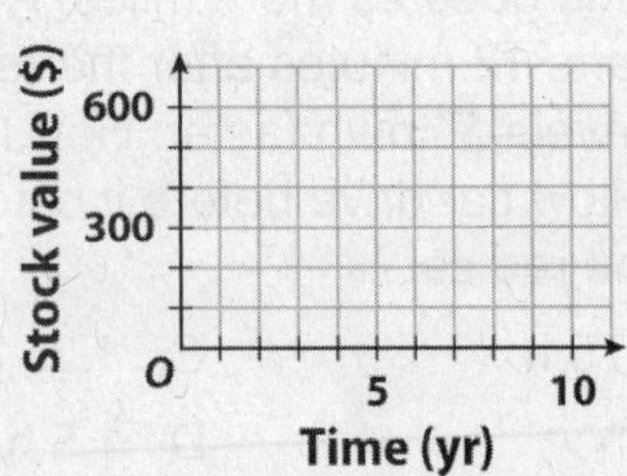

    answer: ________________

16. Determine the expression you can substitute for x in $8x + 4y = 6$ to solve the system below.

$$\begin{cases} 8x + 4y = 6 \\ -17y = 5 - x \end{cases}$$

    ____

17. Find the solution to the system of equations below.

$$\begin{cases} 10y = 25x - 35 \\ 25x + 15y = 10 \end{cases}$$

    ____

18. A system of two linear equations has no solution. Describe the graph of this system.

    ____

    ____

Name ______________________ Date ______________ Class______________

UNIT 3

Solving Equations and Systems of Equations

Unit Test: D

1. Solve the equation for x.

$$15 + 2x = 5 + 3x$$

A 4

B 5

C 10

2. A black car and a green car are traveling at the same speed. The black car drives 3 hours. The green car drives 3.5 hours and goes 25 miles farther than the black car. Use x for the speed of the cars. In the time the green car goes $3.5x$ miles, the black car goes $3x + 25$ miles. Which equation can be solved to find how fast the cars are going?

A $3x + 25 = 3.5x$

B $3x - 25 = 2.5x$

C $3x = 3.5x + 25$

3. Pilar and Ramesh left a 20% tip after having dinner. The amount of the tip was \$5. Pilar's dinner cost \$15. Which equation can you use to find x, the cost of Ramesh's dinner?

A $0.2(x + 15) = 5$

B $20x + 15 = 5$

C $2x + 15 = 5$

4. For the equation $21 + 3x = 3x + k$, which value of k will create a false equation with no solutions?

A $3x$

B 15

C 21

5. To start solving the system of equations below, which number would you multiply the equation $-2x - 5y = -1$ by?

$$\begin{cases} -2x - 5y = -1 \\ 4x + 2y = 8 \end{cases}$$

A 2

B 4

C 8

6. A system of linear equations is graphed below.

$$\begin{cases} y = -2x + 6 \\ y = 4x \end{cases}$$

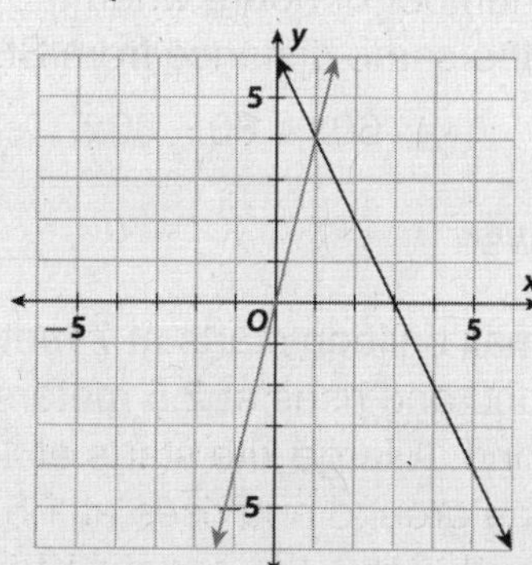

Which point is the solution?

A (−1, −4)

B (−1, 4)

C (1, 4)

7. Which expression can you substitute for x in $12x + y = 5$ to solve the system below?

$$\begin{cases} x = 6 - y \\ 12x + y = 5 \end{cases}$$

A $5 - 12y$

B $5 + y$

C $6 - y$

8. Which is the solution to $\begin{cases} -x + 3y = 1 \\ x - 2y = 2 \end{cases}$?

Start by adding the equations.

A (8, 3)

B (8, −3)

C (−8, 3)

9. The graph of a system of two linear equations is a pair of lines that intersect at the point (5, 7). How many solutions does the system have?

A 0

B 1

C infinitely many

Name ____________________ Date ____________________ Class ____________________

UNIT 3

Solving Equations and Systems of Equations

10. A train leaves St. Louis traveling west at 60 miles per hour. An hour later, another train leaves St. Louis traveling east at 80 miles per hour. Solve the equation to find the number of hours when the two trains are the same distance from St. Louis.

$$60x + 60 = 80x$$

answer: ____________________

11. A small balloon starts at 7 meters off the ground and rises at 2.5 meters per second. A large kite starts at 12 meters off the ground and rises at 1.5 meters per second. Solve the equation to find how many seconds it takes the kite and the balloon to be at the same height.

$$7 + 2.5x = 12 + 1.5x$$

answer: ____________________

12. Evelyn saves 40% of her earnings for college. This year, she earned $200 more than last year, and she saved $900. Complete and solve the equation to find x, her earnings last year.

$$0.4(x + 200) = 900$$

solution: ____________________

13. An equation that results in a true statement has infinitely many solutions. Does the equation below have infinitely many solutions?

$$3(2 + x) = 3x + 6$$

____

14. Solve the system of equations. Start by multiplying the second equation by 2. Then subtract the first equation from the second.

$$\begin{cases} 2x + 4y = 22 \\ 3x + 2y = 21 \end{cases}$$

____

15. Kim bought $100 worth of stock and gained $25 per year. Ari bought $400 worth of stock and lost $35 per year. Use x for time and y for stock value. Graph the equations that represent each situation. The first one is done for you.

Kim: $y = 100 + 25x$

Ari: $y = 400 - 35x$

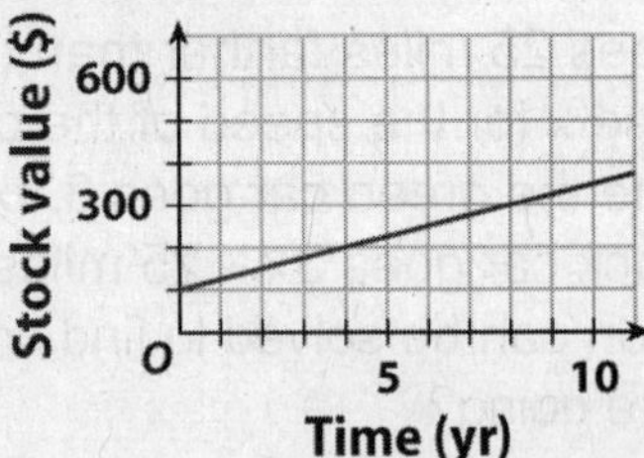

When did Kim and Ari have the same amount of stock value?

answer: ____________________

16. Write the expression you can substitute for x in $4x + 2y = 3$ to solve the system below.

$$\begin{cases} 4x + 2y = 3 \\ x = 4 - 6y \end{cases}$$

____

17. Find the solution to the system of equations below. Start by adding the equations.

$$\begin{cases} -x + 2y = -2 \\ x + 3y = 2 \end{cases}$$

____

18. The graph of a system of two equations is a pair of parallel lines with no points of intersection. Does the system have a solution?

____

Name ______________________ Date ______________ Class ______________

UNIT 3

Solving Equations and Systems of Equations

Performance Task

Answer the questions.

1. Mikhael and Hema are planning the annual school fundraiser. They want to earn more this year than they did last year. Last year, they earned \$4,000. 80% of the earnings went directly to the school and 20% was spent on the cost of the fundraiser. This year, they want \$4,000 to go directly to the school.

   a. Write and solve an equation to find how much more they need to earn this year before paying for costs.

   ____

   b. What is the total amount they need to earn this year?

   ____

2. Mikhael and Hema want to hire a professional DJ to play music during the event. DJ Kay-Cee charges \$100 plus \$50 per hour. DJ Fab Fred charges \$150 plus \$30 per hour.

   a. Write an equation to find the number of hours at which DJ Kay-Cee and DJ Fab Fred would charge the same amount.

   ____

   b. Solve your equation and write the answer.

   ____

3. Mikhael bought refreshments. Sandwiches were \$3 each and bottles of water were \$0.75 each. He spent \$318.75 on a total of 200 items.

   a. Write a system of equations to model the situation.

   ____

   b. Solve the system algebraically to find how many sandwiches and how many bottles of water Mikhael bought.

   ____

4. Mikhael, Hema, and 5 friends will help run the event. They will wear either a red shirt or a red baseball cap during the event. They want to spend exactly \$40. Shirts cost \$8 each and caps cost \$4 each.

   a. Write a system of equations to model the situation.

   ____

   b. Graph the system using the grid at the right.

   c. What is the solution and what does it represent?

   ____

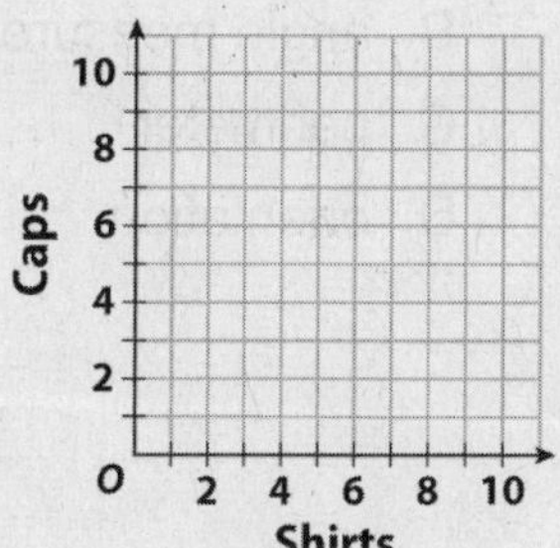

Name ______________________ Date ______________ Class ______________

UNIT 4

Transformational Geometry

Unit Test: A

Use the triangle for 1–10.

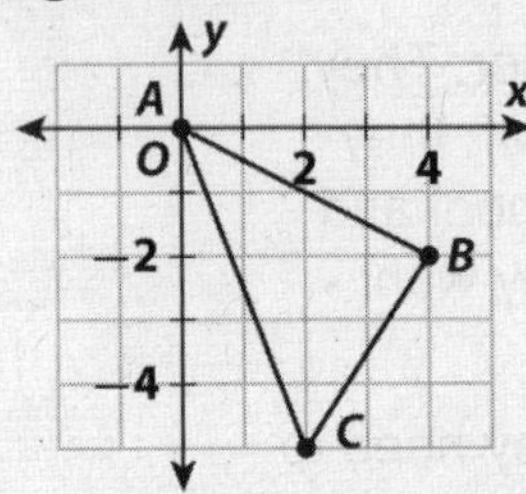

1. ΔABC is translated 2 units right and 1 unit down. What is the new location of point *C*?

   A (1, –7) C (2, –5)

   B (1, –3) D (4, –6)

2. Which property changes when a figure is translated?

   A side lengths

   B angle measures

   C location

   D perimeter

3. Which translation moves a triangle 4 units to the right and 8 units up?

   A $(x, y) \rightarrow (x + 4, y + 8)$

   B $(x, y) \rightarrow (x - 4, y + 8)$

   C $(x, y) \rightarrow (x + 8, y + 4)$

   D $(x, y) \rightarrow (x + 8, y - 4)$

4. ΔABC is reflected across the *x*-axis. What is the new location of point *B*?

   A (–4, –2) C (4, –2)

   B (–4, 2) D (4, 2)

5. Which property changes when a figure is reflected across a line?

   A side lengths

   B angle measures

   C perimeter

   D orientation

6. ΔABC is rotated 90° clockwise about the origin. In what quadrant is $\Delta A'B'C'$, the image of the original triangle?

   A Quadrant I

   B Quadrant II

   C Quadrant III

   D Quadrant IV

7. ΔABC is rotated 90° counterclockwise with the origin as center of rotation. Where is the image of point *A*?

   A (0, 0) C (2, –4)

   B (4, –2) D (2, 4)

8. What is the result of the transformation below?

   $$(x, y) \rightarrow (-x, y)$$

   A reflection across the *x*-axis

   B reflection across the *y*-axis

   C 90° rotation clockwise

   D 90° rotation counterclockwise

9. A figure is translated, rotated, or reflected. Describe its image.

   A same shape, larger size

   B same shape, smaller size

   C same size, same shape

   D same size, different shape

10. ΔABC is dilated using a scale factor of 2. What happens to its angle measures?

    A They double in size.

    B They do not change.

    C They become half as great.

    D It depends on the center of the dilation.

11. A figure is dilated. Describe its image.

    A same size

    B similar

    C congruent

    D reflected

Name ______________________ Date ______________ Class______________

UNIT 4

Transformational Geometry

Use the triangles for 12–21. Write ordered pairs to show the new locations of the vertices.

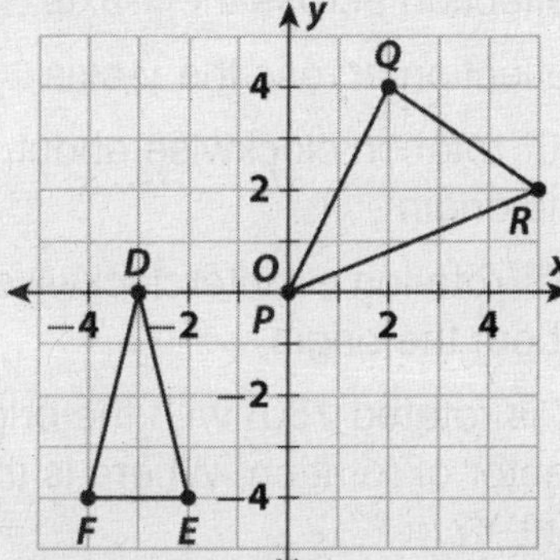

12. Translate ΔDEF 5 units to the right.

D'(______), E'(______), F'(______)

13. Reflect ΔDEF across the x-axis. Which point does not move?

____

14. Rotate ΔDEF 180°. Use point D as the center of rotation.

D'(______), E'(______), F'(______)

15. Write the coordinates of the vertices of ΔDEF.

D(______), E(______), F(______)

Now apply the transformation below.

$(x, y) \rightarrow (-x, y)$

D'(______), E'(______), F'(______)

16. Apply the translation below to ΔDEF.

$(x, y) \rightarrow (x - 10, y + 8)$

D'(______), E'(______), F'(______)

17. Translate ΔPQR 2 units left and 3 units down.

P'(______), Q'(______), R'(______)

18. Reflect ΔPQR across the y-axis.

P'(______), Q'(______), R'(______)

19. Rotate ΔPQR 90° clockwise. Use point P as the center of rotation.

P'(______), Q'(______), R'(______)

20. Write the coordinates of the vertices of ΔPQR.

P(______), Q(______), R(______)

Now apply the transformation below.

$(x, y) \rightarrow (-x, -y)$

P'(______), Q'(______), R'(______)

21. Apply the transformation below to ΔPQR. Describe the result.

$(x, y) \rightarrow (2x, 2y)$

P'(______), Q'(______), R'(______)

____

____

Use the information below for 22–24.

Square $ABCD$ has vertices at $A(-6, 0)$, $B(0, 6)$, $C(6, 0)$, and $D(0, -6)$.

22. Dilate $ABCD$ by a scale factor of 3. Use the origin as the center of the dilation. What are the coordinates of points A', B', C', and D'?

____

23. What shape is figure $A'B'C'D'$?

____

24. When a figure is dilated how does its image relate to the original figure?

____

Name ______________________ Date ____________ Class ____________

UNIT 4

Transformational Geometry

Unit Test: B

Use the triangles for 1–10.

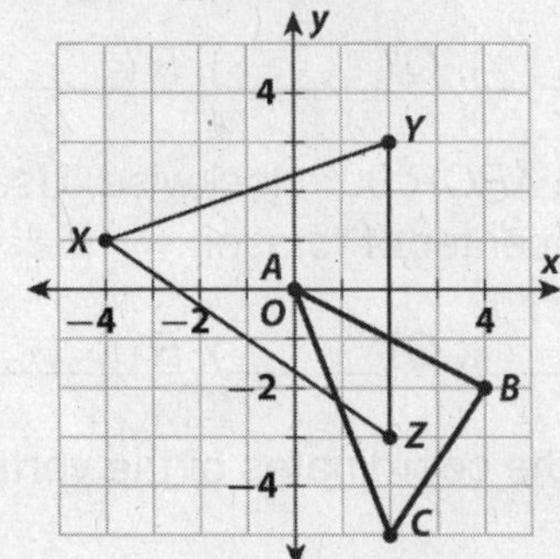

1. ΔABC is translated 5 units left and 2 units up. Where is point C', the image of point C?

   A (−3, −3) C (4, −10)

   B (0, −10) D (7, −3)

2. ΔABC is translated 10 units right and 2 units down. Which property changes?

   A location

   B orientation

   C area

   D perimeter

3. Which translation moves point X so that its image is on the y-axis?

   A $(x, y) \rightarrow (x + 4, y + 8)$

   B $(x, y) \rightarrow (x - 4, y + 8)$

   C $(x, y) \rightarrow (x + 8, y + 4)$

   D $(x, y) \rightarrow (x + 8, y - 4)$

4. ΔXYZ is reflected across the y-axis. What are the endpoints of segment $Y'Z'$?

   A (−2, −3), (−2, −3)

   B (−2, 3), (−2, −3)

   C (2, 3), (2, −3)

   D (2, 3), (−2, −3)

5. ΔABC is reflected across a horizontal line through (0, 2). Which property changes?

   A side lengths

   B angle measures

   C perimeter

   D orientation

6. Which transformation takes point B to (2, 4)?

   A reflection across the x-axis

   B reflection across the y-axis

   C 90° rotation clockwise about the origin

   D 90° rotation counterclockwise about the origin

7. ΔXYZ is rotated 180° with the origin as the center of rotation. Where is the image of point Y?

   A (−3, −2) C (2, 3)

   B (−2, −3) D (3, 2)

8. Which transformation reflects a figure across the y-axis?

   A $(x, y) \rightarrow (-x, y)$

   B $(x, y) \rightarrow (-x, -y)$

   C $(x, y) \rightarrow (-y, x)$

   D $(x, y) \rightarrow (y, -x)$

9. Triangle XYZ is dilated. Which word(s) describe its image $X'Y'Z'$?

   A congruent

   B same size

   C rotated

   D similar

10. The transformation below is applied to ΔXYZ.

    $$(x, y) \rightarrow (0.5x, 0.5y)$$

    What are the coordinates of point X'?

    A (−4, 1) C (0.5, −2)

    B (−2, 0.5) D (4, −1)

11. Which transformation does not produce a congruent image?

    A translation

    B rotation

    C dilation

    D reflection

Name ______________________ Date ______________ Class ______________

UNIT 4

Transformational Geometry

Use the triangles for 12–21. Write the coordinates of the vertices.

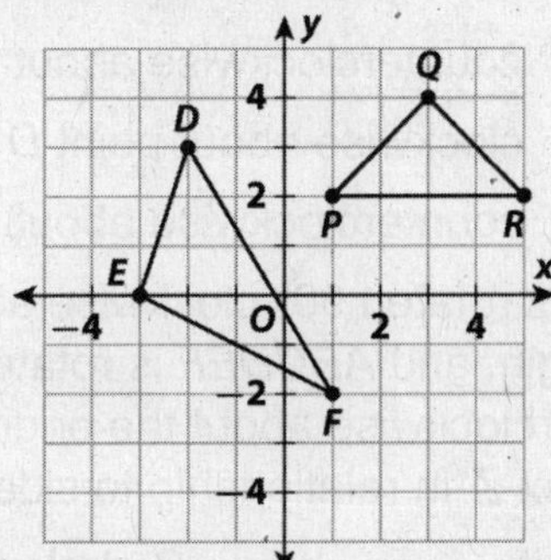

12. Translate ΔDEF 4 units to the right and 2 units down.

 D'(______), E'(______), F'(______)

13. ΔDEF is reflected across the x-axis. Which vertex stays in the same location?

 ____

14. Rotate ΔDEF 90° clockwise. Use the origin as the center of rotation. Where is the image of point D?

 ____

15. Apply the transformation below to ΔDEF. Describe the result.

 $(x, y) \rightarrow (-x, y)$

 D'(______), E'(______), F'(______)

 ____

 ____

16. Apply the translation below to both triangles.

 $(x, y) \rightarrow (x - 10, y + 8)$

 D'(______), E'(______), F'(______)

 P'(______), Q'(______), R'(______)

17. Translate ΔPQR so that point P' coincides with point F.

 ____

18. Reflect ΔPQR across the y-axis.

 P'(______), Q'(______), R'(______)

19. Rotate ΔPQR 90° counterclockwise. Use point P as the center of rotation.

 P'(______), Q'(______), R'(______)

20. Apply the transformation below to ΔPQR. Describe the resulting rotation.

 $(x, y) \rightarrow (-x, -y)$

 P'(______), Q'(______), R'(______)

 ____

21. Apply the transformation below to ΔPQR. Describe the result.

 $(x, y) \rightarrow (3x, 3y)$

 P'(______), Q'(______), R'(______)

 ____

 ____

Use the information below for 22–24.

Rhombus $ABCD$ has vertices at $A(-6, 0)$, $B(0, 8)$, $C(6, 0)$, and $D(0, -8)$.

22. Dilate $ABCD$ by a scale factor of 1.5. Use the origin as the center of the dilation. What are the coordinates of points A', B', C', and D'?

 ____

23. What type of figure is $A'B'C'D'$?

 ____

24. Compare the original rhombus and its image under the dilation by a scale factor of 1.5.

 ____

Name ______________________ Date ______________ Class ______________

UNIT 4

Transformational Geometry

Unit Test: C

Use the polygons for 1–11.

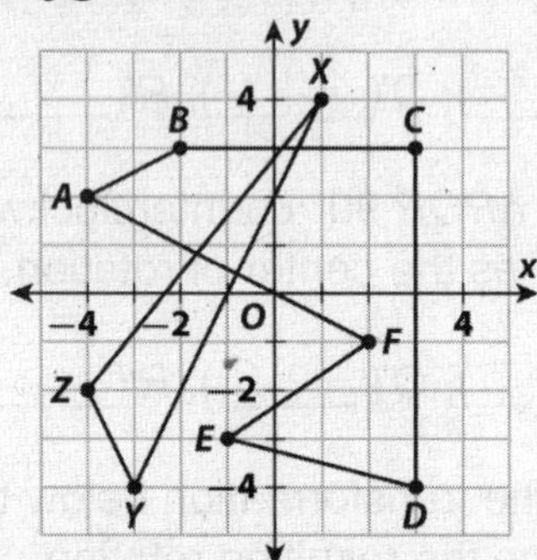

1. The triangle is translated so that the image of vertex *X* coincides with point *E*. What are the coordinates of *Y'*?

   A (−5, −11) C (−1, −3)

   B (−3, −4) D (1, 4)

2. Hexagon *ABCDEF* is translated so that the image lies completely in the first quadrant. Which property does this translation change?

   A side lengths

   B angle measures

   C location

   D perimeter

3. The triangle is translated 4 units down and 8 units to the right. Which translation returns it to its original location?

   A $(x, y) \rightarrow (x - 8, y + 4)$

   B $(x, y) \rightarrow (x - 4, y + 8)$

   C $(x, y) \rightarrow (x + 4, y - 8)$

   D $(x, y) \rightarrow (x + 8, y - 4)$

4. The hexagon is reflected across the *y*-axis. How many points do **not** change location?

   A 0 C 4

   B 2 D 6

5. ΔXYZ is reflected across the vertical line that contains segment *CD*. What are the coordinates of *Z'*?

   A (−2, 12) C (4, −2)

   B (2, −12) D (12, −2)

6. Which rotation moves point *F* to (6, −3)?

   A 90° clockwise about point *C*

   B 90° counterclockwise about point *C*

   C 90° clockwise about point *D*

   D 90° counterclockwise about point *D*

7. ΔXYZ is rotated 90° clockwise about the origin, and *ABCDEF* is rotated 90° counterclockwise about the origin. Where is vertex *Z'* in relationship to side *C'D'*?

   A on it C below it

   B above it D to the left of it

8. Which transformation applied to the hexagon will make *D'* coincide with *Y*?

   A $(x, y) \rightarrow (-x, y)$

   B $(x, y) \rightarrow (x, -y)$

   C $(x, y) \rightarrow (-y, x)$

   D $(x, y) \rightarrow (y, -x)$

For 9–11, the hexagon is dilated by a scale factor of 3, centered at the origin.

9. Which sides are part of the same line?

   A $\overline{AB}$ and $\overline{A'B'}$ C $\overline{EF}$ and $\overline{E'F'}$

   B $\overline{BC}$ and $\overline{B'C'}$ D $\overline{FA}$ and $\overline{F'A'}$

10. How far to the right must *A'B'C'D'E'F'* be translated so that point *A''* lands on $\overline{C'D'}$?

    A 8 units C 21 units

    B 10 units D 29 units

11. The area of *A'B'C'D'E'F'* is 225 square units. What is the area of *ABCDEF*?

    A 25 square units C 75 square units

    B 50 square units D 125 square units

12. In which transformation is the size of the image different from the size of the original figure?

    A translation 3 units right and 3 units up

    B reflection about the *x*-axis

    C rotation of 90 degrees clockwise

    D dilation by a scale factor of 2

Name ______________________ Date ______________ Class ______________

UNIT 4

Transformational Geometry

Use these figures for 13–25. Record transformations by identifying the coordinates of the vertices of each image.

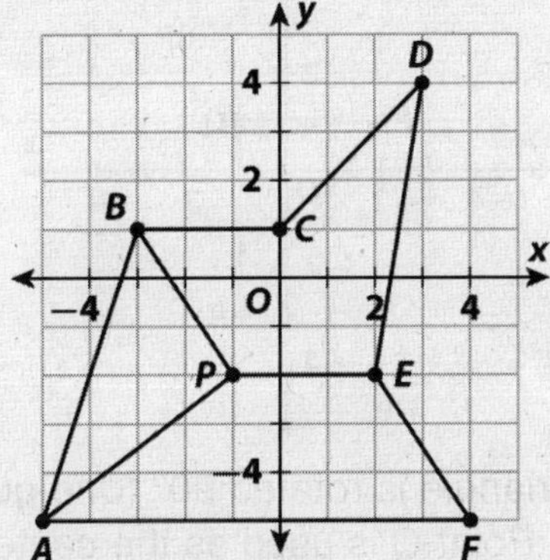

13. Translate ΔABP so that vertex A' coincides with point D.

____

14. Reflect the trapezoid across the x-axis and then across the y-axis.

____

15. Rotate the pentagon 90° clockwise about the origin.

____

16. Apply the transformation below to the entire figure and describe the result.

$(x, y) \rightarrow (-x, y)$

____

____

____

17. Apply the transformation below to the entire figure and describe the result.

$(x, y) \rightarrow (x - 10, y + 8)$

____

____

18. The midline of a trapezoid is a segment that is equidistant from the bases. Translate the trapezoid so that its midline is on the x-axis.

____

19. Reflect the triangle across the y-axis and then translate it 3 units down and 2 units right.

____

20. Rotate the entire figure 180° about point D.

____

21. Apply the transformation below to the entire figure and describe the result.

$(x, y) \rightarrow (-x, -y)$

____

____

____

22. Apply the transformation below to the entire figure and describe the result.

$(x, y) \rightarrow (4x, 4y)$

____

____

____

Dilate the figure by a scale factor of 0.5. Use point P as the center of the dilation.

23. Write the coordinates of the image vertices.

____

24. What always stays the same under a dilation by a scale factor greater or less than 1?

____

25. Will the area of pentagon BCDEP be the same as the area of its image? Explain.

____

Name ______________________ Date ______________ Class ______________

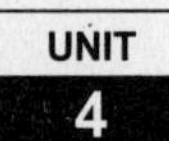

Transformational Geometry

Unit Test: D

Use the triangles for 1–5.

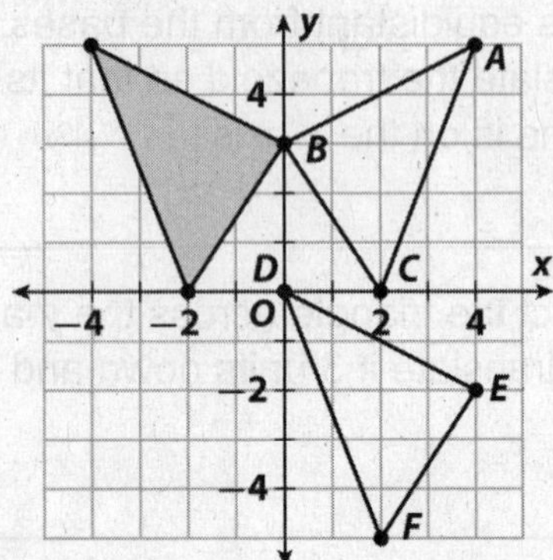

1. Which triangle is a translation of the gray triangle?
   A ΔABC
   B ΔDEF
   C neither
2. ΔDEF is translated 5 units straight up so that point F lands on the x-axis. Where does point D land?
   A (0, 5) B (5, 0) C (5, 5)
3. The translation below is used on all three triangles.
   $$(x, y) \rightarrow (x, y + 1)$$
   What happens to the triangles?
   A They all move 1 unit to the right.
   B They all move 1 unit to the left.
   C They all move 1 unit up.
4. Which triangle is a reflection of the gray triangle?
   A ΔABC
   B ΔDEF
   C neither
5. Which triangle has the same orientation as the gray triangle?
   A ΔABC
   B ΔDEF
   C neither

Use the triangle for 6–11.

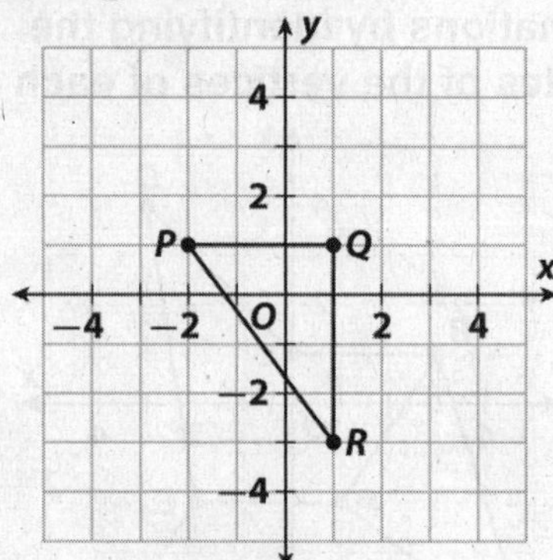

6. The triangle is rotated 90° (one-quarter turn). Point Q is used as the center of this rotation. Which describes the new position of side PQ?
   A vertical
   B horizontal
   C slanted
7. The triangle is rotated 180° with point Q as the center of rotation. What is the new position of point P?
   A (–2, 1) B (1, 4) C (4, 1)
8. The translation below is used on the triangle.
   $$(x, y) \rightarrow (x + 4, y + 4)$$
   What is the new location of point R?
   A (1, 5) B (5, 1) C (4, 4)

ΔPQR is dilated by a scale factor of 2. The center of the dilation is (0, 0).

9. How does the image of triangle PQR relate to triangle PQR?
   A It is smaller. C It is the same size.
   B It is larger.
10. The new location of point P is (–4, 2). What is the new location of point Q?
    A (2, 2) B (2, –4) C (4, 4)
11. Triangle PQR and its image are the same shape but not the same size. What word do you use to describe this?
    A congruent B dilated C similar

Name ______________________ Date ______________ Class ______________

UNIT 4

Transformational Geometry

Use the triangles for 12–17.

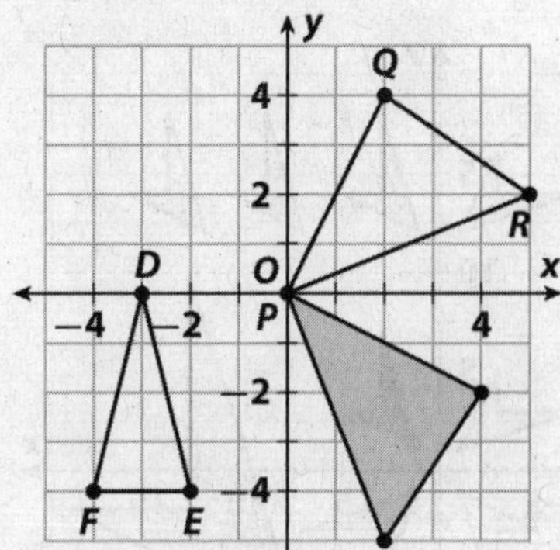

12. Translate ΔDEF 1 unit to the right. Write the ordered pairs for the new vertices.

_________, _________, _________

13. Reflect ΔDEF across the x-axis. Write the ordered pairs for the new vertices.

_________, _________, _________

14. The gray triangle is a 90° rotation of ΔPQR. Is the direction of rotation clockwise or counterclockwise?

____

15. Apply the translation below to ΔDEF. Write the ordered pairs for the new vertices.

$$(x, y) \rightarrow (x, y + 4)$$

_________, _________, _________

16. Apply the reflection below to ΔPQR. Write the ordered pairs for the new vertices.

$$(x, y) \rightarrow (-x, y)$$

_________, _________, _________

17. Describe a translation to ΔPQR so that point P lands on top of point D.

____

Use the grid for 18–20. Draw your answers on the grid and label each one with the problem number.

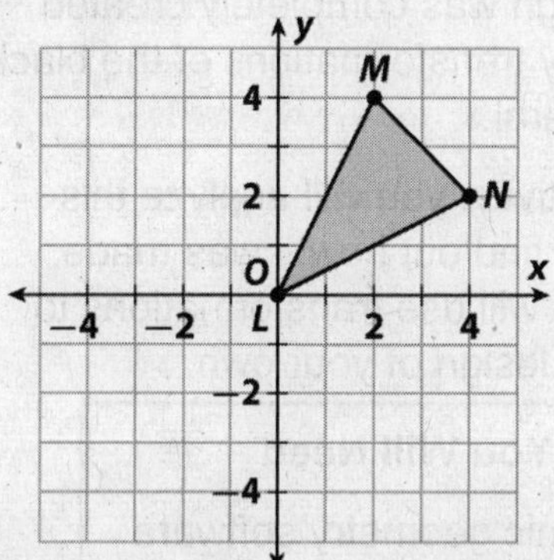

18. Reflect ΔLMN across the y-axis.

19. Rotate ΔLMN 90° clockwise about the origin.

20. Rotate ΔLMN 180° about the origin.

Use the figure for 21–24.

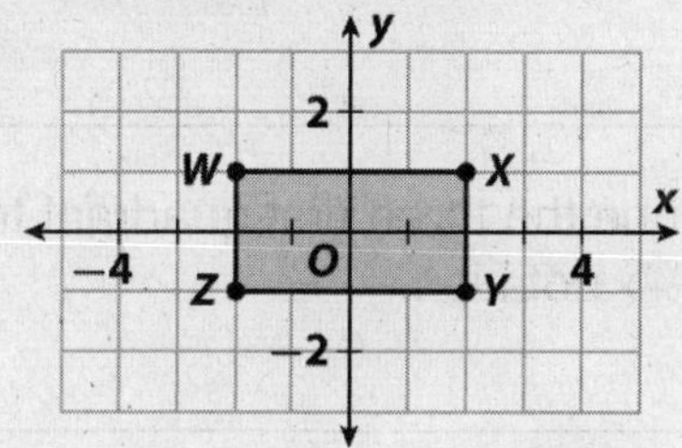

21. Dilate the rectangle using a scale factor of 2. Use the origin as the center. Draw your answer on the grid.

22. How did the length and width change?

____

23. Label the new rectangle W', X', Y', Z'. Write the ratio of WX to $W'X'$.

_________ to _________

24. Compare the new rectangle to the original rectangle. Their areas are different, but what stays the same?

____

Name ______________________ Date ______________ Class ______________

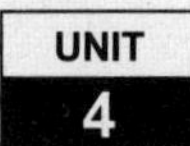

Transformational Geometry

Performance Task

Designing with Transformations

This design was completely created using only transformations of the black quadrilateral.

In this activity, you will analyze this design to find out how it was made. Then you will use transformations to create a design of your own.

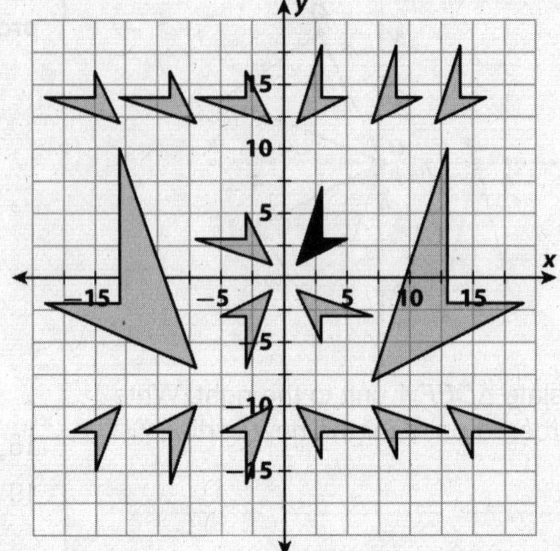

You Will Need

- dynamic geometry software
  OR
- graph paper, a ruler, and colored pencils

Start by solving these problems.

1. The top three figures in the first quadrant were made with translations. Describe how these were made in words.

   ____

2. Describe the three first-quadrant translations using the $(x, y) \rightarrow$ notation.

   ____

3. The three figures around the origin were created with rotations. Describe the three rotations in words.

   ____

4. Describe the three rotations using the $(x, y) \rightarrow$ notation.

   ____

5. The two large figures were made with a dilation, a translation, and a reflection. Describe how these were made.

   ____

   ____

   ____

6. Now create a design of your own on a separate sheet of paper. Use all four types of transformations: translations, reflections, rotations, and dilations. Record the transformations you use.

Name ______________________ Date ______________ Class ______________

UNIT 5

Measurement Geometry

Unit Test: A

1. In the figure below, which angle pair is a pair of corresponding angles?

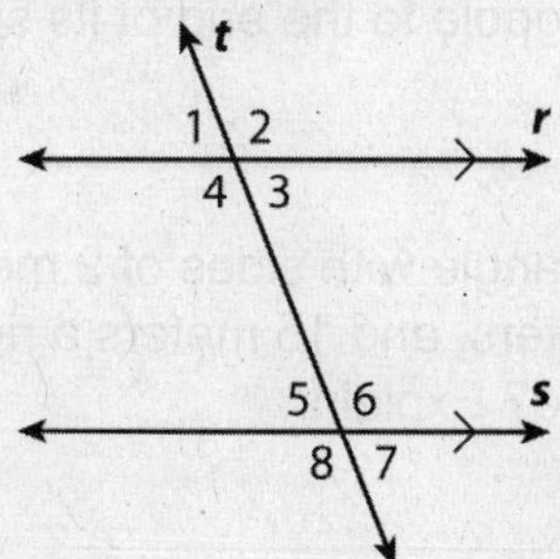

A ∠1 and ∠3 C ∠5 and ∠6
B ∠2 and ∠4 D ∠4 and ∠8

2. The measures of the three angles of a triangle are given by 4*x*, 2*x*, and 6*x*. What is the measure of the smallest angle?

A 15° C 60°
B 30° D 90°

3. What is the value of *h* in the triangle below?

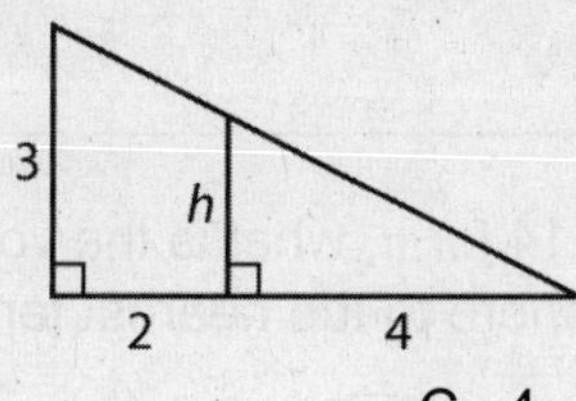

A 2 C 4
B 3 D 6

4. What is the length of the unlabeled side?

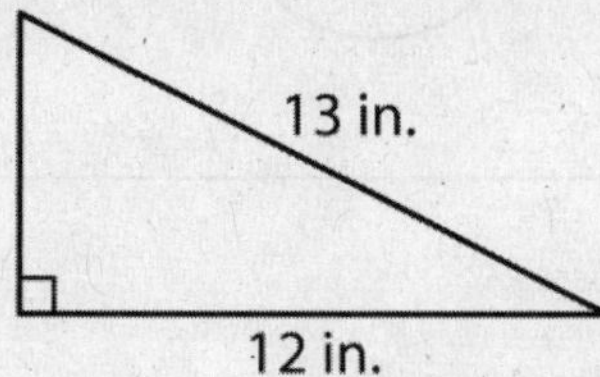

A 5 in. C 16 in.
B 7 in. D 25 in.

5. Which set of lengths are the side lengths of a right triangle?

A 1, 9, 12 C 5, 10, 20
B 3, 4, 5 D 7, 11, 13

Use the grid for 6–7.

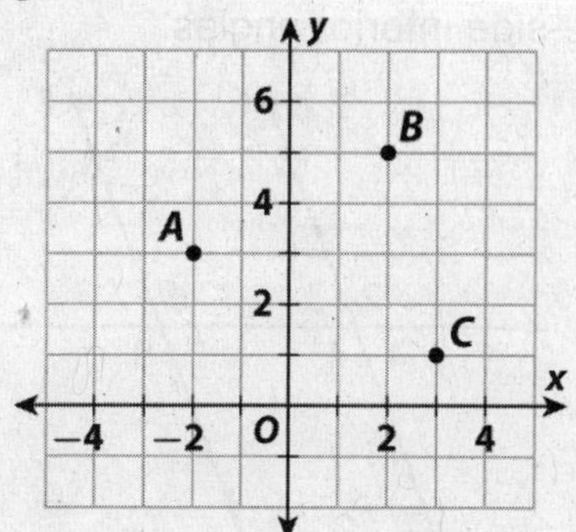

6. What is the distance between point *B* and point *C*?

A 2 units C 8.6 units
B 4.1 units D 15 units

7. What is the distance between point *A* and point *C*?

A 5 units C 5.6 units
B 5.4 units D 29 units

8. Using 3.14 for π, what is the volume of the cylinder below to the nearest tenth?

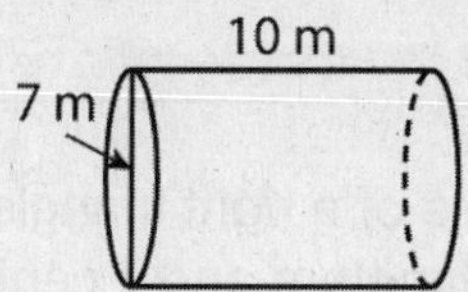

A 109.9 m^3 C 384.7 m^3
B 219.8 m^3 D 1538.6 m^3

9. A cone-shaped paper cup is 2.5 inches high and has a radius of 1.5 inches. What is its volume to the nearest hundredth?

A 3.93 in^3 C 7.85 in^3
B 5.89 in^3 D 16.77 in^3

10. Using 3.14 for π, what is the volume of a ball with a radius of 3 centimeters?

A 7 cm^3 C 113 cm^3
B 13 cm^3 D 127 cm^3

Name ______________________ Date ______________ Class ______________

UNIT 5

Measurement Geometry

11. In the figure below, name one pair of same-side interior angles.

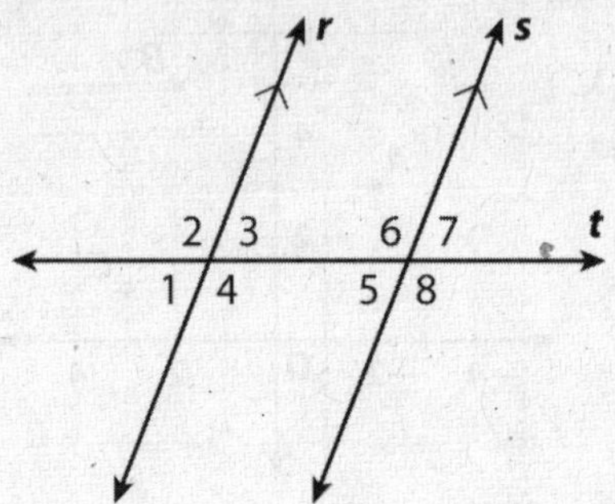

____

12. What is the measure of $\angle DBA$ in the diagram below?

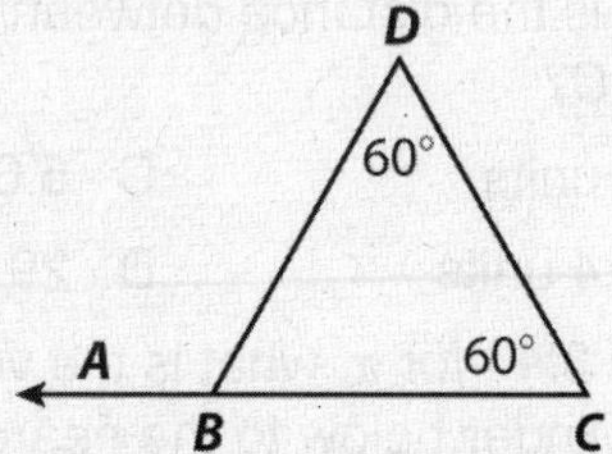

____

13. Two sides of a right triangle have lengths of 4 centimeters and 7 centimeters. The third side is **not** the hypotenuse. How long is the third side?

____

14. A fence is 6 feet tall. A rope is attached to the top of the fence and fastened to the ground 5 feet from the base of the fence. What is the length of the rope?

____

15. A right triangle has legs that measure 4 centimeters and 9 centimeters. What is the length of the hypotenuse in centimeters?

____

16. A flagpole is 10 feet tall. Its shadow is 12 feet long. How far is it from the top of the flagpole to the end of its shadow?

____

17. Is a triangle with sides of 9 meters, 12 meters, and 15 meters a right triangle? Explain.

____

18. A cylinder has a radius of 6 inches and a height of 4 inches. What is its volume rounded to the nearest tenth?

____

19. Using 3.14 for π, what is the volume, to the nearest tenth, of a cone that has a height of 10 feet and a base with radius 3 feet?

____

20. Using 3.14 for π, what is the volume of the sphere to the nearest tenth?

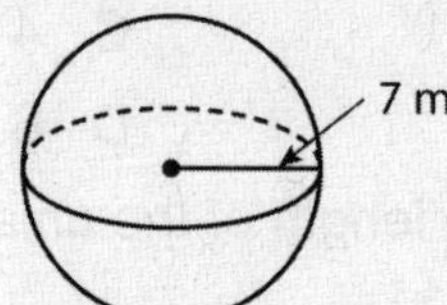

____

Name ______________________ Date ______________ Class ______________

UNIT 5

Measurement Geometry

Unit Test: B

1. In the figure below, which angle pair is a pair of alternate interior angles?

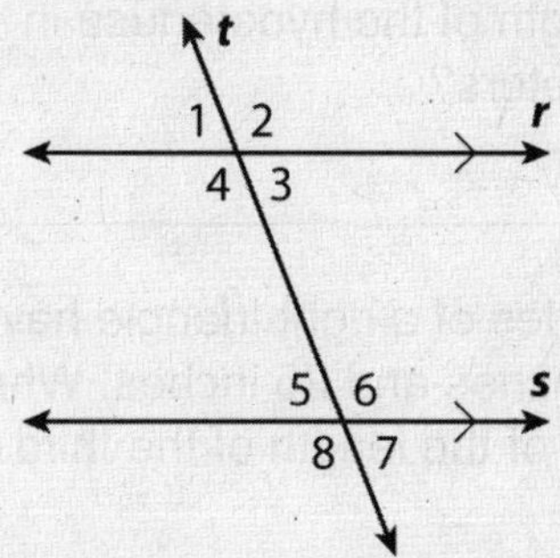

A ∠3 and ∠4 C ∠3 and ∠6

B ∠3 and ∠5 D ∠4 and ∠5

2. The measures of the three angles of a triangle are given by $4x - 1$, $2x + 1$, and $6x$. What is the measure of the largest angle?

A 15° C 59°

B 31° D 90°

3. What is the value of *h* in the triangle below?

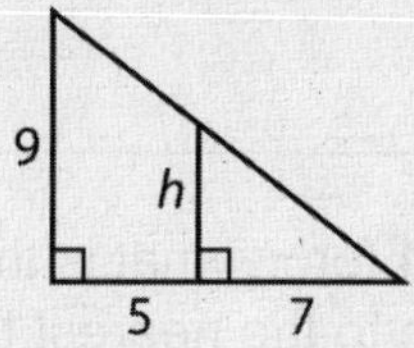

A 1.7 C 6.43

B 5.25 D 12.6

4. What is the length of the unlabeled side?

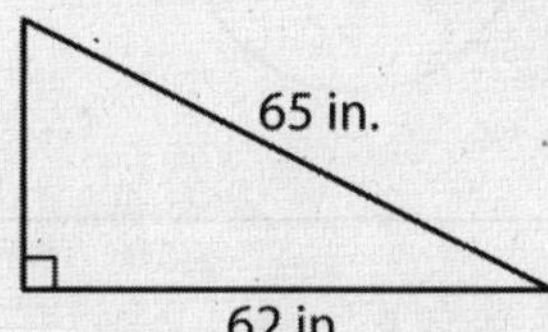

A 19.5 in. C 45.2 in.

B 36.7 in. D 89.8 in.

5. Which set of lengths are the side lengths of a right triangle?

A 9, 15, 17 C 20, 30, 40

B 14, 23, 25 D 15, 36, 39

Use the grid for 6–7.

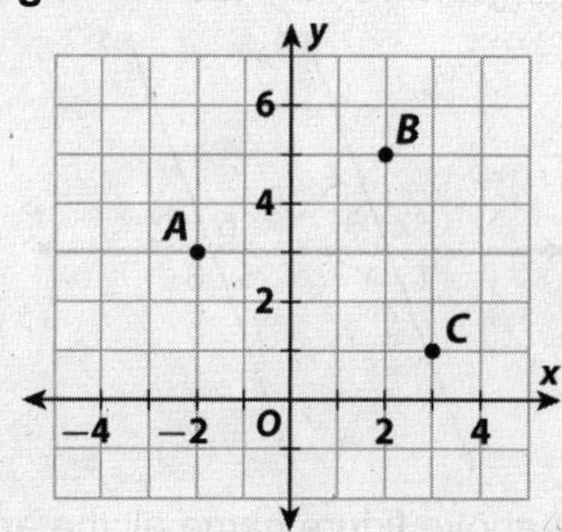

6. What is the distance between point *A* and point *C*?

A 4 units C 5.4 units

B 5.1 units D 25 units

7. What is the distance between point *A* and origin?

A 2 units C 3.6 units

B 3 units D 13 units

8. Using 3.14 for π, what is the volume of the cylinder below to the nearest tenth?

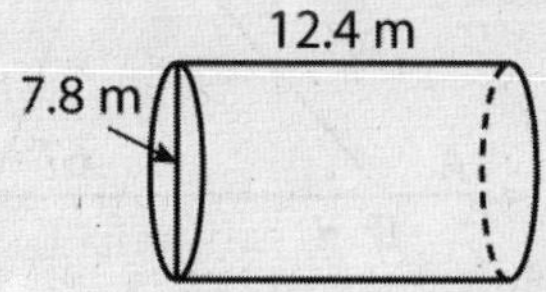

A 96.7 m^3 C 592.2 m^3

B 151.6 m^3 D 2368.9 m^3

9. A cone-shaped paper cup is 2.5 inches high and has a diameter of 3 inches. What is its volume to the nearest hundredth?

A 3.93 in^3 C 7.85 in^3

B 5.89 in^3 D 16.77 in^3

10. Using 3.14 for π, what is the volume of a ball with a diameter of 7 centimeters?

A 134 cm^3 C 539 cm^3

B 180 cm^3 D 789 cm^3

Name ________________ Date ________________ Class ________________

UNIT 5

Measurement Geometry

Use the diagram for 11–12.

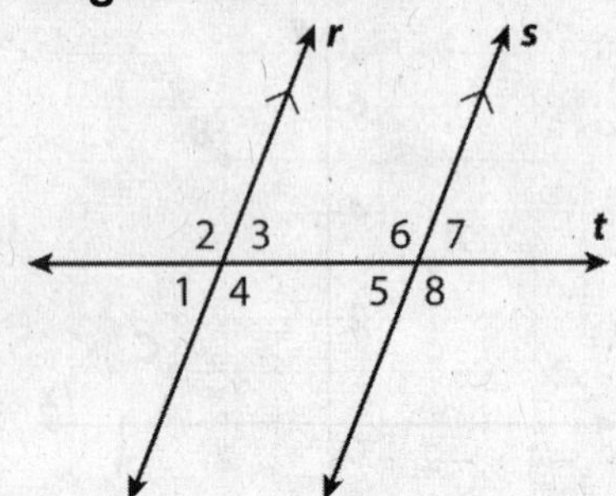

11. In the above figure name all the angles that are congruent to $\angle 8$.

____

12. What is another set of congruent angles?

____

13. What is the measure of $\angle DBA$ in the diagram below?

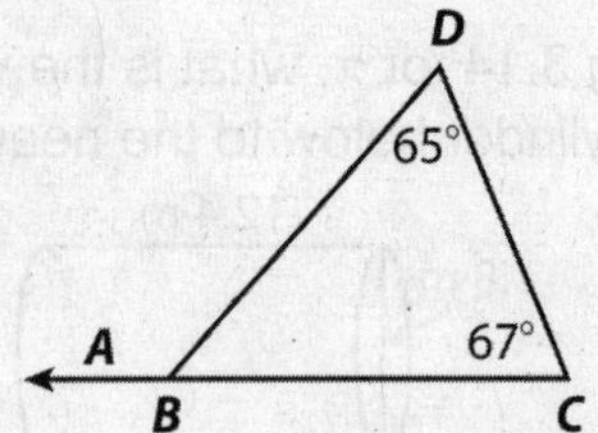

14. Two sides of a right triangle have lengths of 46 centimeters and 23 centimeters. The third side is **not** the hypotenuse. How long is the third side?

____

15. A fence post is 13 feet tall. A chain is attached to the top of the fence post and fastened to the ground 7 feet from the base of the fence post. What is the length of the chain?

____

16. A right triangle has legs that measure 7 centimeters and 6 centimeters. What is the length of the hypotenuse in centimeters?

____

17. Two sides of a right triangle have lengths of 75 inches and 25 inches. What is the square of the length of the third side?

____

18. A cylindrical metal tin has a diameter of 12 inches and a height of 4 inches. What is its volume rounded to the nearest tenth?

____

19. Using 3.14 for π, what is the volume, to the nearest tenth, of a cone that has a height of 16 feet and a base with radius 5 feet?

____

20. Using 3.14 for π, what is the volume of the sphere to the nearest tenth?

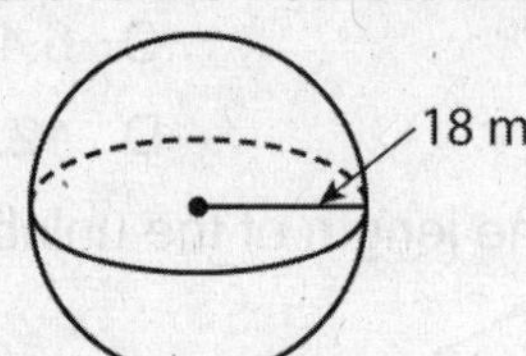

____

Name ______________________ Date ______________ Class ______________

UNIT 5

Measurement Geometry

Unit Test C

1. In the figure below, ∠3 measures $5x°$. What is the measure of the angle that forms a same-side interior angle pair with ∠3, when $x = 13$?

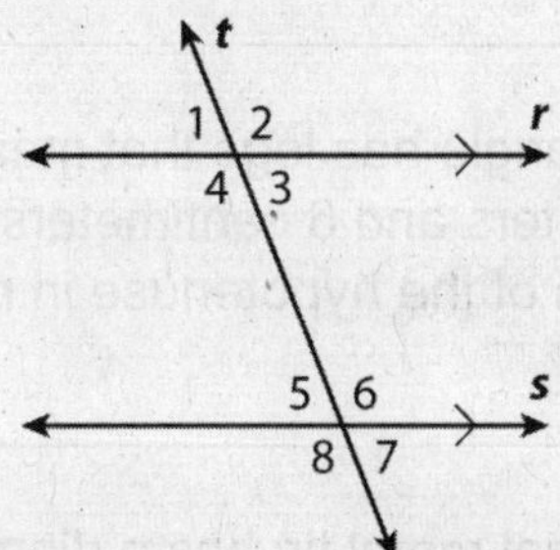

A 65° C 115°

B 90° D 135°

2. The measures of the three angles of a triangle are given by $18x - 7$, $12x + 9$, and $4x$. What is the measure of the largest angle?

A 5.2° C 71.9°

B 21° D 87.3°

3. A triangle is similar to the ones shown below but has a base length of $12 + h$. What is its height?

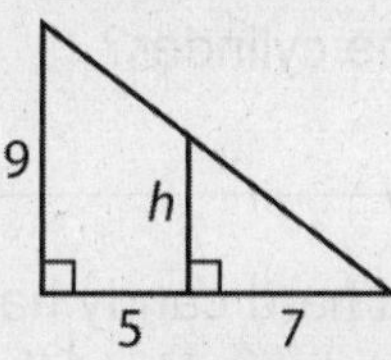

A 5.25 C 17.25

B 12.94 D 36

4. What is the minimum length of fence that could surround a triangular garden plot with the dimensions below?

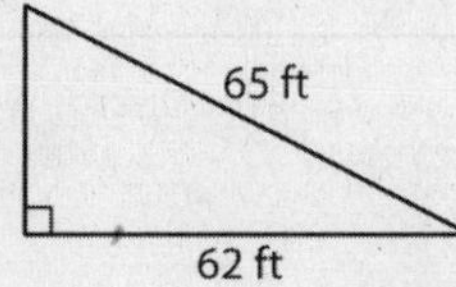

A 19 ft C 165.7 ft

B 146.5 ft D 180 ft

5. Which set of lengths are the side lengths of a right triangle?

A 11, 15, 27 C 21, 32, 41

B 20, 52, 48 D 15, 36, 49

Use the grid for 6–7.

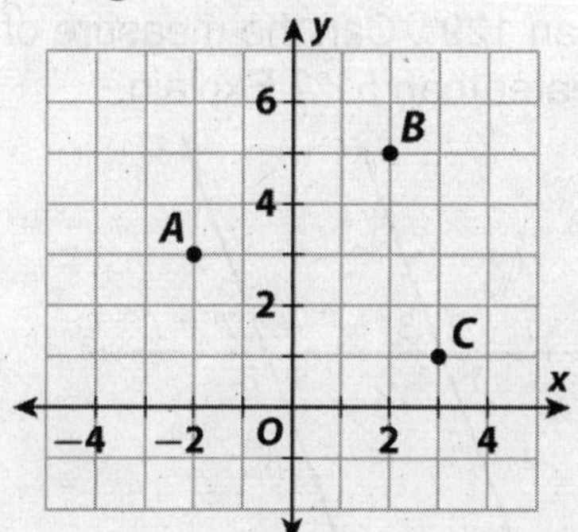

6. What is the perimeter of the triangle formed by points A, B, and C?

A 4.5 units C 14 units

B 5.3 units D 25 units

7. Move point C to (4, 1). How does this affect the perimeter of ΔABC?

A less than C equal to

B less than or equal to D greater than

8. A storage tank has the dimensions shown below. How many storage tanks are needed to contain 60,000 cubic meters of liquid?

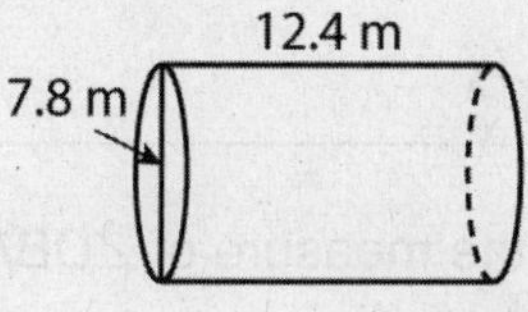

A 99 C 102

B 100 D 105

9. A cone-shaped paper cup is 10 centimeters high and has a diameter of 8 centimeters. Using this cup, about how many servings can you get from 1 liter (1000 cubic centimeters) of water?

A 4 C 9

B 6 D 10

10. How much air is needed to fill a ball with a diameter of 7 centimeters?

A 134 cm^3 C 539 cm^3

B 180 cm^3 D 789 cm^3

Name ____________________ Date ____________ Class ____________

UNIT 5

Measurement Geometry

11. In the figure below, the measure of ∠4 is greater than 129°. Can the measure of ∠5 be greater than 51°? Explain.

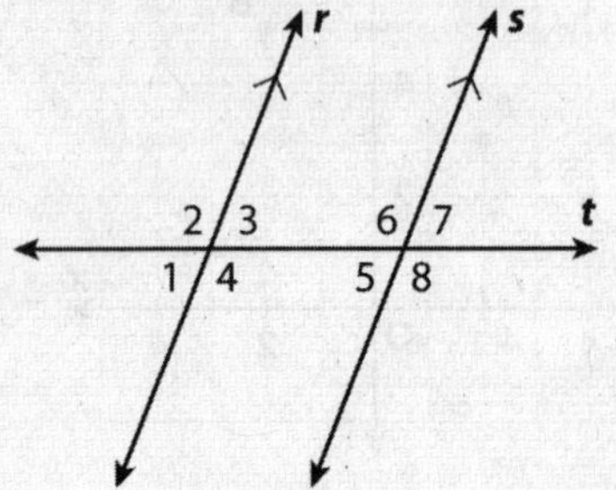

____

Use the diagram for 12–13.

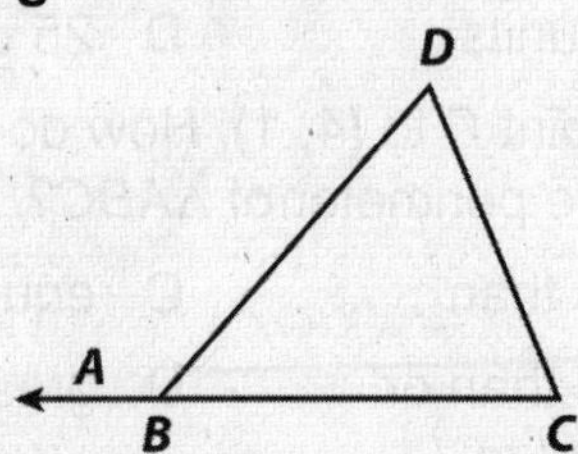

12. In the above diagram ∠DBC measures 5 degrees less than ∠C, and ∠D measures 8 degrees more than ∠C. What is the measure of each angle of the triangle?

____

13. What is the measure of ∠DBA?

____

14. Two sides of a right triangle have lengths of $46x$ cm and $23x$ cm. The third side is **not** the hypotenuse. How long is the third side in terms of x?

____

15. A 54-foot cable is hung from the top of a building that is 52 feet tall. The cable needs to be fastened 12 feet from the base of the building. Is the cable long enough? Explain.

____

16. For the situation in problem 15, what is the length of the shortest cable that would work?

____

17. A right triangle has legs that measure 7 centimeters and 6 centimeters. What is the length of the hypotenuse in meters?

____

18. A cylindrical metal tin has a diameter of 12 inches and a height of 4 inches. An ounce of popcorn takes up about 45 cubic inches of space. How many tins are needed to contain 1000 ounces of popcorn?

____

19. A paper cone has a height of 16 centimeters and a base with radius 5 centimeters. The contents of two such paper cones fit into a cylinder with a radius of 3 centimeters. What is the height of the cylinder?

____

20. A spherical hard candy has a liquid center. The diameter of the candy is 1.25 inches. The thickness of the hard outer core of the candy is 0.25 inch. Using 3.14 for π, how much liquid is needed to fill the candy center?

____

Name ______________________ Date ______________ Class ______________

UNIT 5

Measurement Geometry

Unit Test: D

1. In the figure below, which of the following angles is congruent to $\angle 1$?

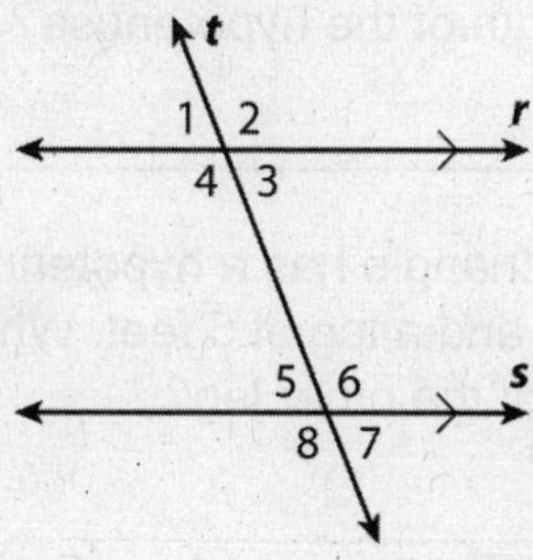

A $\angle 2$ B $\angle 3$
C $\angle 4$

2. Two angles of a triangle measure 45° and 90°. What is the third angle measure?

A 30° B 45°
C 90°

3. Which length correctly replaces the question mark in the proportion below?

$$\frac{3}{?} = \frac{h}{4}$$

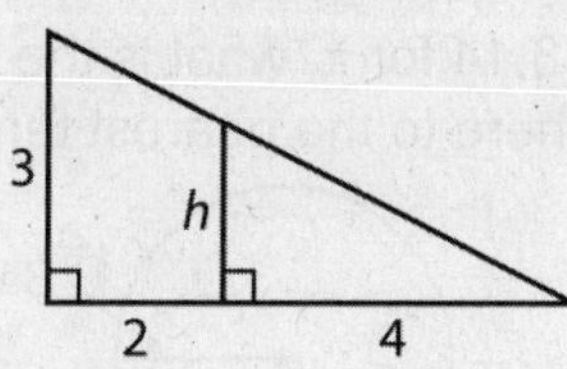

A 2 B 4
C 6

Use the triangle for 4–5.

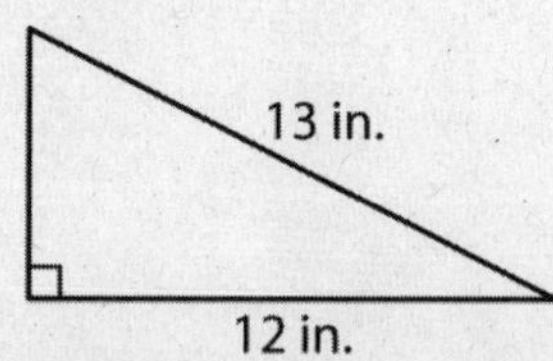

4. Which equation finds the missing length?

A $x^2 + (13)^2 = (12)^2$

B $x^2 + (12)^2 = (13)^2$

C $(13)^2 + (12)^2 = x^2$

5. What is the missing length?

A 4 in. B 5 in.
C 25 in.

6. Which side lengths form a right triangle?

A 1, 2, 3 B 3, 4, 5
C 5, 6, 7

7. Using the distance formula $d = \sqrt{(x_2 - x_1)^2 + (y_2 - y_1)^2}$, what is the distance between point B and point C?

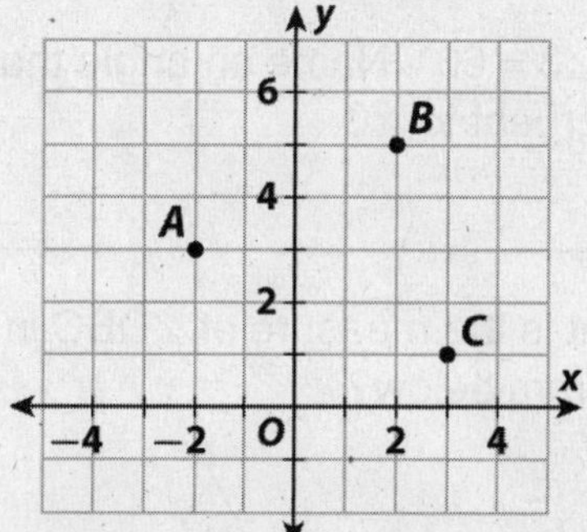

A 2.1 units B 4.1 units
C 8.6 units

8. Using the formula $V = \pi r^2 h$, what is the volume of the cylinder below?

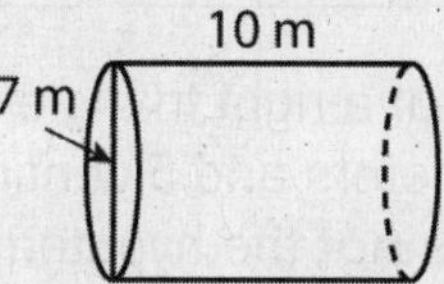

A $70.1\pi \text{ m}^3$ B $122.5\pi \text{ m}^3$
C $490\pi \text{ m}^3$

9. A cone is 3 inches high and has a base with an area of 7 square inches. What is the volume of the cone?

A 7 in^3 B 9 in^3
C 21 in^3

10. Using the formula $V = \frac{4}{3}\pi r^3$, what is the volume of a ball with a radius of 3 units?

A 4π cubic units
B 12π cubic units
C 36π cubic units

Name ______________________ Date ______________ Class ______________

UNIT 5

Measurement Geometry

11. In the figure below, name one pair of congruent angles.

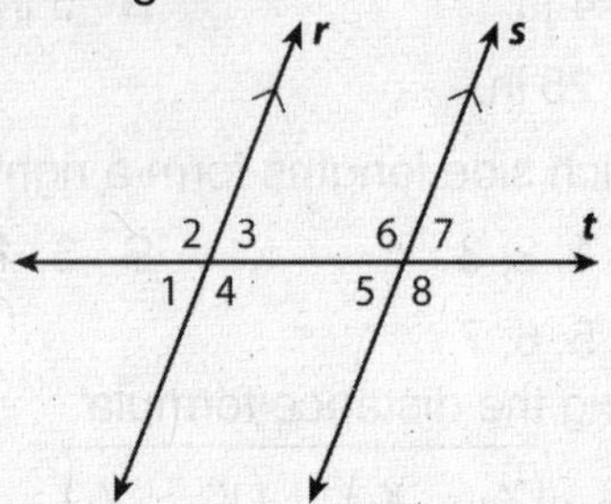

____

12. Let $\angle 3 = 60°$. Name an angle that is **not** congruent to $\angle 3$.

____

13. What is the measure of $\angle DBC$ in the diagram below?

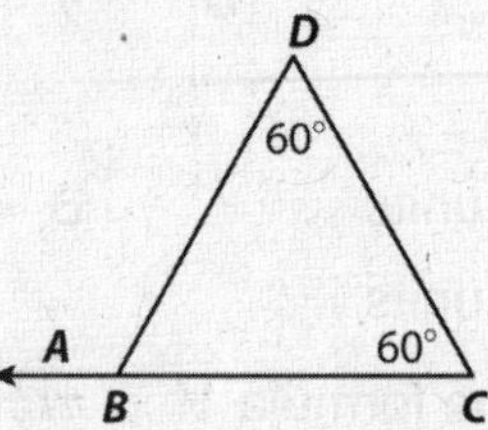

____

14. Two sides of a right triangle have lengths of 2 centimeters and 5 centimeters. The third side is **not** the hypotenuse. How long is the third side?

____

15. A fence is 10 feet tall. A stick leans against the fence as shown. What is the length of the stick?

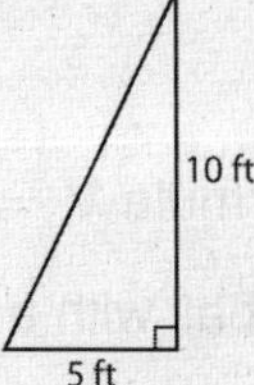

____

16. A right triangle has legs that measure 1 centimeter and 3 centimeters. What is the length of the hypotenuse?

____

17. A right triangle has a hypotenuse of 10 feet and a leg of 6 feet. What is the length of the other leg?

____

18. A cylinder has a height of 4 inches and a base with an area of 113 square inches. What is its volume?

____

19. What is the volume of a cone that has a height of 10 feet and a base with an area of 9 square feet?

____

20. Using 3.14 for π, what is the volume of the sphere to the nearest tenth?

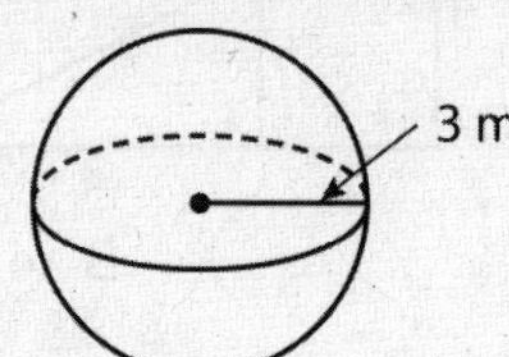

____

Name ______________________ Date ______________ Class______________

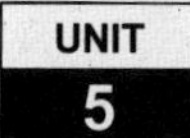

Measurement Geometry

Performance Task

Answer the questions. Round all answers to the nearest tenth. Use 3.14 for π.

1. Kevin is making a set of candles to give as a gift. The first candle is a triangular prism with a height of 17 centimeters.

   a. The base is a triangle with two angles measuring 90° and 65°. What is the measure of the third angle?

   ____

   b. The base has legs measuring 11 centimeters and 12 centimeters. What is the length of its hypotenuse?

   ____

   c. Kevin makes a second candle shaped like a triangular prism, with the same height as the first candle. The base is a triangle similar to the base of the first candle, except with the shorter leg 2 centimeters longer than the shorter leg of the first candle. What are the side lengths of the base of the second candle?

   ____

2. Next, Kevin makes a cylinder-shaped candle. He uses a metal can as a mold. The can has a radius of 6 centimeters and a height of 18 centimeters. How much wax is needed to fill the metal can?

   ____

3. Kevin then makes several cone-shaped candles. He uses a cone mold that has a height of 15 centimeters and a diameter of 10 centimeters. How much wax is needed to make 3 cone-shaped candles?

   ____

4. Lastly, Kevin makes a candle in the shape of a sphere. He uses two bowls as molds, filling them with wax, letting them dry, and then gluing the hemispheres together to make one sphere. Each bowl has a diameter of 16 centimeters. How much wax is needed to make one spherical candle?

   ____

Name ______________________ Date ______________ Class ______________

UNIT 6

Statistics

Unit Test: A

1. Which scatter plot could have a trend line whose equation is $y = -x + 8$?

A
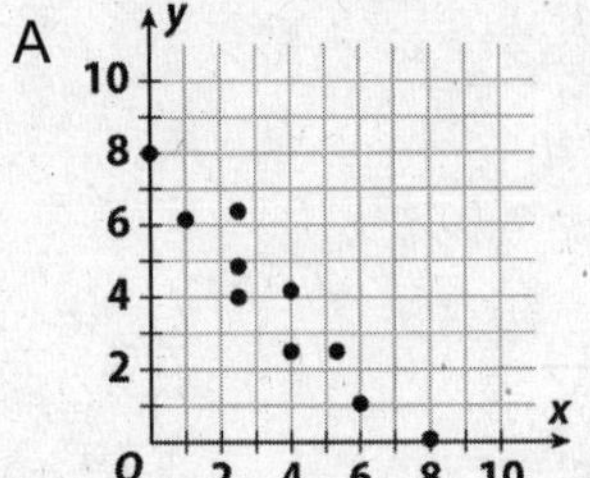

C
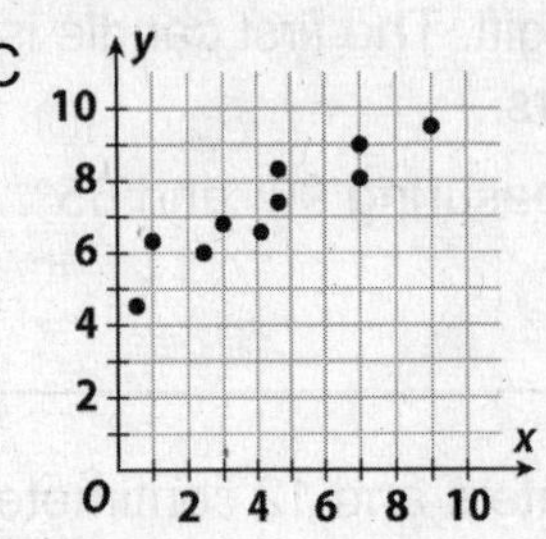

B
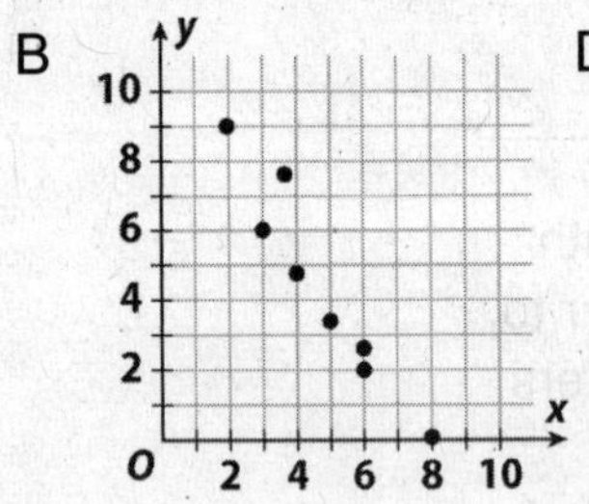

D
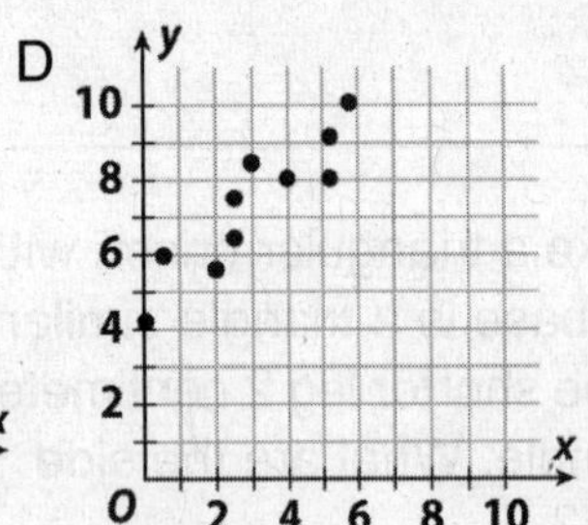

2. Which of the following is **not** shown on the scatter plot below?

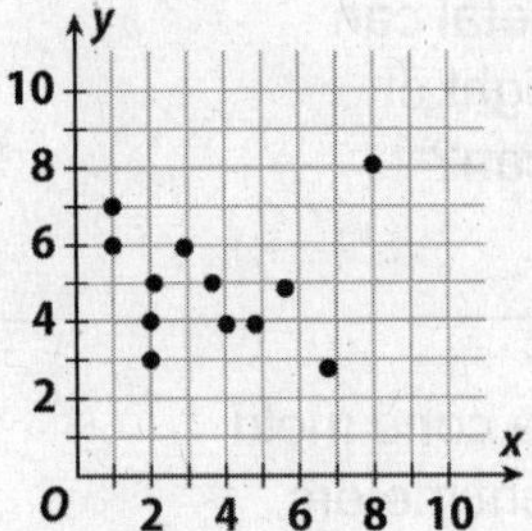

A a cluster

B negative association

C positive association

D an outlier

3. For the data shown in the scatter plot below, which point is an outlier?

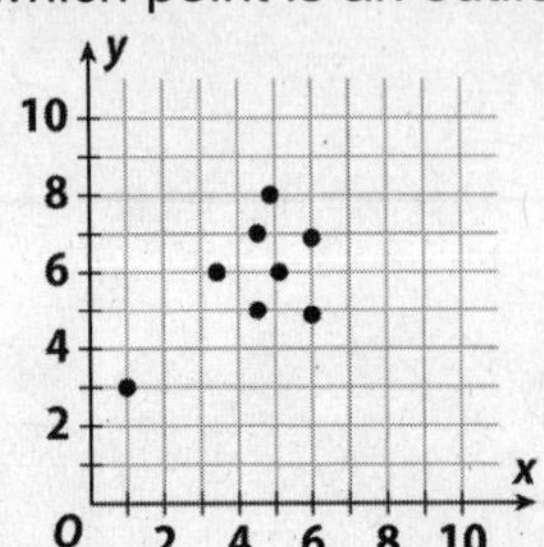

A (1, 3) C (5, 8)

B (6, 5) D (8, 6)

4. Marisol graphed a scatter plot of the number of hours she rode her bicycle (x) and the distance traveled (y). She drew the trend line and calculated its equation to be $y = 10x + 4$.

What is the predicted distance Marisol rode her bicycle if she rode for 2.5 hours?

A 20 C 29

B 25 D 30

Use the table for 5–7.

An online shopping service collects data on their customers. One set of information the service collects is whether customers live in rural or urban areas and whether they pay by credit card or debit card. The results for 100 customers are shown on the table below.

	urban	rural	total
credit card	65	13	78
debit card	4	18	22
Total	69	31	100

5. What is the joint relative frequency of customers from a rural area who pay by debit card?

A 13% C 31%

B 18% D 22%

6. What is the marginal relative frequency of rural customers?

A 13% C 31%

B 18% D 69%

7. What is the conditional relative frequency of customers from a rural area who use debit cards?

A 4% C 22%

B 6% D 58%

Name ______________________ Date ______________ Class ______________

UNIT 6

Statistics

Use the table for 8–11.

A restaurant kept track of lunches and dinners served on two weekend days. The results are shown on this two-way relative frequency table.

Day	Lunches	Dinners	Total
Saturday	42	58	100
Sunday	36	14	50
Total	?	72	150

8. How many lunches did the restaurant serve over the weekend? ______

9. Show each set of meals a percent of the total. Round to the nearest percent. Use the table below.

Day	Lunches	Dinners	Total
Saturday	%	%	%
Sunday	%	%	%
Total	%	%	%

10. What is the joint relative frequency of Sunday lunches? ______

11. What is the marginal relative frequency of dinners on the weekend? ______

Use the table for 12–16.

Time on Internet	30	60	90	60	20	80
Time on Phone	60	30	30	40	80	20

The table shows the amount of time six students in Mr. Havershaw's class spend on the Internet and on the phone each night.

12. Make a scatter plot of the data and draw a trend line.

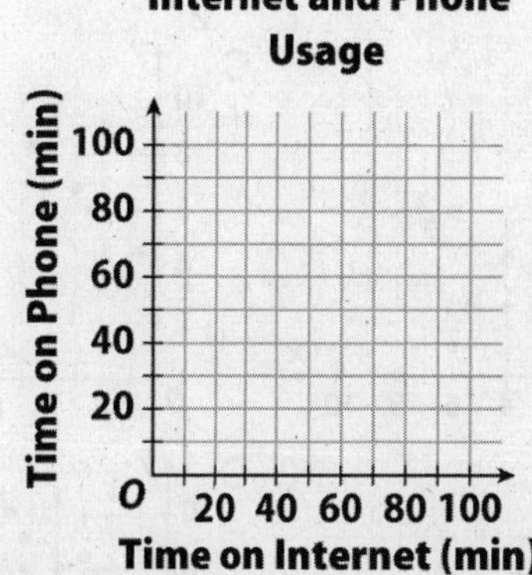

13. Write an equation for the trend line.

____

14. What type of association does the trend line show?

____

15. Predict the amount of time a student will use the Internet if she uses the phone for 45 minutes.

____

16. Are there any limitations to using the linear model to predict the amount of time spent on the Internet and the phone? Explain.

____

____

Name ______________________ Date ______________ Class ______________

UNIT 6

Statistics

Unit Test: B

1. Which scatter plot could have a trend line whose equation is $y = \frac{1}{2}x + 5$?

A
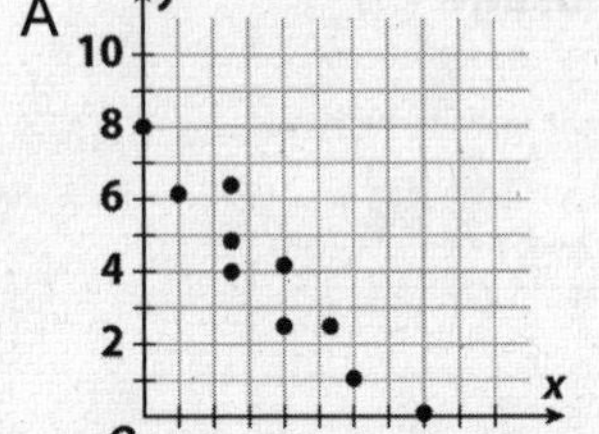

C
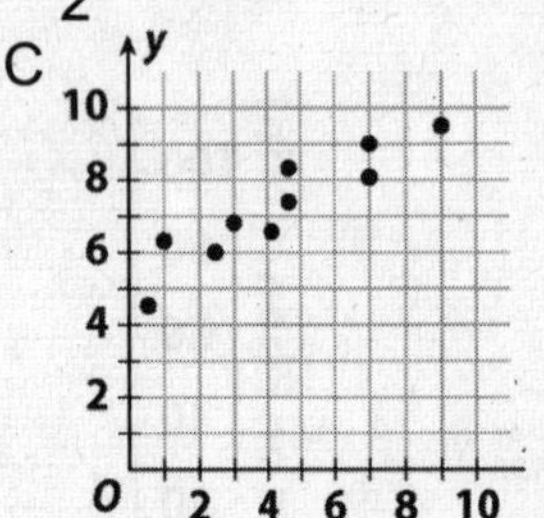

B
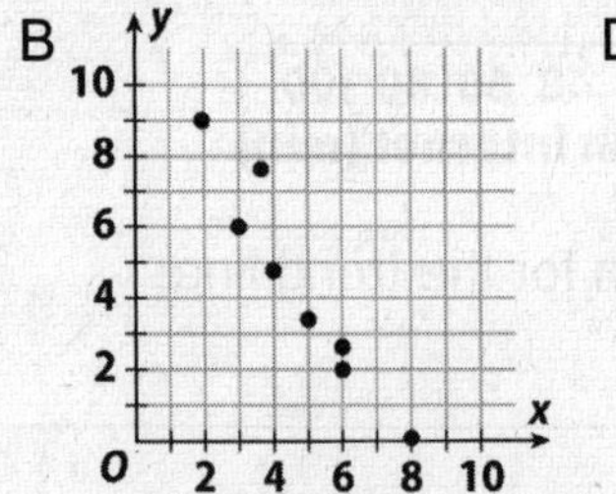

D
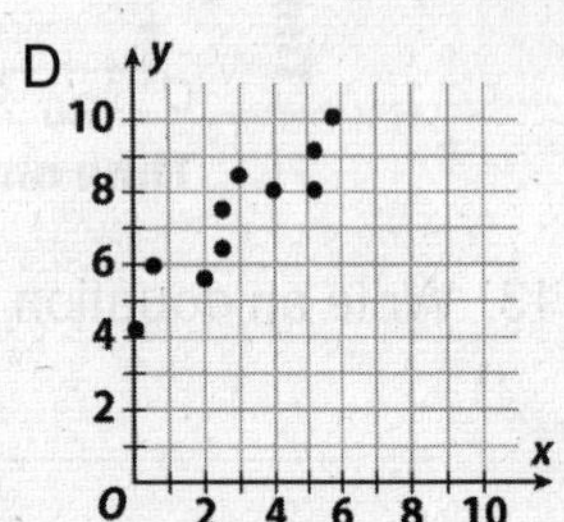

2. Which of the following is **not** shown on the scatter plot below?

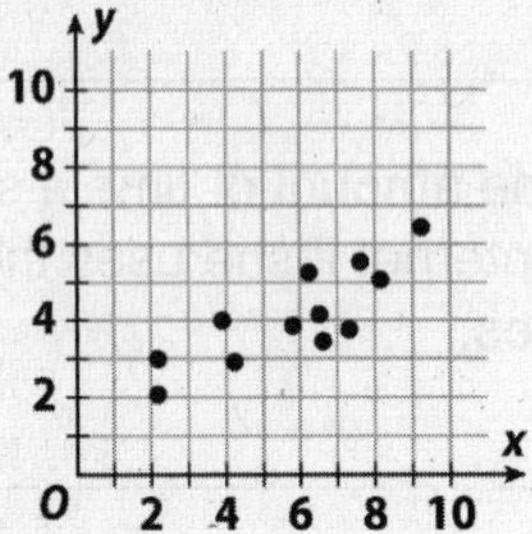

A a cluster
B a linear relationship
C positive association
D an outlier

3. For the data shown in the scatter plot below, which point is an outlier?

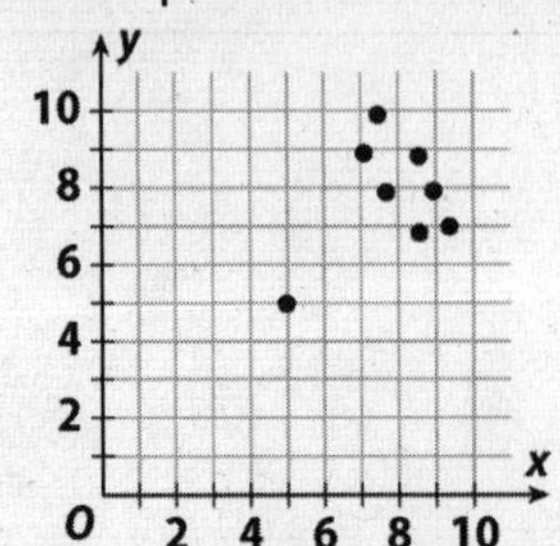

A (5, 9) C (5, 5)
B (9, 6) D (9, 8)

4. Oskar graphed a scatter plot of the number of hours he drove his car (x) and the distance traveled (y). He drew the trend line and calculated its equation to be $y = 50x + 2$.

What is the predicted distance Oskar drove if he drove for 3.5 hours?

A 175 C 180
B 177 D 201

Use the table for 5–7.

A sporting goods store collects data on their customers. One set of information the store collects is whether customers are male or female and whether they carry or ship their purchases. The results for 150 customers are shown on the table below.

	Male	Female	Total
Carry	47	51	98
Ship	22	30	52
Total	69	81	150

5. What is the joint relative frequency of female customers who ship their purchases?

A 15% C 35%
B 20% D 51%

6. What is the marginal relative frequency of customers who carry their purchases?

A 31% C 65%
B 34% D 98%

7. What is the conditional relative frequency of female customers who ship their purchases?

A 20% C 37%
B 30% D 63%

Name ______________________ Date ______________ Class______________

UNIT 6

Statistics

Use the table for 8–11.

A junior high school kept track of student absences from two classes for two semesters. The results are shown in this two-way relative frequency table.

Class	Semester 1	Semester 2	Total
101	18	?	45
102	26	27	53
Total	44	54	98

8. How many student absences should be recorded for Class 101 in Semester 2?

____

9. Show each set of absences as a percent of the total. Round to the nearest percent. Use the table below.

Class	Semester 1	Semester 2	Total
101	%	%	%
102	%	%	%
Total	%	%	%

10. What is the joint relative frequency of absences from Class 102 in Semester 1?

____

11. What is the marginal relative frequency of absences in Semester 2?

____

Use the table for 12–15.

Circumference (ft)	15	20	35	40	45	20
Height (ft)	15	20	17	22	28	12

The table shows the circumference and height of six trees in a forest.

12. Make a scatter plot and draw a trend line.

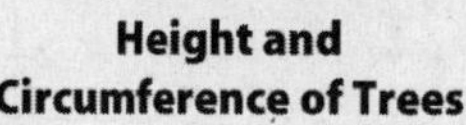

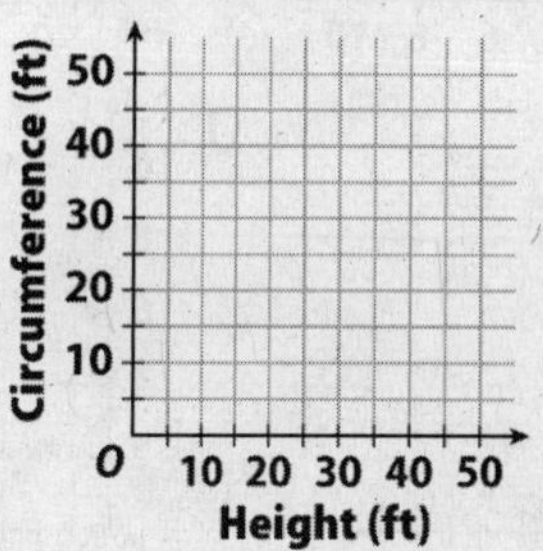

13. Write an equation for the trend line.

____

14. What type of association does the trend line show?

____

15. Predict the height of a tree that has a circumference of 40 feet.

____

Name ______________________ Date ______________ Class ______________

UNIT 6

Statistics

Unit Test: C

1. Which scatter plot could have a trend line whose equation is $y = -\frac{3}{2}x + 12$?

A
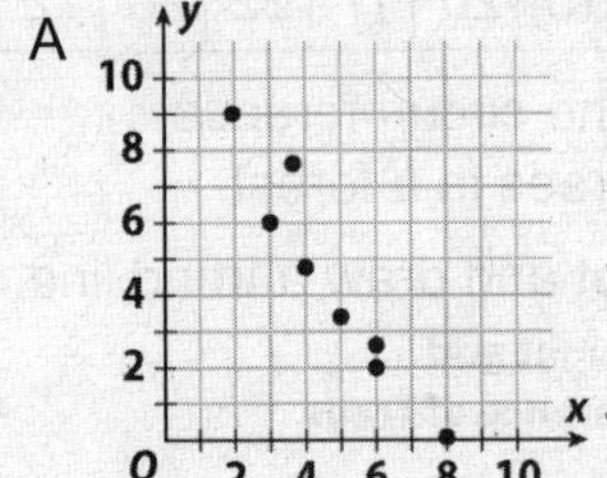

C
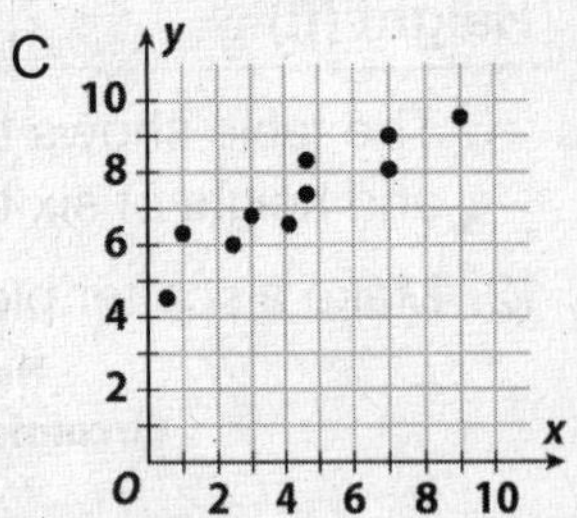

B
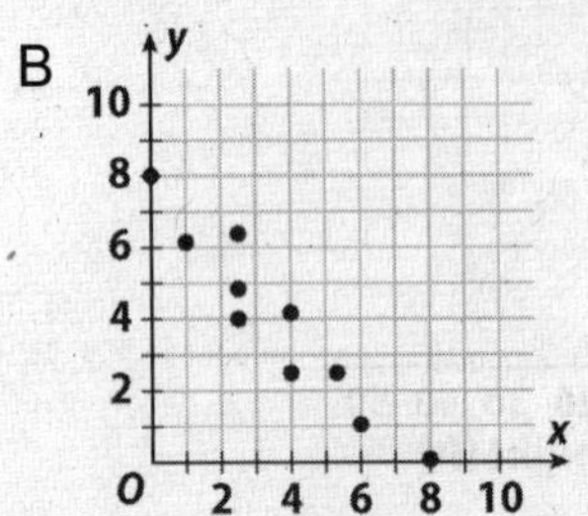

D
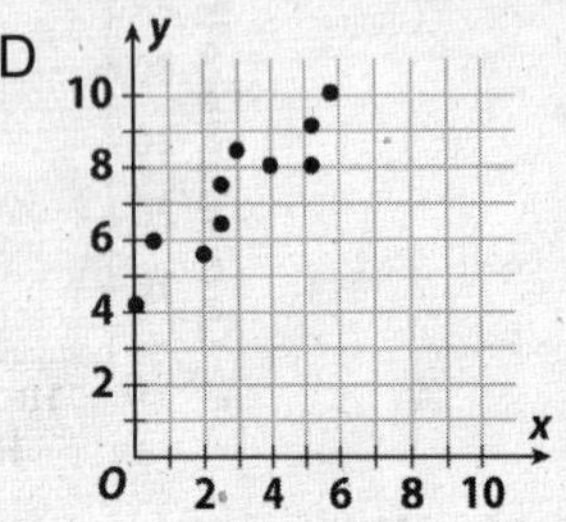

2. Which of the following is shown on the scatter plot below?

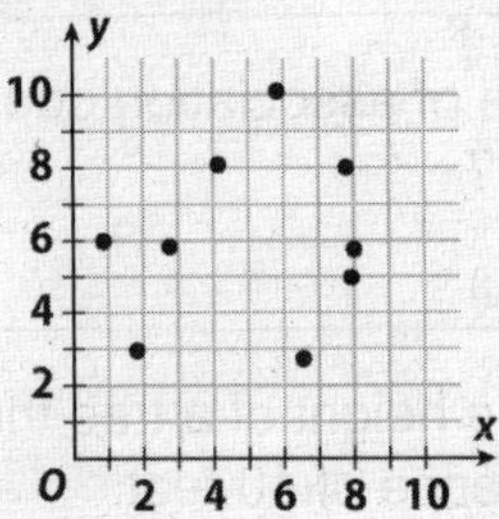

A a cluster

B negative association

C no association

D an outlier

3. For the data shown in the scatter plot below, which point is an outlier?

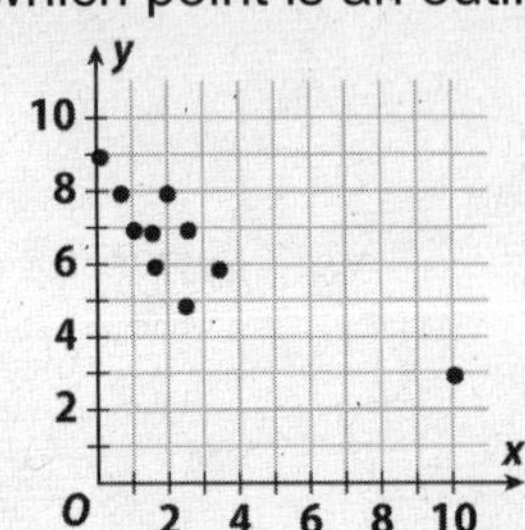

A (0, 9)
C (3, 8)

B (6, 10)
D (10, 3)

4. Fernando graphed a scatter plot of the number of hours he drove his car (x) and the distance traveled (y). He drew the trend line and calculated its equation to be $y = 39.4x + 12.2$.

What is the predicted distance Fernando will drive if he drives for 1.25 hours?

A 49.25
C 61.45

B 51.60
D 70.21

Use the table for 5–7.

A busline collects data on their passengers. One set of information the bus company collects is whether passengers are children, adults, or seniors and whether they take daytime or evening buses. The results for 250 passengers are shown on the table below.

	Daytime	Evening	Total
Children	34	7	41
Adults	76	61	137
Seniors	53	19	72
Total	163	87	250

5. What is the joint relative frequency of adult passengers who take the bus at night?

A 8%
C 45%

B 24%
D 71%

6. What is the marginal relative frequency of passengers who take daytime buses?

A 30%
C 47%

B 33%
D 65%

7. What is the conditional relative frequency of senior passengers who ride the evening buses?

A 8%
C 33%

B 22%
D 29%

Name ______________________ Date ______________ Class______________

UNIT 6 Statistics

Use the table for 8–11.

A fruit stand kept track of the number of peaches, strawberries, and melons sold in July and August. The results are shown in this two-way frequency table.

Fruit	July	August	Total
Peaches	63	62	125
Strawberries	76	59	136
Melons	33	57	89
Total	?	?	350

8. How many pieces of fruit were sold in July? In August? ______________

9. Complete the relatively frequency table below. Round to the nearest tenth of a percent.

Fruit	July	August	Total
Peaches	%	%	%
Strawberries	%	%	%
Melons	%	%	%
Total	%	%	%

10. What is the marginal relative frequency of the peaches, strawberries, and melons that were sold in August?

____

11. What is the conditional relative frequency of strawberries among the fruit sold in July? ________

Use the table for 12–16.

Temperature (°F)	70	80	85	90	82.5	75
Glasses Sold	40	45	60	80	50	50

The table shows daily high temperatures and iced tea sales at a local cafe.

12. Make a scatter plot of the data and draw a trend line.

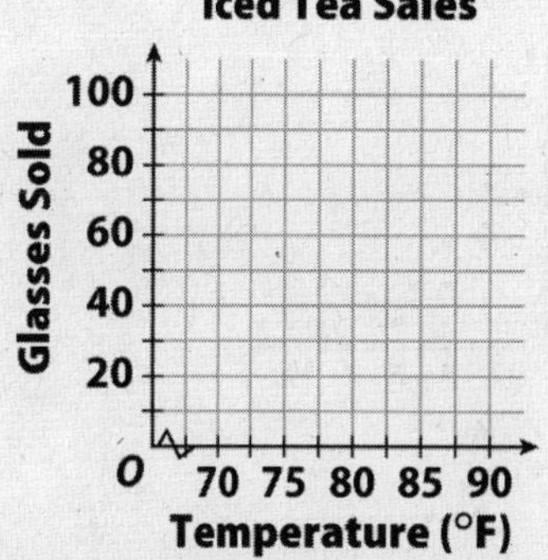

13. Write an equation for the trend line.

____

14. What type of association does the trend line show?

____

15. Predict the sales of iced tea when the outside temperature is 60°F.

____

16. Are there any limitations to using the linear model to predict the sales of iced tea given the outside temperature? Explain.

____

____

____

Name ______________________ Date ______________ Class ______________

UNIT 6

Statistics

Unit Test: D

1. Which scatter plot could have a trend line with the equation below?

$$y = x + 4$$

A
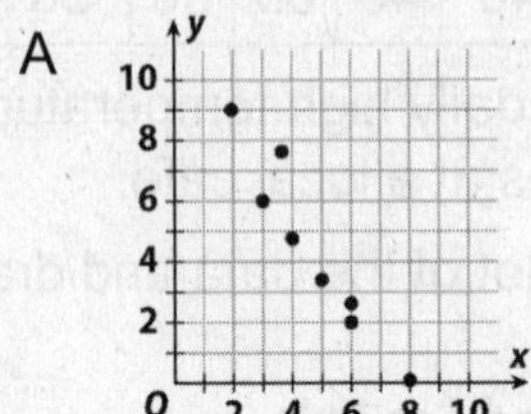

B
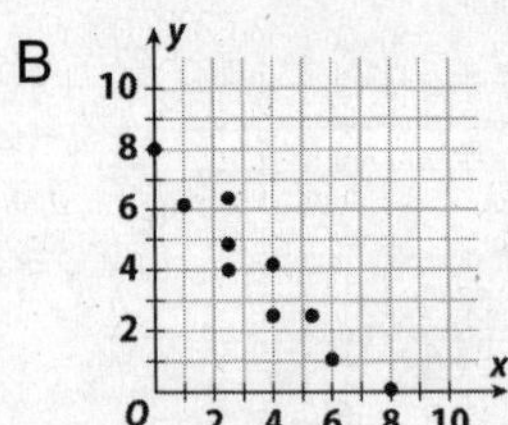

C
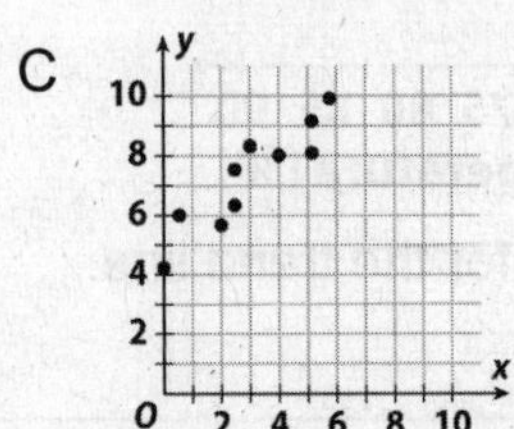

2. Which of the following is **not** shown on the scatter plot below?

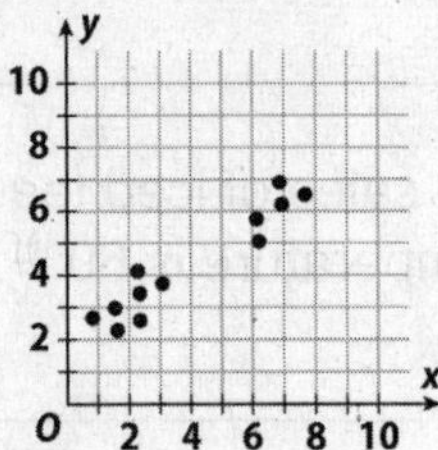

A a cluster

B positive association

C an outlier

3. For the data shown in the scatter plot below, which point is an outlier?

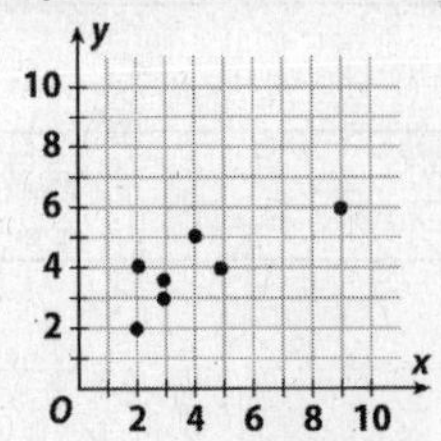

A (2, 2)

B (9, 6)

C (5, 4)

4. Chris found the equation of a trend line. The equation is shown below.

$$y = 3x + 10.$$

If x is 5, what is the predicted value of y?

A 10

B 15

C 25

Use the table for 5–7.

A phone company collects data on their customers. One set of information the company collects is whether customers use cell phones or land lines primarily and their ages. The results for 100 customers are shown on the table below.

	under 50	over 50	total
cell	70	5	75
land line	5	20	25
total	75	25	100

5. What is the joint relative frequency of cell phone customers over 50?

A 5%

B 20%

C 25%

6. What is the marginal relative frequency of customers under 50 who use cell phones?

A 75%

B 80%

C 93%

7. What is the conditional relative frequency of landline customers over 50?

A 20%

B 25%

C 80%

Name ________________________ Date ______________ Class ______________

UNIT 6

Statistics

Use the table for 8–11.

An advertising agency kept track of newspapers delivered to two sides of town in one day. The results are shown in the table.

Newspaper	East	North	Total
New Times	11	9	20
Main St. Journal	13	17	30
Total	24	?	50

8. How many newspapers were delivered on the North side that day? ________

9. Show each number of newspapers as a percent of the total. Use the table below.

Newspaper	East	North	Total
New Times	%	%	%
Main St. Journal	%	%	%
Total	%	%	%

10. What is the joint relative frequency of the Main Street Journal delivered to the North side? (Hint: Use the North side column and the Main Street Journal row.)

____

11. What is the marginal relative frequency of East side deliveries? ________

Use the table for 12–16.

Practice Hours	3	4	5	4	3	2
Goals Scored	2	1	4	3	3	1

The table shows the average number of hours 6 members of a soccer team practiced each week. It also shows the number of goals each player scored during the season.

12. Make a scatter plot of the data and draw a trend line.

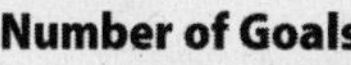

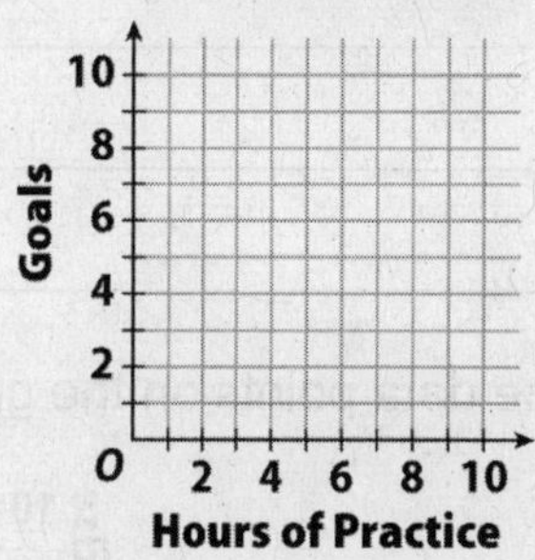

13. Write an equation for the trend line.

____

14. What type of association does the trend line show?

____

15. Another player practiced 10 hours each week. Predict the number of goals she scored.

____

16. Can you always use this linear model to predict the number of goals a player will score based on the number of hours he or she practices, or are there limitations to the model? Explain.

____

____

____

Name ______________________ Date ______________ Class ______________

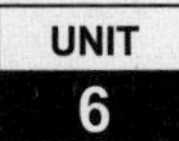

Statistics

Performance Task

Eldridge School has 150 students. A sample of 8 students were surveyed about their study and exercise habits. The results are shown in the table.

Weekly Student Study and Exercise Habits

Hours of Study	4	10	8	0	6	3	5	3
Hours of Exercise	3	0	1	10	4	5	3	6

1. For the students surveyed, what was the average number of hours of study per week? What was the average number of hours exercised per week? Show your work.

____

____

____

____

2. Graph the data points on the grid below. Sketch the trend line.

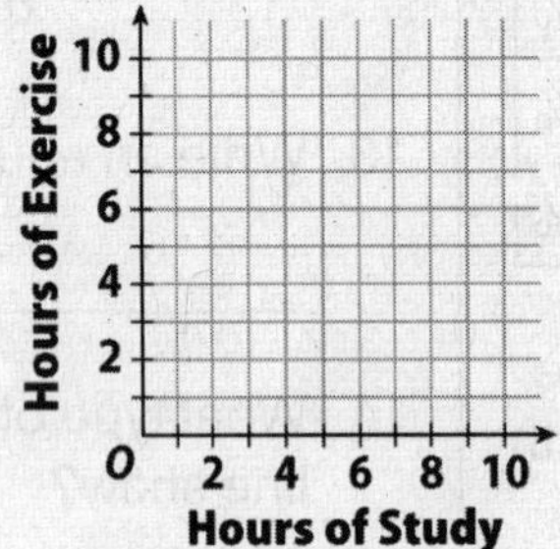

3. What is the equation of the trend line?

____

4. What kind of association is shown between hours of exercise and hours of study?

____

5. Make a conjecture about the total number of hours spent on studying and exercise by the students surveyed.

____

6. Is the sample a good representation of the entire school? Explain.

____

____

Name ______________________ Date ______________ Class ______________

Benchmark Test Modules 1–6

1. The square root of a number is 6. What is the other square root of this number?

   A –6

   B –3

   C 3

   D 36

2. A square acre of land is 4,840 square yards. The length of one side of the square is between which of the following?

   A 14 yd and 48 yd

   B 69 yd and 70 yd

   C 98 yd and 100 yd

   D 124 yd and 139 yd

3. Which of the following numbers is an integer but **not** a whole number?

   A –6.7

   B –5

   C 0

   D 4.2

4. How is the number below written in scientific notation?

   80

   A 8×10^2

   B 80×10^2

   C 80×10^1

   D 8.0×10^1

5. A global study of sea life has recorded 232,620 different species of animals. What is this number of species written in scientific notation?

   A $2,3262 \times 10^5$

   B 2.3262×10^2

   C 2.3262×10^5

   D 2.3262×10^6

6. On average, the people in the United States use about 2.53×10^6 plastic bottles every hour. What is this amount written in standard form?

   A 25.30 bottles

   B 25,330 bottles

   C 253,300 bottles

   D 2,530,000 bottles

7. The square root of a number is between 5 and 6. Which of the following could be the number?

   A 11

   B 21

   C 31

   D 42

8. Which of the following is equivalent to 5^{-3}?

   A –125

   B $-\frac{1}{125}$

   C $\frac{1}{125}$

   D 125

9. Each human hair has a width of about 6.5×10^{-4} meter. What is this width written in standard form?

   A 0.00065 m

   B 0.000065 m

   C 0.0000065 m

   D 0.00000065 m

10. Alex is writing a number in scientific notation. The number is greater than one million and less than ten million. Which number will Alex use as the exponent of 10?

    A 8

    B 7

    C 6

    D 5

Name ______________________ Date ______________ Class ______________

Benchmark Test Modules 1–6

11. Which of the following is **not** true?

A $\sqrt{27}+2<\sqrt{9}+4$

B $3\pi>9$

C $\sqrt{24}+3<\sqrt{10}+6$

D $8-\sqrt{36}<\sqrt{9}+\sqrt{3}$

12. Which number is plotted on the number line below?

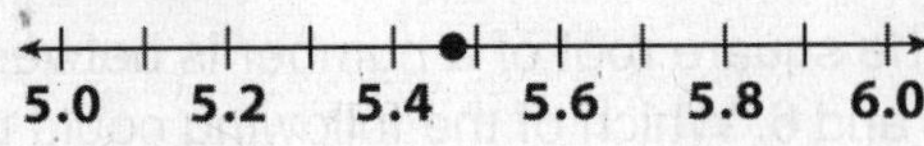

A $\frac{169}{30}$ C 5.14

B $\pi+1.6$ D $\sqrt{20}+1$

13. What is the value of the expression $\frac{(7-5)^2}{[(3+2)^2]^2}$?

A $\frac{4}{625}$ C $\frac{4}{225}$

B $\frac{4}{525}$ D $\frac{4}{125}$

14. Carlos can type 228 words in 4 minutes. Which equation represents the number of words Carlos types per minute?

A $y=\frac{1}{228}x$ C $y=57x$

B $y=\frac{1}{57}x$ D $y=228x$

15. Which of the following lists shows the numbers below in order from **greatest** to **least**?

$0.56,\ 5\times10^{-4},\ 6\times10^{-2},\ 0.006,\ 0.065$

A $0.56,\ 6\times10^{-2},\ 0.065,\ 0.006,\ 5\times10^{-4}$

B $0.56,\ 0.006,\ 0.065,\ 6\times10^{-2},\ 5\times10^{-4}$

C $0.56,\ 6\times10^{-2},\ 0.006,\ 0.065,\ 5\times10^{-4}$

D $0.56,\ 0.065,\ 6\times10^{-2},\ 0.006,\ 5\times10^{-4}$

16. Which equation represents the relationship shown in the table below?

x	−2	0	2	4
y	−13	−7	−1	5

A $y=-x-9$ C $y=-7x$

B $y=3x-7$ D $y=-3x+7$

17. Lexi earns $7 for each pillow she sews. Which table represents this proportional relationship?

A

Pillows	3	6	9
Earnings ($)	10	13	16

B

Pillows	4	6	8
Earnings ($)	28	42	54

C

Pillows	5	7	9
Earnings ($)	35	49	63

D

Pillows	6	8	10
Earnings ($)	42	59	63

18. What is the slope of the line below?

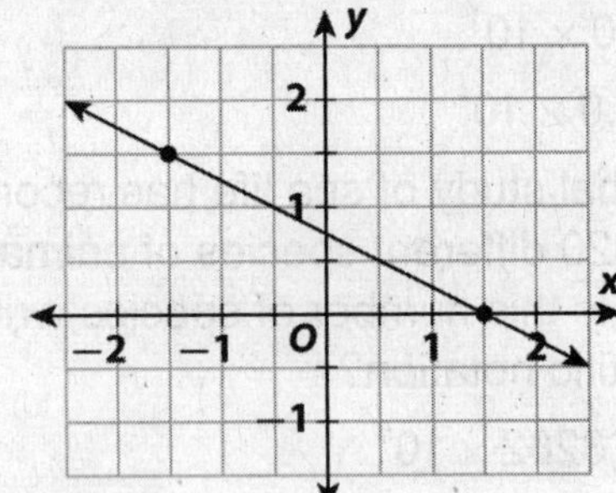

A −2 C $\frac{1}{2}$

B $-\frac{1}{2}$ D 2

Name ______________________ Date ______________ Class ______________

Benchmark Test Modules 1–6

19. Which equation shows a non-proportional relationship?

A $y = 4x + 0$ C $y = 4x + 5$

B $y = -4x$ D $y = \frac{1}{4}x$

20. Which of the following is the equation of the graph shown below?

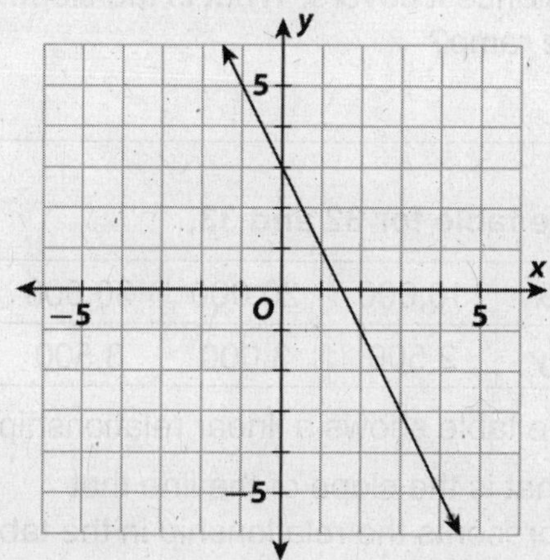

A $y = -2x + 3$

B $y = -2x + 1.5$

C $y = 2x + 3$

D $y = 2x + 1.5$

21. Russia has estimated natural gas reserves of 5.5×10^{13} cubic meters. The United States has estimated reserves of 9.0×10^{12} cubic meters. What are the combined natural gas reserves of the two countries?

A 6.4×10^{12}

B 6.4×10^{13}

C 6.4×10^{14}

D 6.4×10^{25}

22. The table below represents a linear relationship.

x	2	3	4	5
y	4	7	10	13

What is the y-intercept of the line?

A −4 C 2

B −2 D 3

23. Which graph shows a linear relationship?

A

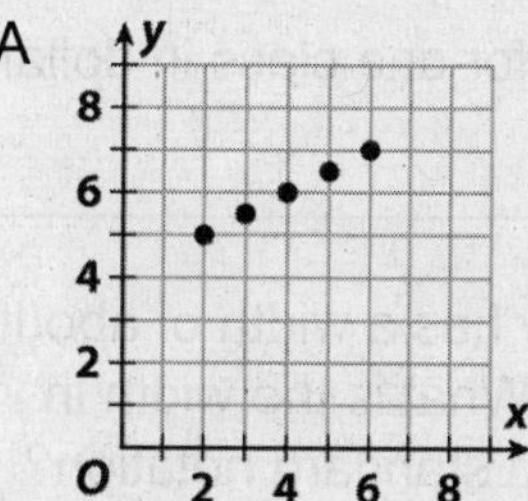

B

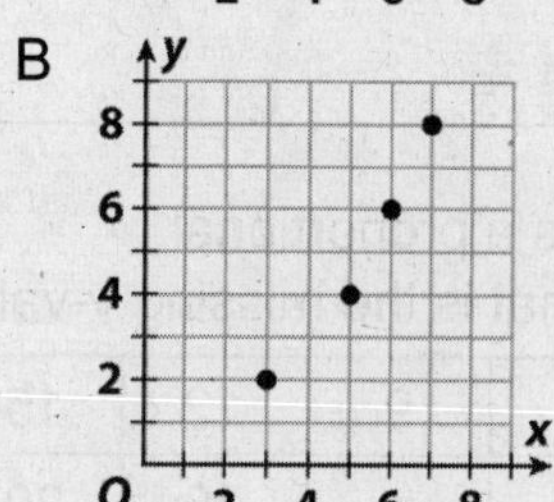

C

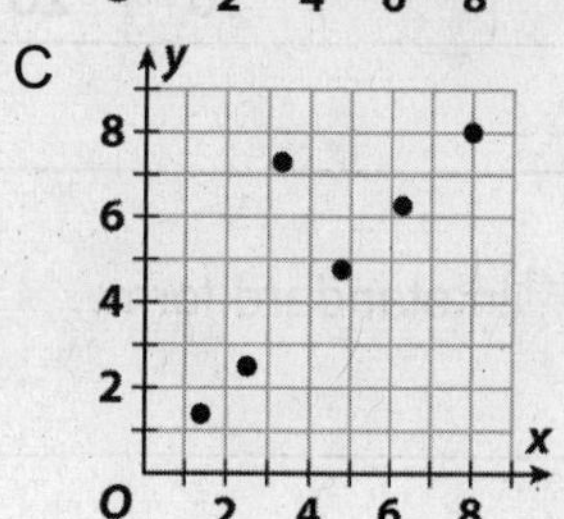

D

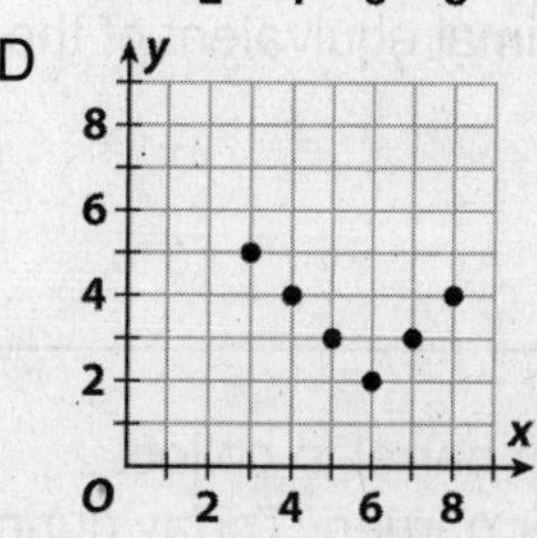

Name ______________________ Date ______________ Class ______________

Benchmark Test Modules 1–6

24. In 7 hours, operators at a call center make 4,732 telemarketing calls. How many calls did the center make per hour?

____

25. An art school charges a materials fee in addition to a fee per class. The equation below represents the total cost *y* of *x* classes.

$$y = 40x + 25$$

What is the fee for one class in dollars?

____

26. A drinking straw has a width of about 5×10^{-3} meter. What is the width in meters written in standard notation?

____

27. The table shows a proportional relationship. What is the missing *y*-value?

x	3	9	12	15
y	4		16	20

____

28. Write 4.67×10^{-1} in standard form.

____

29. What is the decimal equivalent of the fraction $\frac{27}{24}$?

____

30. Gina uses a rain barrel to collect rainwater for her garden. Today during a major storm, Gina began to record the amount of water in the rain barrel. Her data for the first five hours of the storm is shown in the table below.

Hours	2	3	4	5
Gallons	5	6.5	8	9.5

Suppose it continues to rain at the same rate. How many gallons of water will there be in Gina's barrel after 13 hours?

____

31. The entrance ramp to an arena rises 4.5 feet for every 50 feet of horizontal distance it covers. What is the slope of the ramp?

____

Use the table for 32 and 33.

x	10,000	20,000	30,000
y	2,500	3,000	3,500

The table shows a linear relationship.

32. What is the slope of the line that represents the relationship in the table? Write your answer as a decimal.

____

33. What is the *y*-intercept of the line that represents the relationship in the table?

____

34. The graph shows the amount of rainfall in Holcomb during the first six months of the year. During which month did the least amount of rain fall?

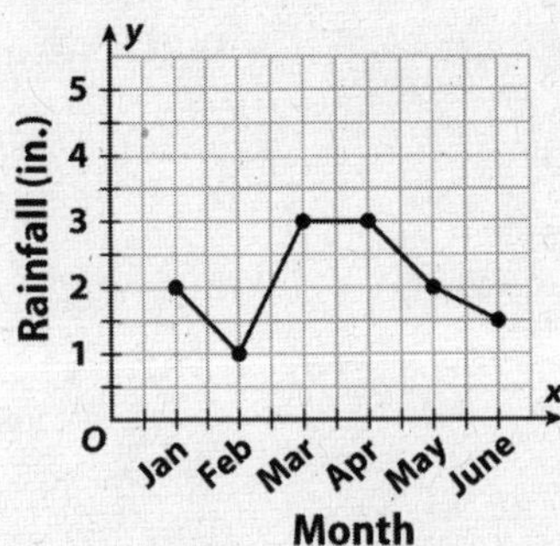

____

Name ______________________ Date ____________ Class____________

Mid-Year Test Modules 1–8

1. What is the value of x in the equation: $2x - 15 = -3x + 5$?

   A 2 C 4
   B 3 D 5

2. Which statement is false?

   A All whole numbers are integers.
   B No real numbers are irrational numbers.
   C All whole numbers are rational numbers.
   D All integers greater than 0 are whole numbers.

3. It costs $12.50 to see a movie at a theater near Jason's house. It costs only $1.95 to rent a DVD from an online service. A DVD player costs $125. To the nearest whole number, how many movies must Jason watch on DVD instead of at the theater before he recovers the cost of the DVD player?

   A 11 C 110
   B 12 D 120

4. Which equation below has no solution?

   A $2(2x + 1) = 4x + 2$
   B $3x + 7 = x$
   C $3x + 6 = x + 2$
   D $5x + 1 = 5x - 3$

5. The square root of a number is 8. What is the other square root of this number?

   A –8 C 4
   B –4 D 64

6. How is the number below written in scientific notation?

   120

   A 1.2×10^1
   B 12×10^1
   C 1.2×10^2
   D 12×10^2

7. Which equation represents the relationship shown in the table below?

x	–2	0	2	4
y	–2	2	6	10

   A $y = -2x$
   B $y = -2x - 2$
   C $y = x + 2$
   D $y = 2x + 2$

8. What is the slope of the line below?

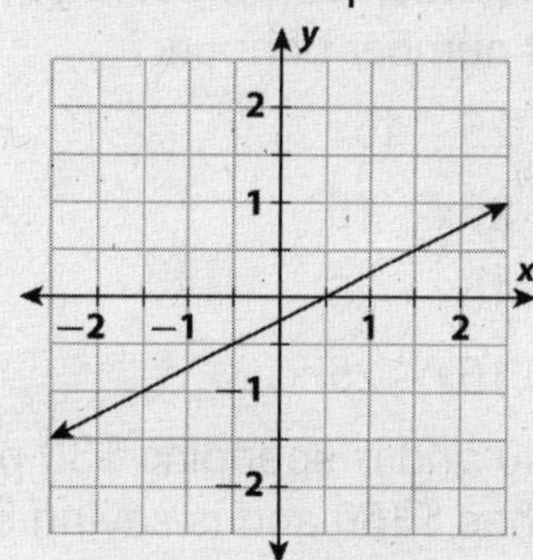

   A –2 C $\frac{1}{2}$
   B $-\frac{1}{2}$ D 2

9. Which equation shows a non-proportional relationship?

   A $y = -2x$
   B $y = \frac{1}{2}x$
   C $y = 2x + 0$
   D $y = 2x + 2$

10. A car and a truck are moving at the same speed. The car drives 2 hours. The truck continues for another half hour at the same speed and goes 20 more miles. What is the speed at which the car and the truck were traveling?

   A 10 mph
   B 20 mph
   C 40 mph
   D 60 mph

Name ______________________ Date ______________ Class ______________

Mid-Year Test Modules 1–8

11. The fees charged by two bicycle shops are shown in the table below.

Bicycle Rentals	Cost
Eastside Bikes	\$10 deposit plus \$20 per hr
Westside Bikes	\$25 deposit plus \$15 per hr

There is a certain number of rental hours at which the costs at the two shops are equal. Which equation below could you use to find that number of hours?

A $10 - 20x = 25 - 15x$

B $10x + 20 = 25x + 15$

C $20x + 10 = 15x + 25$

D $20x - 10 = 15x - 25$

12. Nabor has \$800 and is spending \$30 per week. Rashid has \$150 and is saving \$20 per week. In how many weeks will Nabor and Rashid have the same amount of money?

A 5 weeks

B 6 weeks

C 11 weeks

D 13 weeks

13. What is the value of x in the equation shown below?

$$10\left(\frac{3}{5}x + 4\right) = 10\left(\frac{3}{10}x + 7\right)$$

A 10 C 13

B 12 D 15

14. What is the value of p in the equation shown below?

$7p + 4 = 3p - 12$

A −4 C 2

B −2 D 415

15. Which graph shows a linear relationship?

A
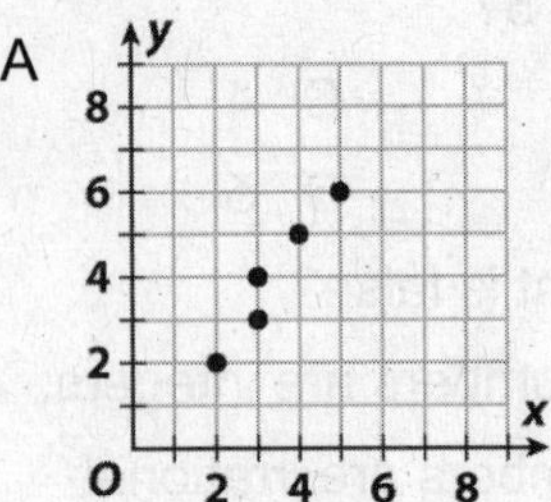

B
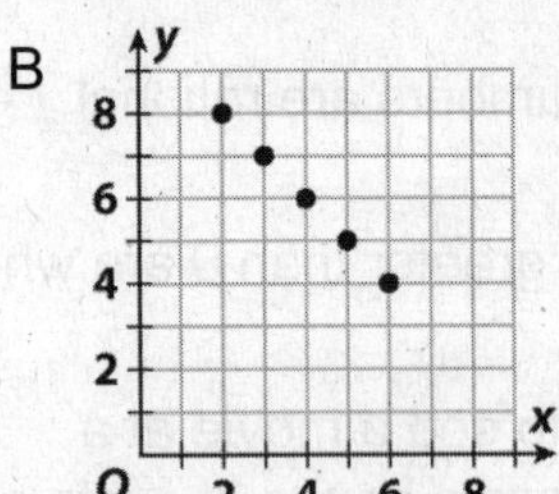

C
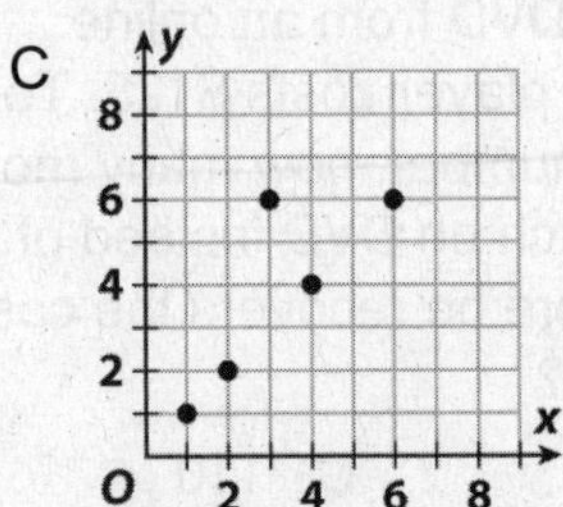

D
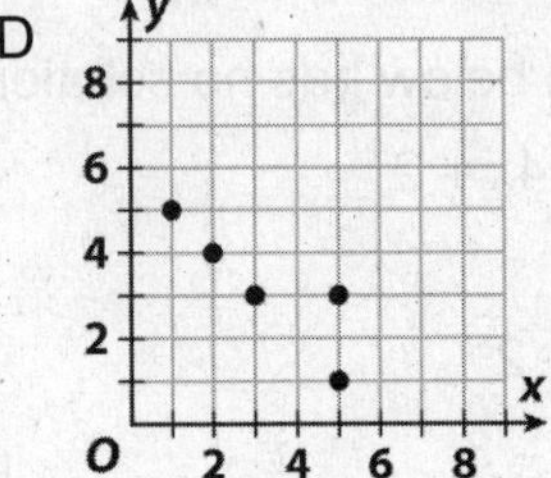

16. What is the solution to the system of equations shown below?

$$\begin{cases} 3x - y = 6 \\ 6x + y = 12 \end{cases}$$

A (−2, 0) C (0, 2)

B (0, −2) D (2, 0)

Name ______________________ Date ______________ Class ______________

Mid-Year Test Modules 1–8

17. Alyssa found two different companies to fix her leaky roof. To compare their rates, she made the table shown below.

Company	Rate
Drip No More	\$50 plus \$80 per hr
Ready Roofer	\$75 plus \$70 per hr

Alyssa estimates she needs 3 hours of repair work. She chooses the company that is less expensive for the 3 hour job. How much will Alyssa spend on the roof repair?

A \$210

B \$240

C \$285

D \$290

18. Sid and Libby are planning to sell pies at a local fair. They spend \$200 to rent a table at the fair. Their costs for ingredients, other supplies, baking, and packaging are \$3.00 per pie. Sid and Libby plan to sell the pies for \$8 each. How many pies must they sell at the fair before they start making a profit?

A 32 pies

B 40 pies

C 64 pies

D 80 pies

19. What is the solution to the equation shown below?

$$3.5(x - 2) = 12 - 0.5x$$

A $x = 1.25$

B $x = 2.5$

C $x = 3.5$

D $x = 4.75$

20. Which number is plotted on the number line below?

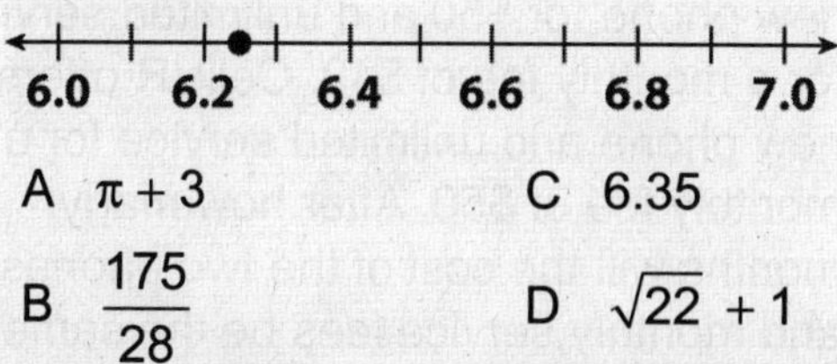

A $\pi + 3$

B $\frac{175}{28}$

C 6.35

D $\sqrt{22} + 1$

21. Which of the following lists shows the numbers below in order from **least** to **greatest**?

$$0.65,\ 6 \times 10^{-4},\ 6 \times 10^{-2},\ 0.065$$

A 6×10^{-4}, 6×10^{-2}, 0.065, 0.65

B 0.65, 0.065, 6×10^{-2}, 6×10^{-4}

C 6×10^{-2}, 6×10^{-4}, 0.065, 0.65

D 6×10^{-4}, 0.065, 6×10^{-2}, 0.65

22. Which expression can you substitute in the indicated equation to solve the system of equations shown below?

$$\begin{cases} x + 2 = -2y \\ 3x - 2y = 10 \end{cases}$$

A $-2y - 2$ for x in $3x - 2y = 10$

B $-2y + 2$ for x in $3x - 2y = 10$

C $2y - 2$ for x in $3x - 2y = 10$

D $2y + 2$ for x in $3x - 2y = 10$

23. Which step could you use to start solving the system of equations shown below?

$$\begin{cases} 2x - 3y = 27 \\ 11x + 6y = 21 \end{cases}$$

A Multiply $2x - 3y = 27$ by 2 and subtract it from $11x + 6y = 21$.

B Multiply $2x - 3y = 27$ by 2 and add to $11x + 6y = 21$.

C Add $2x - 3y = 27$ to $11x + 6y = 21$.

D Divide $11x + 6y = 21$ by 2 and subtract it from $2x - 3y = 27$.

Name ______________________ Date ______________ Class ______________

Mid-Year Test Modules 1–8

24. Rafi is upgrading his cell phone and monthly service plan. Triax Cell offers a new phone for \$50 and unlimited service for a monthly fee of \$40. CellUR offers a new phone and unlimited service for a monthly fee of \$50. After how many months will the cost of the two phones and monthly service fees be the same?

____

25. What is the value of x in this equation?
$6x - 35 = -5x + 9$

____

26. What is the value of the expression shown below written as a fraction in its simplest form?
$$\frac{(9-7)^3}{[(2+1)^2]^2}$$

____

27. For the equation $4(2x - 4) = 8x + k$, what value of k will create an equation with infinitely many solutions?

____

28. What is the solution to the system of linear equations shown in the graph?

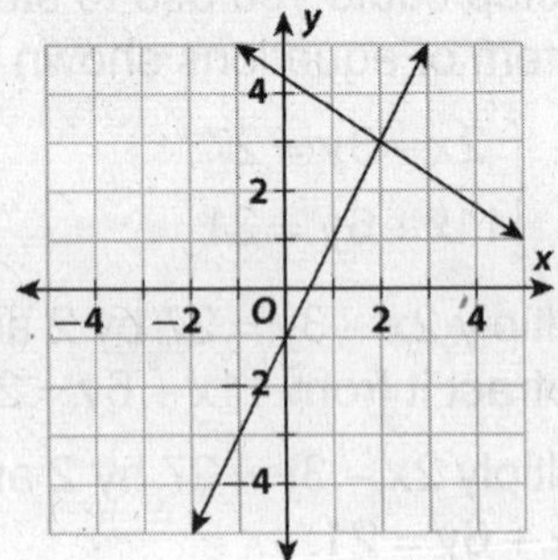

____

29. What is the value of 3^{-3} written as a fraction?

____

30. Curtis has \$600 and is spending \$30 per week. Rachel has \$200 and is saving \$50 per week. In how many weeks will Curtis and Rachel have the same amount of money?

____

31. What is the solution to the system of equations shown below?
$$\begin{cases} 2y - x = 4 \\ 2y + x = 8 \end{cases}$$

____

32. Mike and Mikela left a 15% tip on their bill for dinner together. The amount of the tip was \$10.50. Mike's dinner cost \$40. If x represents the cost of Mikela's dinner, what equation can be written to represent this situation?

____

33. The graph shows the noontime temperatures in Minnox during the first week of April. What is the difference between the least and the greatest temperature during this week?

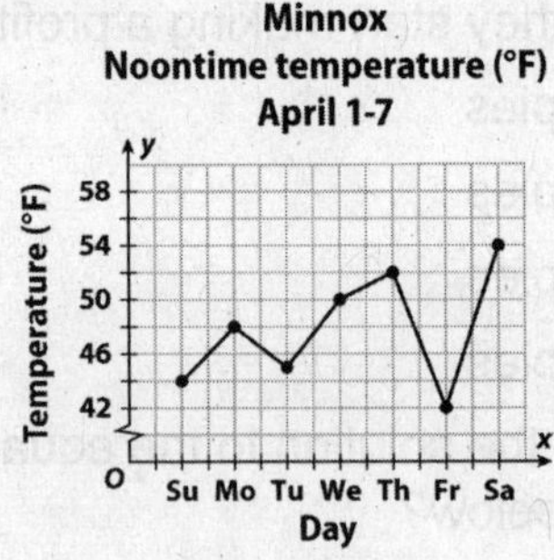

____

34. Saudi Arabia has proven oil reserves of 2.63×10^{11} barrels. Kuwait has proven oil reserves of 9.78×10^{10} barrels. Canada has proven oil reserves of 1.789×10^{11} barrels. What are the combined proven oil reserves of the three countries?

____

Name ______________________ Date ______________ Class______________

Benchmark Test Modules 9–13

1. Which translation moves a triangle 6 units to the right and 3 units down?

   A $(x, y) \rightarrow (x + 6, y - 3)$

   B $(x, y) \rightarrow (x - 6, y + 3)$

   C $(x, y) \rightarrow (x + 3, y + 6)$

   D $(x, y) \rightarrow (x + 3, y - 6)$

2. Which property changes when a figure is reflected across a line?

   A side lengths

   B angle measures

   C perimeter

   D orientation

3. What is the result of the transformation below?

   $$(x, y) \rightarrow (-x, y)$$

   A reflection across the *x*-axis

   B reflection across the *y*-axis

   C 90° rotation clockwise

   D 90° rotation counterclockwise

4. A polygon is translated 7 units to the right and 2 units down. Which translation returns it to its original location?

   A $(x, y) \rightarrow (x - 7, y + 2)$

   B $(x, y) \rightarrow (x - 2, y + 7)$

   C $(x, y) \rightarrow (x + 2, y - 7)$

   D $(x, y) \rightarrow (x + 7, y - 2)$

5. A quadrilateral with vertices at $H(-5, 8)$, $J(0, 10)$, $K(4, 0)$, and $L(-8, -3)$ is reflected across the *y*-axis. Which point does **not** change location?

   A point *H*

   B point *J*

   C point *K*

   D point *L*

Use the figure for 6 and 7.

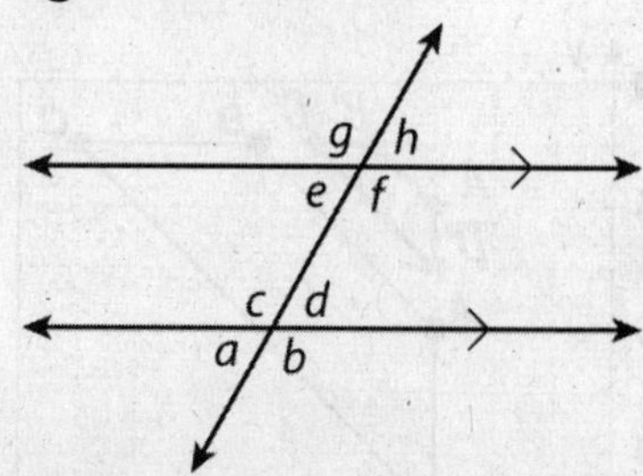

6. Which angle pair is a pair of corresponding angles?

   A $\angle h$ and $\angle c$

   B $\angle b$ and $\angle f$

   C $\angle b$ and $\angle d$

   D $\angle a$ and $\angle f$

7. Which angle pair is a pair of alternate interior angles?

   A $\angle d$ and $\angle h$

   B $\angle c$ and $\angle e$

   C $\angle d$ and $\angle e$

   D $\angle e$ and $\angle f$

8. What is the length of the third side of the triangle below?

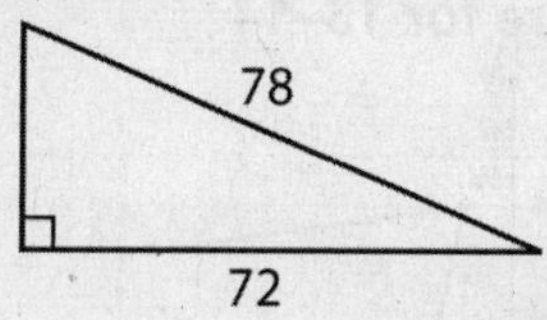

   A 27 C 29

   B 28 D 30

9. A sphere has a diameter of 7.3 centimeters. What is the volume of the sphere? Use 3.14 for π.

   A 203.59 cm^3 C 865.93 cm^3

   B 313.7 cm^3 D 916.14 cm^3

10. Which of the following sets of measurements could be the side lengths of a right triangle?

    A 27, 35, 43

    B 26, 34, 42

    C 25, 33, 41

    D 24, 32, 40

Name ______________________ Date ______________ Class______________

Benchmark Test Modules 9–13

Use the dilation for 11–12.

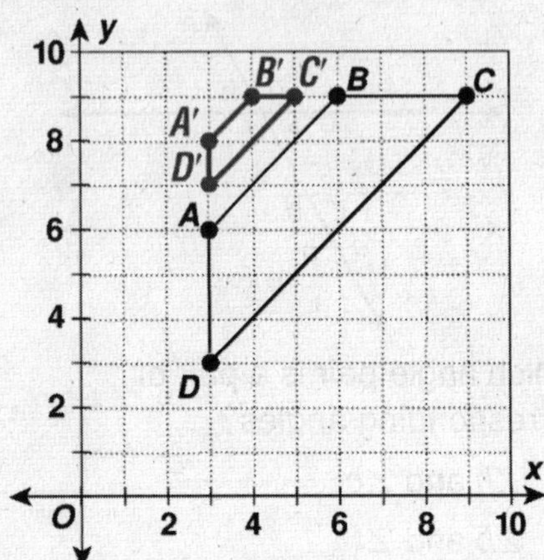

11. What is the scale factor?

A $\frac{1}{3}$ C $\frac{2}{3}$

B $\frac{3}{2}$ D 3

12. What are the coordinates of the center of the dilation?

A (0, 0) C (3, 6)

B (3, 0) D (3, 9)

Use the figure for 13–14.

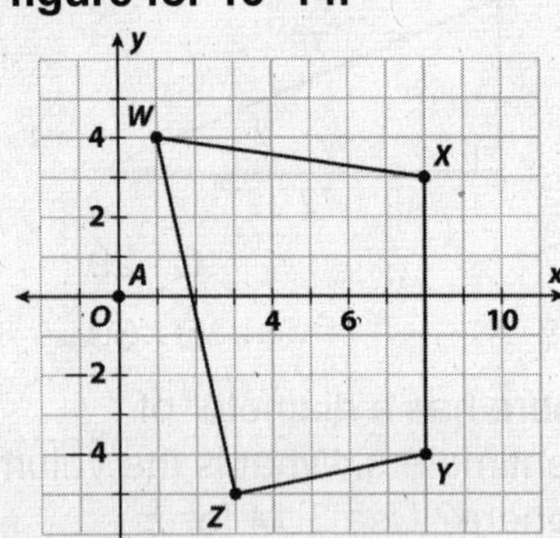

13. Which dilation centered at the origin would create line segment $X'Y'$ with endpoints at (12, 4.5) and (12, –6)?

A $(x, y) \rightarrow (0.5x, 0.5y)$

B $(x, y) \rightarrow (1.5x, 1.5y)$

C $(x, y) \rightarrow (2.5x, 2.5y)$

D $(x, y) \rightarrow (3.5x, 3.5y)$

14. Quadrilateral *WXYZ* is dilated by a scale factor of 3.5 with the origin as its center. What are the coordinates of the vertices of Quadrilateral *W′X′Y′Z′*?

A (3, 12), (24, 9), (24, –12), (9, –15)

B (3.5, 12), (28, 9), (28.5, –12), (10.5, –15)

C (3.5, 14), (28, 10.5), (28, –14), (10.5, –17.5)

D (3, 14), (24, 10.5), (24, –14), (9, –17.5)

15. A cone has a height of 8 inches and a diameter of 6.4 inches. What is the volume of the cone? Use 3.14 for π.

A 78.15 in.^{3}

B 85.74 in.^{3}

C 243.97 in.^{3}

D 342.97 in.^{3}

16. A cylinder in an engine has a height of 6.5 inches and a diameter of 4.8 inches. The engine has six identical cylinders. What is the volume of all the cylinders in the engine? Use 3.14 for π.

A 39.19 in.^{3}

B 96.46 in.^{3}

C 117.56 in.^{3}

D 705.36 in.^{3}

17. A post for a mailbox is 5 feet tall. A brace is attached to the top of the post and the other end of the brace is set into concrete on the ground, 4 feet from the base of the post. What is the length of the brace?

A 4.7 ft C 6.4 ft

B 5.3 ft D 6.7 ft

Name ________________________ Date ______________ Class______________

Benchmark Test Modules 9–13

18. On the grid below, what is the distance between point W and point Z to the nearest tenth?

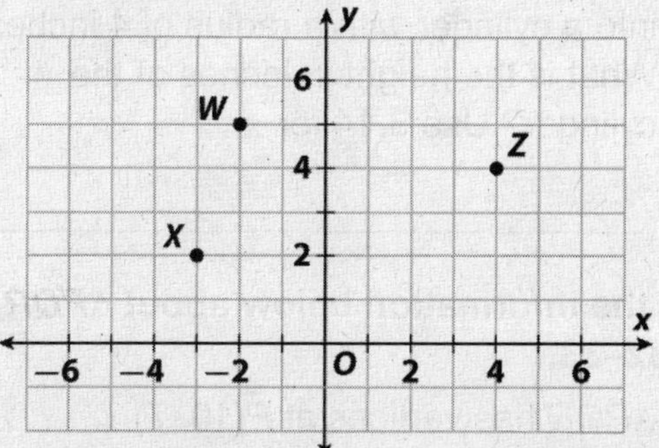

A 7.2 units
C 6 units
B 6.1 units
D 5.8 units

Use the figure for 19–20.
$\triangle ABC$ is similar to $\triangle DEF$.

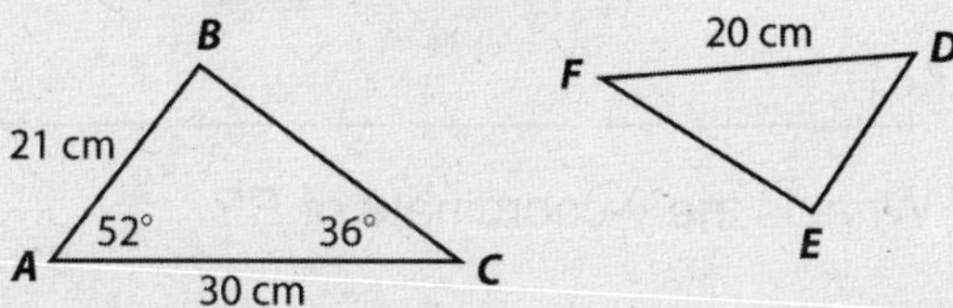

19. What is the measure of $\angle DEF$?

A 88°
C 92°
B 90°
D 128°

20. What is the length of line segment $\overline{DE}$?

A 7 cm
C 21 cm
B 14 cm
D 28 cm

Use the figure for 21–23.

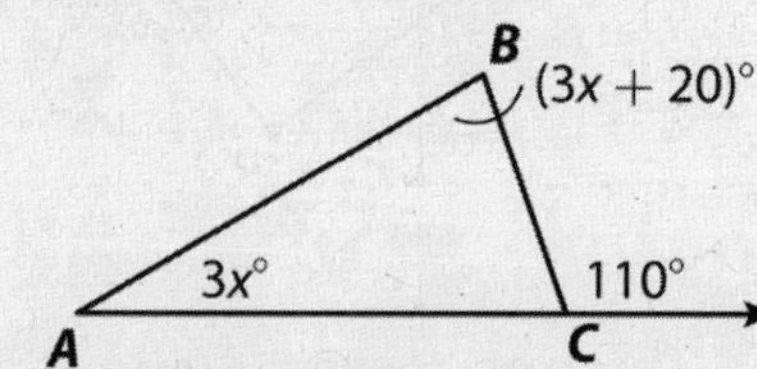

21. What is the measure of $\angle BAC$?

A 15°
C 45°
B 30°
D 70°

22. What is the measure of $\angle ABC$?

A 15°
B 45°
C 65°
D 70°

23. What is the measure of $\angle ACB$?

A 15°
B 45°
C 65°
D 70°

24. What is the value of h in the triangle shown below?

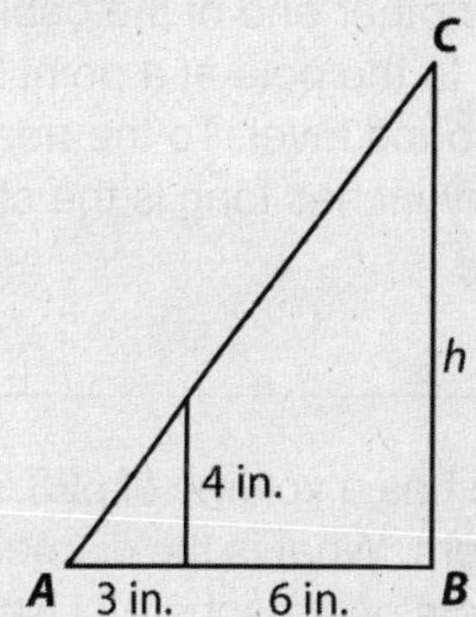

A 9 in.
B 10 in.
C 12 in.
D 15 in.

25. A rectangle has vertices (6, 4), (2, 4), (6, –2), (2, –2). What are the coordinates of the vertices of the image after a dilation with the origin as its center and a scale factor of 2?

A (9, 6), (3, 6), (9, –3), (3, –3)
B (3, 2), (1, 2), (3, –1), (1, –1)
C (12, 8), (4, 8), (12, –4), (4, –4)
D (15, 10), (5, 10), (15, –5), (5, –5)

Name ______________________ Date ______________ Class ______________

Benchmark Test Modules 9–13

26. A paint company packages its paints in cylindrical cans that have a diameter of 6.6 inches and a height of 8 inches. One gallon of liquid takes up 231 cubic inches of space. The manufacturer fills each can with 1 gallon of paint. To the nearest hundredth, how many cubic inches of space is left in the can?

____

27. A telephone pole is installed so that 25 feet of the pole are above ground level. A stabilizing cable is anchored to the ground 44 inches from the base of the pole. The other end of the cable is attached to the pole at a point 20 feet above ground level. To the nearest inch, how many inches long is the stabilizing cable?

____

28. A sphere has a volume of 523.33 cubic centimeters. What is the diameter in centimeters of the sphere? Use 3.14 for π.

____

29. What is the measure in degrees of angle A?

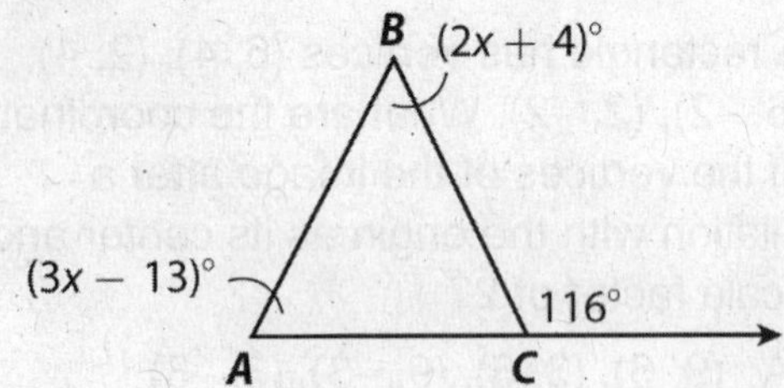

____

30. Two sides of a right triangle have lengths 60 feet and 75 feet. The third side is not the hypotenuse. What is the length in feet of the third side?

____

31. A cone-shaped funnel has a height of 8 inches and a radius of 3 inches. The contents of four such funnels fit exactly into a cylinder with a radius of 4 inches. What is the height in inches of the cylinder? Use 3.14 for π.

____

Use the information below about ΔPQR for 32–33.

ΔPQR has vertices at $P(10, 7)$, $Q(18, 0)$ and $R(7, -7)$.

The translation below is applied to the triangle.

$$(x, y) \rightarrow (x - 5, y + 6)$$

32. What is the x-coordinate of P''?

____

33. What is the y-coordinate of P''?

____

Use the figure for 34–35.

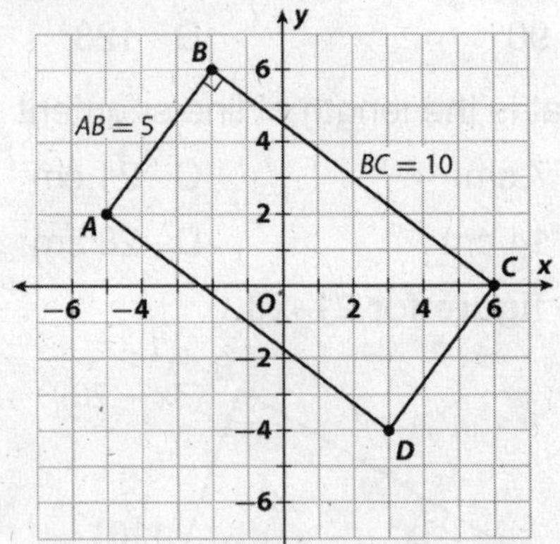

34. Rectangle $ABCD$ is reflected across the x-axis. What is the y-coordinate of D'?

____

35. The rectangle is rotated clockwise about the origin so that the coordinates of A' are (2, 5). How many degrees are in the rotation?

____

Name ______________________ Date ______________ Class ______________

End-of-Year Test

1. Which label or labels could replace "A" in the diagram below?

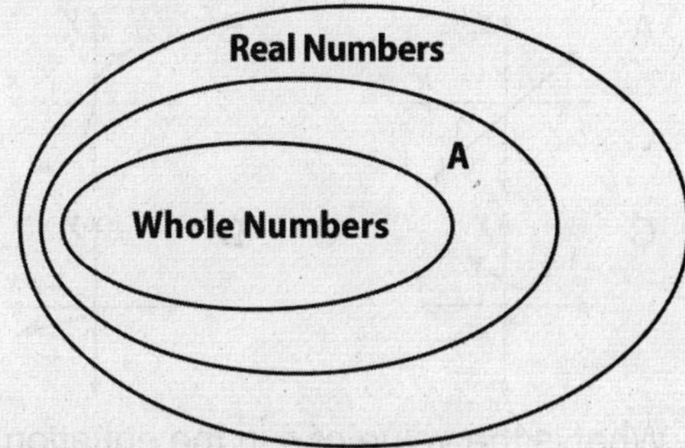

A Rational Numbers only

B Rational Numbers or Integers

C Integers only

D Irrational Numbers

2. Between which two integers does the value of $\sqrt{88}$ lie?

A 1 and 2 C 9 and 10

B 8 and 9 D 87 and 89

3. James wrote the number 8,980,000 in scientific notation. Which number did he write?

A 8.98×10^{-6} C 89.8×10^{5}

B 8.98×10^{-5} D 8.98×10^{6}

4. The gray figure is the image of the black figure after a dilation.

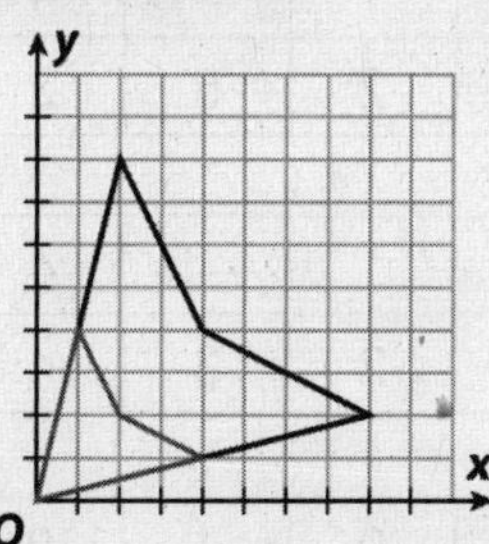

Which represents the dilation?

A $(x, y) \rightarrow \left(\frac{1}{4}x, \frac{1}{4}y\right)$

B $(x, y) \rightarrow \left(\frac{1}{2}x, \frac{1}{2}y\right)$

C $(x, y) \rightarrow (2x, 2y)$

D $(x, y) \rightarrow (4x, 4y)$

5. The lengths in centimeters of four line segments are shown below.

$$3.12,\ 3.24,\ 3\frac{1}{4},\ \sqrt{10}$$

Which list shows the lengths in order from **least** to **greatest**?

A $3.12,\ 3\frac{1}{4},\ 3.24,\ \sqrt{10}$

B $3.12,\ \sqrt{10},\ 3.24,\ 3\frac{1}{4}$

C $\sqrt{10},\ 3.12,\ 3.24,\ 3\frac{1}{4}$

D $3.12,\ 3.24,\ 3\frac{1}{4},\ \sqrt{10}$

6. A figure is dilated by a factor of 2. Which statement about the dimensions of the image is true?

A The perimeter of the original figure is multiplied by 4. The area is doubled.

B The perimeter and area of the original figure are doubled.

C The perimeter of the original figure is multiplied by 4. The area is multiplied by 8.

D The perimeter of the original figure is doubled. The area is multiplied by 4.

7. The points $A(0, 0)$, $B(2, 2)$, $C(3, 3)$ and $D(5, 5)$ all lie on the line $y = x$. Ana calculated the slopes of $\overline{AB}$ and $\overline{CD}$. What can she conclude?

A The slopes are the same.

B The slope of $\overline{AB}$ is greater than the slope of $\overline{CD}$.

C The slope of $\overline{CD}$ is greater than the slope of $\overline{AB}$.

D The slopes of $\overline{AB}$ and $\overline{CD}$ are negative.

Name ______________________ Date ______________ Class ______________

End-of-Year Test

8. What is the slope of the line described by the data in the table below?

x	−1	1	3	5
y	3	8	13	18

A $\frac{2}{5}$ C $\frac{5}{4}$

B $\frac{2}{3}$ D $\frac{5}{2}$

9. Which equation shows the relationship in the table below?

x	5	8	9	11
y	10	16	18	22

A $y = 2x$ C $y = 2x + 1$

B $y = 3x$ D $y = 3x + 3$

10. Which of the following is the equation of the line graphed below?

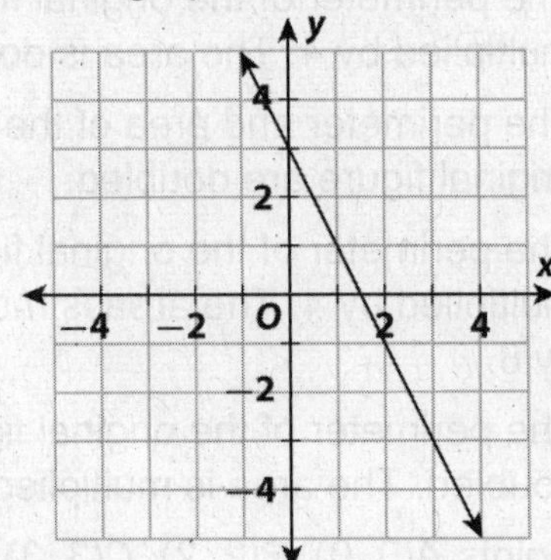

A $y = -2x + 3$ C $y = -3x + 3$

B $y = -2x + 5$ D $y = -3x + 2$

11. Marcus sells homemade pies for \$10.50 a pie. It costs \$1.25 for the ingredients to bake each pie. Marcus bought a new oven for \$800. About how many pies must Marcus bake and sell before he recovers the cost of the oven?

A 68 C 87

B 76 D 640

12. Which of the following graphs shows a linear relationship?

A 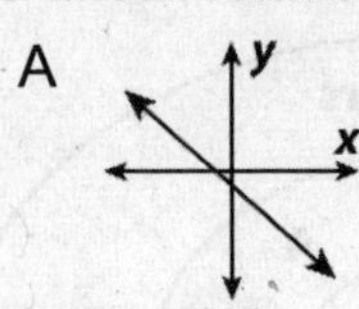

B 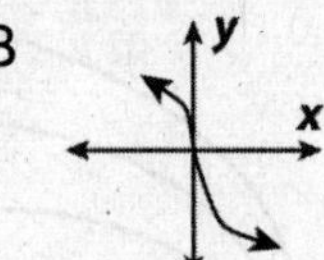

C 

D 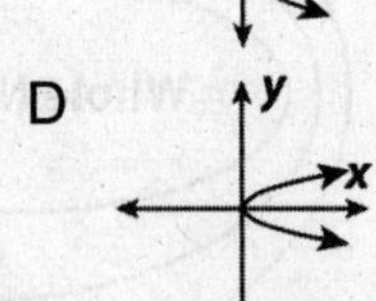

13. What is the value of n in the equation: $8n + 9 = -n + 5$?

A −45

B $-\frac{4}{9}$

C 5

D 45

14. Which of the following equations represents a proportional relationship?

A $y = 3x$ C $y = \frac{3}{x}$

B $y = \frac{1}{2}x + 1$ D $y = x + \frac{1}{2}$

15. Which of the following tables represents a function?

A

x	1	1	4	5
y	2	5	2	6

B

x	1	−1	4	5
y	2	3	4	−3

C

x	0	1	2	2
y	2	3	3	4

D

x	0	1	2	1
y	−1	0	1	3

Name ____________________ Date __________ Class __________

End-of-Year Test

16. Kenneth graphed the triangle *A'B'C'* by dilating triangle *ABC*. Which of the following **must** be true?
    A The ratios of corresponding sides of *ABC* and *A'B'C'* are equal.
    B The area of *A'B'C'* is greater than the area of *ABC*.
    C Triangle *ABC* is congruent to triangle *A'B'C'*.
    D Triangle *ABC* is a isosceles triangle.

17. A cell phone company charges $40 for the phone plus a monthly service charge of $25. The equation below describes the cost *y* after *x* months.

    $$y = 25x + 40$$

    Which is true of the relationship between *x* and *y*?
    A It is linear and proportional.
    B It is linear and non-proportional.
    C It is not linear and proportional.
    D It is not linear and non-proportional.

18. A cheetah's speed was timed over a 50-yard distance. The cheetah was clocked running 60 miles per hour. Which equation shows the relationship between the distance, *y*, and time, *x*, the cheetah runs?
    A $y = 50x$ B $y = 60x + 50$
    C $y = 50x + 60$ D $y = 60x$

19. Which expression can you substitute in the indicated equation to solve the system of equations shown below?

    $$\begin{cases} 4x + 3y = 4 \\ 3x + y = -2 \end{cases}$$

    A $-3x - 2$ for y in $4x + 3y = 4$
    B $-3x + 2$ for y in $4x + 3y = 4$
    C $3x - 2$ for y in $4x + 3y = 4$
    D $3x + 2$ for y in $4x + 3y = 4$

20. What is the solution to the system of equations shown below?

    $$\begin{cases} -2x + 5y = -12 \\ 4x + 3y = -2 \end{cases}$$

    A (−2, 1) C (−1, −2)
    B (−1, 2) D (1, −2)

21. Ryan drew a cylinder and a cone with identical bases and heights. Which of the following is true?
    A The volumes are the same.
    B The volume of the cylinder is three times the volume of the cone.
    C The volume of the cone is three times the volume of the cylinder.
    D The volume of the cylinder is four-thirds the volume of the cone.

22. How can the diagram below be used to explain the Pythagorean theorem?

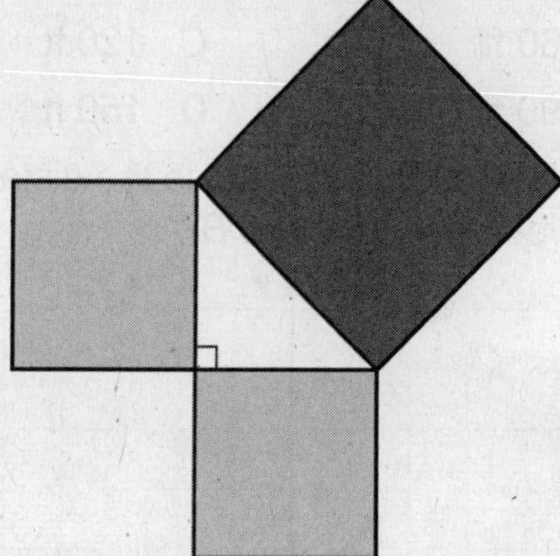

    A The area of the black square is equal to the sum of the areas of the gray squares.
    B The sum of the areas of the gray squares is less than the area of the black square.
    C The perimeter of the triangle is equal to one-fourth of the total perimeter of the three squares.
    D The area of the black square is equal to the area of the triangle.

Name ______________________ Date ______________ Class______________

End-of-Year Test

23. A sphere has a radius of 6 centimeters. What is the volume of the sphere?

   A 72π cm^3 C 200π cm^3

   B 144π cm^3 D 288π cm^3

24. The figure shows two parallel lines intersected by a transversal. What is the measure of $\angle CGH$?

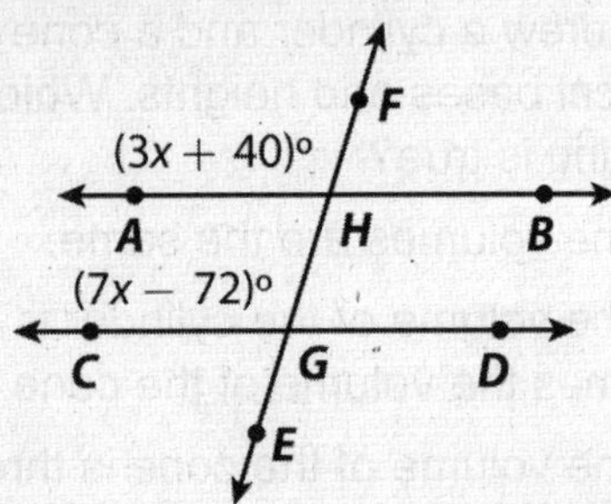

   A 28° C 124°

   B 62° D 151°

25. A diagonal shortcut across a rectangular lot is 130 feet long. The lot is 50 feet long. What is the other dimension of the lot?

   A 60 ft C 120 ft

   B 90 ft D 150 ft

26. On the grid below, what is the distance between points *A* and *B*?

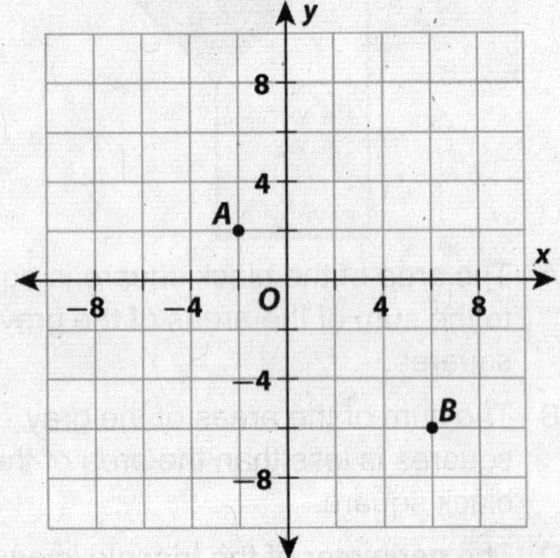

   A 8.2 units C 10.8 units

   B 9.9 units D 11.3 units

27. A tank holds 50 cubic feet of gas to heat a home. The table shows the amount of gas left in the tank after each of five consecutive weeks. What is the rate of change?

Week	1	2	3	4	5
Gas (ft^3)	44	38	32	26	20

   A −12 ft^3 per week

   B −6 ft^3 per week

   C 6 ft^3 per week

   D 12 ft^3 per week

28. The equation below can be used to represent which of the following situations?

$$2x + 5 = 3x$$

   A The price of five boxes of apples is $5.

   B The price of two boxes of apples and a $5 drink equals the price of three boxes of apples.

   C The price of three boxes of apples and a $5 drink equals the price of two boxes of apples.

   D The price of two boxes of apples equals the price of a $5 drink.

29. Alexander rides his bicycle at a speed of 8 miles per hour. Which graph represents this relationship?

A
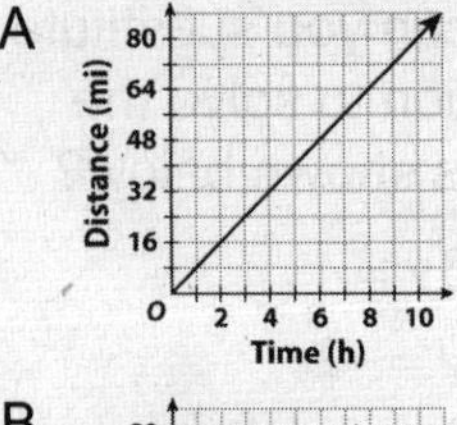

C
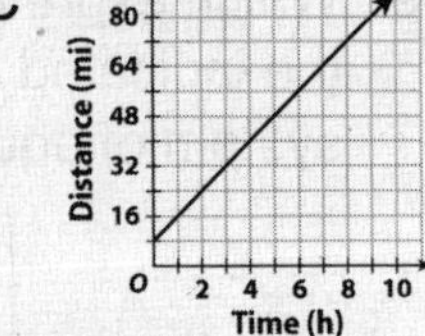

B
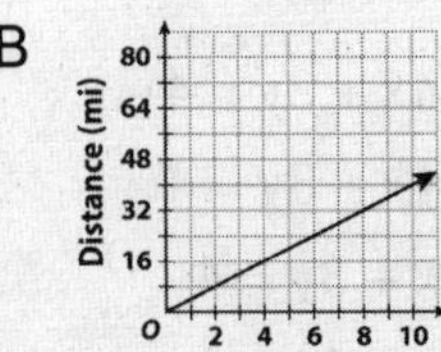

D
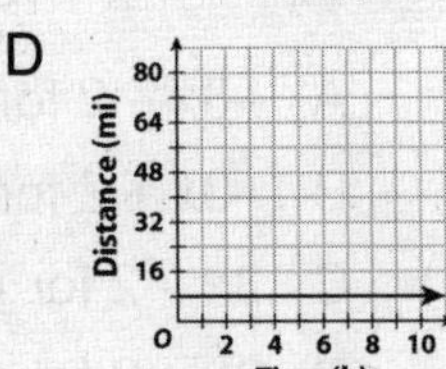

Name ______________________ Date ______________ Class ______________

End-of-Year Test

30. The measures of three angles of a triangle are $(2x)°$, $(3x)°$ and $(x + 60)°$. What is the value of x?

    A 20 C 40

    B 30 D 50

31. What is the solution of the system of equations graphed below?

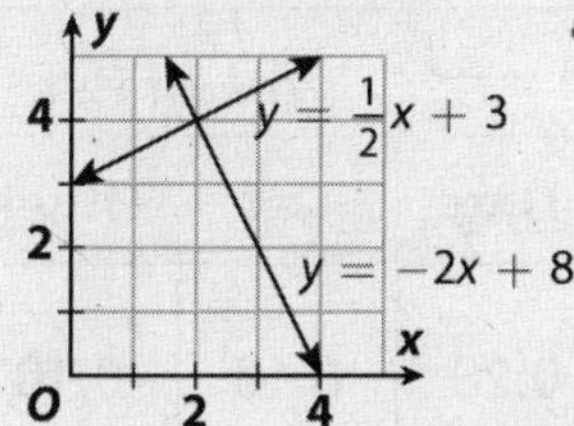

    A (–1, 1) C (2, 2)

    B (2, 4) D (0, 3)

32. Under which transformation is orientation **not** preserved?

    A translation C reflection

    B dilation D rotation

33. Daria applied a transformation to triangle ABC to obtain triangle $A'B'C'$. The two triangles are **not** congruent. Which of the following could be the transformation Daria applied?

    A translation C reflection

    B dilation D rotation

34. Which of the following best describes the number of solutions to the system of equations shown below?

$$\begin{cases} 2x + 3 = y \\ -4y + 8x = -12 \end{cases}$$

    A no solutions

    B one solution

    C two solutions

    D infinite solutions

35. Which expression represents 81?

    A 3^3 C 3^5

    B 3^4 D 3^6

36. The vertices of a triangle are located at the points $A(1, 1)$, $B(2, -3)$ and $C(5, 0)$. The triangle is translated 4 units down, then reflected across the x-axis to obtain triangle $A'B'C'$. What are the coordinates of the vertices of triangle $A'B'C'$?

    A $A'(-1, 3)$, $B'(-2, 7)$, $C'(-5, 4)$

    B $A'(-1, -3)$, $B'(-2, -7)$, $C'(-5, -4)$

    C $A'(1, -3)$, $B'(2, -7)$, $C'(5, -4)$

    D $A'(1, 3)$, $B'(2, 7)$, $C'(5, 4)$

37. Isobel obtained an image of triangle WXY under a dilation with a scale factor of 3. Which of the following describes the area and perimeter of the new figure?

    A The original area is multiplied by 9, and the perimeter is multiplied by 3.

    B The original area is multiplied by 3, and the perimeter is multiplied by 3.

    C The original area is divided by 9, and the perimeter is divided by 3.

    D The original area is divided by 3, and the perimeter is divided by 3.

38. Which of the following best describes the relationship between the data displayed in the scatter plot and in the trend line below?

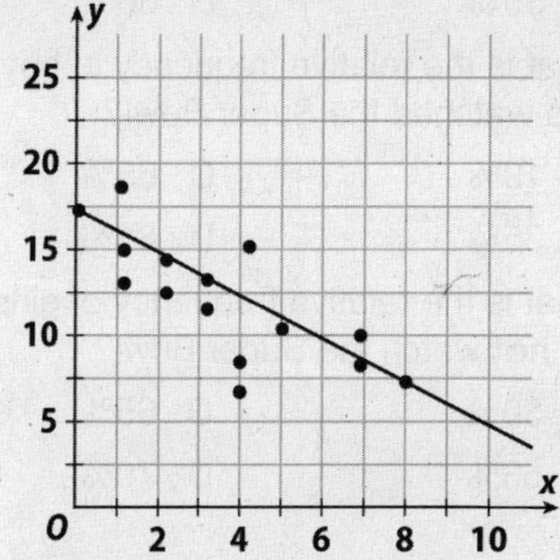

    A positive linear association

    B negative linear association

    C no association

    D quadratic association

Name ______________________ Date ______________ Class ______________

End-of-Year Test

Use the situation and table for 39–43.

Fran collected data from students about whether they watched the latest Super Bowl game. The table below shows the results of Fran's survey. Round answers to the nearest whole percent.

	Watched	Did Not Watch	TOTAL
Boys	85	20	105
Girls	45	?	95
Total	130	70	200

39. Of the students surveyed, how many watched the Super Bowl?

A 70 C 130
B 85 D 200

40. Of the students surveyed, how many girls did **not** watch the Super Bowl?

A 45 C 70
B 50 D 85

41. What is the relative frequency of students who watched the Super Bowl?

A 23% C 43%
B 35% D 65%

42. What is the relative frequency of boys who watched the Super Bowl?

A 19% C 65%
B 35% D 81%

43. What is the relative frequency of girls who did **not** watch the Super Bowl?

A 50% C 65%
B 53% D 70%

Use the situation and table for 44–47.

Thomas collected data from students about the type of pet they preferred: dog, cat, or other. The two-way relative frequency table below shows the results of Thomas's survey. Round answers to the nearest hundredth.

	Type of Pet			
School	**Dog**	**Cat**	**Other**	**Total**
Middle School	0.26	0.18	0.10	0.54
High School	0.25	0.15	0.06	0.46
Total	0.51	0.33	0.16	1.00

44. What is the joint relative frequency of high-school students that prefer having a dog?

A 0.15 C 0.25
B 0.18 D 0.26

45. What is the joint relative frequency of middle-school and high-school students that prefer a pet other than a dog or cat?

A 0.06 C 0.15
B 0.10 D 0.16

46. What is the marginal relative frequency of students surveyed that are in middle school?

A 0.10 C 0.26
B 0.18 D 0.54

47. What is the conditional relative frequency that a student prefers a cat as a pet, given that the student is in high school?

A 0.15 C 0.31
B 0.28 D 0.33

Name ______________________ Date ______________ Class ______________

End-of-Year Test

48. A sphere has a radius of 2 inches. What is the volume of the sphere to the nearest tenth?

A 16.8 in.^2 C 33.5 in.^2

B 16.8 in.^3 D 33.5 in.^3

49. The mass of Earth in kilograms is 5.97×10^{24}, and the mass of the Moon is 7.35×10^{22}. What is the sum of the masses of Earth and its moon?

A 6.0435×10^{22} C 6.0435×10^{24}

B 6.0435×10^{23} D 6.0435×10^{46}

50. If the triangle shown is rotated 180°, what are the coordinates of Point *F*?

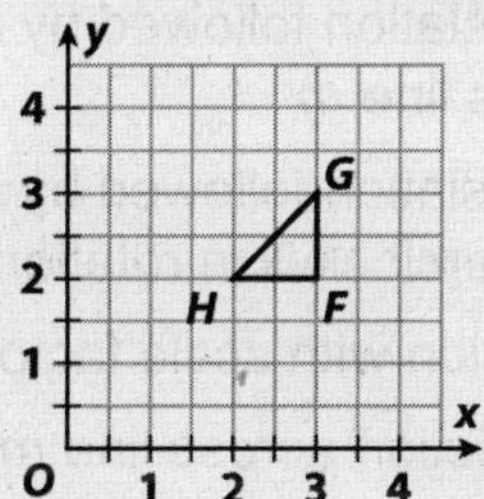

A (1, 1) C (2, 1)

B (–3, –2) D (–3, –1)

51. What value of *x* is the solution to the equation?

$-5(x - 5) = 2(-4x + 5)$

A –15 C 5

B –5 D 15

52. What is the value of *x* in the solution to the system of equations shown below?

$$\begin{cases} 7x + y = 14 \\ -2x - 6 = y \end{cases}$$

A –7 C 4

B –4 D 7

53. Which graph below shows a linear equation with a slope of 2 and a *y*-intercept of –2?

A

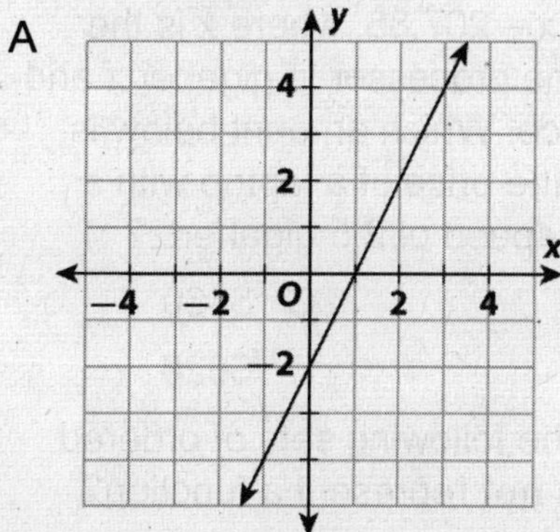

B

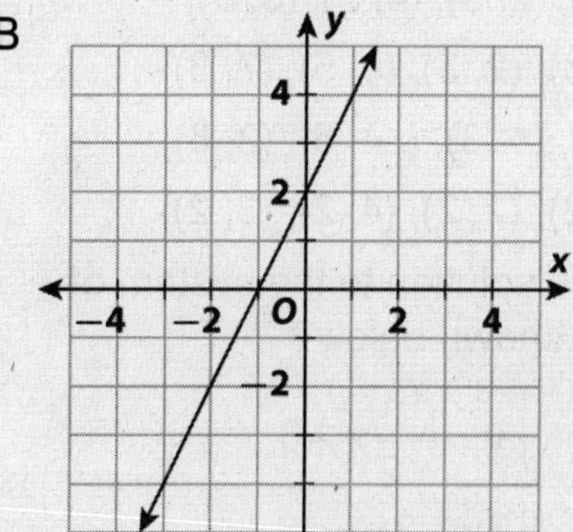

C

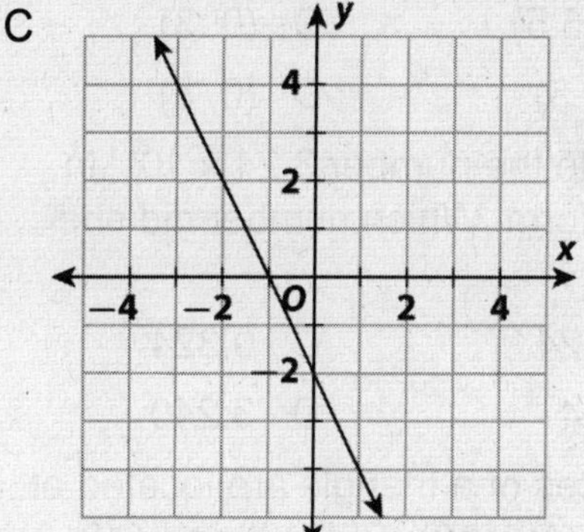

D

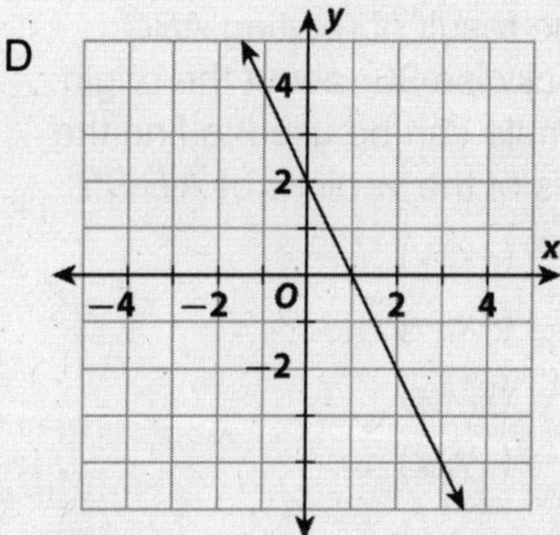

End-of-Year Test

54. Lourenço analyzed prices of laptop computers based on the speed of the processor. He calculated the trend line to be $y = 101x + 207.85$, where x is the speed of the processor in gigahertz and y is the price. Which amount below is closest to the price of a laptop with a processor speed of 2.5 gigahertz?

 A $309 C $460

 B $455 D $620

55. Which of the following sets of ordered pairs does **not** represent a function?

 A {(1, 2), (2, 3), (4, 5), (3, 3)}

 B {(–1, 3), (2, 3), (6, 5), (7, 3)}

 C {(1, 2), (1, 3), (–4, 5), (3, 8)}

 D {(–1, 2), (2, 2), (4, 2), (3, 2)}

56. What is the solution to the system of equations shown below?

$$\begin{cases} y = -\frac{1}{2}x - 6 \\ 2y - 3x = -8 \end{cases}$$

 A (–1, –5.5) C (0, 3)

 B (–1, 5.5) D (0, 8)

57. Erica wrote the number 3.24×10^{-3} in standard form. Which number did she write?

 A 0.00324 C 0.324

 B 0.0324 D 3,240

58. The vertices of a triangle are located at the points $A(-1, 0)$, $B(-2, 2)$ and $C(3, 3)$. $A'B'C'$ is the result of rotating ABC counterclockwise 90° about the origin. Which formula can be used to find the coordinates of the vertices of $A'B'C'$?

 A $(x, y) \rightarrow (-x, y)$

 B $(x, y) \rightarrow (-x, -y)$

 C $(x, y) \rightarrow (y, -x)$

 D $(x, y) \rightarrow (-y, x)$

59. Jerlyn applied a sequence of transformations to obtain triangle $X'Y'Z'$ from triangle XYZ as shown below.

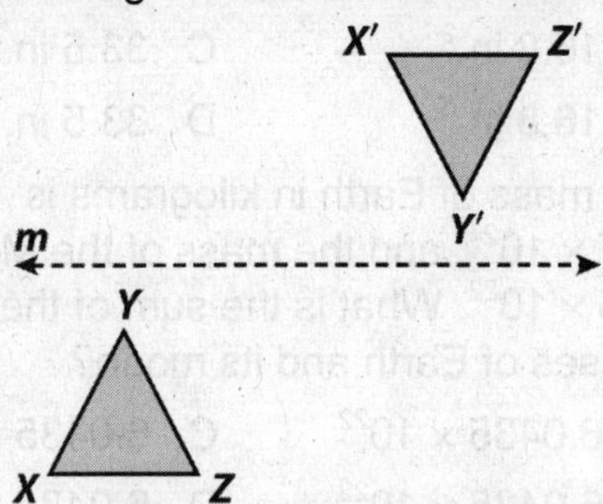

Which of the following describes the sequence of transformations?

 A a translation followed by a reflection across line m

 B a translation followed by a 180° counterclockwise rotation

 C a dilation with scale factor 2

 D a reflection across line m followed by a 180° counterclockwise rotation

60. Lisa analyzed the scatter plot below.

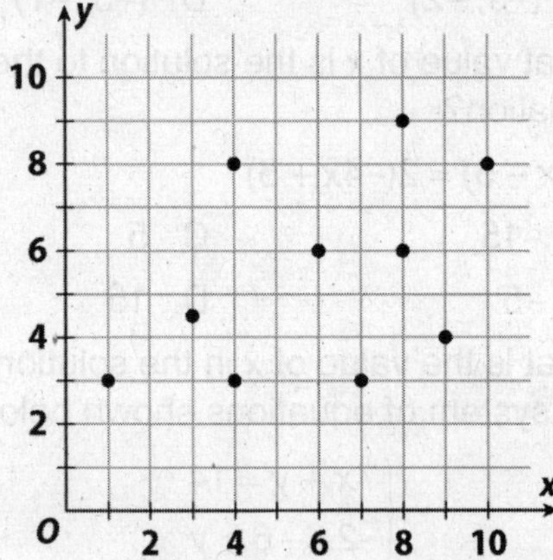

Which of the following best describes the relationship between the two variables?

 A positive linear association

 B negative linear association

 C nonlinear association

 D no association

Name ______________________ Date ______________ Class ______________

End-of-Year Test

Solve.

61. Amman drew a rectangle with a perimeter of 36 units. He then performed a dilation with a scale factor of 3. What is the perimeter in units of the resulting image? Show your work.

____

62. What is the x-value of the solution to the system of equations shown below?

$$\begin{cases} y = 3x + 5 \\ 2y = 4x + 24 \end{cases}$$

____

63. Elizabeth wrote the number 8.45×10^{-2} in standard form. Which number did she write?

____

64. At the café, Rebecca can choose to earn $10 per hour plus a $60 starting bonus or to earn $12 per hour with no starting bonus. After how many hours of work will she earn the same amount under both payment options? Write the equation to solve the problem. Solve.

____

65. The point (–2, –3) is rotated 180° counterclockwise about the origin. What is the y-coordinate of the resulting image?

____

66. What is the slope of the line described by the data in the table below? Show how you find the slope.

x	–2	0	4	12	16
y	5	6	8	12	14

____

67. The volume of a cone is 242.1 cubic centimeters. A cylinder has the same base and height as the cone. What is the volume in cubic centimeters of the cylinder? Explain how you found the volume.

____

68. At a fruit stand, Rajendra can purchase three apples and one orange for the same price as five apples. The price of the orange is $0.84. What is the price in dollars of each apple? Write and solve the equation.

____

69. To the nearest tenth, what is the distance in units between the points (–3, 2) and (5, 6)?

____

70. Samantha deposited $650 into a savings account that pays 3.5% interest compounded annually. After 6 years what will be the value of her investment in dollars?

____

71. How many units long is $\overline{XZ}$?

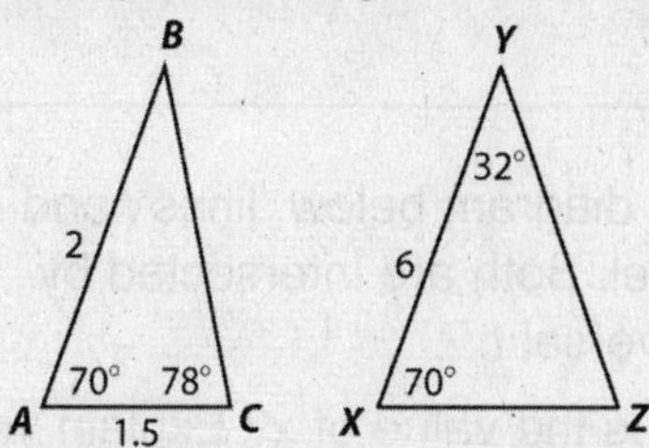

____

72. At a farmer's market the price of a basket of apples is based on the number of apples it contains. A basket that contains 12 apples costs $3.75. What is the price for a basket that contains 18 apples? Show your work.

____

Name ____________________ Date ____________ Class ____________

End-of-Year Test

73. What is a *y*-intercept? What is the *y*-intercept of the line graphed below?

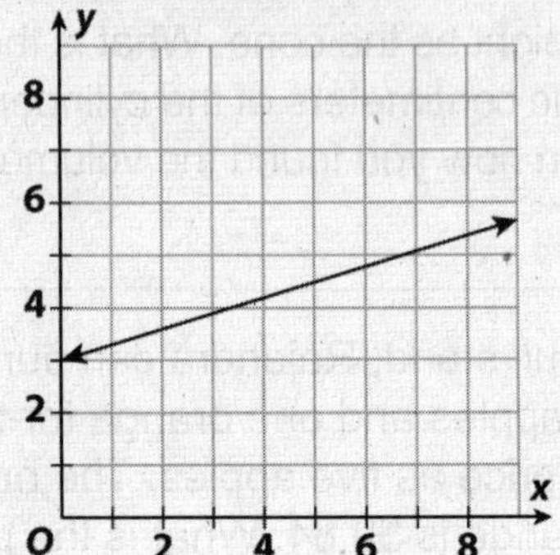

____

74. Beth has a rectangular yard that measures 12 feet by 18 feet. She wants to put a fence along the diagonal of the yard. To the nearest tenth, how many feet long will the fence be?

____

75. At a supermarket, the price of a carton of blueberries varies directly with its weight. A carton that weights 0.5 pound costs $4.25. What is the price in dollars of a carton of blueberries that weighs 0.75 pound? Show your work.

____

____

76. In the diagram below, lines *l* and *m* are parallel. Both are intersected by transversal *t*.

What is the value of *x*? Explain your reasoning.

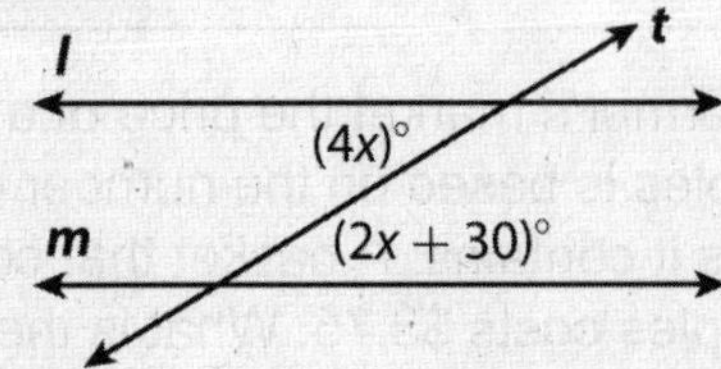

____

77. What is the value of *x* in the equation below?

$$\frac{1}{2}x + 5 = \frac{1}{4}x + 8$$

____

78. What is the *y*-value of the solution to the system of equations graphed below?

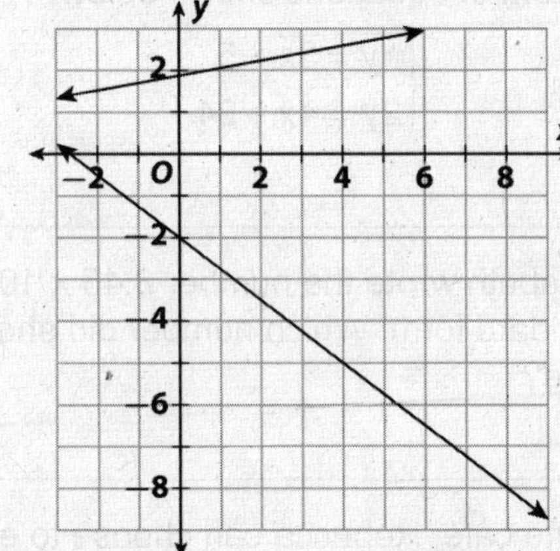

____

79. What is the value of *x* in the diagram below? Show your work.

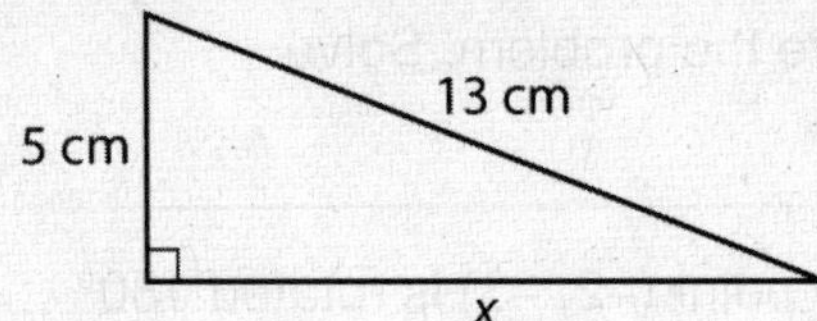

____

80. Grant filled a cylindrical tank with water. The tank has a base radius of 1.2 meters and a height of 3 meters. To the nearest tenth, how many cubic meters of water are in the tank?

____

Answer Key

Placement Test

1. B
2. C
3. D
4. D
5. A
6. B
7. C
8. C
9. A
10. C
11. D
12. B
13. C
14. A
15. D
16. D
17. A
18. C
19. B
20. A
21. C
22. A
23. C
24. D
25. B
26. A
27. D
28. B
29. C
30. D
31. A
32. B
33. B
34. D
35. A

Answer Key

Beginning-of-Year Diagnostic Test

1. B Correct

   The diagram shows set "A" to be a subset of the set of integers. The only answer choice that is a subset of the set of integers is the set of whole numbers.

   TEST PREP DOCTOR: Students who answered **A** may have forgotten that the set of integers is a subset of the set of rational numbers. Students who answered **C** did not realize that some negative numbers are not integers, so the set of negative numbers cannot be a subset of the set of integers. Students who answered **D** did not understand the diagram or did not realize that the set of irrational numbers is not a subset of the set of integers.

2. B Correct

   Since $49 < 50 < 64$, you can conclude that $\sqrt{49} < \sqrt{50} < \sqrt{64}$, or $7 < \sqrt{50} < 8$. The value of $\sqrt{50}$ is between integers 7 and 8.

   TEST PREP DOCTOR: Students who answered **A** or **C** may have made a computation error. Students who answered **D** found the integers that 50 falls between, rather than $\sqrt{50}$.

3. D Correct

   To write a number in scientific notation, write it as the product of a number from 1 up to 10 and a power of 10. To write 6,240,000 in scientific notation, move the decimal point left six places to get 6.24. The number of places the decimal point was moved is the power of 10, so the power of 10 is 6. The number in scientific notation is 6.24×10^6.

   TEST PREP DOCTOR: Students who answered **A** or **B** may have made a computational error. Students who answered **C** chose a number that is equal to 6,240,000 but not one that is written in scientific notation. (In order for it to be in scientific notation, it must be a product of a power of 10 and a number greater than or equal to 1 and less than 10.)

4. C Correct

   The vertices of the gray square are (0, 0), (9, 0), (9, 9) and (0, 9). The corresponding vertices in the black square are (0, 0), (3, 0), (3, 3) and (0, 3). Each coordinate of the gray square is 3 times its corresponding coordinate in the black square. The correct transformation is $(x, y) \rightarrow (3x, 3y)$.

   TEST PREP DOCTOR: Students who answered **A** may not have realized that the gray figure is the image of the black figure after a dilation. Students who answered **B** or **D** may have counted incorrectly or made a computational error.

5. A Correct

   Convert all numbers to decimal form before comparing. $3\frac{1}{5}$ is equal to 3.2. To compare decimals, compare digits in corresponding place values, going left to right.

   TEST PREP DOCTOR: Students who answered **B** may have made a computational error. Students who answered **C** did not realize that $3\frac{1}{5}$ is greater than 3.1. Students who answered **D** ordered the numbers from greatest to least.

6. A Correct

Dilation by a scale factor of 3 multiplies the perimeter of the shape by 3, and the area of the shape by $3^2 = 9$, since area is a two-dimensional measurement.

TEST PREP DOCTOR: Students who answered **B** may not have realized that area is a two-dimensional measurement, and that the scale factor needs to be squared when applying it to the area. Students who answered **C** may not have realized that dilation by a scale factor causes the perimeter to be multiplied by the scale factor. Students who answered **D** may have confused area and perimeter.

7. A Correct

All four points are on the line $y = x$, so the slope between any two of the points is the same. This can be confirmed algebraically: the slope of $\overline{AB}$ is $\frac{1-0}{1-0} = 1$, and the slope of $\overline{CD}$ is $\frac{3-2}{3-2} = 1$.

TEST PREP DOCTOR: Students who answered **B, C** or **D** may have miscalculated the slopes of $\overline{AB}$ or $\overline{CD}$, or may not have realized that, when four points are on the same line, the slopes between any two of the points will be the same.

8. D Correct

Slope between points (x_1, y_1) and (x_2, y_2) is equal to $\frac{\Delta y}{\Delta x} = \frac{y_2 - y_1}{x_2 - x_1}$.

Choose points (0, 2) and (1, 4). The slope is $\frac{4-2}{1-0} = 2$.

TEST PREP DOCTOR: Students who answered **A** may have reversed the order of two coordinates in the slope formula. Students who answered **B** may have calculated the slope as $\frac{\Delta x}{\Delta y}$ rather than $\frac{\Delta y}{\Delta x}$. Students who answered **C** found the negative reciprocal of the slope.

9. C Correct

The table shows a proportional relationship in which y is always equal to 3 times x. The equation that represents this is $y = 3x$.

TEST PREP DOCTOR: Students who answered **A** may have made a computational error. Students who answered **B** did not find the correct proportional relationship. Students who answered **D** did not notice that y is equal to $3 \bullet x$ for all points in the table.

10. D Correct

The slope m between the points (0, 2) and (1, 4) is $\frac{4-2}{1-0} = 2$. The equation becomes $y = 2x + b$. The y-intercept, 2, is equal to b. The equation of the line is $y = 2x + 2$.

TEST PREP DOCTOR: Students who answered **A** incorrectly calculated the slope of the line. Students who answered **B** did not recognize that the y-intercept of the line is +2, not −2. Students who answered **C** incorrectly calculated the slope of the line and did not identify the correct y-intercept.

11. C Correct

Subtract the cost of the ingredients from the sales price of a pie to find Carmella's profit from each pie sold.

$10 – $2 = $8

Divide the cost of the oven by $8.

$\frac{600}{8} = 75$

So, Carmella must bake 75 pies to recover the cost of the oven.

TEST PREP DOCTOR: Students who answered **A** added the cost of the ingredients to the price of a pie, instead of subtracting it. Students who answered **B** did not subtract the cost of ingredients from the price of a pie. Students who answered **D** may have made a computation error.

12. B Correct

The graph of a linear relationship is the graph of a line. The only graph that is not a line is the graph in choice B.

TEST PREP DOCTOR: Students who answered **A**, **C**, or **D** did not know that a graph that shows a linear relationship is the graph of a line, or may have forgotten what the graph of a line looks like.

13. A Correct

$8n + 9 = -n$

$8n + n = -9$

$9n = -9$

$n = -1$

TEST PREP DOCTOR: Students who answered **B** or **D** may have made a computation error. Students who chose **C** made a sign error in isolating the variable.

14. A Correct

A proportional relationship has the equation $y = cx$, where c is a constant. The only equation shown that is a proportional relationship is $y = 5x$.

TEST PREP DOCTOR: Students who chose **B** or **D** did not realize that proportional relationships have the form $y = cx$. Students who answered **C** may have thought that an equation that involves a fraction is a proportional relationship.

15. B Correct

In order for a relation to be a function, each *x*-value must map to only one *y*-value. Looking at each table, all of the *x*-values must be different. This is only true for the set of points in choice B.

TEST PREP DOCTOR: Students who answered **A** may have thought that a function was a relation in which each output is unique. Students who answered **C** or **D** may have forgotten the definition of a function.

16. A Correct

When a shape is dilated, the ratios of the corresponding sides of the image and the original shape are equal.

TEST PREP DOCTOR: Students who answered **B** may not have realized that some dilations can decrease the area of the original figure. Students who answered **C** did not realize that dilations can change the size of the original figure. Students who answered **D** did not realize that dilations can be performed on shapes other than isosceles triangles.

17. B Correct

A linear relationship between variables *x* and *y* has an equation in the form $y = mx + b$, where m and b are constants. The equation $y = 30x + 50$ is in this form. A proportional relationship means that *y* varies directly with *x*, or that the "*b*" in the linear relationship is equal to zero (that is, the equation takes the form $y = mx$). The given equation does not take this form. It is linear but non-proportional.

TEST PREP DOCTOR: Students who answered **A** may have forgotten the definition of proportional relationship. Students who answered **C** or **D** failed to recognize that the relationship is linear.

18. A Correct

Every hour, the distance the leopard runs increases by 50 miles. This is a direct variation relationship in the form $y = 50x$.

TEST PREP DOCTOR: Students who answered **B** or **D** did not realize that the speed of the leopard, 50mi/h, is equal to the slope of the equation of the line. Students who answered **C** did not realize that the distance the leopard runs is not increased by any amount.

19. B Correct

You can substitute $-3x - 2$ for y in $4x + 3y = 4$. Then solve for x, and substitute the x value into one of the equations to solve for y.

TEST PREP DOCTOR: Students who answered **A** substituted $-3x - 2$ for the wrong variable. Students who answered **C** or **D** substituted the wrong expressions for the wrong variables.

20. C Correct

Multiply the second equation by 2, then add the equations to eliminate the x variable.

$$\begin{cases} -4x + y = -1 \rightarrow -4x + y = -1 \\ 2x + 2y = -2 \rightarrow 4x + 4y = -4 \end{cases}$$

$$5y = -5$$

$$y = -1$$

Substitute the y value into $-4x + y = -1$ to find x.

$$-4x + (-1) = -1$$

$$-4x - 1 = -1$$

$$-4x = -1 + 1$$

$$-4x = 0$$

$$x = 0$$

The solution to the system is (0, –1).

TEST PREP DOCTOR: Students who answered **A** or **B** may have made computation errors when solving for the variable. Students who answered **D** transposed the variables when writing the answer as a coordinate pair.

21. B Correct

When the dimensions (base and height) of a cylinder and a cone are the same, the volume of the cylinder is three times the volume of the cone. This can be seen by looking at the formulas for the volumes of a cylinder and a cone: $V_{cylinder} = \pi r^2 h$ and

$$V_{cone} = \frac{1}{3}\pi r^2 h.$$

TEST PREP DOCTOR: Students who answered **A** did not realize that even though the height and radius of the two shapes are the same, the volumes of the two shapes are different. Students who answered **C** reversed the relationship between the volume of a cylinder and the volume of a cone. Students who answered **D** may have confused the formula for the volume of cone with the formula for the volume of a sphere.

22. D Correct

The diagram shows a right triangle with leg lengths of 3 units and 4 units and a hypotenuse 5 units long. The equation $3^2 + 4^2 = 5^2$ is a correct statement of the Pythagorean theorem based on the diagram.

TEST PREP DOCTOR: Students who answered **A** did not realize that the Pythagorean theorem is not an inequality. Students who answered **B** or **C** may not have realized that in the formula for the Pythagorean theorem, the sum of the squares of the lengths of the legs equals the square of the length of the hypotenuse.

23. A Correct

The formula for the volume of a sphere is $V = \frac{4}{3}\pi r^3$. Substitute $r = 3$ to obtain $V = \frac{4}{3}\pi \cdot 3^3 = 36\pi$.

TEST PREP DOCTOR: Students who answered **B** multiplied by an additional factor of 2. Students who chose **C** may have forgotten the formula to calculate the volume of a sphere. Students who chose **D** multiplied by an additional factor of 8.

24. B Correct

When a pair of parallel lines is intersected by a transversal, corresponding angles are congruent, so $\angle 2$ and $\angle 5$ are congruent.

TEST PREP DOCTOR: Students who answered **A**, **C** or **D** chose angle pairs that are supplementary, not congruent.

25. C Correct

Use the Pythagorean theorem to calculate the length of the other side of the lot.

$$60^2 + x^2 = 100^2$$
$$3{,}600 + x^2 = 10{,}000$$
$$x^2 = 6{,}400$$
$$x = 80$$

TEST PREP DOCTOR: Students who answered **A** found the difference in the two given measurements. Students who answered **B** may have assumed that the length and width of the lot are the same. Students who answered **D** may have made a calculation error.

26. C Correct

Make each point an endpoint of the hypotenuse of a right triangle. The other vertex of the triangle is (3, 0). The legs of the triangle measure 3 and 4. Calculate the length of the hypotenuse using the Pythagorean theorem. $3^2 + 4^2 = 9 + 16 = 25 = 5^2$. The distance between the points is 5 units.

TEST PREP DOCTOR: Students who answered **A** or **B** gave the length of a leg of the right triangle that can be drawn using the two given points as the endpoints of the hypotenuse. Students who answered **D** may have forgotten to take the square root after using the Pythagorean theorem.

27. C Correct

The slope of the data in the table is equivalent to the unit rate. So find the unit rate of the data in the table to find the slope. The household uses 80 cubic feet every 2 weeks, or 40 cubic feet every week. So, the unit rate is 40 ft^3/wk, and the slope is 40.

TEST PREP DOCTOR: Students who answered **A** may have made a computation error and misinterpreted the unit rate as a negative number. Students who answered **B** misinterpreted the unit rate as a negative number. Students who chose **D** did not notice that the table data begins with 2 weeks, so the gas used needs to be divided by 2 to find the unit rate.

28. A Correct

The equation says that four times a number equals 15 more than twice the number. The situation that matches this is the situation in choice A.

TEST PREP DOCTOR: Students who answered **B** switched "2*x*" and "4*x*" in the equation. Students who chose **C** ignored the "2*x*" in the equation. Students who answered **D** did not realize that the situation requires the use of two different variables.

29. B Correct

Riding a bicycle at a rate of 5 miles per hour means that the distance y increases by 5 for every increase of 1 in x. This a direct variation relationship with equation $y = 5x$. The graph is a line with slope 5 that passes through the origin.

TEST PREP DOCTOR: Students who answered **A** may have miscalculated the slope of the line. Students who answered **C** did not realize that this situation is a direct variation relationship and that the y-intercept of the graph must be 0. Students who answered **D** did not realize that the line graphed is the line with equation $y = 5$, not the line with equation $y = 5x$.

30. B Correct

Add the measures of the angles, set the sum equal to 180°, and solve for x.

$$x + 2x + 3x = 180$$
$$6x = 180$$
$$x = 30$$

TEST PREP DOCTOR: Students who answered **A** may have made a calculation error or may have divided by 9 instead of 6. Students who answered **C** or **D** may have made a calculation error when adding the measures of the angles together.

31. C Correct

The solution of the graphed system is the point at which the two lines intersect. The solution is (1, 4).

TEST PREP DOCTOR: Students who answered **A** chose the y-intercept of one of the lines. Students who chose **B** chose the y-intercept of the other line. Students who chose **D** chose the x-intercept of one of the lines.

32. C Correct

Orientation is not preserved under a reflection.

TEST PREP DOCTOR: Students who answered **A** may not have realized that orientation is preserved under a translation. Students who answered **B** may not have realized that orientation is preserved under a dilation. Students who answered **D** may not have realized that orientation is preserved under a rotation.

33. B Correct

Dilation is the only transformation of the ones listed that does not preserve size. Images under dilation are not congruent to the original shape.

TEST PREP DOCTOR: Students who answered **A** did not realize that images under a translation are congruent to the original shape. Students who answered **C** did not realize that images under a reflection are congruent to the original shape. Students who answered **D** did not realize that images under a rotation are congruent to the original shape.

34. D Correct

Solve the system by multiplying the first equation by 2 and adding the equations.

$$\begin{cases} 2x + y = 3 \rightarrow 4x + 2y = 6 \\ -4x - 2y = -6 \rightarrow -4x - 2y = -6 \end{cases}$$
$$0 = 0$$

The result is $0 = 0$, which is a true statement indicating that the system has infinitely many solutions.

TEST PREP DOCTOR: Students who answered **A**, **B** or **C** either solved the system incorrectly or need to review how to interpret the results of special systems of equations.

35. D Correct

$$2^6 = 2 \times 2 \times 2 \times 2 \times 2 \times 2 = 64$$

TEST PREP DOCTOR: Students who answered **A**, **B**, or **C** made a computation error or need to review the rules of exponents.

36. A Correct

A translation of 5 units down subtracts 5 from the y-coordinate of each vertex of the triangle: $A' = (0, -4)$; $B' = (2, -1)$; and $C' = (3, -5)$.

TEST PREP DOCTOR: Students who answered **B** added 5 to the y-value of each point rather than subtracting it. Students who answered **C** subtracted 5 from the x-value of each point rather than from the y-value of each point. Students who answered **D** added 5 to the x-value of each point rather than subtracting 5 from the y-value of each point.

37. B Correct

The area of the original shape will be multiplied by 9 to get the area of the image under a dilation with scale factor 3.

$15 \times 9 = 135 \text{ cm}^2$

The perimeter of the original shape will be multiplied by 3 to get the perimeter of the image.

$20 \times 3 = 60 \text{ cm}$

TEST PREP DOCTOR: Students who answered **A** did not square the scale factor before multiplying it by the area. Students who answered **C** may have made a calculation error. Students who answered **D** multiplied the perimeter by 9 rather than by 3.

38. A Correct

The data points move up as they go from left to right, and they resemble a straight line. The relationship is a positive linear association.

TEST PREP DOCTOR: Students who answered **B** did not realize that data points that slope upward from left to right show a positive trend. Students who chose **C** did not realize that the association is positive. Students who chose choice **D** did not realize that the association is linear.

39. C Correct

The total number of students who watched the Super Bowl is 120.

TEST PREP DOCTOR: Students who answered **A** chose the number of girls who watched the Super Bowl. Students who answered **B** chose the number of boys who watched the Super Bowl. Students who answered **D** chose the total number of students surveyed.

40. C Correct

The number of girls who did not watch the Super Bowl is 60.

TEST PREP DOCTOR: Students who answered **A** chose the number of boys who did not watch the Super Bowl. Students who answered **B** chose the number of girls who watched the Super Bowl. Students who answered **D** chose the total number of students who did not watch the Super Bowl.

41. D Correct

Divide the number of students who watched the Super Bowl by the number of students surveyed and write the answer as a percent.

$\frac{120}{200} = 0.6 = 60\%$

TEST PREP DOCTOR: Students who answered **A** chose the relative frequency of boys who did not watch the Super Bowl. Students who answered **B** may have made a computation error or need to review how to calculate relative frequency from data in a table. Students who answered **C** chose the relative frequency of girls who watched the Super Bowl or the relative frequency of students who did not watch the Super Bowl.

42. B Correct

The relative frequency of boys who watched is the number of boys who watched divided by all who watched. $\frac{80}{120} = 0.666 = 66.7\%$

TEST PREP DOCTOR: Students who answered **A** or **D** may have made a computation error or need to review how to calculate relative frequency from data in a table. Students who answered **C** chose the relative frequency of students who watched the Super Bowl.

43. B Correct

The relative frequency of girls who did not watch is the number of girls who did not watch divided by all who did not watch. $\frac{60}{80} = 0.75 = 75\%$

TEST PREP DOCTOR: Students who answered **A** or **C** may have made a computation error or need to review how to calculate relative frequency from data in a table. Students who answered **D** chose the relative frequency of students who watched the Super Bowl.

44. C Correct

A joint relative frequency in a two-way relative frequency table tells you what portion of the entire data set falls into the intersections of a particular value of one variable and a particular value of the other variable. The joint relative frequency of students surveyed who are boys and prefer comedy movies is 0.3, or 30%.

TEST PREP DOCTOR: Students who answered **A, B,** or **D** chose the joint relative frequencies of other combinations of variables and need to review the concept of joint relative frequency.

45. B Correct

A joint relative frequency in a two-way relative frequency table tells you what portion of the entire data set falls into the intersections of a particular value of one variable and a particular value of the other variable. The joint relative frequency of students surveyed who prefer movies other than comedies or dramas is 0.2, or 20%.

TEST PREP DOCTOR: Students who answered **A, C,** or **D** chose the joint relative frequencies of other combinations of variables and need to review the concept of joint relative frequency.

46. C Correct

A marginal relative frequency in a two-way relative frequency table tells you what portion of the entire data set represents a particular value of just one variable. The marginal relative frequency of students surveyed who prefer dramas is 0.3, or 30%.

TEST PREP DOCTOR: Students who answered **A, B,** or **D** chose the marginal relative frequencies of other variables and need to review the concept of marginal relative frequency.

47. C Correct

A conditional relative frequency in a two-way relative frequency table is found by dividing a frequency that is not in the Total row or Total column by the frequency's row total or column total. The conditional relative frequency that a student prefers dramas, given that the student is a girl is $\frac{0.2}{0.5} = 0.4 = 40\%$.

TEST PREP DOCTOR: Students who answered **A, B,** or **D** chose the conditional relative frequencies of other combinations of variables and need to review the concept of conditional relative frequency.

48. C Correct

The formula for the volume of a sphere is $V = \frac{4}{3}\pi r^3$. Substitute $r = 1$ to obtain $V = \frac{4}{3}\pi \bullet 1^3 = \frac{4}{3}\pi$.

TEST PREP DOCTOR: Students who answered **A** chose the expression that represents the area of a circle with a radius of 1 inch. Students who chose **B** may have forgotten the formula to calculate the volume of a sphere. Students who chose **D** chose the expression that represents the circumference of a circle with a radius of 1 inch.

49. C Correct

Rewrite the masses so they have the same exponent, then add the terms.

$6 \times 10^{24} + 7 \times 10^{22}$
$= 6 \times 10^{24} + 0.07 \times 10^{24}$
$= 6.07 \times 10^{24}$

TEST PREP DOCTOR: Students who answered **A** subtracted the terms and the exponents. Students who answered **B** rewrote the masses incorrectly or made a computation error. Students who chose **D** added the numbers and the exponents.

50. D Correct

If the triangle is rotated 90° clockwise about the origin, it would be in Quadrant IV.

TEST PREP DOCTOR: Students who answered **A** chose the same quadrant the triangle is in. Students who answered **B** may have rotated the triangle counterclockwise about the origin. Students who chose **C** may have rotated the triangle 180° about the origin.

51. D Correct

Use the distributive property to simplify both sides of the equation, then add like terms to isolate the variable and find the solution.

$4(x - 1) = 2(x + 1)$
$4x - 4 = 2x + 2$
$4x - 2x = 2 + 4$
$2x = 6$
$x = 3$

TEST PREP DOCTOR: Students who answered **A** may have made a computation error. Students who answered **C** made a sign error when adding and subtracting terms to isolate the variable. Students who chose **B** may have made a computation error.

52. D Correct

Eliminate the y-variable by adding the equations.

$$\begin{cases} 7x + y = 14 \\ -2x - y = 6 \end{cases}$$
$$5x = 20$$
$$x = 4$$

TEST PREP DOCTOR: Students who answered **A**, **B** or **C** may have made a computation error in solving the system.

53. A Correct

The first graph shows a linear equation with a positive slope and a negative y-intercept.

TEST PREP DOCTOR: Students who answered **B** chose the graph showing a linear equation with a positive slope and a positive y-intercept. Students who answered **C** or **D** chose graphs showing linear equations with negative slopes.

54. B Correct

Substitute $x = 2$ into the equation for the trend line.

$y = 103 \bullet 2 + 205$
$= \$411$

TEST PREP DOCTOR: Students who answered **A** added $103 + $2 + 205. Students who answered **C** multiplied $205 by 2 and added $103. Students who chose **D** added $103 and $205, then multiplied by 2.

55. C Correct

A function is a set of ordered pairs for which each input has only one output. When looking at the ordered pairs, pay attention to where the x-values are the same. If the x-values in the table repeat then the relation is not a function.

TEST PREP DOCTOR: Students who answered **A** may have forgotten the definition of a function. Students who chose **B** or **D** did not realize that if the outputs are the same then the relation could still be called a function.

56. A Correct

Both equations are solved for y. Set the expressions for y equal to each other to find the value of x that satisfies the system.

$3x - 6 = 2x$

$-6 = -x$

$x = 6$

Substitute $x = 6$ into one of the equations and solve for y.

$y = 2x$

$y = 2 \bullet 6$

$= 12$

The solution to the system is (6, 12).

TEST PREP DOCTOR: Students who answered **B** reversed the x- and y-coordinates of the solution. Students who answered **C** or **D** correctly calculated the value of x, but may have made a computational error when calculating the value of y (or may have forgotten how to find the y-coordinate of the solution to the system).

57. A Correct

When multiplying 1.5 by 10^{-3}, move the decimal point in 1.5 three places (since the power of 10 is –3) to the left (since the power of 10 is negative). Moving the decimal point in 1.5 three places to the left produces 0.0015.

TEST PREP DOCTOR: Students who answered **B** or **C** did not move the decimal enough places to the left. Students who answered **D** did not move the decimal point in the correct direction.

58. B Correct

The algebraic formula for a counterclockwise rotation of 180° about the origin is $(x, y) \rightarrow (-x, -y)$.

TEST PREP DOCTOR: Students who answered **A** chose the formula for reflecting in the y-axis. Students who answered **C** chose a formula for a rotation of 270° counterclockwise about the origin. Students who answered **D** chose a formula for rotating 90° counterclockwise about the origin.

59. C Correct

Triangle A is mapped to triangle B by a reflection across the x-axis followed by a reflection across the y-axis. To see this, you can look at one vertex of triangle A and see how it moves. (–5, –1) in triangle A is mapped to (5, 1) in triangle B. A reflection in the x-axis sends (–5, –1) to (–5, 1). Reflecting (–5, –1) across the y-axis yields (5, 1). This check does not work for any of the other transformations given.

TEST PREP DOCTOR: Students who answered **A** did not realize that two translations do not turn a figure upside-down shown. Students who chose **B** did not realize that a 90° rotation does not turn a figure upside-down. Students who chose **D** did not realize that a dilation changes the size of a shape, and that the figures shown in the diagram are the same size.

60. B Correct

The data points approximate a line so the trend is linear. The association is negative because as x increases the y-value decreases.

TEST PREP DOCTOR: Students who answered **A** did not realize that the *y*-values decrease as the *x*-values increase. Students who chose **C** did not recognize the linear pattern or did not remember what *linear* means. Students who answered **D** did not recognize that the association between the variables is linear.

61. D Correct

Dilating a rectangle by a scale factor of 2 multiplies the perimeter by 2. The new perimeter is $22 \bullet 2 = 44$.

TEST PREP DOCTOR: Students who answered **A** divided the perimeter by 2 instead of multiplying. Students who answered **C** subtracted 2 from the perimeter instead of multiplying by 2. Students who answered **D** added 2 instead of multiplying by 2.

62. A Correct

Both equations are solved for *y*. Set the expressions for *y* equal to each other to find the value of *x*.

$3x + 20 = 5x + 2$

Subtract $3x$ from each side.

$20 = 2x + 2$

Subtract 2 from each side.

$18 = 2x$

Divide each side by 2.

$x = 9$

Substitute $x = 9$ into the first equation.

$y = 3 \bullet 9 + 20 = 47$

The solution to the system is (9, 47).

TEST PREP DOCTOR: Students who answered **B** substituted $x = 9$ into the second equation but forgot to add 2. Students who answered **C** substituted $x = 9$ into the first equation but forgot to add 20. Students who answered **D** made a calculation error when finding the value of *x*.

63. D Correct

When multiplying 2.3 by 10^3, move the decimal point in 2.3 three places (since the power of 10 is 3) to the right (since the power of 10 is positive). Moving the decimal point of 2.3 three places to the right yields 2,300.

TEST PREP DOCTOR: Students who answered **A** or **B** moved the decimal point in the wrong direction. Students who answered **C** did not move the decimal enough places to the right.

64. B Correct

Let x= the number of hours Padma works. Under the first payment option, Padma will earn $12x + 100$ dollars for working *x* hours. Under the second option, she will earn $16x$ dollars for working *x* hours. Set the two expressions equal to find the value of *x*.

$12x + 100 = 16x$

$100 = 4x$

$x = 25$ h

For 25 hours of work, Padma's pay will be the same under both payment plans.

TEST PREP DOCTOR: Students who answered **A** gave the difference in hourly rates between the two payment options. Students who answered **C** made a mistake in writing the expressions that represent Padma's pay. Students who answered **D** subtracted 16 from 100, two numbers given in the problem.

65. B Correct

To rotate a point 180° counterclockwise use the rule $(x, y) \rightarrow (-x, -y)$. The point $(-2, -3)$ is mapped to $(2, 3)$.

TEST PREP DOCTOR: Students who answered **A** found the image of a reflection of the point $(-2, -3)$ across the x-axis. Students who chose **C** found the image of a reflection of the point $(-2, -3)$ across the y-axis. Students who chose **D** reversed the x- and y-coordinates.

66. B Correct

Find m and b in the equation $y = mx + b$.
Use two points from the table to calculate the slope m.

$$m = \frac{8-5}{0-(-1)} = \frac{3}{1} = 3$$

Since the point (0, 8) is in the table, the y-intercept (b-value) is equal to 8. The equation of the line is $y = 3x + 8$.

TEST PREP DOCTOR: Students who answered **A** switched the sign of the slope. Students who answered **C** or **D** did not correctly calculate the y-intercept of the line.

67. C Correct

Since the volume of the cone is 300 cm^3, we know $\frac{1}{3}\pi r^2 h = 300$. The cylinder has the same radius and height. The formula for the volume of a cylinder is $V = \pi r^2 h$. Multiply the volume of the cone by 3.

$\pi r^2 h = 3(300) = 900$ cm^3

TEST PREP DOCTOR: Students who answered **A** found two-thirds of the volume of the cone. Students who answered **B** did not realize that the volume of the cone is one-third the volume of the cylinder. Students who answered **D** multiplied the volume of the cone by 9 instead of by 3.

68. A Correct

Let x = the price of the pear. The price of 6 pears and an apple equals $6x + 0.80$ since the price of the apple is 0.80. The price of 8 pears is $8x$. Set the two prices equal and solve for x.

$$6x + 0.80 = 8x$$
$$2x = 0.80$$
$$x = 0.40$$

The price of a pear is \$0.40.

TEST PREP DOCTOR: Students who answered **B** made an error in calculating the price. Students who answered **C** did not divide by 2 in the last step of the solution or did not set up the problem correctly. Students who answered **D** multiplied by 2 in the last step of the solution instead of dividing.

69. B Correct

Create a right triangle that has the segment with endpoints $(-3, 3)$ and $(1, 2)$ as the hypotenuse. The legs of the triangle measure $|-3 - 1| = 4$ and $|3 - 2| = 1$. Use the Pythagorean theorem to find the length of the hypotenuse, which is the distance between the points. $4^2 + 1^2 = d^2$

$$d = \sqrt{4^2 + 1^2}$$
$$= \sqrt{17}$$
$$\approx 4.1$$

TEST PREP DOCTOR: Students who answered **A** miscalculated the length of one side of the triangle to be 2 rather than 4. Students who chose **C** calculated the lengths of the sides of the triangle to be 2 and 5 or made a calculation error. Students who chose **D** calculated the lengths of the sides of the triangle to be 4 and 5 or made a calculation error.

70. B Correct

Let x equal the price of a notebook. The price of two notebooks plus a \$40 backpack translates to the expression "$2x + 40$". The price of 10 notebooks is equal to "$10x$". The question says that these two quantities are equal, so $2x + 40 = 10x$.

TEST PREP DOCTOR: Students who answered **A** chose an expression in which the price of two notebooks is $40 more than the price of 10 notebooks. Students who answered **C** chose an expression in which the sum of the prices of 2 notebooks and 10 notebooks equals $40. Students who answered **D** chose an expression in which the price of 10 notebooks is $40 less than the price of 2 notebooks.

71. C Correct

The triangles are similar, so the ratios of the lengths of corresponding sides are equal. The ratio of *AB* to *XY* equals 4:8 or 1:2, so the ratio of *AC* to *XZ* is also equal to 1:2. Since *AC* equals 3, the value of *XZ* must equal $3 \bullet 2 = 6$.

TEST PREP DOCTOR: Students who answered **A** divided *AC* by 2 instead of multiplying. Students who chose **B** did not realize that the ratios of corresponding sides of similar triangles are equal. Students who answered **D** added 4 to the value of *AC* (probably because *XY* is 4 more than *AB*).

72. B Correct

The unit price of an apple is $\$6 \div 12 = \$0.50$, so 18 apples is $18 \times \$0.50 = \$9$.

TEST PREP DOCTOR: Students who answered **A** or **C** may have made a computation error. Students who answered **D** divided 12 by 6 to find an incorrect unit rate of $2.

73. B Correct

The *y*-intercept of a line is the *y*-value of the point at which the line crosses the *y*-axis. According to the graph, the line crosses the *y*-axis at the point (0, –3), so the *y*-intercept is –3.

TEST PREP DOCTOR: Students who answered **A** found the *x*-intercept of the line. Students who answered **C** found the slope of the line. Students who answered **D** made a calculation error or did not realize that the *y*-intercept of the line is negative.

74. C Correct

Use the Pythagorean theorem to calculate the length of the diagonal of the rectangle.

$$20^2 + 48^2 = 400 + 2{,}304 = 2{,}704$$

The length of the diagonal is $\sqrt{2704} = 52$, so the fence will be 52 feet long.

TEST PREP DOCTOR: Students who answered **A** found the difference in the length and width of the yard. Students who answered **B** found the average of the length and the width of the yard. Students who answered **D** found the perimeter of the yard.

75. C Correct

20 is greater than 16 and less than 25, or $16 < 20 < 25$. This implies that $\sqrt{16} < \sqrt{20} < \sqrt{25}$, or $4 < \sqrt{20} < 5$. The only lettered point between 4 and 5 on the number line is point *C*.

TEST PREP DOCTOR: Students who answered **A** may have thought that the value of $\sqrt{20}$ is between and 2 and 3. Students who chose **B** or **D** made a mistake when calculating the value of $\sqrt{20}$ or did not know how to use the number line.

76. A Correct

When parallel lines are intersected by a transversal, the alternate interior angles formed are congruent. The marked angles are alternate interior angles. Set their measures equal to each other to find the value of x.

$3x = 2x + 15$

$x = 15$

TEST PREP DOCTOR: Students who answered **B** found the value of $2x$ or forgot to divide by 2. Students who answered **C** found the measure of each of the labeled angles $(3x)°$ and $(2x + 15)°$. Students who answered **D** found the supplement of the labeled angle ($135° = 180° - 45°$).

77. D Correct

Subtract $0.5x$ from each side of the equation.

$20 = 0.1x$

Divide both sides by 0.1.

$x = 200$

TEST PREP DOCTOR: Students who answered **A** may have made a calculation error or reversed a sign. Students who chose **B** or **C** did not properly divide by 0.1 in the last step of the solution.

78. B Correct

The solution to a system of equations is the point or points at which the graphs intersect. The lines graphed intersect at the point (3, 1), so (3, 1) is the solution to the system.

TEST PREP DOCTOR: Students who answered **A** reversed the values of x and y. Students who answered **C** or **D** found the y-intercept of one of the lines.

79. A Correct

Use the Pythagorean theorem to find the length of the leg labeled x.

$8^2 + x^2 = 10^2$

$64 + x^2 = 100$

$x^2 = 36$

$x = 6$ cm

TEST PREP DOCTOR: Students who answered **B** found the average of the given lengths of the triangle. Students who answered **C** found the perimeter of the triangle. Students who answered **D** made a mistake using the Pythagorean theorem.

80. C Correct

Find m and b in the equation $y = mx + b$.

Use two points from the table to calculate the slope m.

$$m = \frac{1-3}{0-(-1)} = \frac{-2}{1} = -2$$

Since the point (0, 1) is in the table, the y-intercept (b-value) is equal to 1. The equation of the line is $y = -2x + 1$.

TEST PREP DOCTOR: Students who answered **A** calculated the slope correctly but may have made a calculation error when finding the y-intercept of the line. Students who chose **B** or **D** did not calculate the slope correctly or may have forgotten how to find the equation of a line.

MODULE 1 Real Numbers

Module Quiz 1: B

1. C
2. D
3. B
4. A
5. C
6. D
7. D
8. C
9. D
10. A
11. B
12. A
13. terminating; the denominator is a power of 2
14. 2.0625
15. $0.3\overline{6}$
16. 6
17. $\frac{3}{2}, -\frac{3}{2}$
18. between 9.3 and 9.4
19. 15.81
20. rational number, real number
21. $\sqrt{320}, \sqrt{321}, \sqrt{322}, \sqrt{323}, \sqrt{324} = 18, \sqrt{325}$; $\sqrt{324}$ is a rational number
22. area of triangle, volume of sphere
23. volume of sphere, surface area of sphere
24. negative numbers
25. 5
26. $4\pi, \sqrt{150}, 11\frac{4}{9}$

Module Quiz 1: D

1. B
2. B
3. C
4. C
5. B
6. A
7. A
8. A
9. B
10. B
11. A
12. C
13. repeating
14. 12.31
15. $0.58\overline{3}$
16. 1515
17. 12, −12
18. between 6 and 7
19. 9
20. irrational number
21. $\sqrt{10}, \sqrt{12}, \sqrt{14}, \sqrt{16}, \sqrt{18}, \sqrt{20}$; $\sqrt{16} = 4$, so it is not irrational.
22. area of circle, volume of sphere, surface area of sphere
23. area of triangle, perimeter of square, volume of sphere, surface area of sphere
24. Distances and lengths are always nonnegative numbers.
25. 10 or 11
26. 3π

MODULE 2 Exponents and Scientific Notation

Module Quiz 2: B

1. C
2. C
3. D
4. C
5. D
6. C

7. D
8. B
9. D
10. B
11. C
12. B
13. D
14. The first factor is not less than 10.
15. 365,000
16. 10^{10}
17. 5.84×10^4
18. 1.9×10^8
19. 8.43×10^{-6} m
20. 0.00007024 cm
21. Answers will vary. Sample answer: 0.00065, 6.5×10^{-4}
22. 2.25×10^{-5} m
23. 8
24. 0.000016 m
25. 4
26. 1.6×10^{-2} m
27. $\sqrt{75}$, $4.\overline{3}$, $\frac{20}{13}$, $\frac{\pi}{4}$
28. 5.23×10^7

Module Quiz 2: D

1. C
2. C
3. A
4. C
5. B
6. A
7. B
8. B
9. B
10. A
11. C
12. A
13. C
14. 6
15. 10,000; 52,000
16. 4.7×10^3
17. 2.86×10^3
18. 8,500,000
19. –3
20. 4
21. 7×10^{-4}
22. 0.014
23. 8,900 m
24. 0.025 m
25. 1,400,000,000 m
26. grain of salt
27. $\sqrt{30}$
28. 5.19×10^7

MODULE 3 Proportional Relationships

Module Quiz 3: B

1. C
2. C
3. A
4. D
5. B
6. C
7. D
8. B
9.

Time (weeks)	10	15	25
Savings ($)	40	60	100

10. $k = 4$; $y = 4x$
11. $15 per h
12. Students' graphs should show the equation $y = -\frac{4}{3}x$, passing through (0, 0) and (3, –4).
13. unit rate for Object A is 2.5 m/s; unit rate for Object B is $\frac{2}{3}$ m/s.
14. Object C's unit rate is 1.5 m/s. C is moving faster than B, but slower than A.
15. 50 mi
16. 0.000181 m

Module Quiz 3: D

1. B
2. B
3. C
4. B
5. A
6. B
7. B
8. A
9.

Time (weeks)	10	20	25
Savings ($)	100	200	250

10. $y = 10x$
11. $40/h
12. $\frac{4}{3}$
13. 5 m/s
14. Object A. The line has a steeper slope.
15. 50 mi
16. 0.000017 m

MODULE 4 Nonproportional Relationships

Module Quiz 4: B

1. D
2. D
3. B
4. D
5. A
6. C
7. C
8. A
9.

Shirts	1	5	10	50
Cost ($)	52	100	160	640

10. $-\frac{1}{2}$, -3
11. 1, -1
12. $-\frac{4}{3}$, 2

13. Sample answer:

x	0	1	2	5
y	-2	-1.6	-1.2	0

12. and 13.

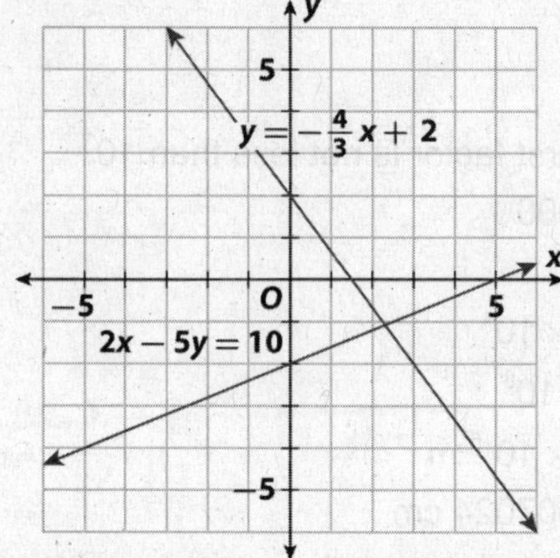

14. linear: *B, C, D*; proportional: *B*
15. Steve: $y = 250 - 25x$;
Chelsea: $y = 30x + 30$
16. Students will graph one of these lines depending on which equation they chose.

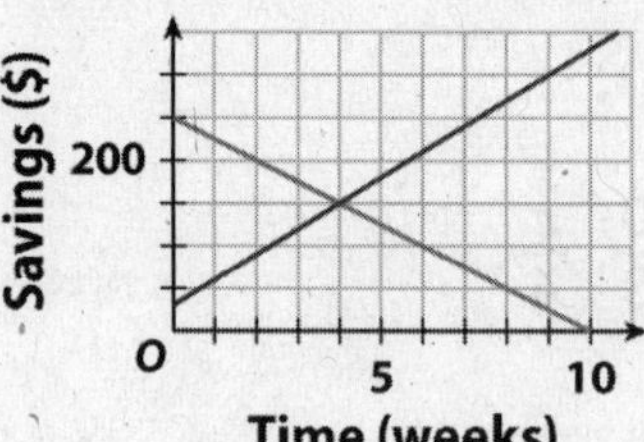

17. <

Module Quiz 4: D

1. C
2. B
3. A
4. C
5. A
6. B
7. B
8. A
9.

Shirts	1	2	3	4
Cost ($)	52	64	76	88

10. 8
11. $\frac{1}{2}$

12. 2, −3

13. Sample answer:

x	0	1	2	3
y	−3	−2	−1	0

12. and 13.

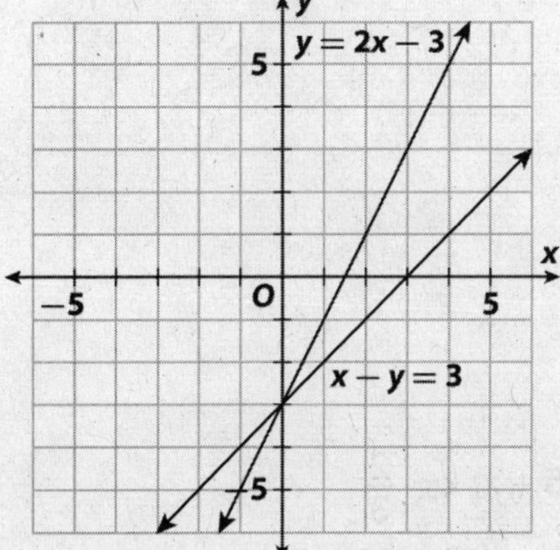

14. line B; It is a straight line passing through (0, 0).

15. $y = 250 - 25x$; $y = 30x + 30$

16. No, neither line goes through origin.

17. >

MODULE 5 Writing Linear Equations

Module Quiz 5: B

1. C
2. A
3. B
4. C
5. C
6. $y = 4x - 7$
7. $y = 2x - 1$
8. $y = -2x + 2$
9. $y = \frac{1}{2}x - 2$
10. $m = -\frac{5}{2}$
11. $y = 2x + 4$
12. $y = -2x + 3$
13. $12.04/h

Module Quiz 5: D

1. C
2. B
3. A
4. C
5. B
6. C
7. C
8. B
9. $y = x - 2$
10. $m = \frac{2}{3}$
11. $d = 3t$
12. $m = -\frac{1}{2}$
13. 12, 14, 16
14. $y = x + 1$
15. $b = -1$
16. $c = 6t$
17. Answers will vary, but must be of the form $y = a$, where a is a constant, e.g. $y = 1$.
18. $\frac{1}{5}$

MODULE 6 Functions

Module Quiz 6: B

1. D
2. B
3. D
4. A
5. A
6. B
7. The equation for Claire's account is $y = -15x + 480$. Marshall pays $18 per month. Claire pays $15. So, Claire's dues are $3 cheaper per month.
8. After 32 months Claire's account will equal $0. After about 30.6 months Marshall's account will equal $0. So Claire can pay her dues for more months.

9.

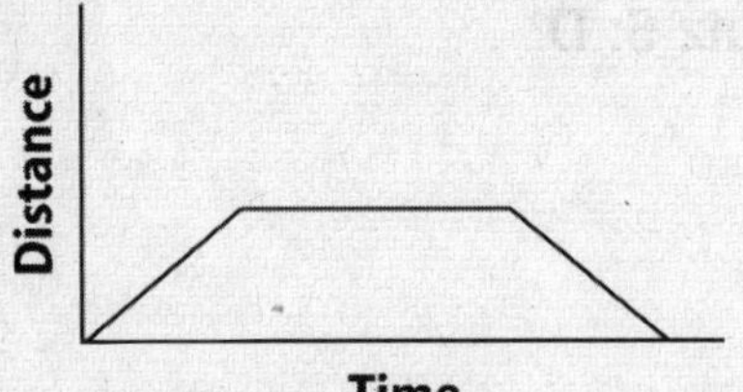

10. 1; choose two points on the line, (0, –2), (2, 0);

    $\text{slope} = \frac{y_1 - y_2}{x_1 - x_2} = \frac{-2-0}{0-2} = \frac{-2}{-2} = 1.$

11. $y = \frac{10}{3}x$; 240 pages

12. $y - 2 = 4(3x + 5)$

    $y - 2 = 12x + 20$

    $y = 12x + 22$; nonproportional

Module Quiz 6: D

1. A
2. C
3. A
4. C
5. C
6. B
7. A
8. C
9.

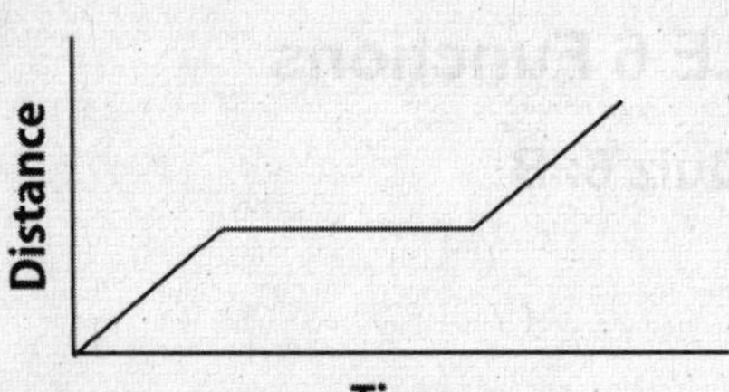

10. not a function
11. function
12. $\frac{1}{2}$
13. nonproportional
14. $y = 6x + 5$
15. Their cost per lawn mowed is the same, however, Service A charges $20 per month even if it does not mow that month.

MODULE 7 Solving Linear Equations

Module Quiz 7: B

1. C
2. C
3. D
4. B
5. C
6. B
7. C
8. C
9. A
10. C
11. $4x + 3 = 5 + x$; $x = \frac{2}{3}$
12. $500 - 30x = 150 + 20x$; 7 years
13. $0.\overline{33}$ is a rational number because it can be written as a ratio of two integers, $\frac{1}{3}$.
14. $x = \frac{8}{3}$
15. $2.5x + 7.7 = 4.7x$; 3.5 mph
16. $0.1(x + 250) = 5{,}000$; $49,750
17. $x = \frac{156}{23}$
18. zero solutions
19. 16
20. 1.5×10^7

Module Quiz 7: D

1. A
2. B
3. C
4. A
5. B
6. B
7. C
8. C
9. A
10. $3x - 5 = 2x$; $x = 5$
11. $15 + 2x$; 7 years
12. rational

13. $x = -14$
14. $x = 4$; 4 mph
15. $x = 49{,}750$; $49,750
16. $x = 12$
17. 16
18. 1×10^6

MODULE 8 Solving Systems of Linear Equations

Module Quiz 8: B

1. D
2. A
3. B
4. B
5. B
6. A
7. C
8. D
9. Steve: $y = 250 - 25x$
   Chelsea: $y = 30 + 30x$

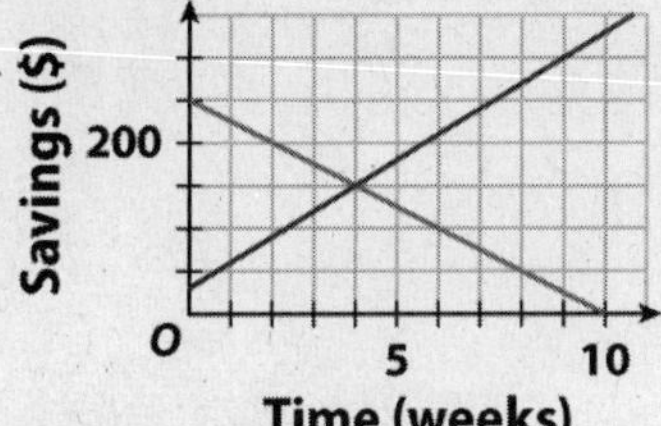

   Steve and Chelsea have the same amount of money in 4 weeks.
10. 25 – y
11. (3, –1)
12. $\frac{5}{4}$, π, $3\sqrt{3}$
13. a notebook is $1.50; a pen is $0.75
14. adult ticket is $11; children's ticket is $7.50
15. Yes, the graphs are the same line so the system has infinitely many solutions.
16. 9

Module Quiz 8: D

1. C
2. A
3. B
4. C
5. A
6. A
7. B
8. B
9. Larissa $y = 250 - 25x$, Chucho: $y = 30 + 30x$; in 4 weeks
10. $25 - y$
11. (3, –1)
12. $\frac{1}{4}$, $\sqrt{3}$, π
13. (5, 1)
14. (4, 2)
15. Sample answer: (–1, 1)
16. 6

MODULE 9 Transformations and Congruence

Module Quiz 9: B

1. D
2. A
3. A
4. B
5. B
6. C
7. D
8. B
9. Quadrant III
10. Quadrant IV
11. Quadrant II
12. They are all congruent to the original triangle.
13. $\frac{\sqrt{13}}{3}$, 2.3, $\sqrt{11}$
14. (–2, 0), (–5, 0), (–5, 2)
15.

16. Sample answer: No. To get the coordinates of the new trapezoid, you multiply each x-coordinate by -1, then switch the x- and y-coordinates.
17. $(-4, -3)$, $(-7, -3)$, $(-5, -5)$, and $(-2, -5)$
18. 87°

Module Quiz 9: D

1. A
2. C
3. A
4. C
5. A
6. C
7. C
8. B
9. B
10. Quadrant IV
11. Quadrant II
12. Quadrant IV
13. It is congruent to the original figure.
14. (4, 2), (4, 5), and (6, 5)
15. $-\sqrt{2}$, 2.5, 7
16.

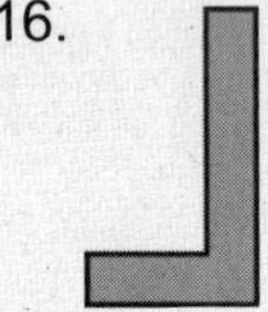

17. yes
18. $(-1, 1)$, $(-1, 5)$, $(-4, 1)$
19. 44°

MODULE 10 Transformations and Similarity

Module Quiz 10: B

1. B
2. C
3. C
4. B
5. C
6. A
7. D
8. No
9.

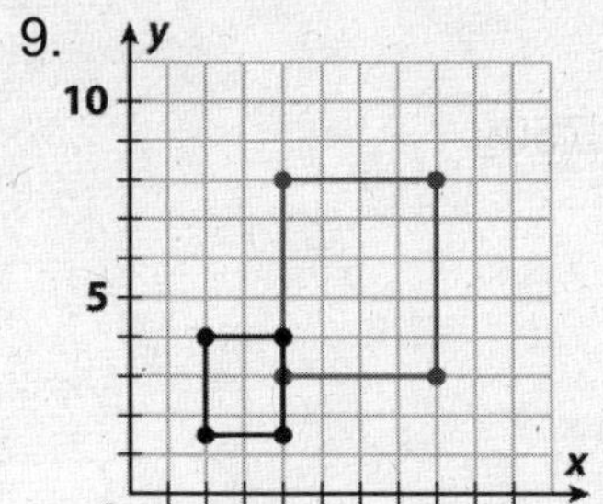

$(x, y) \rightarrow \left(\frac{1}{2}x, \frac{1}{2}y\right)$

10.
$$\begin{aligned} 6 + 3x &\le 2x - 1 \\ 6 - 6 + 3x &\le 2x - 1 - 6 \\ 3x &\le 2x - 7 \\ 3x - 2x &\le 2x - 2x - 7 \\ x &\le -7 \end{aligned}$$

11. $P(P'R'S'T') = 3 \times 2\,(x + y)$.
12. $A(P'R'S'T') = 3x \times 3y$ or $9xy$
13. larger; smaller

Module Quiz 10: D

1. C
2. B
3. C
4. A
5. C
6. A
7. B
8. C
9. Students' letter should be upright and reversed.

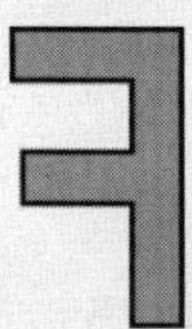

10. Sample answer: When you multiply any number by a decimal or fraction less than 1, the answer is less than the original number, so the dilation would be smaller than the original figure.
11. Sample answer: The transformation is a reflection because each point of the image is the same distance from the y-axis as the corresponding point in the original figure but on the opposite side.

12. Dilate $A'B'C'D'$ by a scale factor of $\frac{1}{4}$.

13. It is smaller than the original figure because the scale factor is less than 1.

14. Check students' triangles and images.

MODULE 11 Angle Relationships in Parallel Lines and Triangles

Module Quiz 11: B

1. C
2. B
3. B
4. A
5. D
6. C
7. D
8. 9 in.
9. Ashley
10. 2 mi/h
11. 98°
12. 139°
13. 123°
14. 123°
15. No. The angle measures for the triangle on the left are 60°, 62°, and 58°. The angle measures for the triangle on the right are 62°, 62°, and 56°. The triangles have only one pair of congruent angles so they are not similar.

Module Quiz 11: D

1. B
2. B
3. C
4. C
5. B
6. B
7. A
8. C
9. No, they are not similar because only one angle of the triangles is congruent. The angle measures in the triangle at left are 46°, 90°, and 44°. In the triangle at right, the angle measures are 46°, 38°, and 96°.
10. No, it is not a function because there are two different outputs (6 and 14) for the same input (12).
11. $117 = 81 + b$
    $36 = b$
    $\angle b = 36°$
12. 53 mph
13. Sample answer:

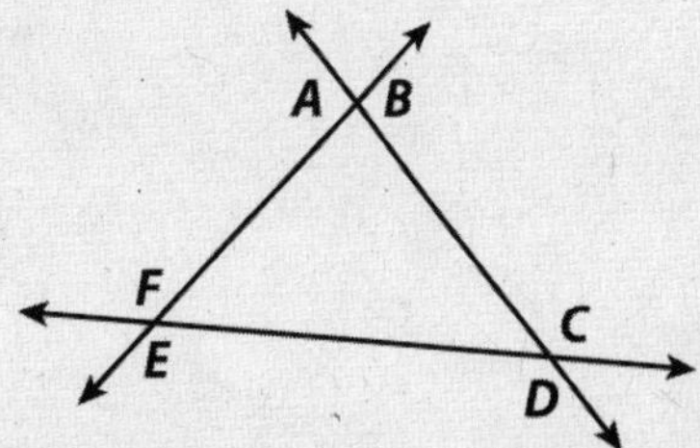

MODULE 12 The Pythagorean Theorem

Module Quiz 12: B

1. C
2. A
3. B
4. C
5. C
6. D
7. C
8. B
9. C
10. C
11. 45
12. 26.6 cm
13. 71.1 in.
14. 24.2 in.
15. No. Sample explanation: None of these expressions are equal to 30: $\sqrt{12^2 + 15^2}$, $\sqrt{12^2 + 18^2}$, $\sqrt{15^2 + 18^2}$
16. 17 units

17. $PR \approx 8.2$, $QR \approx 4.2$, $PQ \approx 7.1$

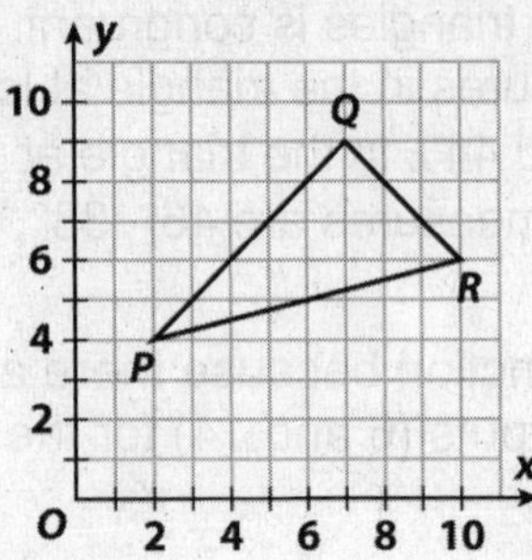

18. 71.9 ft

19. 40

Module Quiz 12: D

1. A
2. B
3. B
4. C
5. A
6. A
7. C
8. B
9. C
10. B
11. 20
12. 41 cm
13. 100 in.
14. 17.3 in.
15. Yes. The lengths 3, 4, and 5 make a right triangle because $3^2 + 4^2 = 5^2$.
16. 17 units
17. $EF = 6$, $FG = 8$, $EG = 10$

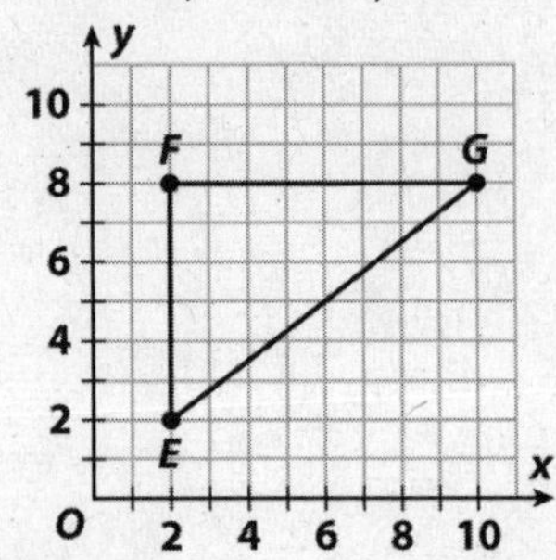

18. 50 ft
19. 30

MODULE 13 Volume

Module Quiz 13: B

1. B
2. D
3. A
4. B
5. C
6. D
7. B
8. B
9. $V \approx (3.14)(1.75^2)(1.25)$

   $V \approx 12.02 \text{ in.}^3$

   $V \approx (3.14)(1.2^2)(1.25)$

   $V \approx 5.65 \text{ in.}^3$

   $12.02 - 5.65 = 6.37 \text{ in.}^3$ difference
10. Entire funnel:

    $V \approx \frac{1}{3}(3.14)(4^2)(9) \approx 150.72 \text{ in.}^3$

    Tip: $V \approx \frac{1}{3}(3.14)(0.5^2)(1) \approx 0.2617 \text{ in.}^3$

    $150.72 - 0.2617 \approx 150.5 \text{ in.}^3$
11. No, the triangles have only one congruent angle so they are not similar. The angles of the left triangle measure 60°, 58°, and 62°. The angles of the right triangle measure 60°, 59°, and 61°.
12. $713.21 \div 3.14 = 227.14$

    $5.2^2 = 27.04$

    $227.14 \div 27.04 = 8.4$

    The height is about 8.4 inches.
13. Two cylinders with the same diameter may or may not have the same volume, depending on the two heights. The same is true for two cones. Two spheres with the same diameter will have the same volume because the formula doesn't use any other dimension.
14. No, $20^2 + 48^2 \neq 54^2$, so it cannot be a right triangle.

Module Quiz 13: D

1. C
2. A
3. B
4. C

5. C

6. B

7. $V = \frac{1}{3}\pi r^2 h$

$V = \frac{1}{3}(3.14)(2^2)(18)$

$V = \frac{1}{3}(3.14)(4)(18)$

$V = \frac{1}{3}(3.14)(72)$

$V = \frac{1}{3}(226.08)$

$V = 75.36 \text{ in.}^3$

8. Sample answer: The πr^2 part of the formula is the base. I know because that's the formula for the area of a circle.

9. Sample answer: The cylinder has a greater volume. The formula for the volume of a cylinder is $V = \pi r^2 h$, and the formula for the volume of a cone is $V = \frac{1}{3}\pi r^2 h$. So if a cone and cylinder have the same height and radius, the volume of the cone is $\frac{1}{3}$ the volume of the cylinder.

10. $a^2 + b^2 = c^2$

$6^2 + 8^2 = c^2$

$36 + 64 = c^2$

$100 = c^2$

$\sqrt{100} = \sqrt{c^2}$

$10 = c$

The hypotenuse is 10 in. long.

11. Sample answer: Find the volume of the cone. Then find the volume of the sphere and divide it in half. Add the volume of the cone and the volume of half the sphere.

MODULE 14 Scatter Plots

Module Quiz 14: B

1. B
2. A
3. B
4. C
5. D
6. D
7. B
8. A
9. Answers will vary. Sample answer: It is not a good model because people stop growing after they reach adulthood.
10.

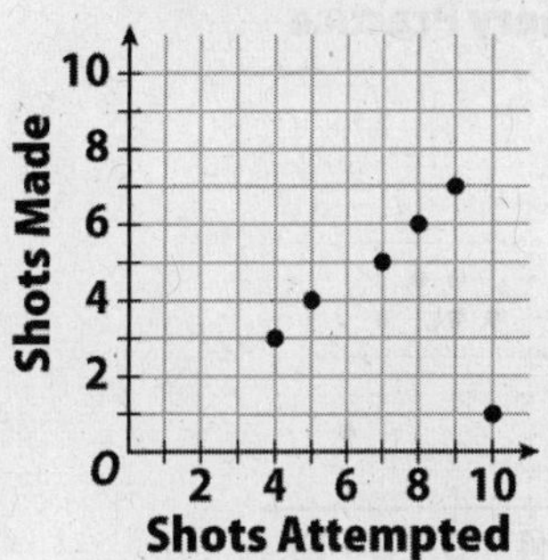

11. No. None of the data points are clustered together.
12. Yes. The point (10, 1) is an outlier; there are no other data points near it.
13. Devon; 10 mi
14.

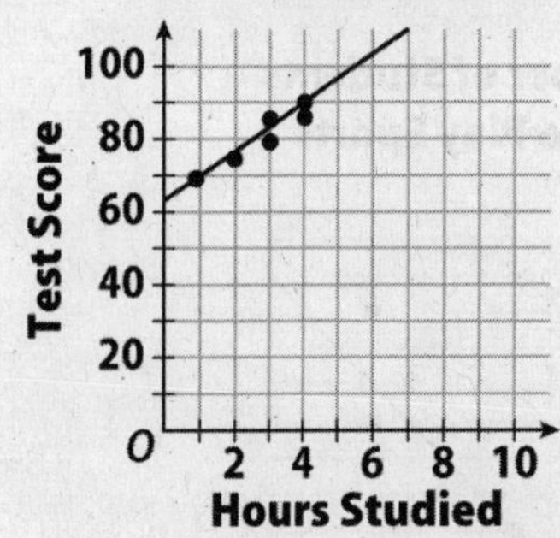

15. Sample answer: $y = \frac{20}{3}x + \frac{190}{3}$

16. positive association
17. 96.7%
18. Answers will vary. Sample answer: Yes, the number of hours that a student can study in one night is limited.

Module Quiz 14: D

1. A
2. B
3. A
4. B
5. A
6. C
7. A
8.

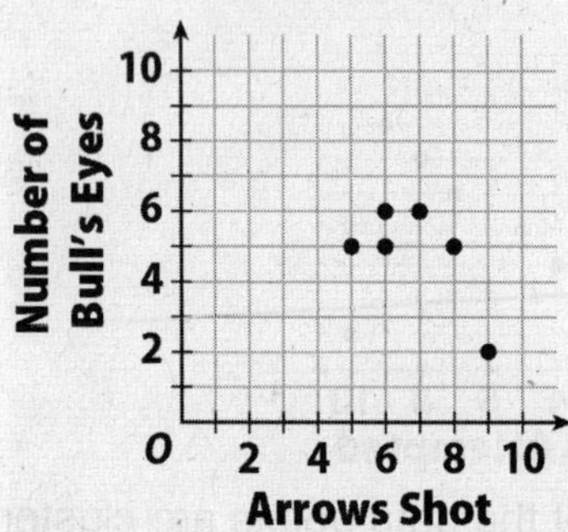

9. Yes. Most of the points are located near each other.
10. Yes, (9, 2) is far from the other data points.
11. 120 mi
12. 130
13.

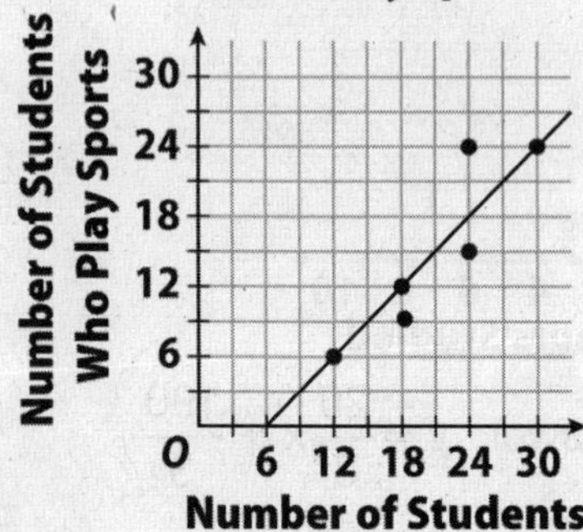

14. Sample answer: $y = x - 6$
15. positive association
16. 34
17. Yes, (25, 3) will be far from the other data points, so it would be an outlier.

MODULE 15 Two-Way Tables

Module Quiz 15: B

1. B
2. C
3. A
4. D
5. C
6. B
7. D
8. B
9. 32
10. 14
11. 48
12. 0.5 or 50%
13. 0.55 or 55%
14. No, being a boy has a 40% relative frequency while wanting a \$10 ticket has a 50% relative frequency.
15. 0.24 or 24%
16. 0.36 or 36%
17. 0.625 or 62.5%
18. 0.67 or 67%
19. Sample answer: I leave home, walk to the park. I rest for a while. I walk back home.

Module Quiz 15: D

1. B
2. C
3. B
4. A
5. B
6. B

7. A
8. B
9. 8
10. 3
11. 4
12. 0.55 or 55%
13. 0.44 or 44%
14. No, being a girl has a 60% relative frequency while wanting baked chicken has a 45% relative frequency
15. 1,000
16. 0.26 or 26%
17. 0.6 or 60%
18. 0.28 or 28%
19. Sample answer: I left home and walked to the corner, then I turned around and walked back home.

Answer Key

Unit Tests and Performance Tasks

UNIT 1 Real Numbers, Exponents, and Scientific Notation

Unit 1 Test: A

1. B
2. C
3. C
4. D
5. D
6. D
7. A
8. C
9. B
10. A
11. A
12. 12.25
13. $0.\overline{7}$
14. Sample answer: They both have 4 in the tenths place. But the decimal form for $\frac{4}{9}$ is a repeating decimal with every place to the right being a 4. The decimal form for $\frac{2}{5}$ has only one decimal place.
15. 20, –20
16. 12.2
17. The expressions -4^3 and 4^{-3} have the same base, but different exponents. $-4^3 = -64$ and $4^{-3} = \frac{1}{64}$
18. Answers will vary. Sample answer: A = irrational numbers, B = real numbers
19. Answers will vary. Sample answers: –2, –1, 0, 1
20. at about $11\frac{2}{3}$
21. 1.728×10^{15}
22. 1,400,000,000
23. 0.0000084 m
24. 4.0×10^2

Unit 1 Test: B

1. A
2. A
3. D
4. D
5. C
6. A
7. B
8. B
9. C
10. D
11. B
12. 4.375
13. $0.4\overline{16}$
14. Both have 25 in the first two decimal places, but $\frac{1}{4}$ is a terminating decimal, while $\frac{25}{99}$ is a repeating decimal.
15. $\frac{1}{4}, -\frac{1}{4}$
16. 6.32
17. They have the same exponent, but different bases. $(-5)^5 = -3{,}125$ and $5^5 = 3{,}125$.
18. Answers will vary. Sample answer: A = whole numbers, B = integers, C = real numbers
19. Answers will vary. Sample answers: 7, 8, 9, 10
20. between 3.4 and 3.5, but closer to 3.4
21. 2.28×10^2
22. 19
23. 0.0000000053
24. 2.86×10^2

Unit 1 Test: C

1. B
2. D
3. C
4. D

5. B
6. B
7. A
8. D
9. A
10. B
11. C
12. 3.3125
13. 6
14. The numerator has a factor of 7.
15. $-\sqrt{34.68}$, -5.89
16. 7
17. Yes. A positive number raised to a negative power remains positive. For example, $2^{-3} = \left(\frac{1}{2}\right)^3 = \frac{1}{8}$
18. Answers will vary. Sample answer: Every integer *n* can be written as a ratio in the form $\frac{n}{1}$. So, every integer is rational. A number cannot be both rational and irrational.
19. Answers will vary. Sample answer: $\sqrt{80}$
20. The expression is undefined because the denominator equals 0.
21. 4×10^2
22. 1,400,000,000
23. 7
24. about 2×10^{35} times larger

Unit 1 Test: D

1. B
2. B
3. C
4. C
5. B
6. C
7. A
8. C
9. A
10. B
11. B
12. 6.27
13. $0.8\overline{3}$
14. 333
15. 6, –6
16. 8
17. positive
18. whole number, integers
19. Answers will vary. Sample answers: 4, 5
20. about halfway between 5 and 6
21. 2.86×10^8
22. 1,400,000,000
23. 0.0024 m
24. grain of sand

Unit 1 Performance Task

1. 0.125 in., 0.0034 m, 0.34 cm; Sample answers: 1.25×10^{-1} in., 1.04×10^{-2} ft, 3.4×10^{-1} cm
2. 2 is rational, π is irrational; $\pi > 2$
3. 40,074,156 m: 40,100,000 m: 4.01×10^7 m
4. 11,790,000,000; 1.18×10^{10}; Sample answer: about 12 billion
5. Possible speed: 200 m/h;
   $\frac{40{,}100{,}000}{200} = 200{,}500;$
   $\frac{200{,}500}{24} = 8{,}354;$ about 8,354 days
6. Answers will vary. Students should discuss rounding methods, calculation steps, and reasons for the choice of ant speed.

UNIT 2 Proportional and Nonproportional Relationships and Functions

Unit 2 Test: A

1. C
2. B
3. B
4. A
5. A
6. A
7. C
8. D

9. Rider A: 30 km/h; Rider B: 24 km/h
10. Rider A: $y = 30x$; Rider B: $y = 24x$
11.

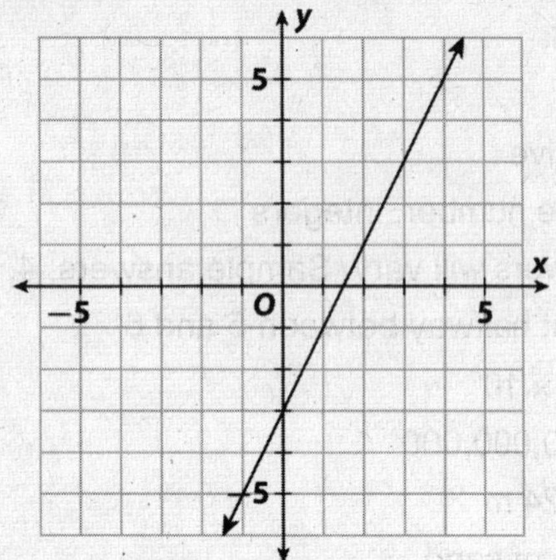

12. 3; 5
13. 75; 150
14. Car A; The graph is a straight line.
15. Car A. It gets home in 10 hours. Car B takes more than 12 hours to get home.

Unit 2 Test: B

1. B
2. C
3. D
4. B
5. C
6. A
7. A
8. D
9. Rider A = 30 km/h, Rider B = 24 km/h
10. Rider A: $y = 30x$, 450 km

    Rider B: $y = 24x$, 360 km
11.

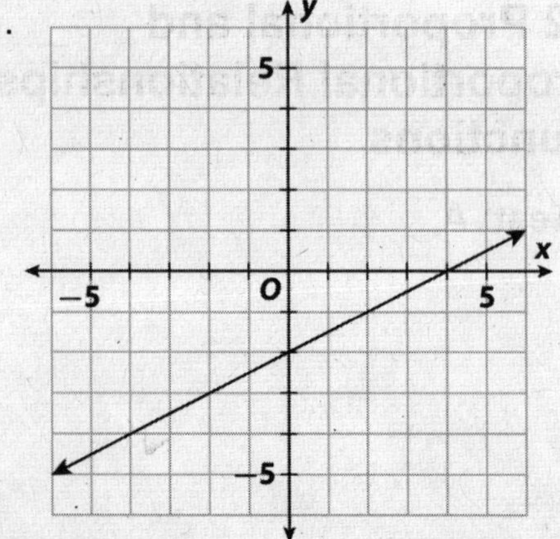

12. slope = $\frac{1}{2}$, y-intercept = −2
13. slope = 75, y-intercept = 150
14. A is linear, B is not. Neither is proportional.
15. Car A. Sample answer: Car A gets home in 13 hours. Car B takes more than 14 hours.

Unit 2 Test: C

1. A
2. C
3. A
4. D
5. C
6. B
7. C
8. B
9. Sample answers: Both are travelling at a constant rate of speed. Rider A is going 30 km/h; Rider B is going 24 km/h. Rider A's speed is 25% faster than Rider B's speed.
10. Rider A: $y = 30x$, 5 hours; Rider B: $y = 24x$, 6.25 hours
11. Numbering on scales may vary.

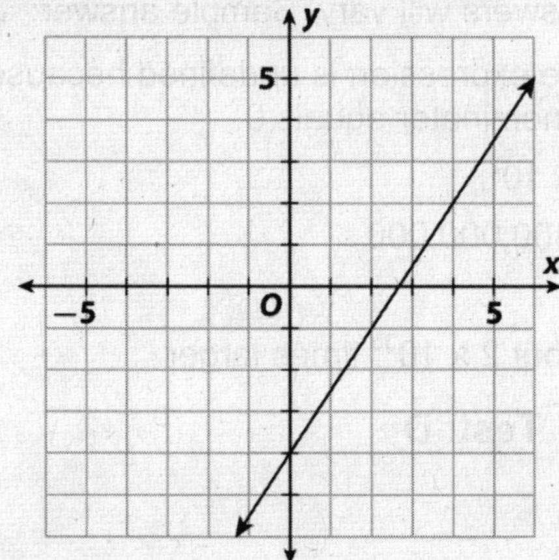

12. $\frac{3}{2}$, −4
13. straight line, slope = 75, y-intercept = 150; the person is saving $75 per month. The initial deposit was $150.
14. A is linear, B is not. Neither is proportional.
15. Car A

Unit 2 Test: D

1. B
2. C
3. A
4. B
5. B
6. A
7. A
8. C
9. slope is 20; speed is 20 km/h
10. $y = 20x$
11.

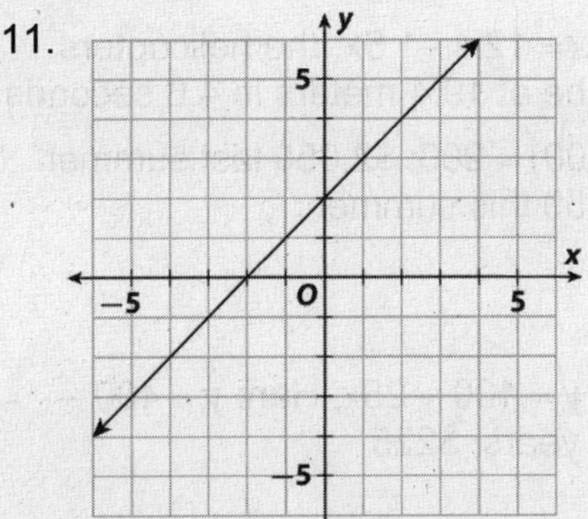

12. 5
13. 75; 150
14. Sample answers: Car B does not drive the same number of miles per hour. The speed is not constant.
15. Car A. It gets home in 10 hours.

Unit 2 Performance Task

1.

Years (t)	200	400	500
Cost (c)	$1,000	$2,000	$2,500

Graphs for 1. and 3.

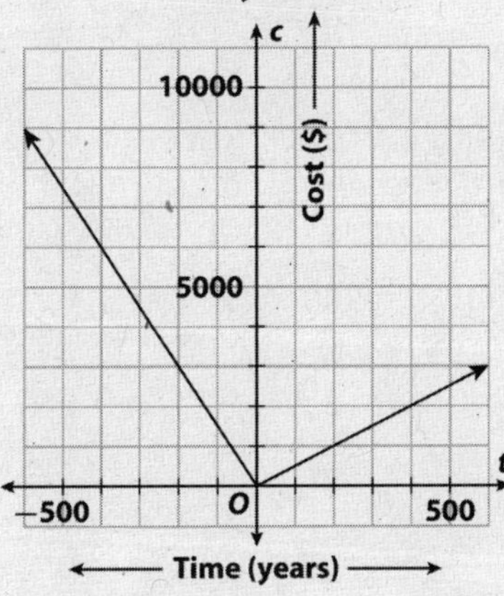

2. $c = 5t$
3.

Years (t)	–200	–400	–500
Cost (c)	$3,000	$6,000	$7,500

4. $c = -15t$
5. Sample answer: The values for time going backward are negative, but the cost will always be positive. So, the constant of proportionality must be negative.
6. forward: $c = t + 2{,}000$; backward: $c = -t + 2{,}800$

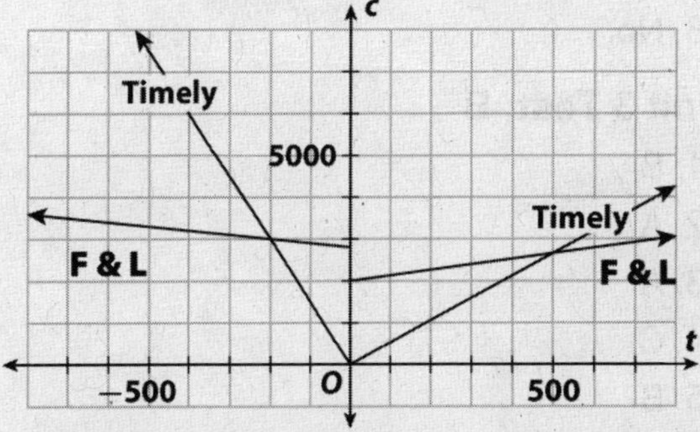

7. All of the functions are linear. The Timely functions are proportional; the First and Last functions are not proportional.
8. Traveling to the future, when $t > 500$ years; traveling back in time, when $t < -200$ years.

UNIT 3 Solving Equations and Systems of Equations

Unit 3 Test: A

1. C
2. A
3. A
4. C
5. B
6. D
7. C
8. A
9. B
10. $80x$; in 3 h
11. $12.4 + 1.5x$; in 5.1 s
12. 900; $22,300
13. 6

14. adult ticket is \$5.50, children's ticket is \$3.50

15. in 5 years

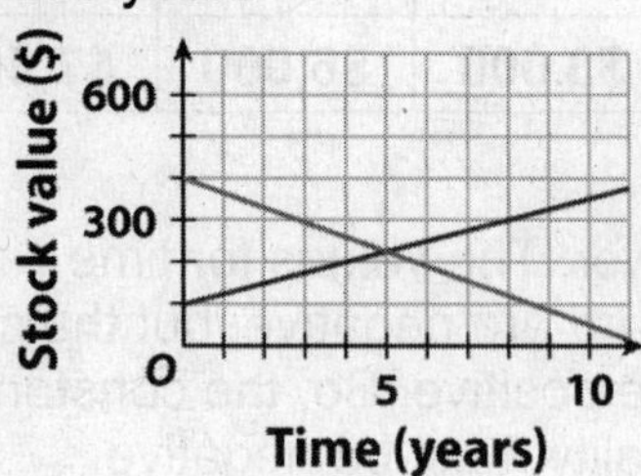

16. $4 - 6y$

17. (1, –1)

18. No.

Unit 3 Test: B

1. B
2. A
3. A
4. C
5. B
6. D
7. C
8. A
9. B
10. $60x + 60 = 80x$; in 3 hours
11. $7.3 + 2.6x = 12.4 + 1.5x$; in 4.6 seconds
12. $0.4(x + 200) = 900$; \$2,050
13. 6
14. adult ticket is \$5.50, children's ticket is \$3.50
15. Art: $y = 100 + 25x$; Kiley: $y = 400 - 35x$; in 5 years

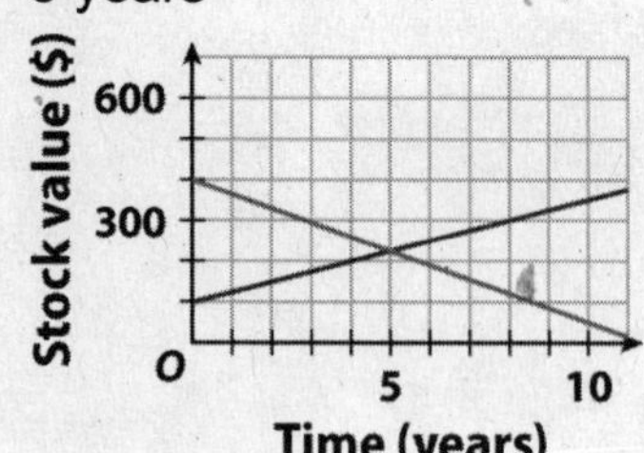

16. $4 - 6y$
17. (1, –1)
18. No, the system has no solution since there is no point of intersection between the graphs of the two linear equations.

Unit 3 Test: C

1. B
2. B
3. C
4. C
5. C
6. D
7. C
8. A
9. D
10. $60x + 60 = 80x$; at 3:45 P.M.
11. $7.3 + 2.6x = 12.4 + 1.5x$; the helicopters will both be at 19.4 meters in 4.6 seconds
12. $0.4(x + 200) = 900$; \$2,050 last summer and \$2,250 this summer
13. 27
14. \$20
15. Babette: $y = 100 + 25x$; Han: $y = 400 - 35x$; in 5 years; \$225

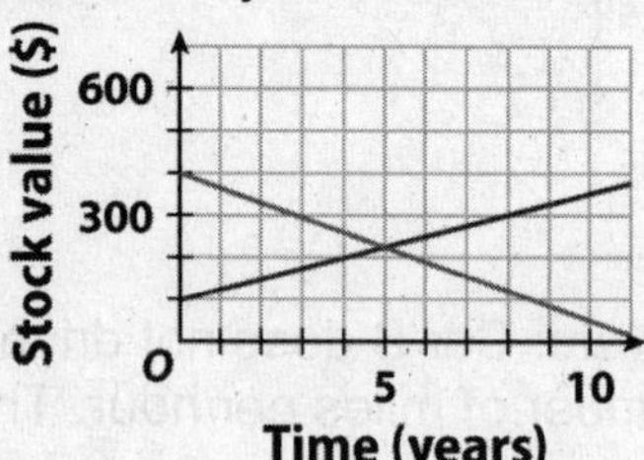

16. $5 + 17y$
17. (1, –1)
18. It is a pair of parallel lines.

Unit 3 Test: D

1. C
2. A
3. A
4. B
5. A
6. C
7. C
8. A
9. B
10. 3 h
11. 5 s
12. \$2,050
13. yes

14. (5, 3)

15. in 5 years

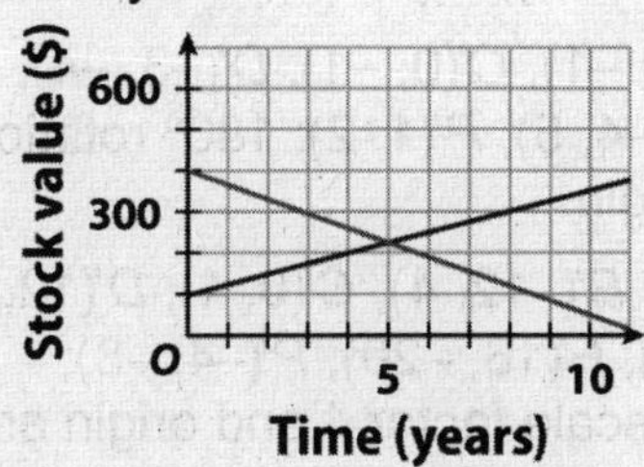

16. 4 – 6y

17. (2, 0)

18. No.

Unit 3 Performance Task

1. a. 0.8(4,000 + x) = 4,000; $1,000

   b. $5,000

2. a. 100 + 50x = 150 + 30x;

   b. 2.5 h

3. a. $\begin{cases} x + y = 200 \\ 3x + 0.75y = 318.75 \end{cases}$

   b. 75 sandwiches and 125 bottles of water

4. a. $\begin{cases} x + y = 7 \\ 8x + 4y = 40 \end{cases}$

   b.

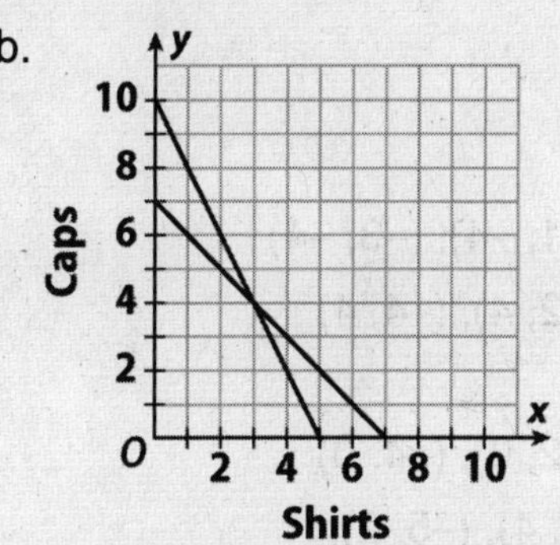

   c. The solution is (3, 4). It means that 3 people will get red shirts and 4 people will get red caps.

UNIT 4 Transformational Geometry

Unit 4 Test: A

1. D
2. C
3. A
4. D
5. D
6. C
7. A
8. B
9. C
10. B
11. B
12. $D'(2, 0)$, $E'(3, -4)$, $F'(1, -4)$
13. point D
14. $D'(-3, 0)$, $E'(-4, 4)$, $F'(-2, 4)$
15. $D(-3, 0)$, $E(-2, -4)$, $F(-4, -4)$;
    $D'(3, 0)$, $E'(2, -4)$, $F'(4, -4)$
16. $D'(-13, 8)$, $E'(-12, 4)$, $F'(-14, 4)$
17. $P'(-2, -3)$, $Q'(0, 1)$, $R'(3, -1)$
18. $P'(0, 0)$, $Q'(-2, 4)$, $R'(-5, 2)$
19. $P'(0, 0)$, $Q'(4, -2)$, $R'(2, -5)$
20. $P(0, 0)$, $Q(2, 4)$, $R(5, 2)$;
    $P'(0, 0)$, $Q'(-2, -4)$, $R'(-5, -2)$
21. $P'(0, 0)$, $Q'(4, 8)$, $R'(10, 4)$; dilation with scale factor 2 and origin as center
22. (–18, 0), (0, 18), (18, 0), (0, –18)
23. a larger square
24. It is similar.

Unit 4 Test: B

1. A
2. A
3. A
4. B
5. D
6. D
7. B
8. A
9. D
10. B
11. C
12. $D'(2, 1)$, $E'(1, -2)$, $F'(5, -4)$
13. point E
14. (3, 2)
15. $D'(2, 3)$, $E'(3, 0)$, $F'(-1, -2)$; reflection across y-axis

16. $D'(-12, 11)$, $E'(-13, 8)$, $F'(-9, 6)$; $P'(-9, 10)$, $Q'(-7, 12)$, $R'(-5, 10)$
17. $P'(1, -2)$, $Q'(3, 0)$, $R'(5, -2)$
18. $P'(-1, 2)$, $Q'(-3, 4)$, $R'(-5, 2)$
19. $P'(1, 2)$, $Q'(-1, 4)$, $R'(1, 6)$
20. $P'(-1, -2)$, $Q'(-3, -4)$, $R'(-5, -2)$; 180° rotation with the origin as center
21. $P'(3, 6)$, $Q'(9, 12)$, $R'(15, 6)$; dilation with scale factor 3 and origin as center
22. (−9, 0), (0, 12), (9, 0), and (0, −12)
23. a larger rhombus
24. The image is a similar, larger rhombus.

Unit 4 Test: C

1. A
2. C
3. A
4. A
5. D
6. C
7. B
8. A
9. D
10. C
11. A
12. *D*
13. $A'(3, 4)$, $B'(5, 10)$, $P'(7, 7)$
14. $A''(5, 5)$, $P''(1, 2)$, $E''(-2, 2)$, $F''(-4, 5)$
15. $B'(1, 3)$, $C'(1, 0)$, $D'(4, -3)$, $E'(-2, -2)$, $P'(-2, 1)$
16. $A'(5, -5)$, $B'(3, 1)$, $C'(0, 1)$, $D'(-3, 4)$, $E'(-2, -2)$, $F'(-4, -5)$, $P'(1, -2)$; reflection across the *y*-axis
17. $A'(-15, 3)$, $B'(-13, 9)$, $C'(-10, 9)$, $D'(-7, 12)$, $E'(-8, 6)$, $F'(-6, 3)$, $P'(-11, 6)$; translation 10 units left and 8 units up
18. $A'(-5, -1.5)$, $P'(-1, 1.5)$, $E'(2, 1.5)$, $F'(4, -1.5)$
19. $A''(7, -8)$, $B''(5, -2)$, $P''(3, -5)$
20. $A'(11, 13)$, $B'(9, 7)$, $C'(6, 7)$, $D'(3, 4)$, $E'(4, 10)$, $F'(2, 13)$, $P'(7, 10)$
21. $A'(5, 5)$, $B'(3, -1)$, $C'(0, -1)$, $D'(-3, -4)$, $E'(-2, 2)$, $F'(-4, 5)$, $P'(1, 2)$; 180° rotation about the origin
22. $A'(-20, -20)$, $B'(-12, 4)$, $C'(0, 4)$, $D'(12, 16)$, $E'(8, -8)$, $F'(16, -20)$, $P'(-4, -8)$; dilation with scale factor 4 and origin as center
23. $A'(-3, -3.5)$, $B'(-2, -0.5)$, $C'(-0.5, -0.5)$, $D'(1, 1)$, $E'(0.5, -2)$, $F'(1.5, -3.5)$, $P'(-1, -2)$
24. the shape of the image
25. No, it will be greater since the scale factor of 0.5 reduces the image.

Unit 4 Test: D

1. B
2. A
3. C
4. A
5. B
6. A
7. C
8. B
9. B
10. A
11. C
12. (−2, 0), (−1, −4), (−3, −4)
13. (−3, 0), (−2, 4), (−4, 4)
14. clockwise
15. (−3, 4), (−2, 0), (−4, 0)
16. (0, 0), (−2, 4), (−5, 2)
17. 3 units to the left
18. –20.

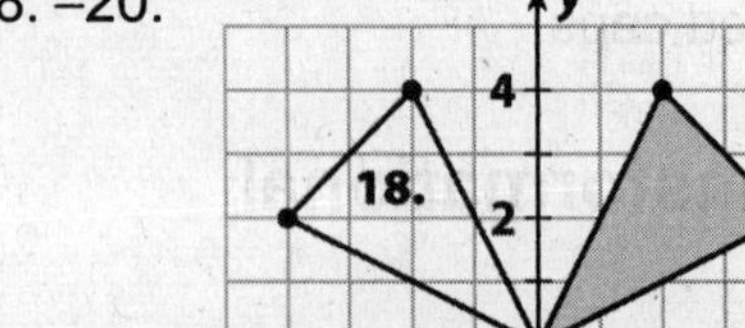

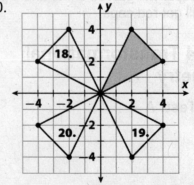

21. 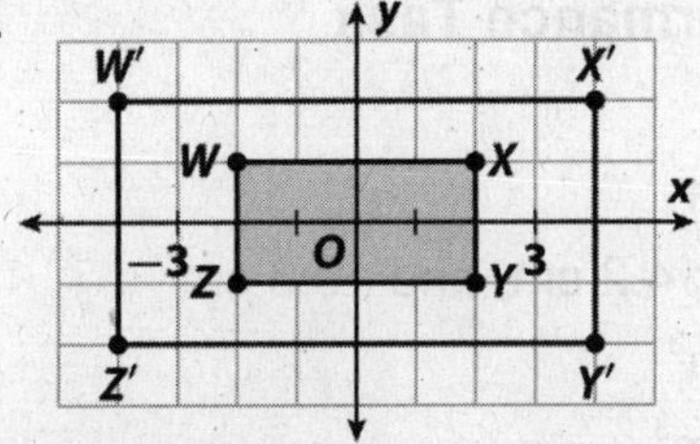

22. They doubled.

23. 1 to 2

24. their shapes

Unit 4 Performance Task

1. 11 units up; 6 units to the right repeated two times
2. $(x, y) \rightarrow (x, y + 11)$; $(x, y) \rightarrow (x + 6, y)$ repeated two times
3. 90° clockwise, 90° counterclockwise, 180°; or quarter-turn clockwise, quarter-turn counterclockwise, half-turn
4. $(x, y) \rightarrow (y, -x)$, $(x, y) \rightarrow (-y, x)$, $(x, y) \rightarrow (-x, -y)$
5. Sample answers: Right figure: a dilation with center at the origin and a scale factor of 3, then a translation of 4 right, 11 down; Left figure: reflection of the large right figure across the *y*-axis
   In algebraic notation: Right figure: $(x, y) \rightarrow (3x, 3y)$ then $(x, y) \rightarrow (x + 4, y - 11)$; left figure: $(x, y) \rightarrow (-x, y)$
6. Answers will vary. Encourage students to use algebraic notation, but accept descriptions given in words.

UNIT 5 Measurement Geometry

Unit 5 Test: A

1. D
2. B
3. A
4. A
5. B
6. B
7. B
8. C
9. B
10. C
11. Sample answers: ∠3 and ∠6, ∠4 and ∠5
12. 120°
13. 5.7 cm
14. 7.8 ft
15. 9.8 cm
16. 15.6 ft
17. yes; $9^2 + 12^2 = 15^2$
18. 452.2 in^3
19. 94.2 ft^3
20. 1,436 m^3

Unit 5 Test: B

1. B
2. D
3. B
4. A
5. D
6. C
7. C
8. C
9. B
10. B
11. ∠2, ∠4, ∠6
12. ∠1, ∠3, ∠5, ∠7
13. 132°
14. 39.8 cm
15. 14.8 ft
16. 9.2 cm
17. 6,250
18. 452.2 in^3
19. 418.7 ft^3
20. 24,416.6 m^3

Unit 5 Test: C

1. C
2. D
3. D
4. B
5. B
6. C
7. D
8. C

9. B

10. B

11. No, ∠4 and ∠5 are same-side interior angles. Since they are supplementary, the sum of their measures is 180°, so if ∠4 measures more than 129°, then ∠5 cannot be more than 51°.

12. ∠C = 59°; ∠B = 54°; ∠D = 67°

13. 126°

14. 39.8x cm

15. Yes; Sample explanation: A 54 foot cable can reach 14.56 feet from the top of a 52-foot building.

16. 53.37 ft

17. 0.092 m

18. 100

19. 7.4 cm

20. 0.22 in^3

Unit 5 Test: D

1. B
2. B
3. C
4. B
5. B
6. B
7. B
8. B
9. A
10. C
11. Sample answers: ∠1 and ∠3, ∠2 and ∠4, ∠5 and ∠7, ∠6 and ∠8
12. any of ∠2, ∠4, ∠6, ∠8
13. 60°
14. 4.6 cm
15. 11.2 ft
16. 3.2 cm
17. 8 ft
18. 452 in^3
19. 30
20. 113.0 m^3

Unit 5 Performance Task

1. a. 25°
   b. 16.3 cm
   c. 13 cm, 14.2 cm, and 19.3 cm
2. 2034.7 cm^3
3. 1,177.5 cm^3
4. 2,143.6 cm^3

UNIT 6 Statistics

Unit 6 Test: A

1. A
2. C
3. A
4. C
5. B
6. C
7. D
8. 78
9.

Day	Lunches	Dinners	Total
Saturday	28%	39%	67%
Sunday	24%	9%	33%
Total	52%	48%	100%

10. 24%
11. 48%
12.

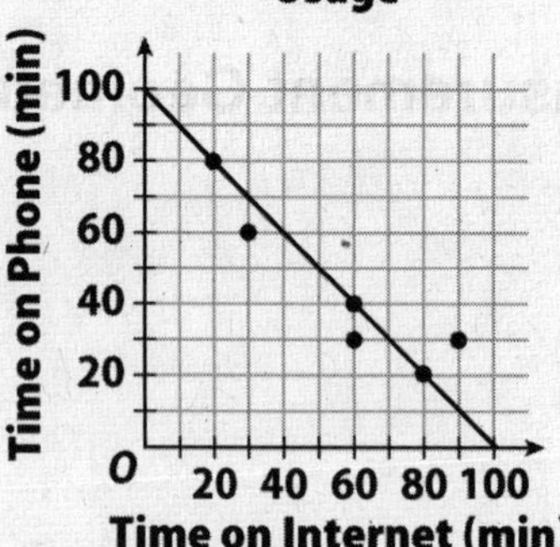

13. Sample answer: $y = -x + 100$
14. negative association
15. Sample answer: 55 min

16. Answers will vary. Sample answer: Yes, the amount of time that a student can talk on the phone and use the Internet is limited.

Unit 6 Test: B

1. C
2. D
3. C
4. B
5. B
6. C
7. C
8. 27
9.

Class	Semester 1	Semester 2	Total
101	18%	28%	46%
102	27%	28%	54%
Total	45%	55%	100%

10. 27%
11. 55%
12.

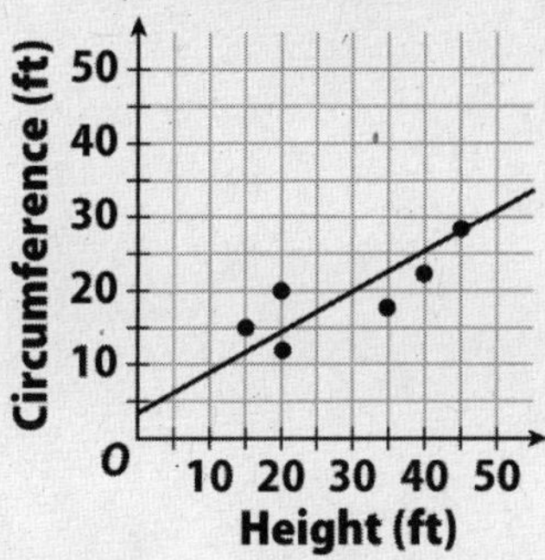

13. Sample answer: $y = 0.55x + 4$
14. positive association
15. Sample answer: about 65 ft

Unit 6 Test: C

1. A
2. C
3. D
4. C
5. B
6. D
7. B
8. 172, 178
9.

Fruit	July	August	Total
Peaches	18%	17.7%	35.7%
Strawberries	21.7%	16.9%	38.9%
Melons	9.4%	16.3%	25.4%
Total	49.1%	50.9%	100%

10. 50.9%
11. 44.2%
12.

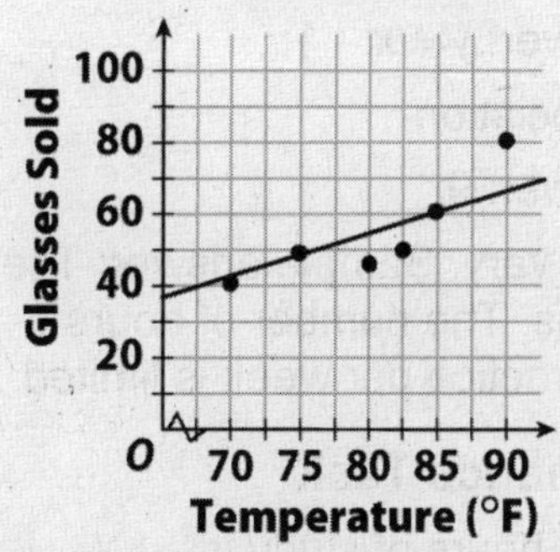

13. Sample answer: $y = x - 25$
14. positive association
15. Sample answer: 35 sales
16. Answers will vary. Sample answer: Yes. The ability to predict sales using the trend line is limited because sales cannot be negative, and because temperatures typically vary within a certain range.

Unit 6 Test: D

1. C
2. C
3. B
4. C
5. A
6. C
7. C
8. 26
9.

Newspaper	East	North	Total
New Times	22%	18%	40%
Main St. Journal	26%	34%	60%
Total	48%	52%	100%

10. 34%

11. 48%

12. 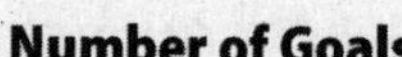

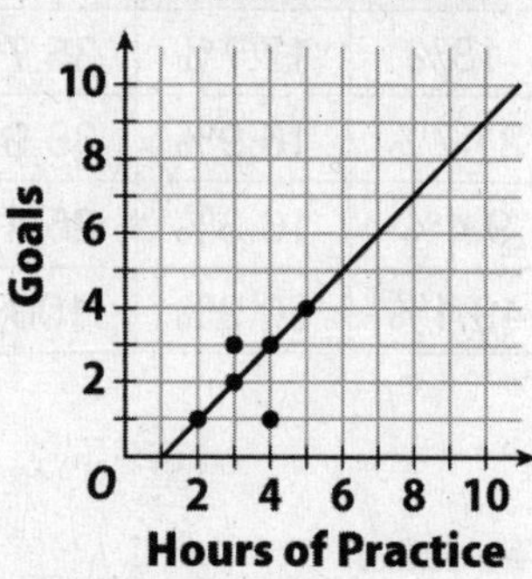

13. Sample answer: $y = x - 1$

14. positive association

15. Sample answer: 9

16. Answers will vary. Sample answer: There are limitations. The number of hours a player can practice per week is limited.

Unit 6 Performance Task

1. The average hours of study is
$$\frac{4+10+8+0+6+3+5+3}{8} = 4.875 \text{ h}.$$
The average hours of exercise is
$$\frac{3+0+1+10+4+5+3+6}{8} = 4 \text{ h}$$

2. 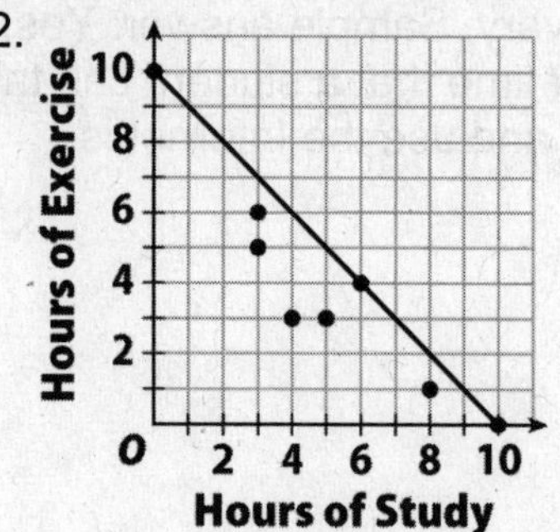

3. Use the points (0, 10) and (10, 0) to get the equation of the trend line.
$y = 10 - x$

4. This is a negative association.

5. Answers will vary. Sample answer: Most students did not spend more than a total of 10 hours studying and exercising.

6. Answers will vary. Sample answer: No. Since only 8 students were surveyed, this is not a representative sample. There are 150 students in the school. 8 students represents roughly 5% of the entire population.

Answer Key

Benchmark Test Modules 1–6

1. A
2. B
3. B
4. D
5. C
6. D
7. C
8. C
9. A
10. C
11. A
12. D
13. A
14. C
15. D
16. B
17. C
18. B
19. C
20. A
21. B
22. B
23. A
24. 676
25. $40
26. 0.005
27. 12
28. 0.467
29. 1.125
30. 21.5
31. 0.09
32. 0.05
33. 2,000
34. February

Answer Key

Mid-Year Test Modules 1–8

1. C
2. B
3. B
4. D
5. A
6. C
7. D
8. C
9. D
10. C
11. C
12. D
13. A
14. A
15. B
16. D
17. C
18. B
19. D
20. B
21. A
22. A
23. B
24. 5 months
25. 4
26. $\frac{8}{81}$
27. –16
28. (2, 3)
29. $\frac{1}{27}$
30. 5
31. (2, 3)
32. $0.15(x + 40) = 10.50$
33. 12 °F
34. 5.397×10^{11}

Answer Key

Benchmark Test Modules 9–13

1. A
2. D
3. B
4. A
5. B
6. B
7. C
8. D
9. A
10. D
11. A
12. D
13. B
14. C
15. B
16. D
17. C
18. B
19. C
20. B
21. C
22. C
23. D
24. C
25. C
26. 42.56
27. 244
28. 10
29. 62°
30. 45
31. 6
32. 5
33. 13
34. 4
35. 90°

Answer Key

End-of-Year Test

1. B
2. C
3. D
4. B
5. B
6. D
7. A
8. D
9. A
10. A
11. C
12. A
13. B
14. A
15. B
16. A
17. B
18. D
19. A
20. D
21. B
22. A
23. D
24. C
25. C
26. D
27. B
28. B
29. A
30. A
31. B
32. C
33. B
34. D
35. B
36. D
37. A
38. B
39. C
40. B
41. D
42. D
43. B
44. C
45. D
46. D
47. D
48. D
49. C
50. B
51. B
52. C
53. A
54. C
55. C
56. A
57. A
58. D
59. A
60. D
61. P = 36; dilating by a scale factor of 3 multiplies the perimeter by 3; So, the new perimeter is $36 \times 3 = 108$ units.
62. $y = 3x + 5$; $2(3x + 5) = 4x + 24$; $6x + 10 = 4x + 24$

    $2x = 14$

    $x = 7$
63. 0.0845
64. $10h + 60 = 12h$

    $60 = 2h$

    $30 = h$

She earns the same amount after 30*h*.

65. 3
66. $m = \frac{y_2 - y_1}{x_2 - x_1}; \frac{6 - 5}{0 - (-2)} = \frac{1}{2}$

67. $V_{\text{cone}} = \frac{1}{3}\pi r^2 h = 242.1$

$V_{\text{cylinder}} = \pi r^2 h = 3\left(\frac{1}{3}\pi r^2 h\right) = 3(242.1) =$

726.3
The volume of the cylinder is 726.3 cubic centimeters.

68. $3x + 0.84 = 5x$ where x is the price of an apple; $x = \$0.42$

69. 8.9

70. 799.02

71. 4.5

72. $3.75 \div 12 = 0.3125$; $18 \bullet 0.3125 = 5.625$ or \$5.63

73. A y-intercept is the y-coordinate of the point where the graph crosses the y-axis; The y-intercept of the line shown is 3.

74. 21.6

75. \$4.25 for 0.5 pound, so the unit rate is \$4.25/0.5 = \$8.50 per pound.
For 0.75 pound: \$8.50(0.75) = 6.375;
The blueberries cost \$6.38.

76. Since the angle whose measure is $(4x)°$ and the angle whose measure is $(2x + 30)°$ are alternate interior angles, they are congruent. $4x = 2x + 30$;
$2x = 30; x = 15$

77. 12

78. 1

79. The triangle is a right triangle. Using the Pythagorean Theorem $5^2 + x^2 = 13^2$;

$25 + x^2 = 169$

$x^2 = 144$

$x = 12$ cm

80. 13.6